WORLD PEACE

VOLUME FIVE

FARMER AND PEACE

Suresh Chandra Mallick
Pritam Mallick

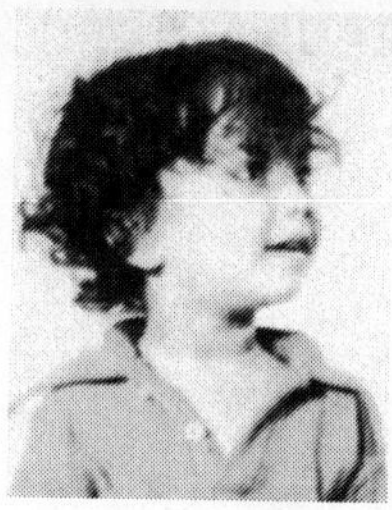

FARMER AND PEACE

Institute of Development Studies and Policy research,
Pritam Bhawan, 93 Dharma Vihar, P.O. Khandagiri,
Bhubaneswar 751030 (Orissa), INDIA

© ISBN: 978-81-924851-4-0

2018

Price: US $

Dedicated to

Mr. Pranab Mukherjee
President of India,
New Delhi

PROLOGUE

The farmers encounter poverty, hunger, illiteracy, unemployment and debt for generations. So, it is necessary to find out the real causes of their sufferings. They dedicate their life for the benefits of the urban people. But they are neglected by the successive governments. They suffer without medicine to cure their diseases. They are poor because their life is not insured for old ages. Many peasants are born in debt, live in debt and die in debt. Let the farmers of all developing and developed countries claim for suitable agricultural policies for achieving justice. They need the State Laws to alleviate their sufferings and they could be the torchbearers of peace in the world.

The United Nations, FAO, the World Bank, IFAD, and the governments have not solved the problems of farmers so far. These institutions have failed miserably to award justice to the peasants. So how could we achieve WORLD PEACE? Why no organization or Government has yet been successful in ameliorating the sufferings of the farmers so far? The farmers work for others; they supply food to city dwellers, hotels, hostels, hospitals, military and business establishments. They produce and supply grains, pulses, vegetables, fruits, milk, meat, fish, chicken, condiments, tea and coffee. But they feel suffocated with state laws in many countries. They are tortured but they do not have the capacity to influence the government. They are poor and live in country side.

The term 'farmer' includes: farmer, small farmer, peasant, sharecropper, agricultural labourer, seasonal worker, poor people and widows residing in rural areas as all of them do some work for agricultural production and depend upon farming for a living. The problem arises because most of them are trying to leave agriculture to earn higher income in the far off urban areas as industrial workers or daily wage earners in construction of roads or buildings. Even the well-to-do farmers are also disgusted with their profession. It is because agriculture has become a **loss-bearing profession** as governments of all countries monitor agricultural prices of cereals and offer higher subsidy to corporations and industrial houses for agricultural inputs.

In this manuscript, attempts have been made to identify the real problems of the farmers and find out the possibilities to solve their problems that could restore WORLD PEACE everywhere.

In the first chapter, the severity of hunger has been explained and the need for farmers' welfare has been emphasized. Chapter II highlights the farmers' problems and distress. The farmers are committing suicides because of poverty, crop loss and bad loan. Chapter III explains the reasons of farmers' revolutions; the reasons are fewer prices of grains, sugarcane, cotton and import of edible oil or forceful eviction of cultivated land for the industrialists by armed police. The chapter-IV explains the defects of agricultural marketing systems in different countries. The farmers need trade justice, suitable trade policy, better price fixation policy, and consumers' welfare measures in marketing operations. The government should also consider the risks and uncertainty in agriculture and should make suitable adjustments in order to award justice to safeguard the economy of farmers. Chapter V explains that demands of the farmers would achieve success provided the farmers stand united, fight and claim their demands through farmers' organizations. Chapter VI illustrates the role of international organizations for farmers have the capacity to demand for their rights though appropriate policy legislation and government patronage. The government should award financial assistance to protect their livelihood and pensioners' benefits to live in peace. The government could assist the farmers to get rid of poverty, illiteracy and exploitation. Chapter VI incorporates that the demands of the farmers in all countries could be easily solved if the farmers have their organizations and political party to demand for policy changes suitable for the farmers. Chapter VII explains that law and practice must save small farmers. Each farmer must be provided rights over land and be free from debt.

We are grateful to Wikipedia, Google in search, and a number of Newspapers for collection of facts on farmers and farm policies. We have referred Journals and Internet during preparation of this manuscript. We acknowledge the contribution of authors, who have studied and opined for the welfare of farmers. We acknowledge the contribution of the world organizations, international organizations and countries for their sustained efforts for the growth of agriculture and for farmers' welfare. We will appreciate for constructive criticism aiming at improvement of the subsequent editions of the book. We will be happy, if a small step towards world peace is contemplated through this Endeavour.

November 21, 2012 Suresh Chandra Mallick

ACRONYMS

A O A.	Agreement on Agriculture
A I K S	All India Kisan Sabha
A C G R.	Annual Compound Growth Rate
Ads:	Advertisements
A. M C Os	Agricultural Marketing and Agricultural Cooperatives
A. M S	Aggregate Measurement Support
A P E C	Asia – Pacific Economic Cooperation
BAAC:	Bank for Agriculture and Agricultural Cooperatives.
BEST	Business Environment for Strengthening Tanzania
B J P	Bharatiya Janata Party
B P L:	Below Poverty Line
C R F	Calamity Relief Fund
C M:	Chief Minister
C A D	Command area Development
C A C P	Commission for Agricultural Costs & Prices
C B D	Convention of Biological Diversity
CPI (M)	Communist Party of India (Marxist)
C. P. P. C. C	Chinese People's Political Consultative Conference

C O S O Ps	Country Strategic Opportunities Programs
C U S T A	Canada- United States Free Trade Agreement
G D P	Gross Domestic Product
E. E. C.	European Economic Cooperation
EU	European Union
F C I	Food Corporation of India
FDR	Franklin Denalo Roosevelt
F R P	Fair and Remunerated Price
F S R	Farmers' Suicide Rate
F T A	Free Trade Association
F O:	Farmers' Organization
GATT	General Agreement on Trade and Tariff
G E	Genetic Engineering
G S. R	General Suicide Rate
G F A R	Global Forum for Agricultural Research
I S O P O M	Integrated Scheme on oilseeds, Pulses, Oil Palm and Maize
I A. A. H	International Alliance against Hunger
I B R D	International Bank for Reconstruction and Development
I. A. T. P	Institute for Agricultural Trade Policy
I C A	International Cooperative Association
I. C. A. C.	International Cotton Advisory Committee
IFAD	International Fund for Agricultural development
I. F. A. P	International Federation of Agricultural Producers
INR	Indian Rupees
I P C	International Planning Committee
I. R.R. I	International Rice Research Institute
I I E D	International Institute for Environment and Development
J. F. F. L S.	Junior Farmer and Field Life School
M A S R	Movement against State Repression
M I D S	Madras Institute of Development Studies
M D Gs	Millennium Development Goals
M S P	Minimum Support Prices

N B F A	National Black Farmers' Association
N C R B	National Crime Records Bureau
N I C s	Newly Industrial Countries
N M B	National Micro-finance Banks
N R E G S	National Rural Employment Guarantee Scheme
N A F T A	North American Free Trade Association
O D A	Official Development Assistance
O C F C U	Oromia Coffee Farmers Cooperative Union
O E C D	Organization for Economic Cooperation and Development
P R A	Participatory rural Appraisal
P G R F A	Plant Genetic Resources for Food and Agriculture
P N P C	Philippines National Peasant Caucus
P R S P	Poverty Reduction Strategy Papers
P D S	Public Distribution System
P S E B	Punjab State Electricity Board
P M O	Prime Minister
P P V F R	Protection of Plant Varieties and Farmers' Rights Act
R o P	Roots of Peace
R D S	Rural Development Strategy
S A S	Situation Assessment Survey of Farmers
S E Z	Special Economic Zone
S P	Special Products
S. S. M.	Special Safeguard Mechanism
S F A	Swiss Farmers Association
S C L C	Southern Christian Leadership Conference
S I A N I	Swedish International Agriculture Network Initiative
S I D A	Swedish International Development Cooperative Agency
S. C. C.	Swedish Cooperative Center
T D	Tender Distribution
T R I P S	Trade Related Aspects of Intellectual Property Rights

U N C E D	United Nations Conference on Environment and Development
U N C T A D	U N Conference on Trade and Development
UN FAO	United Nations Food and Agriculture Organization
U P A	United Political Alliance
U P O V	International Union for Protection of New Varieties of Plants
U S D A	United States Department of Agriculture
W I P O	World Intellectual property Organization
W F S	World Food Summit
W T O	World Trade Organization

+++++

CONTENTS

INTRODUCTION

Seventy-five percent of the world's poor reside in rural areas. Farmers, peasants, sharecroppers', agricultural labourers, landless people and artisans constitute the bulk of the rural poor. Unless they live in peace and are allowed to live in peace by the government, the quest for WORLD PEACE would be impossible at the shortest possible time. The gravity of farmers' economic situations is revealed in the following examples. The farmers of South Korea, United States, United Kingdom and India have challenged the policy makers of their government vis-à-vis the world leaders. Moreover, more than a billion of people are hungry today. Could the United Nations, International Organizations and Governments of all countries find a solution to these problems? It is possible provided the farmers of the world feel that they are fairly treated by the government and agriculture is considered as a profitable enterprise.

South Korea: Lee Kyung Hae, the South Korean co-operative farm leader stabbed himself to death outside WTO talks in Mexico. Wearing a banner declaring 'WTO kills farmers', he was protesting at this undemocratic institution opening his country to cheap imports that had resulted in the price of rice being cut to a quarter, driving him and millions of others off the land even after they had increased productivity. His last words were: "My warning goes out to all citizens that human beings are in an endangered situation. Uncontrolled multi-national corporations and a small number of big WTO members are leading an undesirable globalization that is inhumane, environmentally degrading, farmer-killing, and undemocratic. It should be stopped immediately. Otherwise the false logic of neo-liberalism will wipe out the diversity of global agriculture and be disastrous to all human beings. Farmers in all countries have in common problems of dumping, import surges, and lack of government budgets."

United States: This is supported by American farmer George Naylor, who grows corn and soybeans. He states, "Even when the US breaks its own WTO rules to subsidize its agriculture, it is the corporations buying the cheap crops that reap the benefits. Farmer incomes, even with government payments, are a fraction of what they would be under previous, now defunct programs that more nearly aimed at paying farmers at least our cost of production and required the buyers to pay that price, rather than the American taxpayers. Multinational corporations, like Cargill, Tyson, and Smithfield, that have already destroyed diversified family farming in America by feeding livestock cheap corn and soybean meal in giant polluting feedlots, are further expanding this industrial model to other countries every year.

The European Union: The EU spends more than half of its annual budget (about €53 billion in 2007) in farm subsidies. The money is raised from customs duties, sales taxes and a contribution made by each EU country based on its wealth, which again comes from national tax. We in Europe are paying double for our food — one for higher food prices in the stores and then for the taxes that goes to pay for farm subsidies. Europe farm subsidies started as production incentives in the 1960s, when its goal was to increase the food supply and help farm communities still recovering from the ravages of World War II. The practice of tying subsidies to food production, which led to vast surpluses in the 1980s, was eliminated in a series of reforms, and grants to landowners on the basis of size of land farmed, rather than how much is grown on it.

India: The farmers grow cereals, vegetables, sugarcane or cotton as per advices of university scientists and Agriculture department officials. The government of India sanctions billions of Indian rupees for the development of agriculture in the country. Subsidy in agricultural inputs, subsidy in cereals distribution, free gifts to peasants during flood, cyclone and natural hazards. When the market is glutted with agricultural commodities with no buyers, price of agricultural produce falls below production costs. The farmers cannot repay back the bank loan. They get reminders from banks and non-banking institutions to repay back loan; and the farmers commit suicides.

In India, on an average, 18,000 farmers commit suicides annually even in the 21st century.

The developed countries are managing the farm sector through huge subsidy, promotional activities and encouragement to youths through 'Junior Farmer and Field Life Schools' program. All governments of all countries award subsidies to farm sector because the governments know that agriculture is a losing concern and yet, the farmers are supplying food to all people. Even the Government farms or University farms cannot meet the expenditure incurred in raising crops through sale of farm outputs. In the twenty-first century, massive structures and large number of buildings are being constructed in cities and towns at a faster rate. Moreover, cities are decorated with lawns, gardens and waterfalls. A number of multi sky scrapers are added to each city each year. The rural youths are better engaged in construction work with higher wages in cities. The city-dwellers are the privileged people in all developing countries. In contrast, farmers commit suicides because they face more problems, which they cannot solve.

The causes for loss in farm sector are:

(a) Crop failure due to natural calamities;
(b) Absence of Parity price for rice or wheat as compared to price of gold or cement or land or pay of government servants with a base year;
(c) Government imports cereals, edible oil, sugar or cotton at subsidized rate from other countries that are available at fewer prices because developed countries offer higher subsidies in agriculture;
(d) Heavy burden on borrowed capital;
(e) Corrupt government with wrong policies and false promises;
(f) Absence of effective Farmers' Organizations and majority peasants are poor and hungry;
(g) Vagaries of monsoon and
(h) Poverty of farmers

The governments should examine the **ill effects** of subsidy policy, entry of multinational organizations in agriculture, participation in World Trade Organization, formation of Special Economic Zones, Liberalization of Economy, and industrial policy in their countries.

Let the governments of all developing countries consider the necessity of life insurance policy and pensioners' benefits to all senior citizens' of the country.

The governments should adopt pro-poor, pro-rural and pro-agricultural policy to save the farmers, which are committing blunders and unexpected sins.

The politicians need peoples' support in all elections and it is possible through cheap prices of agricultural commodities particularly in Wheat and Rice. In India, the consumer's price of rice and wheat is only 1 or 3 INR (Indian rupees) per kg. A consumer can avail 35 kg of rice or wheat per month, while he earns 200 INR – 400 INR per day in cities.

Has the government of India studied the causes of farmers' suicides? Does the state policy empower the farmers? The government demands prestige and applauses for increase in agricultural production, subsidy in agriculture, and road connectivity to the villages. The farmers' annual income from agriculture is decreasing each year.

In India an average income of an urban man is about 16 times of a rural man. Each year farmers commit suicide because of loan incurred for agricultural purposes.

The government's policy is a major factor of farmers' suicides. Why the farmers are not yet covered under Pensioner's benefits?

An International Law is necessary to assist the farmers in all countries. Similarly, the farmers in all countries should organize a 'Farmers' Political Party' to stand united and express their sufferings in Parliament for justice.

+++++

Chapter 1

FARMERS NEED PEACE

The problem of malnutrition is a matter of national shame. Despite impressive growth in our GDP, the level of under nutrition in the country is unacceptably high. We have not succeeded in reducing this rate fast enough.

Dr. Manmohan Singh, Prime Minister of India

In most of the countries of the world, the farmers, peasants, agricultural labourers, artisans, and landless people are forced to suffer because they constitute the largest share of population. Most of the sufferers reside in countryside; they have accepted sufferings as a way of life; they know their duties but not rights; they are poor and hungry; they are convinced with false promises of the government servants and politicians; they believe in God and depend upon divine mercy; and they are born in debt, live in debt and die in debt. They are innocent, honest, grateful and active people with restless life. They shed tears, but pray God. They live for others, yet they are tortured. They give alms to the beggars although they do not know their future.

The farmers, peasants and share croppers cultivate land and grow grains, vegetables, fruits, and supply food to the world; they face marketing problems for their saleable surplus; they realize that agriculture has become a loss-bearing profession; yet they are engaged in farming. They are poor, because the governments neglect them continuously. The political parties declare pro-poor policies before the elections but they forget all promises after they assume power in all democracies.

The poor peasants desire to live in peace. But leaders of different political parties need their help for achieving personal mileage. The poor peasants join all uprisings, wars or rebellions; their leaders mislead them. The poor people join military; join anti-government groups such as Terrorists' camps, Naxalites or Maoist organizations for engagement. They are hungry people and could be utilized in all professions or activities. The poor peasants live in remote villages and are devoid of justice lifetime.

If the governments can utilize their services, they can earn their bread and can prove their presence everywhere, but unemployment and hunger have turned these people as negative entities. Most of the school dropouts, farmers' suicides and land cases are associated with these families. Agriculture can create more employment than other sectors such as industry or services. But governments of developing countries neglect agriculture, horticulture, fishery or dairy. These countries are running after industries and industrialists. The Governments in developing countries sell or mortgage thousand acres of land to these industrialists to start mega industries in fertile land. How could food security to the growing population be ensured today and in future?

The government fixes remunerative prices for agricultural commodities, but these prices are neither economical nor profit generating. Government allots subsidy to farm requisites, which are mostly misappropriated by the industrialists, corporations, politicians, touts or government employees. In other words, non-farmers misappropriate funds earmarked for the farmers.

They live like subordinates to all government officials and politicians. Their voices are choked even today. They supply food to the world, but they are hungry.

A farmer leads a life of mental torture and sufferings but his photo is published when he commits suicide because of poverty, social obligations and incapability of repayment of loan. Could the government save the peasants, who have never taken any benefit from the governmental policies? All policies must be framed for the benefits of all citizens.

Why there is subsidy in agriculture? Who is benefited through subsidy? Why the peasants commit suicides in India almost daily? Why the cereals like Rice and Wheat are under-rated? Why parity price is not maintained within agriculture, industry and service sectors? Why parity price is not maintained for gold, petrol or wheat or rice over the years?

The government employees are better off always and treat them as employees of royal families and the political leaders are equating them as kings or monarchs of yester years. So it is the government that creates problems; the government spends huge amounts to solve the problems of the country by creating further problems. Who would guide the activities of the governments?

Avarice for power is so strong that the political or military rulers can kill thousands of poor people to remain in power for decades and generations. But there is a ray of hope that it could be changed through the United Nations Organization or a divine personality or restriction of period of governance through constitutional amendment. To restrict the activities of all governments, an international law could be made for global peace. No citizen needs war, it needs food, shelter and peace.

The world encounters a host of crises engineered by the governments but these governments put all blames on the poor people or peasants.

The peasants, farmers and agricultural labourers believe in God for survival because they encounter hardship throughout life.

Most of the peasants are sharecroppers. They want a piece of land, where they could make huts for their living. They need engagement for productive purposes. Can we provide the bare necessities of life to these uncared people? Can we provide them clean drinking water? Can the farmers be covered under Pensioners' benefits? It is possible.

These people should be awarded right to land, right to work and right to food.

But they are neglected as all lands belong to the state or to the landlords. They are neglected because they are poor and the leaders have 'no time' to hear their grievances. They are hungry because the bureaucrats and politicians are corrupt. They do not get justice because the legal system is more complicated and time consuming. The peasants who grow food for others go to bed hungry. They are uncared for in hospitals, as they cannot purchase medicines. They add old-age quickly as compared to others privileged groups.

They are forcefully evacuated from their ancestral property by the government for industry, port, and irrigation dam, government office without allotment of adequate land or compensation. The budgetary allocations or benefits allotted to the farmers never reach the farmers in full. It is simply diverted to the government officials or contractors without even the knowledge of the farmers. The farmers hear that government would do everything for them. The politicians do more harm to the farmers than the traders even. The problem is 'who would award justice to the farmers, peasants or poor people residing in countryside?

Let the governments and all peace-loving people try to create an era of peace by including these un-privileged people in this great march towards World Peace. This Chapter brings out facts on hunger, farmers, and possibilities of achieving WORLD PEACE.

World Hunger 2011

It is said that War is such a complex event that it is beyond a human's capacity to bring peace. Is the same true for World Hunger?

Every year 15 million children die of hunger. For the price of one missile, a school full of hungry children could eat lunch every day for 5 years.

The crisis of world hunger has been installed in the world since early times, along with conflict; it has been part of human history. Famines and post-conflict food shortages have had devastating effects on world populations. Today, by 2011, world hunger continues to be a major problem of the century.

Billions of people suffer from this world hunger crisis. On the other hand, thousands of government organisations, NGOs, activists, volunteers and professionals continue to work in different programs aimed at ending the World Hunger Crisis. But they fail miserably in solving the problem of hunger and the city expands with sky scrapers by few individuals.

Information on the web is always changing. From the outside, the reality of the situation is unclear. More than 100 million children will die from illness and starvation. Those 100 million deaths could be prevented for the price of ten Stealth bombers, or what the world spends on its military in two days.

Where does the World stand at beginning of 2011 in World Hunger and Agriculture programs? The World Food and Agriculture Organization of the United Nations say: **Global Hunger is declining but still unacceptably high.** They estimate 950 million people are currently undernourished. Of those numbers 578 million belong to Asia and the Pacific, 239 million to Sub-Saharan Africa, 53 million to Latin America and the Caribbean and the rest is divided among other countries.

Environmental scientists say that the World's total food output is more than enough to feed everyone, so malnourishment is caused by an inability or unwillingness to distribute food more evenly. What are the biggest blocks for food distribution? It is caused by political and international regulations, blockades and cost of transport, agriculture and livestock government programs and blocks on import and export.

Why the main challenges act as obstacles? Are there opportunity-plans for major investors to play an effective and positive role in World Hunger and Agriculture? Why the organizations, government and NGOs fail to check world hunger? Billions of dollars have been given as donations for agricultural development, but world hunger continues.

The total world population is 7 billion, but **1.3 billion people** are undernourished. This means that approximately 1: 6 is suffering from hunger. The United Nations has estimated the cost of ending world hunger would be at about US **$195 billion a year**.

Twenty-two countries have pledged to donate this money by contributing 0.7 percent — less than 1 percent — of national income to international aid, but the goal has yet to be reached. Every day thousands die due to world hunger. The Russian Federation is a United Nations (anti-hunger program) member. Russia assists financially as well as makes voluntary contributions to the program.

Every day thousands of dollars is spent on world hunger but it is only a fraction of what is needed. 'Stop the Hunger powered by Real Time Statistics' said that more than **3 million US dollars** were allocated daily in an effort to stop World Hunger. But more than **US $ 21 million** would be needed for success of the program.

(a) Are there new innovations in the field of solving World Hunger?
(b) If there are, why is the world's general public not aware of them?
(c) Why farmers are committing suicides in the Twenty-first century?

Global society is a world of contrasts. When strong economic sections of society are affected by a "crisis" the world community is swiftly taxed to effectively bail out the "crisis", however, world hunger as a crisis has been neglected in the background for a very long time. How are the international community and the general public coping with that idea? Many questions remain unanswered.

A program that effectively manages, money spent versus money on return or value on return (measured in results) is the only program that will end World Hunger. Many people are working on it. Have they found the answers?
The Mercy Corps, the United Nations World Food Program, the Global Network, Action–Against-Hunger, Charity Watch, Freedom from Hunger, and

thousands of other organisations and NGOs work daily with the situation. Muslim Aid calls for a global alliance of governments and NGOs to fight poverty.

Poverty forces a peasant to live a life with hunger, disease and lack of education. It affects a man to live without human rights.

Transport, supply and demand is all met with strong legislation. Nearly half the world arable crop production is fed to livestock, which in turn produce smaller amounts of food. Countries are catalogued and masked behind tags of Least Developed Countries and Developing Countries. The mismanagement remains unexplained.

The World Health Organization estimates that one-third of the world is well fed, one-third is under-fed and one-third is starving. Since you've started reading this article at least 200 people have died of starvation. Over 4 million of people will die this year.

How does politics influence world hunger and agriculture programs? How does economics influence agriculture programs? Is world hunger a crime? One in twelve people worldwide are malnourished, including 160 million children under the age of 5. (FAO)

The Indian subcontinent has nearly half the world's hungry people. Africa and the rest of Asia together have approximately 40 percent, and the remaining hungry people are found in Latin America and other parts of the world. There is saying in South East Asia, "I will not give you fish, I will teach you how to fish." (Hunger in Global Economy)

Water is a major problem in the areas most affected by world hunger. Water is essential for agriculture programs to work.

Food scarcity, global warming, and rocketing food and fuel prices have led to a dangerous global food crisis, plunging an extra 100 million people into poverty each year.

Global food prices have risen by 75 percent in the last decade (since 2000) while wheat prices have increased by a staggering 200 percent. The cost of other items such as rice and soybean has also hit record highs, while corn is at its most expensive in 12 years. (Islamic Relief)

India ranks 67 in a new global hunger index. -- International Food Policy Research Institute (IFPRI).

Uneven distribution of goods and ineffective programs in livestock and agriculture are responsible for world hunger, and economic crisis. We have to answer:

(a) What are the limitations in analyzing the past?
(b) What should never be repeated?
(c) What would an honest and critical analysis reveal?
(d) What is the reliability of all information?
(e) Does the solution to world hunger require a global participation of all levels of society or can a difference be made locally?[1]

Many people are willing to donate or help but have lost faith in NGOs. They find NGOs to be inefficient in delivering goods or unable to cope with mechanisms of local governments. There are numerous documented examples of this occurring, from corruption in aid to misuse of donations and ineffective timing. Examples range from Haiti's Earthquake to Cyclone Nargis or the Pakistan floods of 2010, to name just a few.

---

[1] Prof De Schutter, "World Hunger 2011, Catholic University Louvain, I NEMP Com, Belgium

Conflict and Food Insecurity

Armed conflicts are enemies of food security. There is a well-established correlation between the exposure of countries to external or internal conflicts, and the deterioration or long-term stagnation in their food security. Most conflicts, and especially the internal conflicts that have now become the dominant model of mass violence, mainly affect rural areas and their populations. They disrupt food production through physical destruction and plundering of crops and livestock, harvests and food reserves; they prevent and discourage farming; they interrupt the lines of transportation through which food exchanges, and even humanitarian relief, take place; they destroy farm capital, conscript young and able-bodied males, taking them away from farm work and suppress income earning occupations. The impact of conflicts on food security often lasts long after the violence has subsided, because assets have been destroyed, people killed or maimed, populations displaced, the environment damaged, and health, education and social services shattered; still more awesome are the landmines which litter agricultural land, kill and cripple people and deter them from farming for years –even decades- after all violence has ceased.

2. The last 15 years have seen a large number of food emergencies arising from both natural and human-induced factors. The number of food emergencies has fluctuated from between 20 and 30 in most years, but has tended to increase during the 1990s, particularly during the latter part of the decade. This increase has been associated primarily with a rise of conflicts. Whereas human-induced disasters contributed to only about 10 percent of the total emergencies in 1984, by the end of the century they were a determining factor in more than 50 percent of cases. Of the $1204 M spent by the World Food Program in 2000 for relief operations (compared with $98 M in 1978), $715 M were for man-made

emergencies and protracted operations in support of Internally Displaced People (IDPs) and refugees.

3 The most important impacts of all conflicts, and of all natural disasters, are the suffering, injury and death of men, women and children. Yet, direct material losses are also important, for they undermine the ability of conflict survivors to subsist and recover. This is most obvious in agriculture, where the destruction of crops and livestock results, at best, in reduced food security and at worst, in famine and death. Smallholder agriculture – the basic livelihood of the rural poor – is usually hit the hardest; small farmers and the already poor often lose the few assets and tools they have, joining the masses of hungry population. The economic losses, social disturbance and the disruptions to food supply and access associated with conflicts can be disastrous, especially in low-income countries where there are no effective social safety nets. A recent attempt at measuring conflict-related agricultural output losses for all developing countries showed that they are extensive: for the 28 years from 1970 to 1997, estimated losses amount to almost $121 billion at 1995 prices, or an average of $4.3 billion per year.[2]

This can be compared with the costs of raising nutrition to minimum required levels: using the notional estimate that it would cost approximately $13 per caput/year to provide enough food to feed the undernourished at a minimally adequate level, the same amount of money could have ensured adequate food intake for 330 million undernourished people each year. A decrease in under-nutrition on such a scale would outstrip the combined impact of all food aid. In both the 1980s and the 1990s, conflict-induced losses in developing countries exceeded the value of total food aid of all types to

[2]FAO, The state of Food and Agriculture, 2000

those countries. For the full decade of the 1980s, the former were about $37 billion and the latter $29 billion (both in current prices).[3]

4. While conflicts are the underlying cause of acute or lasting food insecurity situations in many countries, it is equally true that socio-economic inequities and inequalities, systematic ethnic discrimination, denial of human rights, disputes over political participation or long-standing grievances over the allocation of land and other resources, are critical factors that may lead to the outbreak of conflicts, often in combination with poor-governance, exploitation by unfettered ambition or greed. In addition to addressing conflicts when they mature and erupt, at a dramatic human and economic cost, responding to their root causes is a crucial contribution toward the preservation of peace.

Sustainable development, by redressing the inner causes that make society a fertile terrain for conflict, including food insecurity, poverty and lack of human development in its various dimensions, is a building stone for peace. The development of the rural regions, home to most of the world's poor and undernourished, plays an important role in the promotion of a peaceful and stable environment, where opportunities are created for a more equal access to physical, natural, financial and institutional resources for sustainable livelihoods. It is obvious, however, that sustainable development cannot take place in the midst of actual or potential conflict, and that protracted conflicts destroy the achievements of development.

The changing nature of conflicts

5. The downturn in world military expenditure that had followed the end of the cold war came to an end

---

[3] FAO (1996), Food Security and Food Assistance

by 1998. After a decline by 37 percent, world military expenditure rebounded by 2 percent in 1999 and 3 percent in 2000, reaching some $800 billion. The increase took place in all regions, with Africa and South Asia registering the steepest increases among the developing regions (respectively +37 percent and +23 percent from 1998 to 2000), and Russia and the USA accounting for the largest volume increases. New orders placed in the arms trade, the first five ranking suppliers being the permanent members of the Security Council, grew in 2000 for the third consecutive year to $37 billion – nearly 70 percent of it directed to developing countries, a stable pattern of the 1990's·

6. The nature of conflicts has changed markedly in the late part of the twentieth century. The state-against-state model is becoming the exception: of the 56 major armed conflicts registered in the decade 1990-2000[4], only three were of an interstate nature; all others were internal conflicts, even though in 14 of them foreign troops were engaged on one or the other side. Moreover, while the first half of the century was dominated by warfare between rich states, most contemporary conflicts take place overwhelmingly in the world's poorer countries, with Africa and Asia accounting for the greatest number of internal conflicts in the past decade. Civil wars and conflicts are indeed a major cause of development failure in the developing world, a point that is increasingly being emphasized by aid donors and international agencies. Easily tradable natural resources –particularly minerals- can be used to finance warring parties, instead of nurturing development, and "development efforts are not only halted or damaged, but actively targeted and undermined.

7. Technology has always been used to renovate and diversify the array of weapons and other means of

[4] SIPRI Year Book

violence used in conflicts. Arms-rich conflict areas and state disruption fuel the dissemination of weapons of all kinds, and the deadly violence of conflicts appears to have escalated with technology. However, the spread of small arms is also having devastating effects in disputes over land and pastoral issues, even within countries that are not considered to be in conflict. The UN Secretary General Kofi Annan, in addressing the Security Council on the impact of small arms and light weapons on people and societies throughout the world, underlined: "the fact that small arms require such minimal training has surely played a role in the recruitment of some 300,000 child combatants around the world.

8. Information technology, in itself a new target and channel for cyber-terrorism, also makes sophisticated means of communication accessible to violence-prone individuals and groups, and facilitates access to technical information on war and terrorism devices, as well as contacts and networking for organizing violent action, and allows for the dissemination of violence-inducing propaganda.

9. Internal conflicts, be they of an ethnic or revolutionary nature, or associated with a failure of the state or disruptive changes in regime, emerge where politically organized groups, national, ethnic or other minorities, or warlords and other violent elements in society, rebel against governments, often also fighting among themselves. This pattern of conflict makes it increasingly difficult to identify who are the protagonists, and which are the lines of authority through which to seek to mediate and put an end to the conflict.

10. In this new environment it becomes difficult to distinguish combatants from civilians. Combatants are no longer uniformed soldiers under state control. Nor are the combatants the main victims of conflicts: peaceful citizens -women, children, and the elderly-

become the major target (possibly 90 percent of the victims) of the warring parties. In addition to those killed or wounded, up-rooted populations run to millions – about 22 million in 150 countries by the end of 2001, including refugees and asylum seekers outside their home country, as well as returnees and others.

11. The international mechanisms that had been developed to control prevent and resolve conflicts were created to deal with the conventional state-state model of conflict: they have great difficulties in adjusting to the new patterns of collective violence, which mostly takes place within a sovereign territory, with the responsibility of the government being sometimes unclear. At the same time, however, many of the current conflicts have significant regional and international dimensions and implications. Even though the `zone of turmoil' is largely located in developing countries, the industrialized ones are not entirely insulated.

12. The distinction between intra-state and inter-state wars is therefore no longer straightforward. Most wars occurring within a single state tend to transcend its boundaries – affecting neighbouring countries, or with some external or transnational parties located far away from the site of the struggle. Negative spillovers to neighbouring nations result from collateral damage from nearby battles, severance of input supply lines, disruptions to trade, heightened risk perceptions by would-be investors, and resources spent to assist refugees.

In most cases, people flee across immediate borders, sometimes destabilizing entire regions, leading to further conflict and more refugees. Accelerated flows of refugees and asylum seekers, escalating costs of international or regional peace-restoration and maintenance efforts, international terrorism and destabilization of the global economy affect all nations, rich or poor, close to or far away from the war scene. The collapse of tourism and transport sectors that followed the unprecedented 11th September 2001 terrorist attacks in the United States is a striking example of the latter.

Peace, food security and justice

13. Much of deprivation is rural, with seven out of ten of the world's poor (less than $1 income per day) living in rural areas; among those, the undernourished represent the most extreme level and form of poverty and must constitute the priority target of poverty reduction efforts.

14. The various forms of inter-state competition, national, ethnic or religious conflicts, disputes for control over territories or resources, and even the legacy of imperialism and colonialism in modern times, continue to take their toll even after the end of the Cold War, which had for long fed and shaped many of the violent clashes taking place around the world. Conflicts over natural resources, especially minerals, are becoming relatively more frequent

15. In some cases, there is competition for control of highly valuable minerals that also finance war; in other settings, the concentrated ownership of diffuse resources like land and water may lead to conflicts, as underlined by the UN Secretary General: "Recent conflicts and farm invasions in southern African countries and the struggles between pastoralists and sedentary farmers in eastern Africa underline the importance of access to land-based resources by the poor as a basis for peace and sustainable development. Similarly, land concentration, coupled with poverty in Latin America, is one of the key issues underlying long-term conflict in that region. Where the need to meet family food requirements forces people to deplete natural resources or rely on degraded natural resources, ...natural resource

development activities and other land and resource management interventions - can help prevent conflicts that are based on or related to tensions over limited natural resources."[5]

16. Many avenues must be followed to prevent conflicts and restore peace; but to make the resolution of conflicts a lasting outcome and to prevent new fuel being added to the sleeping fire of violence, it is necessary to address not simply conflicts but "the deep-rooted socio-economic, cultural, environmental, institutional and other structural causes that often underlie the immediate political symptoms of conflicts." Food insecurity is one of them.

17. The issue of the ultimate causes of recent or older collective violence and conflicts has been the subject of considerable scrutiny by scholars, and a host of varied interpretations have been proposed: all these theories have used aspects of social transformations as the dominant explanation for violent collective action, in the rural milieu in particular.[6] Modern conflicts, however, illustrate that in many of the poorest countries, severely affected by endemic strife, social convulsions are the result of the dramatic inadequacy of economic development to meet the growing aspirations of rising populations. The deep dissatisfaction of segments of society (both urban and rural) that ultimately challenge the state is a main reason for violence. The inadequate response of the state to such challenges, due to the development of political institutions lagging behind social and economic change, can also be part of the

[5]Report of the UN Secretary General to Security Council on Prevention of armed conflict, June 2001

[6] de Soysa, I. and N.P. Gleditsch (1999), "To cultivate peace: agriculture in a world of conflict", Report of the International Peace Research Institute, Oslo (PRIO)

explanation of violence.[7] Democratic governance on one hand, and vitality of civil society organizations on the other, are critical ingredients for defusing the accumulation of grievances within society.

18. Conflicts are rooted in the sense of frustration, injustice and despair, which pervade large parts of society and are fuelled by poverty, inequality and discrimination. What triggers revolt is not only "absolute" but "relative" poverty as well; and not only does inequality rise in our times –but also the conscience of inequality, which many have-nots identify with injustice. While almost every village and hamlet in the world is now connected through radio, and often television, to global information, these channels of communication carry messages designed to induce higher levels of consumption by those who have the means to acquire them; they ostentatiously display lifestyles and consumer goods that are far beyond the reach of the vast majority of people in poor countries.

One consequence of the globalization of information and communications is that income disparities are now felt not only within the ambit of each national society, but also at a global scale. While there appears to be no generalized and discernable trend in within-country income inequality, international inequality has dramatically increased the gap between the richest and poorest regions –a gap that would appear even greater by comparing individual countries. In 1960, most developing regions had per capita incomes (expressed in Purchasing Power Parity) worth about 1/10th of the average for OECD countries; by the end of the century, the gap for the least developed countries and Sub-Saharan Africa had doubled, to almost 1/20th.

---

[7] Huntington (1968), Political order and changing societies

19. One consequence of these developments in both the level and the awareness of inequality is that large segments of the population, especially the youth, in poor and rich countries alike, become convinced that the world in which they are to live is fundamentally unjust. The fatalist concept that "being poor is your fate, because the world is like that", has lost a lot of ground, making it easier for the promoters of violence to harness support and mobilize full soil quality, water availability, marine environment, science base, provision of training, and tirade barriers owners. The transformation, in recent years, of the meetings of the powerful leaders of the world into risky encounters that mobilize a war-like apparatus of protection shows how quickly the violence of protest against felt inequity has been gaining ground, building upon a widespread new pessimistic perception of the world and how it is governed. But these disturbing trends, that easily capture attention, should not hide the vibrant and growing vitality of civil society organizations in mobilizing themselves voluntarily for enhancing awareness of local and global issues of development, sustainability, justice and peace; for debating new and creative ways of action; for embarking on a multitude of constructive initiatives at the local, national, regional and international levels.

Food security and agricultural development for a peaceful world:

20. The fight for peace, the fight against social insecurity and conflicts, must comprise determined action against poverty, inequality, injustice, and against the most extreme and most dependence-inducing form of poverty – being hungry, insecure of today's and tomorrow's food.

The Committee on Economic, Social and Cultural Rights, in their General Comment on the right to adequate food, prepared in response to the request by the World Food Summit to "clarify the content of the right to adequate food and the fundamental right of everyone to be free from hunger", affirmed that "the right to adequate food is indivisibly linked to the inherent dignity of the human person and is indispensable for the fulfillment of other human rights enshrined in the International Bill of Human Rights. It is also inseparable from social justice, requiring the adoption of appropriate economic, environmental and social policies, at both the national and international levels, oriented to the eradication of poverty and the fulfillment of all human rights for all."[8]

21. Of serious concern, the regular monitoring conducted by FAO of progress towards the 1996 WFS target "to reduce by half the number of undernourished in the world no later than 2015" continues to show that, year after year, such progress is insufficient and uneven. According to the most recent data, the number of undernourished has been declining by 6 million a year on average over the last decade, thereby raising to 22 million per year the size of future reductions required if the target is to be reached on time.[9]

But the same study, noting that a few countries have significantly improved since 1990 their food security situation while the majority has suffered deterioration, reveals once again that where resources are available for agriculture development, hunger recedes, while it gains ground where such resources diminish.

22. Looking ahead, prospective studies conducted by FAO further conclude that it is now becoming unlikely, unless decisive shifts are made in agricultural development and food security policies, that the WFS

---

[8]CESCR 1999

[9] FAO, the State of Food Insecurity, 2001

target would be met by 2015, and possibly even by 2030.[10]

Yet, never before has the world been so well equipped with the financial and technical resources to ensure that all people have adequate access to food. The question then is –does it lack in political commitment?

23. The international community is bracing itself to respond to the new challenges. Throughout the global Conferences of the 1990s and at the Millennium Assembly, the reduction and elimination of poverty and hunger has emerged as the overarching aim of development in the twenty-first century. In the words of the Monterrey Consensus, "peace and development reinforce each other". What had been accepted for centuries as a normal, if regrettable, part of human condition it is now considered a scandal that has to be eradicated? The global conscience, thanks to worldwide instant communications, is alerted to distant losses of life, due to natural or human-caused disasters, that would have gone unnoticed beyond the neighborhood in earlier times. Nowadays, the boundaries of moral concern are those of the planet.

24. Eliminating hunger is not just a moral imperative: it also makes economic sense, increasing productivity, raising incomes, creating jobs and adding to the demand for goods and services throughout the economy. It is also a necessary contribution to the many avenues that need to be followed to reduce violence and promote lasting peace. As concluded in a study commissioned by Future Harvest, a foundation established by former US President Jimmy Carter, "rehabilitation of agriculture is a central condition for development, reducing poverty, and preventing environmental destruction –and for reducing violence. Poor

[10]FAO, " Agriculture towards 2015 - 2030

conditions for agriculture hold grave implications for socio-economic development and sustainable peace. We also see good governance as crucial in building healthy conditions for agriculture, and thus in breaking the vicious cycle of poverty, scarcity and violence. The central issues are not merely technical: they relate directly to the way human beings organize their affairs and how they cope with natural and man-made crises."

25. Policies need to be put in place to promote growth and distribute its benefits broadly across society. Agricultural development, as part of economic and social changes that give the poor greater power over the productive resources and the social factors that shape their livelihoods, is indispensable to the enhanced food security of the rural population and to a more peaceful and stable environment. Equitable growth and pro-poor policies are critical not only to prevent the outbreak of conflicts but also in immediate post-conflict situations.

26. FAO's mandate to raise levels of nutrition and standards of living and to better the condition of rural populations, "and thus to contribute toward an expanding world economy and ensuring humanity's freedom from hunger "charges it with a particular responsibility to help meet the World Food Summit objective of eliminating food insecurity both in its chronic and emergency manifestations, drawing upon synergies and collaboration with the other Rome-based UN agencies, the technical and financial institutions of the UN system, the regional organizations and in partnerships with NGO/CSOs. FAO endeavors to foster sustainable agricultural and rural development, with a particular attention to small-scale producers and the agriculture-dependent rural poor in low-income food-deficit countries. It collects, analyzes and disseminates, for the attention of the international community, data and information

concerning food insecurity and the related potential threats to vulnerable people and groups. It takes action to help disaster-affected rural populations recover the capacity to care for them through agricultural rehabilitation.

27. Peace is a cherished good of humanity. But it is a good that many people have not enjoyed for decades. Millions of people have been deprived of peace for much of their foreshortened life, while an even greater number - possibly all humankind - can feel the threat of being severed from peace and stability - if not for themselves, for their children. Good in itself, true peace, lasting peace - is also a symptom of welfare and happiness, a symptom of people living in harmony with themselves and others. Otherwise peace can be no more than elusive, an appearance maintained through repressed violence, undermined by the sense of frustration and impotence, and which will eventually be threatened by revolt.

28. The call for action to eliminate hunger, poverty and injustice that form the social bed of violence, is getting louder every moment - action at the local and national level by governments, civil societies, and non-governmental institutions and organizations. Action is needed to promote and support the development of well-governed societies, where all segments of society, women and men equally, share rights and obligations equitably. Action is required to remove the social, institutional, political and economic barriers that prevent the most vulnerable from having their voice heard, from participating to decision-making affecting their lives, from accessing productive resources, from enjoying human development and the right to exert their initiative; and for those momentarily or lastingly deprived of the means to sustain their livelihoods, action is needed for them to benefit from national and international solidarity. Action is necessary to incorporate peace-oriented considerations into macro-economic planning

and international financial and structural assistance, and systematically to take into account the ways in which government policies and development aid are likely to influence food security, equity and poverty. The ways and means of such action are those carefully spelled out, five years ago, by the international community assembled to sanction the World Food Summit Plan of Action. Time is running out for making words blossom into deeds.[11]

Taunting the Poor

Indian democracy — with apologies to Abraham Lincoln — is Government of the rich, by the rich, for the rich. The poor and the weak exist to serve the rich. They can be ruthlessly evicted, marginalized and even be killed, if they stand in the way. Even if they are not murdered suddenly and violently, they are slowly sent to the hereafter by the deprivation of livelihood, the denial of adequate nourishment, ill health through the payment of criminally low wages or the denial of rightful wages through governmental corruption and private chicanery.

One would doubtless run into a volley of invectives as one says this. India has free and fair elections. People vote and change Governments. There is a lively, free and much-feared media that regularly exposes corruption and wrongdoing by officials and the politically and economically powerful and has, in some cases, compelled retribution and remedial action by administrative machinery which had remained silent. India has a Constitution that guarantees a comprehensive set of fundamental rights and Directive Principles of State Policy, which lays down the coordinates for enlightened governance.

---

[11]World food summit, Five Years Later, Multi Stake Holder dialogue, June 10-13, 2002

The argument that economic exploitation continues despite all this would be met by the answer that minimum wages have been statutorily provided in many sectors of the economy, the industrial workforce, even drivers and those engaged in public and private sanitation, now enjoy middle-class life styles. The National Rural Employment Guarantee Scheme has hugely benefited the rural poor. The Green Revolution and land reforms have markedly improved the life of farmers. A state-run healthcare system exists almost everywhere; primary education is reaching down to the grassroots level.

All this is true. India is a democracy in a formally institutional and mechanistic sense. While institutions do function, they often do so grossly imperfectly and do not deliver what they are supposed to. An independent judiciary does not help beyond a point, if those without resources cannot access it and if one has to wait for years to receive a judgment. Lawyers' fees are reaching for the skies and not many lawyers are prepared to fight *pro bono* for the poor. Besides, most such lawyers are beyond the reach of the poor in the countryside, and some of them in peripheral urban areas. As for state-run healthcare, one has only to visit Government hospitals and health centers in some part to realize the farce that it is.

A significant section of industrial and service sector workers, no doubt, enjoy middle-class incomes. They, however, represent a fraction of the country's total work force. The rural poor remain exploited and under-nourished because of the corruption that prevails in the NREGS in many States. Even farmers, who have done well, are increasingly driven to suicide by rising costs of inputs, inadequacy of crop insurance facilities, poor returns and the debt burden. Both they and those below the poverty line in rural areas are vulnerable to forcible eviction to facilitate the setting up of industries, mines, and infrastructure like roads. Crooked Government employees and middlemen, even where the amount does not turn it into a cruel joke, usurp compensation.

There are, doubtless, non-Government organizations reaching out to the dis-privileged. While many of them are doing an excellent job, many operate under severe financial constraints. It is hardly a secret that Government employees demand bribes for even sanctioning reimbursements for programs for the benefit of street children. NGOs whose welfare activities exist on paper and whose funds are diverted to private pockets — and there are quite a few of them — are, course, generally flush with money, as they are skilled in the art of greasing palms.

As for the media, the focus is increasingly on entertainment, the celebration of the wonders of the market, and the altruism and excellence of corporate entities. The result is a diversion of the focus of public discourse from the plight of the poor to the titillating world of trivia, the glorious world of endless consumption, including luxurious travel.

How many print publications and television channels report serious, informed debates in Parliament and the State legislatures? How many have run sustained campaigns against the systematic genocide of tribal people and their culture, and the rape of the environment, in the name of development? How many, for example, have opened their pages or programs for an adequate debate on the pros and cons of the UID? The discussions that have occurred have been desultory and far-between.

Long before John Kenneth Galbraith wrote 'The Affluent Society', RH Tawney had said in The Acquisitive Society, published in the 1920s, that in a society with great disparities of wealth, the money that should have been invested on meeting the subsistence needs of the poor ends up catering to the consumption urges of the rich which ensures higher returns. This is precisely what is happening in India. People have money to hire a plane and celebrate a wedding in mid-air, or charter aircraft and take friends on foreign jaunts to celebrate their birthdays, but would not donate the amount thus spent on a hospital for poor children.

The harsh fact that consuming Indians, whose ranks now include those from the middle-class as well, have no time for what Swami Vivekananda called *Daridra Narayan*, or the God that resides in the poor. Worse, a section with money to influence bureaucrats and politicians and run advertising blitzkriegs, is mercilessly dispossessing and evicting the poor and the week.

The poor and the unprivileged are not going to endure their plight passively. Their anger is alienating them implacably from the existing order. They are, in their respective areas, being drawn to the most powerful group that stands for the overthrow of it. It is the Maoists at some places and/or communal, linguistic, ethnic or separatist organizations in some others. Repression will not help.

Extremist violence of one kind or the other is raging in large parts of the country and may spread all over with time. Extremist groups are establishing links among themselves and trying to launch coordinated action. On how many fronts can the security forces fight, particularly if, following American withdrawal from Afghanistan, Pakistan, its arsenal swelled by aid, unleashes both *jihadis* and its conventional forces against India?

One has to switch to a development pattern that does not destitute the poor.[12]

---

[12]Hiranmay Karlekar (2010), "Taunting the Poor", The Pioneer, October 9, 2010

Governance of Food Security

The Director General of the Food and Agriculture Organization of the United Nations, Rome has advised that governance of food security should aim at:

(a) Keep agriculture and food security at top of the international agenda for the eradication of hunger and malnutrition in the world;
(b) Fully understand the factors that affect world food security, the associated risks and remedial actions;
(c) Ensure close links between technical expertise and policy-making;
(d) See that the international community adopts a coherent and systematic approach to food security:
(e) To respond rapidly to situations of food crisis and emergency in order to mitigate their negative effects;
(f) To stimulate investment in agriculture and rural development and mobilize the funding required ensuring the food security of local populations.
(g) To help bolster the governance of food security in a framework of coherence and synergy of policies, strategies and actions at all levels – national, regional and international.[13]

Acting against Hunger

A parliamentary standing committee has recently asked the government to introduce the National Food Security Bill in the winter session of the Lok Sabha. A promise to implement a Bill of this kind was first mooted in President Pratibha Patil's inaugural speech last year when she mentioned the government's

[13]Report of the 36th Session of the Committee on World Food Security (CFS), Rome 18-23 November 2009

intention to provide each family below the poverty line (BPL) with 25 kg of food grains a month at Rs 3 per kg.

The public debate about the "right to food" and the appropriate contents of the Act has continued ever since, and has indeed intensified because food prices keep marching up. In particular, social activists have argued that the right cannot be restricted simply to the BPL families and that the quantity of grain mentioned in the president's speech is quite inadequate.

Perhaps, in response to this, the National Advisory Council (NAC) has recommended that the Act should provide every family in the 200 most disadvantaged districts with 35 kg of rice or wheat at Rs 3 per kg. The NAC also suggested that the benefits of the Act may be restricted to BPL families in the rest of the country, although it also set the target of universal coverage by 2015. Although Sonia Gandhi's presence in the NAC gives its recommendations enormous weight, the government has still been dragging its feet and it is not clear as yet about the contents of the Act in its final form.

Is the government's reluctance to implement the NAC recommendations justified? The answer has nothing to do with the intrinsic merits of such legislation. It needs no statistical facts to convince anyone that vast numbers of our poor go hungry to bed every night although every government in independent India has promised to work tirelessly for the poor! That is why a legal right to food is so important to the poor it forces the government to honour its promises. However, no government should pass a law that simply cannot be implemented. Routine and repeated violations of individual rights debase the very meaning of rights and laws.

In the foreseeable future, even a government with the best of intentions cannot ensure that it provides BPL families throughout the country with the stipulated amount of food grains. The reason for this is not the availability of food as we surely know, Food Corporation of India (FCI) warehouses are stuffed to their capacity. The only real constraint is the lack of any adequate delivery mechanism.

The public distribution system has become an article of faith in India. In fact, even the NAC suggests that grain to the poor should be distributed through the PDS. However, this faith ignores completely the wealth of data establishing the gross inadequacy of the PDS. Consider some of the evidence against the PDS. A recent study shows that two-thirds of the grain allocated to the PDS for distribution to the poor end up in the open market. Contrary to popular belief, large numbers of the poor do not purchase their food grain from the PDS for a variety of reasons lack of PDS outlets especially in the north, absence of BPL cards, the inability to buy in bulk. Not surprisingly, there are estimates showing that the poor receive only 10 per cent of the total food subsidy bill.

Perhaps, the PDS can be improved. But this is not going to happen in a hurry. However, there is no need to wait for the wholesale revamping of the PDS before launching a modified form of the food security Bill. A start can be made by initiating the first component of the NAC recommendation of providing universal coverage to the poorest 200 districts. Incidentally, universal coverage in any given region has the advantage that it abolishes the need to identify BPL families. The restriction on geographical coverage will obviously make it that much easier for the government to ensure that an adequate delivery mechanism is in place in these areas. The Bill can also specify a reasonable timetable within which food security will be extended gradually all over the country.

It is also important to realize the imperative to look for alternatives to the PDS. The government's Economic Survey for the current year set the ball rolling by discussing the system of food stamps. The use of food stamps originated in the US in 1964, and has since then been used in several countries including Sri Lanka, Jamaica, Mexico and Honduras. Under this scheme, the target population is issued coupons or stamps which recipients can exchange for stipulated amounts of food at any shop not just ration shops. The shop owners can then deposit these coupons in their bank accounts and be credited appropriate amounts, which depend on prevailing market prices.

The biggest advantage of food stamps is that it would wipe out the leakages associated with the PDS. Moreover, to the extent that private traders are more efficient than the FCI, there would be a social saving in terms of the lower delivery costs. Of course, the system is not foolproof. But then, the benchmark is the PDS, and so the appropriate question to ask is how any new system compares relative to the PDS.[14]

Appetite for Reform

The UN Food and Agriculture Organization recently warned that food prices worldwide had hit record levels since their first indexing in 1990. More, it said they would spike further. Now, with over two-thirds of China's wheat crop under threat courtesy shortage of rainfall, the prediction looks fewer alarmists than its critics say. More so, since drought-afflicted China's troubles have accompanied weather-related disruption elsewhere as well, such as flood-hit

[14]Bhaskar Dutta, " Acting Against Hunger", The Times of India, Bhubaneswar, August 25, 2010

Australia and other big food-producing nations like the US, Russia, and Brazil. The world, it appears, might need to brace for supply shocks and consequently bigger food bills, which have already caused unrest in many regions including the Arab world.

True, we haven't seen food riots of the kind marking 2008's crisis. But the international situation is worrisome not least because the political counter to be had in protectionist export caps or bans – as in 2007-08 – only aggravates problems in an interdependent world. No country today is self-sufficient and must export or import to help meet its own and others' food needs. So, the issue mandates multilateral thinking on global governance, climate change with special focus on water management as well as aid policies including on transfer of knowhow and technological collaboration to help upgrade farming techniques in developing countries with rising food demand.

India's policy makers correctly say high food inflation is a global and not solely domestic headache. But surely that's no excuse for blinking at India's massively underdeveloped farm sector and creaking supply and public distribution networks. Providing food security to a nearly 1.2 billion-strong nation is a daunting task. The world can't help us unless we help ourselves by striving to eliminate agriculture's deep-rooted systemic weaknesses. Only by modernizing can productivity be raised and delivery glitches plugged. For starters, we need better monsoon readiness, and that includes a vastly expanded and qualitatively improved irrigation cover, which is now limited to just 40 percent of India's cultivable land.

As crucial are regulations – be it on labour or viable land holding size – favourable to promoting large-scale mechanized farming and agro-processing. Indeed, rural India needs massive private sector investment, to be had by building an agriculture-industry interface. Widespread food insecurity is scandalous when huge amounts of perishables go waste annually thanks to inadequate storage and transport infrastructure.

With retail reform, funds can flow to cold chains and warehousing apart from creating profitable marketing opportunities for farmers. Inter-state movement and trade in products need easing as well to help match cross-country demand and supply. Finally, R&D and innovation in farming are a must to help conserve depleting groundwater, improve soil and seed quality and beat back use of harmful fertilizers. Taking a favourable call on genetically modified foods will be key to our launching a long overdue second green revolution.[15]

Hear farmers' call

It has been 60 years since the Indian Parliament held its first session in 1952. In this context, the media reported that the third Lok Sabha (1962-67) had farmer- leaders formed the single largest group in the House. Three five-year plans laid great emphasis on agriculture — building large dams, establishing agricultural universities, undertaking major irrigation works, setting out on the path of the Green Revolution and so on. Subsequent plans laid emphasis on other sectors, whilst also supporting agriculture.

Records show that agriculture grew annually at around one per cent in the pre-Independence era, while it has hovered around three to four per cent in free India. Agricultural contribution to our gross domestic product has fallen from 43 per cent to 16 per cent in the years between 1970 and 2011. However, this fall may also be due to a faster growth in the manufacturing and service sectors.

---

[15]The Times of India, February 15, 2011

Agriculture has become unattractive and stressful, pushing farmers to end their lives rather than endure with hope for a better future.

Problems are multifarious— poor quality seeds, high input costs, lack of sufficient water, unpredictable power supply, absence of timely produce procurement, lack of storage, unavailability and high interest rate of credit facility, inadequate and delayed minimum support price, meager insurance at times of crop failure and lack of permanent land rights.

The youth do not want to inherit this burden resulting in migration to urban areas. It will be cruel to top this brimming cup of woes with our indifference to their plight. The two-day Farmers' Parliament held in New Delhi on May 12-13, 2012 voiced their concerns. They felt that the neglect of agriculture is now complete. This meet has demanded a special session of Parliament to discuss agriculture.

Karnataka had started giving their farmers a separate budget and loans at an interest rate of one per cent. Gujarat is currently holding a month-long "Farmers' Festival" — an annual pre-monsoon preparatory and readiness exercise where every need of the farmer is comprehensively addressed at his village or revenue block so that he confidently takes on the forthcoming crop season.

In the eighth "Farmers' festival" this year, nearly one hundred thousand employees belonging to various ministries, departments, corporations and boards were present in the villages with the farmers. They would help them in getting Soil Health Card, Kisan Credit Card, crop insurance, enrolling for drip irrigation etc. Activities such as de-silting canals and ponds and providing new power substations were taken up in mission mode.

Gujarat now has 107 soil-testing centers. Ten years ago there were only 20 such centers. The four agricultural universities in the state actively participate in this campaign, notwithstanding the fact that their interaction with farmers and extension workers is an ongoing process.

A typical day during this campaign has the morning spent on animal welfare. The cattle are vaccinated, treated and where necessary operated upon, all free of cost. Two hundred and twenty-seven mobile units — vehicles — one each for a taluka (Revenue office) stay for a whole day in a village for each cluster, providing intensive training and information on specific crop/issue.

This year saw the input salesmen — of seeds, fertilizers and pesticides — follow the vehicles offering special discounts. The government provides a subsidized input kit to all marginal farmers. During this festival, the government appealed to the farmers to adopt best agricultural practices. Invariably citing the example of a local progressive farmer worthy of emulation, the chief minister motivates them to strive and succeed, assuring, as if incidentally, that the Gujarat government is fully with them.

Attempts to project Gujarat as an industrialized state continuing to sustain its lead in that and in trade and commerce, thereby diluting its achievements in agriculture, are completely misplaced. In the last 10 years, income from agriculture has tripled even at constant prices (base year: 2001) from 159.75 billion INR to 392.77 billion INR. Gujarat has found itself rightly on the global agricultural map for sustaining a double-digit average growth in the last decade. During the year 2010-11 the state's agriculture grew by 16.6 per cent. Agricultural income totaled 880 billion INR. As of April 2012, over 469 thousand hectares are drip irrigated. In the Vibrant Gujarat

Summit 2013, a separate event is being planned for agriculture.

Today, Kutch, the salty marshland, which was ravaged by an earthquake 10 years ago, is the horticultural hub of Gujarat. The Government of India has declared 2012-13 as "**Horticulture Year**" and provided the National Horticulture Mission an outlay of 18.50 billion INR. But with an outlay of 1.55 billion INR and with a horticultural produce availability of 300 kg/person, while the national average is only 198kg/person, Gujarat has raised the benchmark.

Seven years ago, Kutch produced 125 thousand litres of milk per year. Now, Kutch and Kathiyavad together produce 1500 thousand litres per year, earning 50 million INR daily from the sale of milk. There are more than 100 agricultural produce marketing centers in Gujarat. They are a hub of activity for the farmers. The Gujarat government spent 20 million INR on each of them for providing better facilities to the farmer. Now a farmer can get subsidized nutritious meals and his cattle can get a resting place and water to drink.[16]

Ten years ago, farmers in Gujarat got only 15 power substations each year, but it increased to 150 power substations every year since then. The subsidy for providing power to the farmers is 30 billion INR now as compared to 5 billion INR then. Gujarat is an arid state covering two-thirds area. Thanks to sustained campaigning and concerted efforts, groundwater depletion has halted. The groundwater table has risen — by three meters in some areas and 13meters in some others — closer to the surface. Over 6, 50,000 water-harvesting structures, interlinking of rivers, check dams and canals have contributed to this critical and catalytic change. The people of Gujarat

---

[16] Nirmala Sitharaman (2012), "Hear farmers' call", Deccan Chronicle, May 14, 2012

have contributed to this massive effort through sacrificing time. We may consider agriculture for providing food security to the nation, or for employing the bulk of semiskilled and unskilled workers or for being the fountainhead of our rural economy. Throwing tonnes of money at it is no good.

Commitment, understanding, detailed planning, sustained efforts and visionary leadership make the difference.

PERU: **Farmers' Rights in Peru**

Farmers of Peru acknowledge the importance of their traditional knowledge and its vulnerability, as well as the vulnerability of the crop diversity they are maintaining. Factors contributing to the loss of biological diversity and traditional knowledge included as follows:

(a) The increasing number of frosts and weevils
(b) The introduction of chemical fertilizers and pesticides
(c) Lack of interest among the young farmers for learning about traditional agricultural systems and practices
(d) Out-migration of young men
(e) Environmental pollution through mining
(f) Improved seeds reduce the acreage under native varieties
(g) Climate change and glacial melting
(h) Overgrazing
(i) Social weakening of communities
(j) Free trade agreement with the USA might limit farmers' market access

Most of the farmers participating at the workshops were subsistence farmers. The farmers expected that they would get low prices if they sell their produce in the market. Many farmers mentioned that fair prices could improve their livelihoods. Some farmers emphasized on processing of their produce for better prices. In the post-harvest season fewer prices are offered to the farmers. The farmers believed that they would earn more through processing. Every one emphasized on better and profitable prices. Although they had less knowledge on domestic laws and international agreements, some farmers had heard about Peru's bilateral free trade agreement with the USA. They were worried about free trade agreements, and they expected that the local market might be flooded with cheap potatoes of USA.

Farmers' Rights:

The farmers of the workshop felt that the small farmers or peasants would be marginalized and become powerless and face exclusion. They lamented the authorities' lack of interest in consulting them, and felt they should be allowed to participate when laws and policies were made. They felt that their knowledge of crop management and biodiversity conservation should matter, and that their traditional crops should be valued in the same way as imported varieties. Among other things they believed that their crops should receive more recognition for nutritional value. The experts explained quality of modern varieties. One farmer stated that a good and nutritious diet is the basis for good health; and that the government should recognize this and support farmers who produce nutritious food. Some also expressed the need to know more about the nutritional qualities of the food they produce in order to be able to put together a balanced diet. For this purpose they wanted a laboratory at their disposal where they could test the different varieties.

Prices:

Farmers are more concerned about the market prices of their products. The producers' prices of agricultural commodities are too low to enable the peasants to live with dignity. The farmers wanted the government to recognize their suffering, and they wanted the local authorities to help them obtain better prices. Some farmers felt that the mayors did not care about farmers, and that the municipal authorities were not involved. This situation could be improved, the farmers thought, if the mayors and other municipal authorities are present at farmers' meetings. They also wanted financial help from the municipal budgets to conserve biodiversity, as well as with access to seed and capacity building. One suggestion was subsidies for maintaining varieties. During natural calamities, the government should procure agricultural commodities from local farmers, which could enrich and empower the farmers. But the government emphasizes on food aid of foreign countries.

Relationship to INIA and other authorities:

Financial support for communal seed banks was mentioned as another measure the authorities could implement to strengthen Farmers' Rights. The farmers from Quilcas felt that the funds for INIA's seed banks should go directly to the communities, since INIA and PRONAMACH are not supporting many communities. These farmers also wanted help in securing the rights to their varieties, and thought it would be a good idea to have a committee that could articulate the needs of farmers in relation to the conservation of biodiversity and provide them with support.

Recognition and support to conservative farmers:

The conservation farmers were interested in receiving recognition and support for their work in maintaining such a high a number of varieties, and had many suggestions for how this could be done and their situation improved. One conservation farmer from

Huánuco wanted conservation farmers to be recognized by a special law, while others suggested policies aimed at the maintenance and conservation of agro-biodiversity, and rules and regulations for conservation farmers.

Some farmers expressed their interest in being able to receive loans/ credits from the Agrarian Bank. They felt that there should be an emergency fund for crop failure and that farmers should participate in the Farmers' Rights conventions. It was also suggested that the government should arrange for a quota of guano fertilizer to be distributed to them as organic fertilizer. The conservation farmers of Huánuco and Cuzco wanted financial support from the Ministry of Agriculture for seed exchange fairs, in addition to health insurance, fair prices and greater recognition. It was also suggested that the registry of native varieties should be the responsibility of communities or conservation farmers themselves but that the country data could be managed by INIA, which should provide recognition to the contributors. Access to genetic resources was important to these farmers, and they felt that they should also have access to the *ex situ* resources kept by various institutions.

Many conservation farmers believed that the communities especially concerned with conserving native varieties should work together and form an organization, but they also stressed that the communities needed to collaborate with the authorities.

They wanted their land to be protected, and for this the cooperation of the authorities would be necessary. Many also felt that the land they use in their conservation work should be categorized as a type of biological reserve.

Farmers' suggestions: When asked about what they thought the government should do to realize Farmers'

Rights, promote sustainable use of genetic resources and protect traditional knowledge, the farmers participating in the different workshops had a range of suggestions in addition to those already mentioned. Moreover, they added other important factors which could assist them for a sustainable living.

These factors are as follows:

(a) Respect for farmers and their work
(b) Recognition of, and support to, farmers and farmers' organizations on the part of local, regional and national authorities
(c) Recognition of the importance and value of native crops, instead of replacing them with imported crops
(d) Underline the importance of biological diversity in relation to climate change
(e) Support for *in situ* conservation, in the same way as *ex situ* conservation is supported
(f) Disseminate information, including research results based on materials collected from communities
(g) Disseminate information about the agrarian laws or market laws that affect them
(h) Health insurance for farmers
(i) Subsidies to farmers who grow Andean crops
(j) Fair prices - enough to live a dignified life (some indicated that they would be able to lift themselves out of poverty if potatoes could be sold for S/5.00 (2.5 US) for one kilo.
(k) Help the peasants to improve their products so they can get better prices in the markets
(l) Recognition of the importance of transmitting knowledge to the younger generations
(m) Easier access to long-term loans/credit (with low interest rates)
(n) Irrigation
(o) Farmers' Exchange visits
(p) Research on soil fertility

(q) Support for seed fairs with native varieties, and help them to cover the costs of attending fairs
(r) Reforestation
(s) Improved homes
(t) Making organic fertilizers and guano available at special rates, or for free distribution
(u) Advertise for native potato varieties
(v) Help the farmers for certification of organic products
(w) Policies targeted at small-scale farmer
(x) Machinery for processing
(y) Recognition of farmers' culture and knowledge
(z) A change of relief/aid practices: good-quality seed and propagation material should be distributed on time

The other important factors are:

(a) A register for native potato varieties
(b) Law that favors /protects/recognizes conservation farmers
(c) Crop insurance/agricultural insurance for emergencies protection of areas used for cultivation of native crops (agro-biodiversity reserves)
(d) Access to virus-free native varieties
(e) Access to propagation material and relevant information from gene banks
(f) Access to information about varieties
(g) The Ministry of Agriculture should consult farmers when drawing up seed laws and other legislation affecting farmers – a more bottom–up approach when designing laws and
(h) Facilitate the creation of an organization for all conservation farmers, with its own bylaws.

In short, the five workshops provided valuable insights into the realities and challenges of farming in the exceptionally diverse Andes region. The farmers consulted were deeply concerned about the situation and prospects for further maintenance of their crop diversity. They had a wealth of reflections and suggestions as to necessary measures, many of which are relevant in a Farmers' Rights perspective. In a preparatory workshop prior to the national workshop on Farmers' Rights held in Lima in September 2008, representatives from the five workshops came together to work out the main suggestions to present to decision-makers in the country.

The suggestions of the farmers in the workshops are documented for the planners of the country. These are as follows:

Access to seed:

(a) Seed exchange should be promoted through seed fairs, which should focus on the sharing of seeds and knowledge, rather than prizes.
(b) Capacity-building efforts should focus on the importance of seed exchange.
(c) (c)Activities should be organized (for example by local and regional authorities) that bring farmers together so they can get to know and trust each other, which in turn will foster seed exchange.
(d) Old seed sources known for their high-quality seed should be revived and made official.
(e) Farmers should be provided with the opportunity to participate in activities targeted at removing virus from native varieties and capacity building should be initiated to keep the varieties virus-free.
(f) Farmers should have access to seeds from INIA and CIP, and information about this possibility should be widely disseminated.
(g) Communal seed banks should receive financial and technical support.

(h) The authorities should develop incentives for conservation and sustainable use of crop genetic resources.

Strengthening of local knowledge:

(a) The value of traditional knowledge should be recognized. In particular the traditional management of seeds should receive greater attention and recognition.
(b) Initiatives to foster exchange of knowledge, through exchange visits and the like, should be promoted and supported.
(c) Capacity building should target the young, so that they can learn more about ancestral farming techniques and traditional knowledge.
(d) Cooperation with scientific research should take as their point of departure farmers' realities, and support farmers in their efforts to improve their varieties and farming systems.
(e) As part of the cooperation between farmers and research institutions, farm children should be offered access to higher education in agriculture.
(f) A national coordinating agency should be established for the management of agricultural biodiversity and Farmers' Rights.

Access to markets:

(a) Fair prices should be offered for native varieties, to make them competitive with improved varieties.
(b) Conservation farmers should have access to special low-interest loans through the Agrarian Bank, as well to agricultural insurance.
(c) When varieties are lost, through for example drought, frost or hail, the authorities should have a ready course of action to enable farmers to access emergency funding. This

funding should help them buy local propagating material and ensure that they can retrieve their varieties.

Other suggestions regarding Farmers' Rights:

(a) National agro-biodiversity reserves should be established in order to protect these areas from the threat of mining and other pollution or destruction, and to ensure that Farmers' Rights are respected particularly in these reserves.
(b) Farmers should be compensated for maintaining crop diversity. The funding should be at an equal level with *ex situ* facilities.
(c) Farmers' seed varieties should be registered by the farmers or farming communities themselves.
(d) Information about relevant laws and policies should be disseminated in farming communities.
(e) Farmers should be included in relevant decision-making processes.

This study on farmers' perceptions and Farmers' Rights in Peru is based on the workshops held in Lima in September 2008. The goal of the workshops is to focus on the realization of Farmers' Rights. The approach has been to look into the situations and views of farmers and to draw recommendations for planning.

The realization of Farmers' Rights is a highly relevant issue in Peru due to the country's rich agro-biodiversity and the relative poverty and marginalizing of Peruvian farmers. The workshops showed that the farmers themselves have many ideas as to how this can be done. They are interested in taking part in and organizing projects, as well as participating in the relevant decision-making processes.

The measures needed for realizing **Farmers' Rights** can be grouped into four categories:

(a) Protection of traditional knowledge,
(b) Equitable benefit sharing,
(c) Participation of farmers in decision-making processes
(d) Providing the legal space necessary for farmers to continue their traditional practices of seed saving and exchange.

The following core strategies build on the perceptions and suggestions of the farmers participating in the workshops and the implications of these as analyzed in section 6. For the purpose of realizing Farmers' Rights in Peru these measures from the four different categories are recommended:

Protection of traditional knowledge:

(a) Efforts should be made both to document traditional knowledge in such a way that it cannot be misappropriated, and to keep it alive by sharing it and teaching it to the next generation.
(b) Agro-biodiversity reserves should be introduced to protect the land most important for the cultivation of native varieties in as many communities as possible. This would help keep traditional farming practices and traditional knowledge alive.

Equitable benefit sharing:

(a) Farmers' access to suitable propagating material of good quality should be promoted by providing support to community gene banks, seed fairs and exchange visits, and research into seed systems.
(b) Farmers should have access to research, technology and new techniques through

information dissemination and collaboration with researchers. Bottom–up approaches should inform agricultural research, PPB should be central, and it is important that the resultant varieties are disseminated quickly.

(c) Farmers must to a greater extent be informed about existing possibilities and projects, such as the CIP's repatriation program.

(d) Efforts should be made to get higher prices for farmers' crops, for example by initiating projects providing assistance with processing and marketing.

(e) A support system for Andean crops should be considered to ensure that the incentive system also promotes this type of agriculture.

(f) Pilot villages should be considered as a measure to bolster the conservation and exchange of genetic resources and traditional knowledge.

Participation of farmers in decision-making:

(a) Awareness-raising efforts should be implemented targeting all relevant decision-makers, for example through workshops;

(b) Capacity-building efforts should be implemented targeting farmers in all regions, disseminating information about existing laws and policies as well as political processes and ways to influence the outcome.

(c) National Farmers' Organization should be supported in its efforts to organize farmers engaged in the management of plant genetic resources for food and agriculture to influence legislative and policy processes.

(d) Farmers' organizations should be consulted as part of legislative and policy processes and during their implementation.

(e) Providing legal space for the continuation of traditional practices:

1 A chapter on Farmers' Rights should be included in the Seed Law.
2 A wider farmers' exemption should be tried incorporated into the new P V P law.
3 Projects in farming communities should focus on networking and building trust, to promote seed exchange.

In addition to these recommendations, the Peruvian government should also consider making some institutional changes to facilitate the realization of Farmers' Rights. A central recommendation resulting from the discussions in the workshops is that the role of INIA should be clarified. This can be done by making INIA the sole focal point for implementation of the Plant Treaty at the national level in Peru. Another measure in the category of institutional reform would be to establish an interagency committee to coordinate the different measures for realizing Farmers' Rights launched by various government units.[17]

Let us examine some farmers of different countries to assess their deeds and thoughts on the possibility of peace. The governments neglect the farmers; the former kings and monarchs also neglected them in the past. It is because they are over-occupied with their fieldwork; they are poor and therefore they are accustomed to torture and sufferings. They produce food for the whole world; but the rich people cheat them easily with palatable words. Let us hear their experiences from Zambia, China and Ethiopia.

The Challenges Ahead

The world population was below than I billion in 1798 or say at 1800 AD; it reached 7 billion by 2012 and

[17]Maria Scurrah et al (2008), Farmers' Rights in Peru", back Ground Study 8, Farmers' Rights Project. FNI Report 16/ 2008

would reach 9 billion by 2050. So there is a question mark: Can the farmers of the world provide necessary food stuffs for these growing billions of people? The governments, politicians, administrators and scientists would guarantee food security to all future generations as all of them are specialists in false promises and false reports. Who is actually engaged in cultivation of cereals, fruits, vegetables, fishery, dairy and poultry? He is no other than a farmer, peasant, farm labourer or a rural man or woman.

A farmer is neglected in all countries. None is interested to remain in rural area. The population in cities or towns has crossed more than 50 percent of total population in many countries. Land is snatched away by the governments from the farmers in favour of the industrialists. Land area in agriculture is being squeezed by land mafias in all countries. Urban people are entering to rural areas for acquiring large acreage of land to invest their ill-got money for leisure and pleasure. There is change of climate; water is scanty, and farm labourers are now urban labourers, or slum dwellers. Land rights of farmers are complicated in all developing countries. Corruption is the aim, objective and rule in all countries. Corrupt politicians and corrupt bureaucrats have made the farmers nomads and have forced thousands of farmers to commit suicides by wrong policies, such as subsidy, government procurement, free bicycles, and colored dresses to young kids. The governments train the rural kids for free lunches of inferior quality and quantity in primary schools. In other words, the government is taking all steps to train their minds for free benefits; it encourages the art of begging to all rural people because they are poor.

Why a government would distribute free books, food, and dress to young kids and subsidized seeds, fertilizer, insecticide or irrigation water

to the farmers? It is because government knows that there should be poor people as they are vote-banks for elections.

Food production cannot be increased by increasing subsidy in agriculture; it can be possible by making agriculture, a profitable enterprise. Why the government employees or elected leaders would be allowed higher pay, perks and pensioners benefits with dearness allowances and other benefits during service periods and even after retirement? Let the farmers be assured that their life is secured. Let all inhabitants of the country after 60 years of age get pensioners' benefits, at least 1/10th of the highest bureaucrat?

The farmers do not need sympathy from the government; they need justice. They need favourable prices for their commodities; they simply need profit in agriculture and food security now and in future. They need land rights over cultivated land and residential plots as hereditary rights. They need peace.

Conclusion

All the developing countries should adopt pro-poor, pro-rural and pro-agricultural policies to make the people of the country food secure. A country can be politically, socially and economically independent if it does not depend upon other countries in food production. The farmers, peasants, agricultural labourers, artisans and poor people should be properly engaged for development of the country. Their engagement would establish an era of peace in the country. They can contribute immensely in nation building programs such as food security, free from foreign debt, societal harmony and construction work.

Too much emphasis on industrialization and urbanization causes environmental degradation and war-like situations. It creates uproar, strikes, and evacuations of farmers from parental land, loss of farmland and forestland, unlawful mining, high corruption, smuggling and health hazards of common men. The Governments of all developing countries should award the following free benefits to increase the morale, social status and income of the farmers.

These are:

(a) Life Insurance policy
(b) Health Insurance Policy
(c) Crop Insurance Policy
(d) Cattle Insurance policy
(e) Monthly pension scheme to all senior citizens of the country including farmers
(f) Free Market intelligence service
(g) A piece of land to all landless voters above 21 years of age
(h) Agricultural markets in each cluster of villages
(i) Free saplings of fruit trees to all farm families that are best grown in the locality
(j) Land records must be up to date, clean and clear. The revenue officer should be under strict scanner.
(k) Land cases must be finalized within one year.
(l) All citizens of the country including farmers must have Bank Accounts for safety and satisfaction.
(m) Food Security to all

Moreover farmers of Peru demanded the following terms for the benefit of the farmers. These are:

(a) Farmers right should include prices of saleable commodities could improve their livelihoods.
(b) They emphasized on farmers' rights,
(c) Favourable prices of agricultural commodities,
(d) Support to conservation farmers,
(e) Respect for farmers and their work,
(f) Farmers' exchange visit,

(g) Access to seed,
(h) Strengthening local language,
(i) Access to markets,
(j) Registration of seed varieties for farming communities,
(k) Protection of traditional knowledge,
(l) Equitable benefit sharing, and
(m) Participation of farmers in decision making

Farmers need justice, not charity. They need income, not gifts. They want to keep their heads high. They simply need peace.

Let the farmers feel that the governments are sincerely trying to award justice to them in all countries. But the policy of the government for the farmers and agriculture is nostalgic and disagreeable to the mass. Government plays with the life of millions of poor people, which are engaged in supplying food to all – a path to award peace to all.

The western countries advance excess credit to the developing countries for infrastructure development, but the farmers commit suicides for lack of employment, income generation and government sympathy.

Let all of us live in peace. Let us march ahead with ONE WORLD FAMILY concept in this twenty-first century.

If farmers would be happy, there would be shortage of youths for armed forces; and the challenges of terrorists, Naxalites and Maoists would decline in all developing countries. The rush for war would automatically come down and it is possible even today.

+++++

Chapter II

FARMERS IN DISTRESS

In most of the countries of the world, the peasants, farmers, agricultural labourers, artisans and landless people are the sufferers and they are passing through hardships. If the governments can utilize their services, they can earn their bread and can prove their presence everywherc, but unemployment and hunger have turned those negative entities. All school dropouts, farmers' suicides and land cases could have been avoided if these peasants or agricultural labourers are engaged. Agriculture can create more employment than other sectors such as industry or services. But governments neglect agriculture, horticulture, fishery or dairy. All the governments of developing countries are running after industries and industrialists. The government evicts peasants from their cultivated land for roads, railways and industries; allots thousands of acres of land, mines, and forest areas to industrialists for development of the state. The government is also responsible for unemployment, of youths, societal change and massive corruption. So there should be some restrictions on the activities of the governments. But how it can be done?

In this chapter, facts such as "Farmers encounter Challenges, Seeding control, Farmers' Suicides in India, Farmers' Suicides Worse after 2001, Response to farmers' suicides, and farmers' suicides in India, What a Team of Farm scientists say? Farmers face Problems, Don't pauperize farmers for profit, Seed Wars: The right to refuse, Farmers faces Problems, Economy cuts both ways to Farmers, Government promises to solve farmers' problems, Tanzania Farmers, Farmers Sell Livestock, Zimbabwe Farmers – United amid fears of tobacco ban, Republic of Angola are discussed. These factors speak the pathetic conditions of farmers throughout world. It is high time to take urgent steps to stop or at least reduce the sufferings of the farmers in this twenty-first century to create an era of peace everywhere.

INDIA:
Farmers Encounter Challenges

(a) **Impact of scientific advancement**

The world is advancing in science, technology and media reporting. The young boys and girls have forgotten that their forefathers were under foreign rule and every farmer was working hard to produce grains for his family members. He faced natural calamities such as drought, flood, cyclone, and torrential rainfall. None was helping the farmers to meet his food requirement. People were depending upon forests, domestic animals and rivers for their daily food requirement. There were no roads, no doctor, and no transport facility for moving to distant places even during the mid twentieth century. People regarded the kings, emperors as living Gods.

Today the situation is completely changed. There are schools, colleges, hospitals, and government offices in remote areas. Now the students, women, daily workers and even unemployed youths have mobile phones, two wheelers and pocket money to spend for pleasure and progress. The rising expectation of every person has created a new era in the society. Most of the people have forgotten their duties for the society but they ask for their rights.

The political leaders, businessmen, government officials and traders are exploiting the society to save more wealth at the shortest possible time; this has created dis-contentment in the society. These privileged people are the factors of revolutions in all developing countries. Disparities in income, high sky scrappers' buildings, aero planes, luxury cars and mega industries of some people have annoyed the common man, unemployed youths and the peasants.

(b) **Autocratic governance**

In most of the developing countries, a particular political party rules the county for decades and he hands over the state rule to his progenies. These rulers rule the country as their birthrights. The Arabs are rising against autocratic regimes not only because many of them are poor and unemployed but also because their rulers have failed to respond to a new society with a new economic order.

The French Revolution in 1848, 'New Left' revolution of Belgrade in 1968 and Poland Revolution in 1989 have spread beyond their boundaries. The whole world has become smaller because of transmission of news at a faster rate. The Arab Unrest of 2011 explains that people are fed up with anti-government policies. The government becomes unpopular when poverty, unemployment, injustice and corruption rule the state.

Now corruption, unemployment, industrialization process, mining scam, foreign debt, 2G spectrums Scam, and false propaganda by the government have challenged the very existence of democratic rule in India. Income disparity among all section of people have created unhealthy political atmosphere in the country. Rule by a particular government through corrupt practices have created the growth of Maoists, Naxalites and Terrorists in eight states in India, The Orissa state faces the worst Naxalites problem as they could hijack Mr. R V Krishnan, the Magistrate of Malakangiri District and kept him in forest area for 8 days in captive. Here too the tribal peasants have become the terrorists and they have also helped the magistrate for his safe return. Rapid industrialization process activated by State governments in India has forced the farmers and youths to organize revolutions since 2000 and it is gaining momentum throughout the country.

(c) **The Mining Scam**

The Mining scam in Indian states particularly in Orissa, Chhattisgarh, and Karnataka and Jharkhand states is alarming. There are at least half – dozen cases seeking, among other things, a CBI probe into the siphoning of mineral resources worth thousand billions of INR (Indian Rupees) from the state. This happens when daily one farmer commits suicide for loss of crop and inability of clearing the bank loan. The peasants are suffering mental agony, as a small number of people living like erstwhile kings or emperors. Agriculture has become a loss-bearing profession.

(d) **Unemployment of youths**

There is no assured income of the graduates or post-graduates in the state. There is no guarantee that they would earn an income. This has resulted in late marriages, less family attachment and less regard for the governments among the educated youths.

(e) **Populist planning ruins the Farmers**

Orissa is the poorest state in India. More than 58 percent people belong to BPL (Below Poverty Line) group. The inability of the Government to adopt pro-poor, pro-rural and pro-agricultural policies has resulted in chaos in the country. Neither the Parliament nor the State Assemblies are doing justice to the people. The farmers of the state face difficulty in selling rice (Paddy with Husk) even below the production cost. But the government of India supplies wheat, rice (without husk) at the rate of 3 INR per kilo of rice. The state government sells the same quantity of rice @ 2 INR per kg. This farce is going on for the last couple of years. As a result, the agricultural labourers are not available for manual work in rice or wheat fields. This subsidy in agricultural inputs like fertilizer, seeds or irrigation water and subsidy in cleaned rice and raw wheat has crossed 1, 250, 000 million of Indian rupees. This has created massive storage loss, massive corruption in management and harms the very existence of rice and wheat farming in the state and country.

Forceful Eviction from parental land, undeveloped market structure, shortage of irrigation water, loss bearing cultivation practices, government harassment, import of agricultural commodities from foreign land, lack of insurance facility to farmers, harassment by revenue officials, delay in court cases and entry of corrupt politicians in august houses of Parliament and Assemblies have ruined the democratic countries.

If the government decontrol all agricultural commodities, and stop subsidies, corruption in agriculture could be stopped. But the government should take up the following steps to assist the farmers for sustainable income and they would enrich them through profitable agriculture. The amount of funds allotted to subsidy in agriculture per year should be gainfully utilized for the cause of the farmers, peasants, sharecroppers, agricultural laborers, artisans and poor people, so that ultimately the beneficiaries would lead better and happier life. The farmers and others need the following benefits through government patronage, such as:

(a) Parity price of rice or wheat must be assured or it should be decontrolled.
(b) Subsidy in agriculture should be completely discontinued in all countries.
(c) The advanced countries award more subsidies in agriculture to their farmers for maximization of production that could be used for international trade, politics and free foods to hungry people.

We strongly hope that farmers could be better off provided the governments identify the real peace lovers of the state; they are the farmers. The farmers are best suited to act as the pillars of a strong nation. Unless a country is food secured, the country cannot continue to be an independent country forever.

The seed of Emergency

The seed is the first link in the food chain - and seed sovereignty is the foundation of food sovereignty. If farmers do not have their own seeds or access to open pollinated varieties that they can save, improve and exchange, they have no seed sovereignty - and consequently no food sovereignty.

The deepening agrarian and food crisis has its roots in changes in the seed supply system, and the erosion of seed diversity and seed sovereignty.

Seed sovereignty includes the farmer's rights to save, breed and exchange seeds, to have access to diverse open source seeds which can be saved - and which are not patented, genetically modified, owned or controlled by emerging seed giants. It is based on reclaiming seeds and biodiversity as commons and public good.

Farmer suicides spike in India

The past twenty years have seen a very rapid erosion of seed diversity and seed sovereignty, and the concentration of the control over seeds by a very small number of giant corporations. In 1995, when the UN organized the Plant Genetic Resources Conference in Leipzig, it was reported that 75 per cent of all agricultural biodiversity had disappeared because of the introduction of "modern" varieties, which are always cultivated as monocultures. Since then, the erosion has accelerated.

The introduction of the Trade Related Intellectual Property Rights Agreement of the World Trade Organization has accelerated the spread of genetically engineered seeds - which can be patented - and for which royalties can be collected. Navdanya was started in response to the Introduction of these patents on seeds in the General Agreement on Tariffs and Trade - a forerunner to the WTO - about which a Monsanto representative later stated: "In drafting these agreements, we were the patient, diagnostician (and) physician all in one." Corporations defined a problem - and for them the problem was farmers saving seeds. They offered a solution, and the solution was to make it illegal for farmers to save seed - by introducing patents and intellectual property rights (PDF) on those very seeds. As a result, acreage under GM corn, soya, canola, cotton has increased dramatically.

Threats to seed sovereignty

Besides displacing and destroying diversity, patented GMO seeds are also undermining seed sovereignty. Across the world, new seed laws are being introduced which enforce compulsory registration of seeds, thus making it impossible for small farmers to grow their own diversity, and forcing them into dependency on giant seed corporations. Corporations are also patenting climate resilient seeds evolved by farmers - thus robbing farmers of using their own seeds and knowledge for climate adaptation.

Another threat to seed sovereignty is genetic contamination. India has lost its cotton seeds because of contamination from Bt Cotton - a strain engineered to contain the pesticide Bacillus thuringiensis bacterium. Canada has lost its canola seed because of contamination from Roundup Ready canola. And Mexico has lost its corn due to contamination from Bt Cotton.

After contamination, biotech seed corporations sue farmers with patent infringement cases, as happened in the case of Percy Schmeiser. That is why more than 80 groups came together and filed a case to prevent Monsanto from suing farmers whose seed had been contaminated.

As a farmer's seed supply is eroded, and farmers become dependent on patented GMO seed, the result is debt. India, the home of cotton, has lost its cotton seed diversity and cotton seed sovereignty. Some 95 per cent of the country's cotton seed is now controlled by Monsanto - and the debt trap created by being forced to buy seed every year - with royalty payments - has pushed hundreds of thousands of farmers to suicide; of the 250,000 farmer suicides, the majority are in the cotton belt.

Seeding control

Even as the disappearance of biodiversity and seed sovereignty creates a major crisis for agriculture and food security, corporations are pushing governments to use public money to destroy the public seed supply and replace it with unreliable non-renewable, patented seed - which must be bought each and every year.

Inside Story: Averting a world food crisis

In Europe, the 1994 regulation for protection of plant varieties forces farmers to make a "compulsory voluntary contribution" to seed companies. The terms themselves are contradictory. What is compulsory cannot be voluntary.

In France, a law was passed in November 2011, which makes royalty payments compulsory. As Agriculture Minister Bruna Le Marie stated: "Seeds can be longer be royalty free, as is currently the case." Of the 5,000 or so cultivated plant varieties, 600 are protected by certificate in France, and these account for 99 per cent of the varieties grown by farmers.

The "compulsory voluntary contribution", in other words a royalty, is justified on grounds that "a fee is paid to certificate holders [seed companies] to sustain funding of research and efforts to improve genetic resources".

Monsanto pirates biodiversity and genetic resources from farming communities, as it did in the case of a wheat bio-piracy case fought by Navdanya with Greenpeace, and climate resilient crops and brinjal (also known as aubergine or eggplant) varieties for Bt Brinjal. As Monsanto states, "it draws from a collection of germ-plasm that is unparalleled in history" and "mines the diversity in this genetic library to develop elite seeds faster than ever before".

In effect, what is taking place is the enclosure of the genetic commons of our biodiversity and the intellectual commons of public breeding by farming communities and public institutions. And the GMO seeds Monsanto is offering are failing. This is not "improvement" of genetic resources, but degradation. This is not innovation but piracy.

For example, the Alliance for a Green Revolution in Africa (AGRA) - being pushed by the Gates Foundation - is a major assault on Africa's seed sovereignty.

Agribusiness

The 2009 US Global Food Security Act also called the Lugar-Casey Act, "A bill to authorize appropriations for fiscal years 2010 through 2014 to provide assistance to foreign countries to promote food security, to stimulate rural economies, and to improve emergency response to food crisis, to amend the Foreign Assistance Act of 1961 and for other purposes".

The amendment to the Foreign Assistance Act would "include research on bio-technological advances appropriate to local ecological conditions, including genetically modified technology". The $ 7.7bn that goes with the bill would go to benefit Monsanto to push GM seeds.[18]

Royalties for Monsanto are based on debt, suicidal farmers and the disappearance of biodiversity worldwide.

---

[18] Note: 1 trillion = 1000 billion; 1 billion = 1000 million

An article in Forbes, titled "Why Uncle Sam Supports Franken Foods", shows how agribusiness is the only sector in which US has a positive trade balance. Hence, the push for GMOs is because they bring royalties to the US. However, royalties for Monsanto are based on debt, suicidal farmers and the disappearance of biodiversity worldwide.

Under the US Global Food Security Act, Nepal signed an agreement with USAID and Monsanto. This led to massive protests across the country. India was forced to allow patents on seeds through the first dispute brought by the US against India in the WTO. Since 2004, India has also been trying to introduce a Seed Act which would require farmers to register their own seeds and take licenses. This in effect would force farmers from using their indigenous seed varieties. By creating a Seed Satyagraha - a non-cooperation movement in Gandhi's footsteps, handing over hundreds of thousands of signatures to the prime minister, and working with parliament - we have so far prevented the Seed Law from being introduced.

India has signed a US-India Knowledge Initiative in Agriculture, with Monsanto on the Board. Individual states are also being pressured to sign agreements with Monsanto. One example is the Monsanto-Rajasthan Memorandum of Understanding, under which Monsanto would get intellectual property rights to all genetic resources, and to carry out research on indigenous seeds. It took a campaign by Navdanya and a "Monsanto Quit India" Bija Yatra (seed pilgrimage) to force the government of Rajasthan to cancel the MOU. This asymmetric pressure of Monsanto on the US government, and the joint pressure of both on the governments across the world, is a major threat to the future of seeds, the future of food and the future of democracy.[19]

---

[19]Vandana Shiva (2012), " The Seed Emergency", Deccan Chronicle, Visakhapatnam, February 1, 2012

Farmers' Suicides in India

Farmers in India became the centre of considerable concern in the 1990s when the journalist P Sainath highlighted the large number of suicides among farmers in India. Official reports initially denied the farmer suicides but as more and more information came to light the government began to accept that farmers in India were under considerable stress. On figures there was much debate since the issue was so emotive. The government tried to underplay the cases of farmer deaths, intellectual supporters of the farmers preferred to inflate them. More than 17,500 farmers a year killed themselves between 2002 and 2006, according to experts who have analyzed government statistics. Others traced the increase in farmer suicides to the early 1990s. It was said, a comprehensive all-India study is still awaited, that most suicides occurred in states of Andhra Pradesh, Maharashtra, Karnataka, Kerala and Punjab. The situation was grim enough to force at least the Maharashtra government to set up a dedicated office to deal with farmers' distress.

In 2006, the state of Maharashtra, with 4,453 farmers' suicides accounted for over a quarter of the all-India total of 17,060, according to the National Crime Records Bureau (NCRB). NCRB also stated that there were at least 16,196 farmers' suicides in India in 2008, bringing the total since 1997 to 199,132. According to another study by the Bureau, while the number of farm suicides increased since 2001, the number of farmers has fallen, as thousands abandoning agriculture in distress. According to government data, over 5,000 farmers committed suicide in 2005-2009 in Maharashtra, while 1,313 cases reported by Andhra Pradesh between 2005 and 2007. In Karnataka the number stood at 1,003, since 2005-06 till August 2009. In the last four years, cases in Kerala were about 905, Gujarat 387, Punjab 75 and Tamil Nadu 26. In April 2009, the state of

Chhattisgarh reported 1,500 farmers committed suicide due to debt and crop failure. At least 17,368 Indian farmers killed themselves in 2009, the worst figure for farm suicides in six years, according to data of the National Crime Records Bureau (NCRB).

History

In the 1990s India woke up to a spate of farmers suicides. One of the major reporters of these suicides was the Rural Affairs Editor of *The Hindu*, P. Sainath. The first state where suicides were reported was Maharashtra. Soon newspapers began to report similar occurrences from Andhra Pradesh. In the beginning it was believed that most of the suicides were happening among the cotton growers, especially those from Vidarbha. A look at the figures given out by the State Crime Records Bureau, however, was sufficient to indicate that it was not just the cotton farmer but farmers as a professional category were suffering, irrespective of their holding size. Moreover, it was not just the farmers from Vidarbha but all over Maharashtra who showed a significantly high suicide rate.

The government appointed a number of inquiries to look into the causes of farmers' suicide and farm related distress in general. Subsequently Prime Minister Manmohan Singh visited Vidarbha and promised a package of Rs.110 billion (about $2.4 billion) to be spent by the government in Vidarbha. The families of farmers who had committed suicide were also offered an *ex gratia* grant to the tune of Rs.100, 000 (about $2,000) by the government. This figure kept on varying, depending on how much criticism the government was facing from the media and the opposition parties for being uncaring towards the farmers' plight. Such a high figure was ironic considering that the net average income of a family of farmers in this region was approximately Rs.2700 (about $60) per acre per annum. The economic plight of the farmer might be illustrated with the fact that a farmer having as much as 15 acres (61,000 m^2) of land, and hence considered a well-off farmer, had an income of just a little more than what he would have earned were he to merely get the legal minimum wage for all of the 365 days of the year. Little wonder that despite government efforts at pumping in more money into the suicide belt, the suicide epidemic among farmers remained unabated through 2006-07.

The problems of the farmers were quite comprehensive. There was little credit available. What was available was very costly. There was no advice on how best to conduct agriculture operations. Income through farming was not enough to meet even the minimum needs of a farming family. Support systems like free health facilities from the government were virtually non-existent. Traditionally support systems in the villages of India had been provided by the government. However, due to a variety of reasons the government had either withdrawn itself from its supportive role or plain simple mis-governance had allowed facilities in the villages to wither away.

Causes

In the initial years when farmers distress came to attract public attention it was said that indebtedness through use of Bt Cotton were the main cause for farmers' suicide. Here it is important to notice that in the context of Indian history the moneylender is considered to be a particularly evil person and the farmer an unwitting subject of his machinations. Moreover, in recent times there has been a considerable ideologically driven movement against the use of Bt. crops. As a result the initial cause's indebtedness and Bt Cotton were easily accepted to be the causes of farm suicides. More detailed research by various investigators like Raj Patel, Nagraj, Meeta and Rajivlochan, identified a variety of causes that essentially boiled down to this: India was transforming rapidly into a primarily urban, industrial society with industry as its main source of income; the government and society had begun to be unconcerned about the condition of the countryside; moreover, a downturn in the urban economy was pushing a large number of distressed non-farmers to try their hand at cultivation; the farmer was also caught in a Scissors crisis; in the absence of any responsible counselling either from the government or society there were many farmers who did not know how to survive in the changing economy.

Such stresses pushed many into a corner where suicide became an option for them At least one study from the Punjab also pointed at the dramatic misuse of agricultural chemicals in farmer households in the absence of any guidance on how to correctly use these deadly chemicals and linked it to the rise in farm suicides wherever farm chemicals were in widespread use.

Responses to Farmers suicides

Vidarbha was in the media for a spate of farmer suicides in recent years ostensibly because of the falling Minimum Support Price for cotton. The problem is complex and root causes include lopsided policies of the World Trade Organization and developed nations' subsidies to their cotton farmers which make Vidarbha's cotton uncompetitive in world markets. Consequently Vidarbha is plagued by high rates of school drop outs, penniless widows left in the wake of suicides, loan sharks and exploitation of the vulnerable groups.

The Indian government had promised to increase the minimum rate for cotton by approximately Rs 100 ($2) but reneged on its promise by reducing the Minimum Support Price further. This resulted in more suicides as farmers were ashamed to default on debt payments to loan sharks. "In 2006, 1,044 suicides were reported in Vidarbha alone - that's one suicide every eight hours."

In April 2007 an NGO named Green Earth Social Development Consulting brought out a report after doing an audit of the state and central government relief packages in Vidarbha. The report's conclusions were:

Farmers' demands were not taken into count while preparing the relief package. Neither were civil society organizations, local government bodies, panchayats etc consulted.

The relief packages were mostly amalgamations of exiting schemes. Apart from the farmer helpline and the direct financial assistance, there was scarcely anything new being offered. Pumping extra funds into additional schemes shows that no new idea was applied to solve a situation where existing measures had obviously failed.

The farmer helpline did not give any substantial help to farmers.

The basis for selection of beneficiaries under the assistance scheme was not well-defined. Also, type of assistance to be given led to problems like a farmer needing a pair of bullocks getting a pump set and vice versa (or a farmer who has no access to water sources being given pump sets)

Awareness regarding the package was also fairly low.

The report concluded quite alarmingly that the loan burden of the farmers would double in 2008.[20]

---

[20]Wikipedia, the free encyclopedia

Farmers' Suicides Worsen After 2001

Although National Crime Records Bureau (NCRB) data confirm an appalling 1.5 hundred thousand farm suicides between 1997 and 2005, the figure is probably much higher. Worse, the farmers' suicide rate (FSR) — number of suicides per 100,000 farmers — is also likely to be much higher than the disturbing 12.9 thrown up in the 2001 Census.[21]

In the five years from 1997 to 2001, there were 78,737 farm suicides recorded in the country. On an average, around 15,747 commit suicide each year. But in just the next four years 2002-05, there were 70,507. Or a yearly average of 17,627 farm suicides. That is a rise of nearly 1,900 in the yearly averages of the two periods. Simply put, farm suicides have shot up after 2001 with the agrarian crisis biting deeper.

A comprehensive study of official data on farm suicides by K. Nagaraj of the Madras Institute of Development Studies (MIDS) pins down these and other figures. The data are drawn from the various issues of *Accidental Deaths and Suicides in India*, a publication of the NCRB. But Professor Nagaraj also explains some of the reasons why the actual numbers and farmers' suicide rate (FSR) could be far higher.

In 2001, when the farm suicides were not yet at their worst, the FSR at 12.9 was already higher than the General Suicide Rate (GSR) — suicides per 100,000 populations — at 10.6. But even this higher suicide rate among farmers conceals a far worse reality.

Firstly, the NCRB data seem to underestimate the number of farm suicides. This is because the criteria adopted for identifying a farm suicide at the State

---

[21]Sainath, P. (2007), "Farm Suicides Worse After 2001", The Hindu November 13, 2007

level are quite stringent. For instance, women and tenant farmers tend to get excluded from lists of farmers' suicides. In those lists, only those with a title to land tend to be counted as farmers. On the other hand, the Census data are based on a very liberal definition of 'cultivator.'

The 2001 Census gives data on two categories of cultivators: Cultivators among 'main workers' and those among as 'marginal workers.'

For the first group of cultivators among main workers — farming is the main activity. The second group includes those who practice cultivation only on a sporadic basis. However, both groups get counted as farmers. The net result of this is that while deriving the farm suicide rate from the NCRB and Census data, we are saddled with figures that undercount farm suicides but over count the number of 'farmers.' Hence a value of 12.9 for the FSR is likely to be way below the mark. As Professor Nagaraj points out, If we took only the cultivators among the main workers as farmers, the FSR increases dramatically to 15.8 which is nearly one and a half times the GSR of 10.6 in 2001.

Secondly, the FSR is anchored in 2001 because that is the year of the Census. However, it was not one of the worst years in terms of farm suicides. Farm suicides in that year actually fell when compared to the previous year, 2000. But the very next year, in 2002, farmers' suicides leapt by about 10 per cent. And the number of such deaths peaked in 2004. So while the number of farmers' suicides shows a rising trend after 2001, the number of farmers may well have declined.

The trend of a decline of farmers seems to have begun even earlier. The 1991 Census says there were 111 million cultivators among main workers. This fell to 103 million in the 2001 Census. This decline would surely have sharpened after 2001 as the farm crisis deepened. Certainly farming has no new takers. The Annual Compound Growth rate (ACGR) for all suicides in India over the nine-year period 1997-2005 is 2.18 per cent. This is not very much higher than the population growth rate. For farm suicides, it is much higher, at nearly 3 (or 2.91) percent. An ACGR of 3 per cent in farm suicides is more alarming as it applies to a smaller total of farmers each year. This means the farm suicide rate must have shot up after 2001.

Suicides by farmers went up 27 per cent during 1997-2005. But non-farm suicides went up by 18 per cent. So by all accounts, while the number of farm suicides kept increasing, the number of farmers has fallen since 2001, with countless thousands abandoning agriculture in distress.

Huge differential in numbers

Lastly, whether we take the farm suicide rate as 12.9 or 15.8, it is the figure for the country as a whole. That again hides huge differentials in the numbers and intensity of farm suicides across the country. There are States and regions in the country where the FSR is appallingly high. There are regions where it is mercifully still low.

The researcher divided the States into four groups:

(a) Group I: States with very high general suicide rates.
(b) Group II: States with high general suicide rates and large numbers of farmers' suicides. (This is the most important group.)
(c) Group 3: States with moderate general and farm suicide rates
(d) Group 4: States with low general and farm suicide rates.

What demarcates the Group II States — clearly the worst hit — is also the trend in suicides, which is most dismal there. This key group includes Maharashtra, Andhra Pradesh, Karnataka, and Madhya Pradesh (including Chhattisgarh) and Goa. The ratio of farmers' suicide rate to the general suicide rate was highest in this Group. The overall ratio of this group is 1.7. Which means the farm suicide rate in these States is 70 per cent higher than it is in their whole population.

Of the major States, Maharashtra has the worst figure with a ratio of farmers' suicide rate to general suicide rate of 2.0. That is, one hundred per cent higher. Karnataka follows this with 1.6. Of the smaller States, Kerala (from Group I) has the awful figure of 4.7. But it also shows a decline from 2004. Pondicherry shows up as the worst with 15.4. Of course, the last two have smaller absolute numbers. The trend for Group II is most dismal. The AGCR for farm suicides in these States for the 1997-2005 periods was 5.33. Or nearly double the national figure of 2.9. And if this trend holds, farm suicides in this group as a whole would double every 13 years. Among these States, Maharashtra and Andhra Pradesh would fare even worse.

Political Economy of Farmers' Suicides

Underlying the reports and reactions of officials to the suicides of farmers is a Yuppie social Darwinism. The farmers are presented as failures, as those who did not make it into life's supermarket. A sense of the defeated getting weeded out. Added to this is a feeling that suicide is pathology. Also, suicide is what individuals do for individual reasons. There is no social current or trend underlying it... So far the reports seem to exonerate the scientists and even the government bureaucrats. It is described as a self–inflicted injury like alcoholism. But there is no examination of the larger grammar of forces within which suicide became the answer.... The media also creates pornography of disasters where we sample disasters as spectacles without engaging with them. 'Farmers swallow pesticide' is news right out of Barnum. But there is geology of disquiet beyond this. (Sociologist Shiv Visvanathan)

It would be fair to recognize that the victims of agrarian distress are not only those who have committed suicide and their family members but also those who continue to live there, believing, as do most cultivators, that they have an obligation to the land, to the community, to the state and to the nation to continue to cultivate the land. (Dr. A.R. Vasavi who conducted research on farmers' suicides in Bidar district of Karnataka)

According to the Karnataka State Crime Record Bureau, the total number of suicides in Karnataka among farmers during the period of 1996 – 2000 was 10959--- 8728 male and 2231 female. The year wise figures were 2079 for 1996, 1832 for 1997, 2039 for 1998, 2379 for 1999 and 2630 for the year 2000. (R S Deshpande, EPW, June 29, 2002)

There is a farming crisis and it is arguably the most serious challenge facing India. The World Trade Organization regime has started to make it felt on the ground. Farmers and experts alike feel that India's farm produce could be pushed out of the market place by heavily subsidized imports of agricultural produce. The suicide of a potato farmer of Navalgund in Dharwad district in late 2000, reportedly owing to the crash in the price of the crop, had Karnataka Chief Minister S.M. Krishna calling for "mid-course corrections" in the WTO regime and demanding a White Paper on the impact of the WTO on Indian agriculture.

Although it might be difficult to establish the direct connections between the price of potatoes and the

WTO, Krishna's observations were clearly about a larger process unfolding in the countryside, one that has much to do with WTO - dictated policy decisions that threaten a wide range of crops, agricultural growth and rural livelihoods. This was the first official acknowledgement in India of the crisis facing the agricultural sector. (Parvathi Menon, Feb.2, 2001, Frontline.)

In December 2000, Prakash Singh Badal, the then Chief Minister of Punjab warned:

The implementation of the WTO agreement in the present form would lead to bloodshed in the country. The signing of the WTO amounts to signing the death warrant for the farm sector.

Farming has indeed become a deathtrap for poor farmers of India. Thousands of farmers in the states of Andhra Pradesh, Karnataka, Tamil Nadu, Kerala, Maharashtra, Punjab and Rajasthan have been forced to commit suicide. Rising input costs, declining farm prices due to globalization of agriculture and the increasing indebtedness of the farmers are the prime culprits behind these unnatural deaths.
(Vandana Shiva, Nov. 2001, the Ecologist.)

Following a complaint by the US, the WTO decided in 2000 that India would have to remove trade barriers that previously protected its own, local producers. Ever since, Indian farmers have found it harder and harder to survive. Products that they once produced for the home market are now undercut by cheaper imported alternatives. The country now ships in Indonesian coconuts. The prices of coconuts in India have fallen by 80 percent as a result. Likewise coffee prices have collapsed by over 60 per cent, and the price of pepper has plummeted by 45 percent.

But this is nothing in comparison with the market for edible oil. The Indian edible oil industry has effectively been wiped out. Low import duties have led to highly subsidized US Soya and Palm Oil from Malaysia flooding the market. Imports now account for 70 percent of India's domestic consumption of edible oil.

Prof. Utsa Patnaik who has done extensive research and written many authoritative papers on WTO's impact on Indian agriculture writes, "There used to be controls earlier on the export and import of agricultural products, and these have gone now. The result is that our producers are now exposed to the volatility of global prices. Global commodity prices are always highly volatile. This has to do with supply conditions. In the space of a few months, it is not unusual to see a trebling of prices and then as sharp a drop. If we take the concrete example of rubber or cotton production in the last decade, what actually happened was that when global prices were high, hundreds of thousands of small producers took loans, they even leased in land when they did not own enough, in the hope of making a profit.

What then happened was that if, as in cotton, yields were not up to expectations, or as in rubber, there was a crash in prices, expectations of profit were not realized, and the producers were ruined. The extent of the volatility our farmers have been subjected to, combined with the cutback in institutional credit, has been such that even well to do farmers are facing a problem. That is very clear if we look at farmers in Punjab for instance, where evidence points to increasing levels of indebtedness even in well to do strata. And this is mostly in the informal credit market, since there has been a very substantial crunch in institutional credit. There has been this well-publicized wave of suicides among farmers, of which there have been more than 800 over the last two years in Andhra Pradesh alone, mainly among cotton farmers. That of course is only the tip of the iceberg because there are several hundreds of thousands of farmers who are really mired in debt and are not taking this extreme step. But their position has definitely worsened to the extent that there has been a loss of land and other assets, and family members are forced to do daily wage labour.

Justice P. A. Chowdary who headed the Farmers' Commission of Experts on agricultural crisis in Andhra Pradesh says:

(a) So far climate has been considered as the most unpredictable variable affecting the agricultural sector.
(b) The influence of global market forces, whose behavior are always not amenable to prediction and control, has become another factor affecting the progress and well-being of farmers.

Explaining the various processes behind the farming crisis in India Prof Abhijit Sen who also chairs the National Commission for Agricultural Costs and Prices says, in the background of higher cost increases and lower risk-bearing capacity consequent to reduced public non-price support to agriculture, the opening up of the sector to international trade further increased the sources of uncertainty. Much hope was reposed in the outcome of the WTO agreement, which was expected to increase world prices further and also lead to greater price stability. The developments since the signing of this agreement have belied all earlier expectations, mainly because the developed countries managed to preserve almost all the distortions in international agricultural trade that suited them. World agricultural prices did increase for two years after the agreement was signed in 1994, but have spiraled downwards after 1996. In large part, it is these wild swings in international prices, which are the source of the present distress of Indian farmers. Unaccustomed to the vagaries of world commodity markets, and with reduced ability to cope with such risks, many farmers have been unable to meet obligations which were optimistically built up during years when prices were high.

Most damagingly, policy-makers too were unable to cope effectively with the consequences of international price volatility. Import duties, which had been reduced when world prices were high were increased only after considerable lag after these fell, and, in some cases, for example in the case of edible oils, the increased duties have been unable to neutralize the fall in world price .In a closed economy prices and output tend to move in opposite directions, with higher prices mitigating incomes at times of output decline. But such automatic mitigation is much less in an open economy since world price movements can depress domestic prices even at times of low production. In the 25 years before 1995-96, there were only three years when the terms of trade had declined simultaneously with a drop in the index of agricultural production. But since 1995- 96, the indices of terms of trade and of agricultural production have moved in the same direction every year. This is a direct effect of the implementation of the WTO agreements.

According to a report of National Task Force on Agriculture headed by Sharad Joshi, "Indian farmers are not pampered with free electricity and water as is the common perception. Instead, because of negative subsidies on domestic prices, their net income is much less when compared to their counterparts elsewhere in the World. "The task force has recommended a complete waiver of all loans taken by farmers. The report points out the implications of negative aggregate measurement of support (AMS) and India being one of the few countries in the World to have it. AMS is calculated as the difference between the prices assured by the government in the domestic market and the corresponding prices in a hypothetical free market. According to the figures submitted by the government to the WTO, the AMS is minus 17 percent in the country.

The worth would be 3, 000, 000, 000, 000 INR (or three trillion Indian Rupees). The report says, "The whole question of indebtedness of the Indian farmers needs to be reviewed from an entirely new perspective of negative AMS. Though its one arm was working facilitating credit to the farmers, the other was working to ensure that he would not be able to repay his loans. It is, therefore, necessary that all forcible recovery of debts and sundry dues be suspended and moratorium declared on coercive recovery including electricity dues and arrears of loans." (Sonu Jain, Indian Express, Sept 4, 2002)

The Finance Minister P. Chidambaram says, "The share of agriculture in India's GDP is declining, but population dependent on agriculture is not declining at the same rate. Too many people with too little income, and simple arithmetic will tell you that these people are doomed to be poor... The low levels of agricultural income are directly attributable to low prices. It is fashionable to say that prices of food and food products are high and hurt the common man. The truth is that prices of agricultural products in India are much below World prices... So far as India is concerned, the AMS is negative. That means, notwithstanding input subsidies and minimum support prices, India's farmers bear the burden of a negative subsidy.

India's agricultural producers are subsidizing the consumers... We pay our farmers ridiculously low prices for their produce... A remunerative price must cover the costs of the farmer- producer and have a little surplus in his hands, if he has to come out of the morass of grinding poverty. In that sense, most agricultural products do not get remunerative prices... At the end of a normal year, the farmer finds himself, economically, in the same position, as he was at the beginning – poor and struggling. In a bad year, when the monsoon fails or the crop is affected, he slips further down the ladder. The farming community gets impoverished. Many sink dippers into debt, some commit suicide... The key to removal of rural poverty is agricultural prices. A mature and civilized nation must cherish its agriculture and protect its farmers. If the price for a robust agricultural sector is to pay one rupee more for a Kg of food products, we must be prepared to pay that price."

(P. Chidambaram, Indian Express, Aug. 9, 2002)

At a Farmers' rally in Dindori, Nashik district in Maharashtra in February 2001, farmers said that, "their livelihoods are being destroyed by the new economic policies. Trade liberalization, costs in fertilizer subsidies, reduced infrastructure investment and privatization of the power sector has adversely affected the profitability of agriculture. While costs of inputs like fertilizer and electricity have risen steadily due to cuts in subsidies and privatization, the prices at which farmers sell their produce have declined due to the glut of imported products in the market."... Agriculture has borne the brunt of liberalization on many fronts. Cuts in government spending have resulted in reduced public investment in agriculture as well as smaller subsidies. Dismantling of procurement agencies, greater imports and falling world commodity prices have also reduced profitability".

Dr. Madhura Swaminathan says that "trade liberalization has resulted in bizarre situations where India is exporting wheat at a price cheaper than what most Indians are paying. Wheat from Food Corporation of India godowns (storage platforms) can now be exported at the same price at which it is sold to people classified as living 'below poverty line'. Millions of under- nourished and vulnerable people, who are still classified as being 'above the poverty line' have been told to pay a higher price for wheat than the price at which the government is willing to sell the same wheat to foreign countries." (Dionne Bunsha, Hindu, Feb. 11, 2001)

INDIA: **Farmers' Suicides in different States**

(a)Andhra Pradesh: In Andhra Pradesh, farmers who switched to commercial crops on the government's advice face an uncertain future because of falling prices. Going by the Center's official figures, out of the 495 farmers who ended their lives during the last two years, 385 were from Andhra Pradesh. This means three of every four farmers who committed suicide in India are from Andhra Pradesh. The state government's own estimate of the suicides in the last five years is 1000. "So far climate has been considered as the most unpredictable variable affecting the agricultural sector. But, the influence of global market forces, whose behaviour is always not amenable to prediction and control, has become another factor affecting the progress and well-being of farmers", says Justice P. A. Chowdhary who headed the farmers' commission of experts on Agriculture in Andhra Pradesh.

Echoing the similar view, Communist Party of India (Marxist) State Secretary B. V. Raghavulu says, "The recurring drought in the state was a minor factor behind the distress of people dependent of agriculture compared with the havoc wrought by market forces. The government encouraged farmers to shift from food crops to commercial crops such as tobacco, cotton, chilies and castor seed. Small farmers who did so found themselves ill-equipped to cope with the market, which was governed by the WTO regime. The huge investments made on commercial crops went down the drain, while the dept burden went up. As the old debt is not repaid, the farmer cannot get a new loan. Left with no money, food or sympathy from his fellow villagers, he ends his life. Had he grown a food crop, he would at least have been left with something to eat," says Raghavulu.

Contrary to popular belief, banks harass farmers no less than private lenders by issuing notices for seizure of assets and sometimes even using the police. The A.P. Rythu Sangham Joint Secretary B. Tulasidas says that in drought- prone districts such as Anantapur and Mahabubnagar farmers went in for irrigated-dry crops such as groundnut and cotton on the government's advice, without any guarantee of returns on investment. They realized their mistake when the prices crashed in the market. A crying need, therefore, was the creation of a market stabilization fund. It had not materialized in spite of the government's promise in 2000 to deposit 1,000,000,000 INR (or one billion of Indian Rupees). The farmers' commission has recommended the setting up of a "farmers' distress fund" on the model of the national calamity fund.

(S Nagesh Kumar, Frontline, Jan. 3, 2003)

Agriculture in Anatapur (A P) faces a huge crisis. The crash in groundnut prices has shattered thousands of households. And debt has broken the spirit of many. According to noted journalist P Sainath, "Between 1997 and the end of 2000, 1826 people, mainly farmers, committed suicide in this district. Hundreds did so by swallowing poison. It is because pesticide is available to the peasants. But the data was fudged. As many as 1061-over 58.1 percent of these were recorded as having taken their lives because of 'sickness'. Indeed, hundreds of these deaths went into the records as people killing themselves due to 'unbearable stomach-ache'. This helped conceal the fact that the suicides were mostly of small farmers, pushed over the brink by economic distress. 45 percent of those committing suicide across this whole period were women. (There are a lot of women-headed households in this high-migration area).

"Large number of farmers took their lives after a good crop last season. Now there is a drought. And its impact could worsen rapidly after this month. But it was preceded by far more crucial processes that spurred the suicides. All of them are policy-driven. One of these is debt and its working is quite visible right in Anantapur town. Eenadu is A. P.'s largest daily newspaper. And the advertisements in its local edition tell a story. On many days, the most prominent ads are the same. Banks announce the auctioning of tiny amounts of gold or jewellery owned by small farmers in the district. Often this happens to recover dues ranging from 2500 to 12000 INR. In one case, the sum owned is as low as 316 INR. These farmers took loans from the banks using the only bits of gold or jewellery they owned as collateral. Many have paid back the principal and more. But they have been crushed by the interest. Most are groundnut farmers owning between two and five acres. The crisis brought on by crashing groundnut prices saw no rescheduling of the debt," says Sainath.

The relentlessness of the auctions can be seen in the daily profusion of such ads in Eenadu. On just the first two days of March, 132 villagers had their names listed as those whose meager assets were up for auction. On March 2 alone, seven such ads appeared in Eenadu. They continue to appear with monotonous regularity. The sense of humiliation is a factor in pushing human beings to the brink. So strong is the shame of losing your wife's only gold and jewelers, those auctions are a tough subject to broach.

In Ipperu village alone, over 100 cases of people facing or about to face auctions had been admitted to in that one village. Ipperu has 350 families. Its debt burden is calculated as being in excess of 12 million INR. "That is only the loans from formal sources. Loans from private lenders with far higher interest rates would be much, much greater", says Sailadri Murthy, an ex-official of the B C Corporation. The collapse of rural credit in the 1990s hit farmers everywhere very hard. So, like elsewhere, those here have turned more to moneylenders, who charge interest ranging from 60 percent to 120 percent per annum. Now, large numbers of people have incurred debt for medical reasons too— "health loans". The collapse of the public health system in the 1990s has ensured that. Health, though, is only one element of growing debt. Like elsewhere, soaring input costs have pushed people further down that road.

Today people are selling their crops at far less than what it cost to produce it. Higher output has not helped. Many of those farmers who committed suicide did so after a decent crop." We were encouraged to produce more, and we did. Then they import this palm oil and it finishes us" says Reddy a farmer in Ipperu. Some of the practices adopted have taken their own toll. An unshakable faith in bore wells is one of these. Often, farmers with just five acres of land have invested in as many as 12 to 14 bore wells. Apart from the debt burden this brings, the practice has had a predictable impact on the water- table. All this comes atop decades of neglect of traditional water harvesting systems. So the damage has been severe. Anantapur has always been a low rainfall area. But the region has survived for centuries on thousands of old tanks, many built in the era of Krishnadeva Raya and earlier. One of those great tanks lays stone dry in the Kuderu Mandal".

All sorts of private water structures were allowed to come up on its periphery. You can see the result. If this tank worked at half its capacity, five villages here would have all they need. They would be prosperous. Of course, this reservoir, too, needs repairs. That, though, is not happening," says Mallikarjun, a farmer in Ipperu. "As the role of the tanks diminished, our reliance on bore wells grew," says Durganna. He is one of those who feel too many bores have damaged the village." Now there is no water in Ipperu and nearby villages at 300 feet. Most of the bores have failed. For drinking water, the 350 families here depend on a single bore well that still works." Despite these conditions, good rains helped turn out a decent crop last season... drought. Some of us here had a terrific crop. The groundnut yield was very good. So what happened? We heard there was a lot of palm oil import. That hit us badly. (Venkat Reddy of Mallayagaripalli village in Kadri Mandal expressed his feelings.)

Look at the way our prices have crashed. The season before that too, we had a decent harvest--but all our profits went in paying off interest on our loans... The area under groundnut went up last year to 787 thousand hectares. That was 65000 hectares more than in 1999. The rains were good and so was the yield...the collapse of rural credit. Soaring input costs - Mindless misuse of water resources - The neglect of traditional irrigation systems. Imports of food grains or oils devastated successful farmers. Huge hikes in rates for power that they never got. The breakdown of the public health system - Insensitivity to the fate of the small farmer - they took their lives," Says P. Madhu, General Secretary of the Andhra Pradesh Agricultural Workers Union. So, Anantpur's drought is policy-driven. So are its suicides.

(P. Sainath, the Hindu, April 29, May 6, 2001)

(b)Punjab Ryots embracing death to escape debts

Even as the increasingly debt-ridden farmers in Punjab are being forced to commit suicide, the state government has also candidly admitted now that the economic condition of farmers in Punjab was getting worse. According to the Punjab Agriculture minister Rajinder Kaur Bhattal, farmers are in financial doldrums and the debt liability of farmers in the state is to the tune of 70 billion of INR (or 70,000 million of Indian rupees).

The movement against state Repression (MASR), a human rights group has done extensive research on the issue of farmers' suicide in Punjab. MASR conveyor Inderjit Singh Jaijee, who was the first one to explore the phenomenon of suicide by farmers in Punjab four years back, says that 450 suicides had occurred in just two blocks (Andana and Lehra in Sangarur district) of Punjab since 1990.

(Rajesh Deol, Deccan Herald, Aug. 21-2001)

Debt-related suicides by farmers continued unabated in Punjab's Andana and Lehra blocks of Sangarur district during the previous financial year. These suicides have reportedly been investigated by a human rights body, certified by village Panchayats and verified by the magistracy. According to human rights group- the Movement against State Repression (MASR), that initially highlighted these cases a couple of years ago, the number of suicides in the two blocks could even be higher as many cases go unreported due to social stigma.

The MASR has quoted that last year as many as 56 suicides were reported in the two blocks. The figure could easily range between 70 and 80. As cases have been reported in the adjoining blocks in Mansa and Bhatinda districts, the state figure could be in a few thousands considering that there are 138 blocks in the state.

The MASR has quoted an instance where a farmer of Alampur village had taken his life. Though he took a loan of 300 thousand Indian Rupees from a moneylender, his heirs face an outstanding debt of 1100 thousand Indian Rupees. The MASR has listed incidents where a heavily indebted youth Jagmel Singh of a village in Andana block ended his life on may 4 this year (2002). The same day about 100 kms away, in Chathe Wallah village of Bhatinda district, another farmer, Jagroop Singh also killed himself. Both complained of harassment by moneylenders. While Jagmel Singh complained 'verbally', Jagroop Singh left a suicide note, in which he is said to have written; "I do not know what will become of my children now. Please save them from the money lenders, who killed me?" The MASR has sought that a debt conciliation board be set up immediately in Punjab. It has also sought strict implementation of the principle of 'Dam-Dupat', which was established in 1934, and ensured that no recovery is made for sum larger than twice the amount advanced.

The organization has also drawn attention towards growing social tensions due to heavy debts on farmers, a fact which it claims to have been warning about since the mid-1990s. It again warns that indications were available where the suicide-"violence turned inwards"-is most likely to turn outwards, especially when the government, despite major announcements, has failed to solve the crisis in the farm sector, which faces acute economic stagnation. (The Hindu, June 13, 2002)

The congress claims that the number of suicides in Punjab has reached 3,500. (Baljinder Pal Singh, Indian Express, 22 March 2001).

In an interview to Indian express Punjab C. M. Captain Amarinder Singh said, "There is a misconception that Punjab is a state with rich farmers. The fact is that 52 percent of the farmers have less than two-and-a-half acres and 84 percent has less than seven acres. There is just a handful, which has large holdings. The world regimen is such that these small farmers cannot survive. For example, if the MSP is 760 INR for a particular product, the world prices are 500 INR right now. Hence the crops are not remunerative, threatening the very existence of farmers in the state... Six hundred farmers have killed themselves in the last one-year in my state. In such a situation, one cannot think of withdrawing these subsidies. But once their incomes go up, the subsidies can be phased out. According to a survey conducted by Punjab University, the cost of cultivation of paddy was estimated to be 720 INR per quintal. The support price that was fixed by the government was 610 INR." (Sonu Jain, Indian Express-March 10, 2002)

(c) Karnataka: Reporting on farmers' suicides in Karnataka Supriya wrote, "During 1999-2001, 110 farmers committed suicide in Karnataka. A great deal of attention was drawn to these events in the initial phases, primarily through the media. More recently, however, it appears that suicides of farmers have become part of regular news, generating neither public outrage nor governmental response. In September 2001 alone, 30 farmers committed suicide in different areas of rural Karnataka. The suicides began in some districts of northern Karnataka, and rapidly spread to the southern parts. While poverty is endemic in rural Indian households, the desperate self-expression of poor farmers in these fairly widespread self-killings perhaps marks the onset of intensified deprivations.

Most of the suicides have happened in areas where the primary crop Is toor dal (a local pulse). These are areas of dry land farming where the cost of cultivation is high. While the price of toor dal earlier ranged from 1800 to 2600 INR per quintal, imports of pulses in recent years have pushed prices down to as low as 1200 /quintal. A number of other produce-maize, pulse, oilseeds, coconut and areca nut are now imported at subsidized rates under the O G L. Prices of all of these have fallen, causing great hardship to rural households already at the edge of poverty."

The drop in prices has caused farmers to borrow heavily for production and consumption purposes. A widely noted factor in the current rural distress appears to be the kind of credit that is available to poor farmers. In large parts of Karnataka, cultivation is carried out in a context of high concentration of land, not reflected in land records. Land is leased out to tenant farmers under unprotected and casual forms of tenancy. Lacking any kind of formal title to land, poor peasants are typically perceived as credit - unworthy by commercial banks. Under these circumstances, the marginal peasant is forced to seek loans from non-institutional sources, highly extractive and extortionist in nature, and where interest rates are as high as 60 percent per annum.

There are other ways in which the new market orientation has worked against the interests of poor rural households. For example, in the new context of economic liberalization, the history of low levels of loan recovery from rural households became a major reason for the declining emphasis on social banking in rural areas. Thus there has been a fall in total bank lending to the priority sectors, from 35 percent in 1980-81 to 22 percent in 1997-98. Within this overall decline, agricultural lending fell from 15 percent in 1980-81 to 10 percent in 1996-97. Thus the numerical weight of the poor obviously has not prevented shifts in policies in directions, which are obviously not pro-poor. (Supriya Roy Chowdhary, the Hindu, October 21, 2001)

(d) Cotton farmers' Suicides in Maharashtra

Faced with mounting debt, a failed crop for the second year and declining price, cotton farmers in the Vidharbha region of Maharashtra are resorting to suicide as a way out of misery. More than 80 suicides have been reported since May 2001 in 12 districts, primarily in the Vidharbha region of eastern Maharashtra. A larger number of deaths were reported during 2002 than the previous year after a second crop failure and dipping cotton prices left farmers with no chance to repay their loans. Even a hand-to-mouth existence was rendered difficult by the state government's irregular payments for the cotton it procured last year. In 1997, the Vidharbha region faced a similar crisis when approximately 80 suicide cases were registered officially. Untimely rain had destroyed the kharif crop that year, leaving small farmers with little money and less hope to clear their debts. While the suicides both times may have been triggered by the vagaries of the weather, it is becoming increasingly clear that the root of the problem lies in the economic and other policies adopted by the government.

Prof. Utsa Patnaik says, "Such a crisis of mounting indebtedness and despair is unprecedented in independent India and it is the direct result of trade liberalization, exposure to global volatility and resulting price crashes. Utsa Patnaik, in a paper titled "Deflation and Déjà vu: Indian agriculture in the World economy", says the majority of cotton growers are small farmers. They are highly price-responsive and have been so since colonial times. She says that as world cotton prices improved in the early 1990s and unregulated exports were permitted, hundreds of thousands of farmers expanded the area under cotton. They took large cash advances from traders and loans from banks to meet the extra seed and input costs on vast tracts of rain-fed land.

One and a half million hectares of land was diverted from food grains to cotton from 1991 to 1996. Unfortunately the cotton crop is susceptible to a large variety of pests and the unholy trinity of commission agents, fly-by-night pesticide dealers and seed suppliers. Cotton prices started declining in 1995-96 from 75 cents to an all time low of 35 cents in October 2001.

Adding to the farmers' problems is the increase in cotton imports, particularly from the United States. With the government lifting quantitative restrictions under the WTO treaties, cotton imports from the US increased from 21,221 tons in 1999 to 48,805 tons in 2000. "By permitting imports of cotton at 5 per cent duty, the central government has destroyed the domestic market. Prices have fallen drastically and the only people who have gained are those in the textile industry", says Vijay Javandhia, Leader of the Kisan Sanghatana based in Wardha. There is a glut of cotton in the world market at present. With more than one million tons of stock remaining from last year, cotton prices during the current marketing season are at their lowest since 1973, says the Washington-based International Cotton Advisory Committee (ICAC), an association comprising 42 countries growing and consuming cotton. "These prices, along with a failed monsoon, have been crippling the Indian small farmers," says the ICAC, which assists members in framing policy and providing technical advice.

(e). Rajasthan

On an average, each day last year, at least one farmer in Rajasthan killed himself because of poverty. Media reports based on the field visits indicate that the number may actually be higher because most suicides go unreported. The farmers' suicides in Rajasthan have been more or less consistent over the past five years. Financial hardship forced at least 15 farmers of Rasheedpura and Palthana villages of Sikar district to commit suicide in the last couple of years. Many farmers in these villages poisoned themselves when onion prices crashed.

Gyan Singh, a farmer of Malaisi reportedly killed himself when the onions he sold fetched less than what it had cost to transport them to the market. "Even control through the minimum support price (MSP) frequently fails to help the farmers. In 2001, there was good bajra crop but the delay by the central government in announcing the MSP forced farmers to sell off their produce to traders at prices much lower than the MSP that was announced later. The traders then sold the bajra to the government at the MSP and made good profit. In the last five years 3329 farmers committed suicide in Rajasthan while 505 farmers committed suicide last year in the state. Declining profit is the major cause of farmers' suicides." (Rajesh Sinha and D. K. Singh, The Hindustan Times, reproduced in Grassroots-January 2003)

What a Team of Farm Scientists say?

A team of scientists have analyzed why the farmers always face problems in their lives. These are:

Weak farmers' organizations: Before the era of liberalization, cooperatives thrived as the main farmers' organizations in eastern Africa. However, most cooperatives could not compete in open-market economies and are today weak, dormant or dead (World Bank 1995). With the decline of cooperatives and other farmers' organizations, many farmers lack a collective voice. They cannot to access affordable production inputs such as finance, technology, land and water, and are locked out of markets. As a result, a large number of small-scale farmers live in poverty and cannot Influence policies that affect their livelihoods. Strong and vibrant farmers' organizations can provide opportunities to farmers to effectively play a role in the market economy and benefit from it. However, identifying and promoting authentic farmers' organizations that empower smallholders, is a big challenge for governments and their development partners. Most groups are hastily formed, often with no regard for the social-cultural and economic structures of the farming communities. Such groups are not viable and incapable of serving as channels through which farmers can take part in decision-making.

Lack of economies of scale: Closely related to the problem of weak organizations is a fragmented and small-scale pattern of production. Farmers are not only scattered geographically, but often produce for subsistence or far below potential. Many are locked in a vicious circle of poverty. Extension services in the region compounded the problem by emphasizing support to individual farmers instead of groups that would provide better opportunities to use limited resources more effectively and efficiently.

Production not market oriented: Small-scale farmers mainly aim to increase production and achieve food self-sufficiency, rather than producing for the market and making a profit. This problem could be partly due to the fact that different departments outside agricultural extension are responsible for marketing, processing and value addition of farm produce.

Technology versus social organization: Agricultural extension has emphasized the promotion of technologies that improve production rather than developing institutional arrangements to encourage the adoption of such technologies.

Partial application of "participatory methods": Although many of the countries that had RELMA programs used participatory rural appraisal (PRA) and other "participatory" methodologies to identify farmers' needs, in most cases extension services promoted what was centrally identified as "good". There little regard to the farmers' socio-economic realities and their felt needs. This left little room for subject matter specialists to improvise solutions to challenges facing farmers. The Farmers Organization (FO) approach could correct this it is bottom-up and capable of bringing about greater transparency and accountability in the development process (Hussein 2000).

Disharmony in development extension: In traditional extension approaches, the complex development needs of farmers were not addressed in a holistic manner. For example, community development, veterinary, crop production, marketing and other services were scattered in different departments or ministries. At the field level, the agents of these technical departments operated independently of each other and often gave disconnected or conflicting messages.

Poor farmer-extension-research linkages: Links between farmers, extension services and research are weak, partly because the limitations of farmers' organizations translate into inadequate representation in agricultural research and limited access to extension (IFAP 1995). Well organized farmers' groups and improved communication among them with researchers and extension workers can help overcome this problem and focus efforts of all on solving farmers' problems. Extension messages not matched with farmers' incomes: In many instances, individual farmers cannot afford the technologies promoted. However, if organized in groups, they can pool resources and gradually help one another adopt such technology.[22]

In short, the small and marginal farmers are born in debt, live in debt and die in debt. They are poor because their investment in agriculture is meager; agriculture is subjected to climatic hazards; agricultural produce is perishable or semi-perishable; there is volatile price system and procurement price is less than cost of production; and they do not have storage facility for their grains.

---

[22] Milli Biruma Abaru et al (2006), "Strengthening farmers organizations -The experience of RELMA and ULAMP", World Agro-forestry Centre, Nairobi, Kenya

They are economically, politically and socially poor too. The farmers' organizations are both weak and lack in leadership. The well-to-do farmers are attached to the ruling political parties.

The poor farmers are fighting for survival. The unemployed youths are aimless. They are leaving the states to work elsewhere as they are hungry.

Problems of Farmers

(1) Distress sale of Paddy:

The delay in announcement of the minimum support price (MSP) and the date from which the procurement of Paddy by official agencies would start notwithstanding, farmers bringing paddy to various grain markets in Punjab are being forced to resort to distress sale of their produce. Against the MSP of 530 INR (Indian Rupees) per quintal for common variety and 726 INR for grade A Paddy last year, the farmers are getting between 391 INR and 625 INR per quintal. This is in spite of the fact that the cost of production has gone up substantially this time because of the drought like situation in the State. The farmers not only depended heavily upon diesel-generated water pumps to meet their irrigation requirements but also paid more for common inputs, including fertilizers, diesel, insecticides and pesticides. (Prabhjot Singh, Tribune, September 4, 2002)

(2) Assam farmers hit by bumper vegetable harvest

A bumper vegetable harvest has brought more woes than cheers for thousands of farmers in Assam. Moinuddin Ahmad, 50, was in tears as he rode on a bullock cart on his return journey from the wholesale market in Kharupetia village, about 70 Km. North of Guwahati." I loaded my bullock cart with cabbages before sunrise and reached the market early in the morning. But there were hardly any buyers and the prices crashed beyond imagination. I offered to sell my cabbage for just 25 paise (1/4th of an Indian Rupee) a kg but still there were no takers," Ahmed said. Angry and frustrated Ahmed dumped more than 100 Kg of Cabbage in drain. The entire area smelled of rotten vegetables with farmers dumping their unsold produce near the roadside market. "Farmers like me are doomed. I feel like committing suicide as months of hard labour and money have gone down the drain," Ahmed said. A Kg. of tomato or Cauliflower was selling for less than 50 paise (half of one Indian Rupee) in the wholesale market- a sharp fall compared to recent years. Three years back, at least a dozen tomato cultivators committed suicide in Assam after a similar crash in prices caused by surplus production. (Times of India, Jan 2003)

(3) Steep fall in Turmeric Price hits peasants (Ryots) in Guntur (Andhra Pradesh)

Turmeric, considered the most remunerative of cash crops has brought the growers in a fix with the produce touching the lowest-ever prices. The prices hit rock bottom and are ranging between 700 and 1100 INR a quintal in the current season in the Duggirala Agricultural Market Yard. In fact, the ruling price of turmeric in 1998-99 was 3750 INR a quintal while it was 3000 INR a quintal in 1999-2000. The prices fell to 1800-2000 INR last year. Mr. A. Peddaiah and Mr. Sudershan Reddy, farmers from Akkilareddy palle of Porumamilla mandal in Cuddapah district, who brought their stocks to the yard, said they reaped a yield of 12 quintals per acre. The input costs, excluding the lease amount, came to 24,500 INR per acre. Considering the existing market prices, even the best quality of turmeric was not fetching more than 15,000 INR per acre. If the lease amount was also added to the inputs, the farmers said they lose at least 15000 INR per acre. The returns were half of the investment.

(A. Saye Sekhar, the Hindu, May 21, 2001)

(4) No end to farmers' tales of woe in Mahabubnagar District

Seetaram Naik who owns 20 acres of land in Mahabubnagar district says, "I am here with the salvaged crop. Last year, the sale price of maize was above 480 INR per quintal. This season, there are no takers at even 300 INR per quintal." "Farmers are anguished on two counts. Their current crop is wrecked by the power cuts. And whatever produces that they could salvage of the Kharif does not yield a price that could even partially recover the costs. Paddy raised in most of the rain-fed villages is not yielding the minimum support price of 510 INR to 540 INR per quintal for the two grades of the grain. Same is the case of maize while castor is going for a song in all Market yards. Last year, the Sona Masuri variety per quintal was above 800 INR. But this year not more than 550 INR is being offered. Castor was sold at 1800 INR per quintal last year but farmers are resorting to distress sale of the seed at 1100 INR per quintal this year."

(T. Lakshmipathi, Hindu, November 23, 2000)

Citing the Commission for Agricultural Costs and Prices figures, former Planning Commission member Prof. Y.K. Alag says that the profitability rates for farmers have been declining since 1990. At the same time, the state has reduced its intervention, leaving the farmers at the mercy of free market.[23]

Don't pauperize farmers for profit

Agricultural land is being acquired from farmers at throwaway prices by the Government and is being

---

[23]Center for Environment and Food Security

handed over to builders, who are developing mega projects and selling them to middle class investors. In the process, the farmer is the ultimate loser.

Dimensions of corruption have changed over the recent past. Unchecked globalization and economic development have created a situation where large amounts of unaccounted money are chasing limited available assets. This black money is generated through corruption, deficit financing and several welfare scheme freebies. The major portion of this money is finding its way into the real estate sector. Corrupt politicians, Ministers and bureaucrats, in connivance with builders and developers, are exploiting gullible middle class investors who dream of owning a house.

The Government is acquiring agricultural land from farmers at throwaway prices and is being handed over to builders, who are developing mega projects and with the efforts of their brand managers, dream-sellers and marketing personnel are selling them to middle class investors. Local authorities are part of this racket and are now operating as real estate development companies. They are helping fill the coffers of some corrupt politicians.

When farmers whose land has been acquired come to know of these manipulations at a later stage and find out that the faulty and outdated Land Acquisition Act has not protected their interests, they are bound to agitate. This is what is happening in villages like Bhatta-Parsaul near Greater Noida. And if any corrective action takes place under pressure from courts or due to the agitation of the local people, leading to cancellation of these projects, then the middle class investor's money goes down the drain.

Similar is the situation in the case of land acquired for mining and industrial development. The economic development of the country also suffers. Land acquisition for industrial purposes has become one of the very contentious issues now. Land acquisition, in principle, is governed the by the Land Acquisition Act of 1894. The Act, despite getting amended in 1967 and 1984, does not address the twin issues of rehabilitation and resettlement of the displaced people.

In view of this, the Government of India announced the National Policy on Resettlement and Rehabilitation for Project-Affected Families in 2003, which came into force in February 2004. Later, in order to make the policy more effective and the Act consistent with it, two Bills - the Land Acquisition (Amendment) Bill, 2007, and the Rehabilitation and Resettlement Bill, 2007 - were drafted but have been kept pending without being put up to Parliament.

The Government must immediately take corrective measures. Foremost is the need to pass an amended Land Acquisition Act, taking into consideration proper compensation for farmers not only in monetary terms but also securing their livelihood. This can be done by paying compensation in installments over a longer duration, giving farmers a stake in the future profitability of the development project, and providing some form of employment for the families of those losing land.

To secure the interests of investors and control the real estate development lobby, there has to be regulatory authorities, which will scrutinize all schemes, check disclosures regarding promises and risk factors, and make sure these are backed by proper legal documents. It also has to ensure that developers deliver on their promises and in the event of any dereliction, investor interests are properly protected and they are duly compensated.

An important aspect from the point of view of the national economy is the need to break the nexus between real estate developers, corrupt politicians and their Public Private Partnership projects, which generate black money through corrupt means. Otherwise, over a period of time, a real estate bubble will be created and will lead to unprecedented problems in our economy.

This asset bubble is also the result of the deficit financing to which the Government resorts every year. Experts have said that emerging economies such as Brazil and India face fiscal and current account deficits and a crisis similar to the one triggered by the global financial meltdown is inevitable. The recent chain of events - whether it is the farmers agitation in Uttar Pradesh or the Maoist insurgency in various other parts of the country -- reflect this point. We must immediately act on these issues and check this particular corrupt practice.[24]

In Orissa State (India), 20 platoons of police force are engaged in June 2011 to capture low-lying farmers' land for the South Korean Steel Company by the government. The women and school children are sleeping on the road to dissuade the government machinery and police force not to capture rice fields and beetle-leaf orchards. All political parties (except Congress and BJD party) are demanding the government not to force the poor peasants to vacate homestead land and rice fields for the mega steel plant. But both the ruling political parties have mutual understanding with the POSCO Company since the last eight years.

The Chief Minister, Orissa said that the people of Orissa, which are against industrialization, are state enemies on May 27, 2013 in a meeting held at Jajpur district.

---

[24]Gopal K. Agarwal (2011), Don't pauperize farmers for profit", The Pioneer, Wednesday, June 1, 2011

People, who were present in the meeting, quipped:

Is it a democratic country of the people, by the people and for the People?

Orissa is the poorest state in India, where farmers commit suicides more than other states. Orissa is a state of peasants, hungry and poor people. Government has acquired 4000 acres of agricultural land by police force. It is a fact that POSCO has influenced both the government of Orissa and government of India.

Seed wars: The right to refuse

The minister of environment and forests, Jayanthi Natarajan, informed the Rajya Sabha during the Budget session of Parliament that the ministry of agriculture and the government's regulatory body, called the Review Committee on Genetic Manipulation (RCGM), have been telling the apex regulatory body for GM organisms, the Genetic Engineering Approval Committee (GEAC), to do away with the requirement for state government clearance before trials on GM crops can be conducted in a particular state. This is blatant indeed. Government agencies are telling the top regulatory body to dilute its rules to benefit the seed industry. The seed industry is naturally lobbying for this dilution because the more lax the rules and regulations, the better off they are. But why is the agriculture ministry and the RCGM lobbying for the seed industry's benefit?

Almost all the crops in the pipeline, the 300-odd Bt cotton hybrids and the infamous Bt brinjal and everything following these (Bt rice, Bt okra, Bt tomato... and so on) are products being developed by Mahyco-Monsanto. There is not a single public sector GM variety or hybrid to be seen anywhere. The shameful fudging by government scientists on the allegedly public sector Bt cotton — the Bt Bikaneri

Narma — is known to all. So why are the eager beavers in the agriculture ministry and the RCGM falling over themselves to make the seed industry happy... the farmers be damned? Should one smell a rat here?

If the RCGM is ignorant of the Indian Constitution, surely the agriculture ministry with its myriad bureaucrats and one of the most knowledgeable ministers in the Cabinet knows better? Agriculture is a state subject; just about everyone who has gone to high school knows that. Nothing pertaining to agriculture can be dictated by the Centre and no action related to this field can be implemented in the states without their express consent. So the audacity and defiance that we are witnessing is breathtaking, especially since both the RCGM and the agriculture ministry are asking for the suspension of the mandatory "no-objection certificate" (NOC) before field trials of GM crops can be conducted in the states.

The hubris of the government lobbyists is to be seen in their discussions with the GEAC where the case was made that state governments did not issue NOCs because they were essentially ignorant of the nature of biotechnology and bio-safety, and that these "highly technical issues" were beyond their comprehension. Chief ministers of Bihar, Madhya Pradesh, Kerala, Uttarakhand and Karnataka, please note, it is your ignorance that underlies your refusal to allow the release of GM crops in your state, not your considered opinion expressed in the interest of your people. The agriculture ministry's future plans include educating these state governments till they can be made to fall in line with what the seed industry wants.

As for state government NOCs, let me tell you of an incident where Gene Campaign was involved. This was in Jharkhand, where we detected a clear case of violation of all prescribed bio-safety norms for field trials in the areas where the Mahyco-Monsanto Bt rice was being tested. The testing by the company was done in the middle of the farmers' fields and there was not a single prescribed containment measure in sight, not even a board announcing that a field trial of Bt. rice was underway. Not surprisingly, we found that rice plants in the neighbouring area had been contaminated with the Bt. gene. When members of the Gene Campaign asked for information regarding the trials under the RTI Act, we received, among other documents, a letter from the head of research of the local agriculture university, refusing to monitor the field trials since they had not been informed of the trials and were not involved in its planning and execution. They were asked to come only in the last phase of the crop, to monitor and report on the outcome. Quite rightly, the research staff refused to be a party to whatever manipulations the company had done. As of now, field trials of GM crops are being conducted only in Andhra Pradesh, Gujarat and Rajasthan since these state governments have given permission for the trials.

The governments of Uttarakhand, Bihar, Madhya Pradesh, Kerala and Karnataka have refused permission for trials of GM crops. Some states remain in limbo, where trials are being conducted without any real knowledge of the state government but no explicit denial either. This situation needs clarification. States must retain their jurisdiction over state subjects and be empowered to take the decisions they feel are in the state's interest. If Bihar does not want to allow GM crops, it should be able to do so without someone in Delhi trying to bypass them, or, worse, browbeat them. To protect themselves from future interference of this kind from Central agencies, states must create legal instruments that will explicitly block such motivated attempts to tread on their territory.

The chief ministers' meeting on April 16 revealed the tensions between the Centre and the states with states chafing at the high-handedness of the Centre. This matter of GM crops will only exacerbate the trust deficit. The Centre must back off.[25]

USA

Farmers face Problems

The first Ky-Farm-Start class began in the spring of 2010 with approximately 150 participants in four locations: Western Kentucky, Somerset, Northern Bluegrass and Central Kentucky. A new class is set to begin in early 2011. The program includes face-to-face educational sessions and on-farm demonstrations covering such topics as enterprise evaluation, land-labor resources, nutrient management, farm record keeping, agriculture water quality plans and marketing plans, among others. This Farmer Program, offered by the Kentucky Cooperative Extension Service and backed by a nearly $750,000 U.S. Department of Agriculture grant. The University of Kentucky, Kentucky State University, Kentucky Beef Network and Kentucky Women in Agriculture are partnering to offer the two-year whole-farm management education program, which is designed to give beginning farmers-those who have been farming for 10 years or less-the tools they need to be successful.

Louie Rivers, Jr., director of the Small Farmer Outreach Training and Technical Assistance Program at Kentucky State University opines that the biggest challenge of the beginning-farmers is that they don't have any idea what they're getting into, especially when there are so many rules and regulations thrown at them, plus marketing and everything else about the enterprise. It gets complicated for them.

---

[25] Suman Sahai (2012), " Seed Wars: The right to refuse", Deccan Chronicle, April 24, 2012

Rich Hale is excited about his new endeavor, but he understands the road in front of him won't be without potholes. He just wants to avoid as many as he can. He says, 'I'm working with live animals here. I've got to be a little bit more careful about what I'm doing, because the repercussions are not just going to be on myself. It's going to be on them, too. I want to make sure I do it right, so they're treated the way they're supposed to be treated. I'm hungry for any knowledge that would be available.'

New farmers and ranchers face unique challenges and need educational and training programs to enhance their profitability and long term sustainability. The USDA funded 29 universities and agricultural organizations in 2009. The training and education provided through these grants will help ensure the success of the next generation of farmers and ranchers as they work to feed people in their local communities and throughout the world. Successful beginning farmer programs might be the key to preserving agricultural land and rural communities.

During participants' second year in the program, Kentucky Beef Network and Kentucky Women in Agriculture will help develop the mentorship component of the program, connecting program participants with mentor farmers who have similar enterprise interests. With their mentors' help, beginning farmers will take what they learned in the first year and put it into practice on their own farms, which is critical, according to organizers, in making beginning farmers successful farmers.

Participants also will be on the receiving end of cutting-edge research results from the state's two land-grant institutions through the collaboration of the University of Kentucky and Kentucky State University. This is an opportunity for two institutions to bring together their resources for the betterment of a clientele that desperately needs good, unbiased research and support in these days of trial by fire. To put it simply, we want to be the best helping hand that we can be and to get these farmers to the point where they are assured that they can be a success.

Professor Meyer said the comprehensive online curriculum would live on well past the face-to-face part of the program. It will provide valuable information to farmers who might not have access to Ky-Farm-Start in their counties, and it also will support and supplement the training of those who are enrolled. I really see that as one of the lasting legacies of this project. We'll have an excellent face-to-face curriculum, but following that, we should have this comprehensive online resource for producers to go and continue to access in the future. [26]

USA: **Economy Cuts Both Ways to Farmers**

As farmers gather at the Pennsylvania State Farm Show, which began Saturday, the tough market for dairy will surely be a common topic. Farmers sell milk by the hundredweight, which amounts to a little less than 12 gallons. Last January, they were paid more than $21 per hundredweight. Now they're getting $14.50, with the price expected to drop to $12.61 next month. "I can assure you that take away all the profit and then some," said Joel Rotz, the governmental relations director for the Pennsylvania Farm Bureau and a former dairy farmer.

The culprit might seem surprising: a strong U.S. dollar. A stronger dollar has been one bright spot amid all the recent economic gloom. Yet the weaker dollar had made U.S. agricultural products a bargain for much of the world, leading to high demand for farm products, including those from Pennsylvania. Now demand has plunged. Countries including China and India, which had significantly increased their

[26]Newsroom – meat trade news daily. Co. uk, 15 Oct 2010

consumption of dairy products and meat, have reversed. Lower prices hurt farmers. Several additional forces have dealt a blow to Pennsylvania farmers.

In early 2008, there was much interest in ethanol, which is made from corn and soybeans. Investors including hedge funds invested heavily in corn and soybeans, driving up the prices. When the economy unraveled, investors sold off holdings, causing prices to plummet. The falling prices are good for consumers, but they are causing short-term problems for a lot of local farmers. That's because local farmers who raise animals need more grain than is produced locally and must buy some from outside the area. So they paid high prices for feed but now face a down market as they sell their animals. Likewise with high fuel prices, which affect the cost of running equipment and the cost of fertilizer, which is fuel-intensive to produce. Fuel prices have dropped in recent months, but many farmers signed contracts locking them in at higher prices. The result is farmers facing a market that won't let them recoup investment costs.

Ken Bechtel, 57, farms in partnership with his father, Ken, 87, and his brother, Jay, 54. They farm their own 136 acres plus more than 700 rented acres. They raise hogs and beef cattle, and they grow crops including corn, soybeans, wheat, barley and oats. Having a diverse operation helps them withstand the assorted economic problems affecting local farmers. For example, in recent years, they have sold some of their hogs and cows directly to customers. They have sold hay to people who kept horses for pleasure. But now consumers aren't spending. "People don't seem to have the money they normally would have to buy a hog or a side of beef," the younger Ken Bechtel said.

Hope for farmers:

Still, no one is predicting the collapse of farming or calling for a government bailout. And some new forces are working in farmers' favor. One is rising consumer demand for vegetables, fruits and meats produced close to home. "It's a small niche. But it's an important niche, which we hope will grow," said David Swartz, the director of the cooperative extension office that serves Cumberland and Perry counties. Statewide, one of the big farming stories involves Marcellus shale, which lies below much of Pennsylvania and holds a huge reserve of natural gas. New technology has made it possible to extract the gas. Farmers in some areas, such as Honesdale, have struck it rich.[27]

Thailand:

Government promises to solve farmers' problems

Prime Minister Abhisit Vejjajiva said that the government would put its utmost effort into systematically solving the problems besetting the agricultural sector. In his speech to mark the Royal Ploughing Ceremony Day he said that farmers are very important for the country, and are major food producers for Thai people and the rest of the world. As the planet has only limited farmland, while the world population is increasing, the demand for food will increase. And our farmers can play crucial role on this. If Thailand has a strong agricultural sector and a recognized agricultural institution ready to move the country to sustainability in development, farming would remain a strong fundamental of Thai society.

It is the government's duty to help strengthen the agricultural sector. He admitted that the farmers had suffered from the impact of the global economic crisis over the past year. The government had tried to help by reducing farm expenditure. For the medium and long-term, the government had implemented policies

---

[27]David Wenner, The Patriot News, 10 January, 2009

on farm income guarantees and agricultural product price stabilization, and was making one million unit of state land available for landless farmers to rent at a low rate.

Even though the hardship of farmers had been eased this year on the back of a recovery in the global and Thai economies, several problems still existed - including the current drought and low rice prices. To deal with the low rice price problem, the government has come up with the farm income guarantee scheme. The government is confident that this scheme is the right way to help solve the problem. The next things the government would do for farmers included farm insurance, agricultural career development, farming under the sufficiency economy philosophy, solving rural debt problems and the establishment of a national farmer's council.

Deputy Prime Minister for economic matters Trairong Suwannakhiri said that the Rice Policy Committee has approved a budget of 436.8 million baht to help 200,000 rice farmers who suffered from low market prices against high reference prices from March 15 to April 25 in 2010. The Commerce Ministry and the Bank for Agriculture and Agricultural Cooperatives (BAAC) will assist the affected farmers immediately. He said the Rice Policy Committee had also approved the royal rice project to celebrate the 60th anniversary of the official coronation of His Majesty the King.

The project will distribute 60 million bags of rice to poor people nationwide. The Rice Policy Committee, the Commerce Ministry and the Interior Ministry will supervise the project.[28]

---

[28]Bangkok Post, May 12, 2010

Tanzania Farmers

Farmers have joined hands in Ntuntu ward of Singida rural district, central Tanzania to form a cooperative and edge out middlemen who connive to keep sunflower and millet prices low. The 3,000 member Agricultural Marketing Cooperative Society (AMCOS) is now preparing to buy sunflower and millet produce at three times the price that middlemen have been offering to them.

Using the membership fee of Tshs 2,000 and share price of Tshs 50,000 each from 69 members who have already paid up for AMCOS membership, the cooperative members have opened a bank account and secured a Tshs 150 million loan from the government-ran National Micro-finance Bank (NMB). "Farmers take the produce to a local warehouse and they are issued with a receipt for their produce pending full payment," Willberd Kimario, an Action Aid staff facilitating the farmers says.

The local government has already supported rehabilitation of warehouses at Ntuntu and Ntewa wards for this project.

The Community Development Trust Fund built the warehouses during the era of Mwalimu Nyerere when there was a strong cooperative movement. "The government guarantees the loan from the Bank against the stock in the warehouse and farmers are paid 60 percent of the agreed price on delivery while the rest is paid after the produce has been sold", Willberd explains.

Singida is the highest producers of sunflower and millet in Tanzania. Ntuntu ward alone produced 1,950 tonnes of sunflower and 835 tonnes of finger millet last year in 2009. But middlemen took most of the

profits leaving farmers with barely enough to keep them going.
50-years old Teresia Paulo is among the farmers in the ward that have endured the backbreaking labour only to enrich middlemen. "When the produce was still in the farm, the middlemen came and gave me an advance of Tshs 8,000 for a 70 kg bag of sunflower", she says. "When I harvested the produce, I pleaded with them to increase the price but only stopped at Tshs 10,000". "Since all my four children had been chased from school and were waiting for money to return to school, I ended up selling all the 30 bags of sunflower at Tshs 10,000 per 70 kg and all five millet bags at Tshs 12,000 per 100 kg"

Teresia who is only one of the many farmers says the cooperative could not have come at a better time. AMCOS treasurer, Petro Nkii says the co-operative has already established the buying price of Tshs 21,000 for the 70 kg-Sunflower-bag and Tshs 45,000 for the 100 Kg-millet bag.

This is about three times the price the middlemen offered to farmers. "When prices increase, we will increase the amount of money we pay to farmers but when it reduces, we will take it to private firms in Singida town and extract oil from the seeds so we get maximum value of our produce", Petro says. This is one of the 12 co-operatives that Action Aid has supported the farmers to register in Singida rural district. "We are aiming at helping farmers register cooperatives in each of the 28 wards of Singida Rural district by December this year (2009)", Willberd Kimario says.

AMCOS treasurer says they plan to unite with other cooperatives in the district to establish their own plant for extracting oil from sunflower seeds. Sunflower husks fetch higher prices than oil at Tshs 300 to Tshs 500 per kg in Tanzania. They are used to make animal feeds for chicken, cattle, pigs and also camels in Saudi Arabia where they are exported. Action Aid begun working with farmers and local government to mobilize people to form and join cooperatives after a baseline survey revealed exploitation by middlemen as the key contributor to poverty in the area.

In short, the organization supports awareness on cooperatives, training leadership on management, cooperative law, warehouse receipt system and financial management. Singida farmers unite to get better price for their produce Sunflower and millet farmers in Singida Rural have upped their stake to beat the middlemen who exploit them. [29]

Kyrgyzstan: **Farmers Sell Livestock**

Kalybek, a farmer of Kyrgyzstan, gesturing at his dwindling store of hay outside his home in Jar-Bash village said:

There are no jobs here, no money, And I have to feed and support my four children.

At the beginning of winter, Kalybek had 10 cows. So far in January, he has sold cows at a pace of about two per week. They used to produce milk that he would sell to a local cooperative. But with limited fodder, they have stopped lactating. He now has no income at all, and reports that he is having trouble keeping his home heated.

His story is not uncommon in northern Kyrgyzstan's Chui Oblast. Kanbolsun, a resident of the neighboring village of Internatsionalnoe complains the feed has trebled in price since the winter of 2007-08. Last year, one bale of hay cost 40 soms (one dollar), this fall it cost 100 soms . . . and now it costs 120 soms. My neighbor is selling hay for 130 soms. So I sold my

---

[29]Action aid: Tanzania

cow because I needed to buy coal, and some more hay for the rest of them. By the end of January, Kanbolsun says he will be forced to sell Faina, one of his three remaining heifers. On average, in winter, a cow needs one bale of hay per day.

Exacerbating already difficult times, farmers say that prices for livestock are plummeting. "Now, a good cow costs 16,000 soms (roughly $400). This is the most expensive kind. Last year the same cow cost 30,000 soms ($740), and hay was cheap. Kazakhs used to buy cattle from us. Now, they don't buy from us; (instead) they bring their animals to our bazaars to sell, because they too had a drought and no hay," said Kalybek.

The crisis has been years in the making, according to farmers and experts. "In Kyrgyzstan there was low precipitation over the last three years, so there was already enormous pressure on the feed base. What has worsened the situation in particular this year is the soaring cost of food," said a United Nations official, who spoke on condition of anonymity.

The official, an agricultural expert, worries about the long-term economic impact on some of Kyrgyzstan's poorest citizens. People are in a desperate situation; they're really losing their economic capacity. . . . In normal years a cow produces maybe 12-15 liters of milk a day. Now milk production is at six liters, which makes a big difference, the expert told Eurasia Net. If no action is taken, people will lose parts of their herds, milk production is already significantly reduced and will probably go down, and there will probably be? a high mortality of livestock in early spring with abortions in calving. In the long term, people might lose their economic assets; it will be extremely difficult for the small farming households and small livestock keepers to recover.

The UN has issued a Flash Appeal emergency aid request for this winter. Soaring food and fuel prices, adverse weather conditions and declining remittances, limited the purchasing power of the most vulnerable, and contributed to a precarious food security situation for some. The appeal asks international donors to provide $20 million for emergency food aid, which should take some burden off smallholders unable to feed their animals. But so far, just 11 percent of the request has been received, according to UN figures reported January 22 on reliefweb.int.

"An estimated 800,000 people are considered specifically vulnerable to the effects of water, energy and food insecurity," the appeal states. Kyrgyzstan is home to roughly 5.4 million people.

Sulaiman Mamaev, head of the Livestock and Veterinary Department at the Ministry of Agriculture, denies the situation is dire. When Eurasia Net described the situation in Jar-Bash and Internatsionalnoe, he became defensive and said that People say that just to pour dirt on the Ministry of Agriculture. If farmers are selling their animals, it is due to their personal and private reasons. Chui Oblast is the most successful province and it is not facing such problems.

He later acknowledged, however, that the cost of feed was an issue. The high price of hay and drought are absolutely connected. Last summer we did not have any rain; all the hay burned because of the hot sun. We have never had such high prices for grain products. For example this year the price for one kilogram of bran was six soms, when before the price was 1.5 soms per kilogram. Mamaev indicated that the difficulties would prove fleeting.

He told, "We shouldn't be afraid of them. They will pass. One way to overcome the current troubles would be to breed more cattle, despite the apparent glut in the market, Mamaev suggested.

Villagers in Chui Oblast, however, don't believe there are simple solutions to the present predicament. The problem, Kalybek says, is all related to feed: My cows don't (eat enough to) give milk; they can't deliver babies. If they would, I wouldn't sell them. His needs are immediate, as he and his family are already living hand-to-mouth. I don't have an income. Now I make money by selling my cows. I bought a little bit of coal the other day. We burn it only in the evening when we are getting ready to cook.[30]

Zimbabwe:
Farmers unite amid fears of tobacco ban

The UN World Health Organisation sponsored the gathering. Representatives from 171 countries signatory to the WHO's Framework Convention on Tobacco Control met to discuss additional tobacco consumption: Smoking, controls.

In Zimbabwe, that's bad news. Therefore, the animosity between black and white farmers that President Robert Mugabe's seizure of the latter's farms caused evaporated. "We have to set aside our differences to save the country's economy," The Wall Street Journal quoted Mr. Kevin Cooke as saying. He heads the Zimbabwe Tobacco Association. Tobacco contributes 26 per cent of the Zimbabwe's gross domestic product. Much as tobacco is a major contributor to Zimbabwe's economy, the country, which produced 79,000 metric tons two years ago, is a global minion. China's production, for example, totaled 2,837 thousands, the UN World Food Programme says.

---

[30] David Trilling, Central Asia Coordinator for EurasiaNet and Alina dalbaeva, Reporter, January 22, 2009 from Kyrgyzstan

The Zimbabwean love-in illustrates the tobacco industry's determination to protect itself. The WHO's choice of Uruguay as the "war council's" venue was symbolic. The US tobacco giant, Philip Morris, which earns twice Uruguay's gross domestic product, has sued the country because of strict tobacco controls.

Wish to prioritize

The "war council" replied with a declaration of a "firm wish to prioritize the application of health measures destined to control tobacco consumption." For a start, tobacco manufacturers should disclose additives they use to attract new smokers and these should be restricted or banned. Why? The WHO says tobacco consumption kills slightly more than 5 million people worldwide annually. Moreover, combined, Aids, legal and illegal drugs, road accidents, murder and, suicides don't do that.

The anti-smoking campaign began haltingly in 1960s. Though now fashionable, it's still insipid. Beginning next year, for example, the US Food and Drug Administration will require gory graphics plastered on most surface of a cigarette packet. Presumably, smokers will choke in disgust. The campaign includes blaming tobacco companies for sleek enticement to an addictive commodity. "Quitting smoking is easy. I've done it a thousand times," Mark Twain reportedly said.

That's not all of the tobacco industry's sins. Knowingly, charges go, they've sugarcoated and sold a harmful commodity. Well, scientists discovered the pure form of nicotine in 1826 and soon declared it a poison. Yet governments, always hostage to money people, allowed the tobacco industry to flourish. That includes 30 million farmers and entities that belong to the International Tobacco Growers Association. If only a leader had stood up early and said, "Hasn't someone said tobacco contains poison?" It's the same tale today. Governments continue to treat the tobacco industry as legitimate business, raking in millions in taxes. If only someone would says and mean, "We need to seek ways of dismantling this dangerous industry." Otherwise, the gatherings al Uruguay, the proposed United States gory graphics, Australia and Britain's bland packets with health warnings, et al amount to swinging earrings, too much stationary movement.[31]

Republic of Angola

The Republic of Angola covers an area of 1 247 000 km and is located on the South Atlantic coast of western Africa, bordering Namibia to the south and the Democratic Republic of the Congo and Zambia to the north and east. Angola became independent from Portugal in 1975 after years of fighting and was immediately engulfed in a civil conflict between the Popular Movement for the Liberation of Angola, led first by Agostinho Neto and, from 1979, by José Eduardo dos Santos, and the National Union for the Total Independence of Angola, led by Jonas Savimbi. Peace seemed imminent in 1992 when national elections were held, but fighting was renewed when the National Union rejected the election results. A new peace agreement, the Lusaka Protocol, was signed in 1994, but war resumed in 1998. In April 2002, a cease-fire was called following the death of Savimbi, and, on 21 November 2002, the Government and former rebels signed a peace agreement that definitively ended the conflict. After more than three decades of war, peace has opened the way for reconciliation and reconstruction in Angola, and President Dos Santos has pledged to hold national elections in 2006. The end of the war exposed very high levels of poverty and destruction,

---

[31]Chege mbitiru, "Zimbabwe: Farmers Unite Amid Fears of Tobacco Ban", All Africa. Com, 21 November 2010

especially in rural areas; most social and economic infrastructure had been damaged or destroyed.

Although endowed with rich natural resources, Angola ranked 166 among 177 countries on the Human Development Index for 2004, revealing some of the highest poverty levels in the world. A per capita income of US $ 740 is skewed by the petroleum-dominated economy. In 2002, infant mortality was 154 per 1 000 live births, the under-5 mortality rate was 260 per 1 000 live births, and life expectancy at birth was 41.5 years for men and 38.8 years for women. In rural areas, only a third of the women are literate, compared with 69 percent of men. There has been no official census since 1970, so all population figures are based on projections. The population is estimated to be 13.12 million, with almost half under 15 years of age. There are no recent reliable sources of information about rural poverty in Angola, and existing surveys were conducted at a time when insecurity prevented access to rural areas.

Available data show that, in 2001, 68 percent of the population was living below the poverty line (defined in Angola as less than US $ 1.68 per day), and 15 percent of households were living in extreme poverty (less than US $ 0.75 per day). Poverty was more prevalent in rural areas, where 94 percent of households were poor, compared with 57 percent in urban areas, due to isolation from essential services and markets, as well as the destruction or theft of crops and livestock. In 2002, 35 percent of the population was living in urban areas; it is difficult to quantify how many former rural dwellers have since returned to rural areas.

The Country Strategy Papers has identified the following problems in Angola. These are:

(a) High inflation
(b) Mounting foreign debt
(c) Governance

(d) Low productivity in agriculture
(e) Less investment in agriculture
(f) Unsuitable crop planning / crop by regions
(g) Livestock
(h) Fisheries
(i) Forestry
(j) Public institutions in rural sector
(k) Sector policy and strategies
(l) Decentralization and accountability
(m) Rural Organizations
(n) Access to Land
(o) Access to water for agriculture
(p) Access to farm inputs
(q) Access to output markets
(r) Access to agricultural services
(s) Rural financial services
(t) Food insecurity
(u) Central high lands
(v) Basic social infrastructure and services
(w) Primary education
(x) Portable water and sanitation
(y) Gender – there is significant shortage of men in Angola
(z) Malaria, HIV / AIDS and diseases

Moreover, the farmers face the following problems in Angola. These problems are:

(a) Opportunities and constraints for rural poverty reduction
(b) Knowledge base of farmers
(c) Public administration system
(d) Process and content of National Strategy for Poverty Reduction
(e) Lessons from IFAD's experience in the country
(f) Building a Knowledge base
(g) Country Programs
(h) Justification for the focus on the central highlands
(i) Capacity building

Moreover, the country should find out possibilities of services or assistance in the following programs for bringing a change in the socio-economic conditions of the country. Outreach and Partnership Possibilities with NGOs and the Private Sector are:

(a) Opportunities for Linkages with Other Donors and Institutions
(b) Leveraging co-funding for ongoing and future projects
(c) Action Areas for Improving Portfolio Management
(d) Tentative Lending Framework and Rolling Programme of Work
(e) Areas for Policy Dialogue, and
(f) Monitoring and Evaluation

Food Security: IFAD's overarching goal in post-conflict Angola will be to ensure food security and increase incomes, particularly among the most vulnerable groups in food-insecure areas of the central highlands. The program will contribute to this goal through these objectives:

(a) Increased family-based production of basic food crops among food-insecure groups in the central highlands;
(b) Empowered rural organizations and vulnerable groups demanding appropriate services and infrastructure in *municípios*, including schools, health centers and wells; and
(c) Informed pro-poor policies based on improved knowledge of rural poverty.

The following thrusts are proposed for the peasants:

Food production: Poor rural households will be supported in the production of basic food crops that meet their needs. Given the level of poverty caused by the war, some communities and vulnerable groups (for example, recently settled populations or the populations in areas to which access has been difficult) may initially require free distribution of seeds, tools and other inputs. The lack of access to good-quality seeds appropriate to local conditions is a key constraint, justifying support for local selection, production and distribution systems for planting material that are linked to national research and extension services and respond to the expressed needs of local producers. In the central highlands, livestock may be required for traction.

The diversification of production and income-generating schemes are necessary in order to respond to nutritional needs and to address the limited income and assets of the various segments of the rural population.

Secure access to productive land in the context of the 2004 land legislation, with a focus on vulnerable groups such as women. IFAD will test approaches that involve rural organizations and local authorities in participatory mapping processes and information collection for the identification of community areas under cultivation or fallow and areas of cultural importance. The aim is to mitigate possible conflicts over land reclamation and ownership, particularly in the light of the return of displaced people and former combatants, as well as to promote investment in land through greater security of tenure.[32]

The social empowerment of the rural poor and the strengthening of their organizations are essential for stability in rural areas. Rural organizations will be supported in articulating their needs, building strategies to communicate the demand to meet such needs and forging partnerships with existing service providers, including administrations. IFAD would

---

[32] Republic of Angola, Country Strategy Papers by International Fund for Agricultural Development

advocate for a policy framework conducive to the establishment and autonomous operation of rural organizations.

Conclusion

An individual farmer cannot fight against injustice, atrocity, torture, and even lawlessness in a society where everyone is an on-looker. A poor man is poor because he is poor. A rich man is rich because he can cheat the poor and manipulate government policy, or has the ability to get the work done through unfair means. But a group of farmers can seek for justice through a farmers' organization. In many cases justice delayed is justice denied. But continuous endeavor for farmers' rights could be successful in democracies provided the attempts are justified and approaches are legitimate.

The high technology farm-practices adopted by the rural subsistence farmers has resulted in farmers' suicides, high indebtedness and disasters in all developing countries. Malnutrition remains a major problem. Agricultural research, agricultural extension, financial allocation and land settlement schemes have failed to reach the poor farmers. The scientists have also misguided them to bid farewell to the traditional farming. They now experience the bad effects of modern technology such soil acidity, high cost seed varieties, attack of pests and insects, price fall during post-harvest season and high monthly premium for borrowed tractor or pump sets. The present problems are multiplied each year. These are:

The agricultural labourers are shifting to towns and cities. As a result, land remains fallow for shortage of labourers. Availability of rice @ Re1/ Kilogram of rice for political reasons has made every family beggar.

The government feels honoured when prices of cereals are kept at the lowest. But, it helps the non-farmers residing in cities and towns. The cost of all agricultural inputs is skyrocketing each year.

The traders' associations generally make whimsical decisions to stop trading to control market prices.

There are no registered farmers' political parties to fight against the government in High Courts to safeguard the interests of the farmers.

The fertilizer companies, seeds corporations, government machinery and even research organizations misappropriate the government subsidies / assistance earmarked for development of agriculture.

The government imports food grains even when market is flooded with cereals and undertakes 'Levy Procurement' of cereals during drought years.

Government encourages large-size farms, contracts farming and Special Economic Zones for multinationals against the dying farmers.

Poverty and indebtedness of farmers has resulted in farmers' suicides to the extent of 18, 000 per annum in India alone. The subsidized rice or wheat is intended for the poor but it has resulted in farmers' suicides and it would completely paralyze the farmers and farming systems in India or elsewhere within five years.

When all government servants, members of legislative Assemblies or Members of Parliament enjoy Pensioners' benefits; why the farmers would be debarred from pension which have no savings?

The land problems of all farmers must be finalized within a year of registration of deeds. The record of rights on land should be endorsed to the actual tiller within a year to save the peasants from distress.

Food Security is only possible by pleasing the farming community through remunerative prices per quintal of Rice/Wheat; insurance facility, family pension and free trade of Rice/Wheat, and stoppage of import/export of cereals.

All Fair Prices shops for Rice or Wheat must be closed forever. The dual price system has increased corruption in all countries. The no-income families might be provided two quintals of cereals per family in raw form free of cost in the village itself after procurement of stock by the government.

The drama of fixation of price of agricultural commodities for the country for a 'marketing year', procurement by the government agency, loss of stock for want of adequate storage facility, involvement of rice millers and administered by corrupt government officials must be stopped.

The government should procure food grains for emergency purposes such as flood, cyclone, drought or war for four months only. All the stocks must be exhausted in the same year.

The entry of multinationals in agriculture in developing countries would increase the number of Terrorists, Maoists and Naxalites that have already challenged the powerful countries. Unless the farmers are ensured sustainable income, respect and food security in true terms, agriculture would be forced for un-time collapse in near future in all developing countries.

And, agriculture has become a loss-bearing profession in all developing countries.

Chapter - III

FARMERS AGITATE THROUGHOUT WORLD

The farmers, small farmers, sharecroppers and agricultural labourers work hard in fields to raise bumper crops because their family members depend upon agricultural output. But variability in output and market prices make agriculture very risky and uncertain enterprise. The government allows cheap agricultural credit, low irrigation charges, subsidized seeds, and subsidized fertilizers and free market yards to the farmers to boost production. The government allows subsidized housing loan, constructs village roads for market facility and provides subsidized pump sets for irrigations purposes and tractors for ploughing and transportation. Government fixes support prices for grains, pulses, cotton and jute.

Yet the farmers live from hand to mouth; they are unable to repay back the borrowed funds from the banks and their friends. The farmers of all countries stage road marches in their countries. They have staged road marches before the Group 20 conference held at Cancun in 2011 even. Let the planners and economists find the causes of poverty of the farmers. Let them study the problems of farmers for a solution of their problems.

(a) Why the innocent and poverty-stricken farmers are agitating over the years?
(b) What is the outcome of these agitations?
(c) Why the government allows subsidies to fertilizer, pesticide and pumps sets companies and bear heavy losses in storage of food grains in state-owned corporations? Who pockets subsidies in agriculture?
(d) Why the government allows cheap rate finances to farmers?
(e) Can the government stop farmers' suicides?
(f) Would the governments increase the prices of cereals to boost their agricultural income and allow them profit in agriculture?

Unless agriculture is a profit generating profession, it would cause mass poverty and mass suicides. The peasants and sharecroppers are simply the agricultural workers in their farming practices. They grow crops and expect that they can manage their families smoothly, but any natural disaster like flood, cyclone or diseases and pests could change their future plans and programs. They do not possess credit worthiness, but they get loan from private and public sources to invest in agriculture.

They undertake road marches for expressing their grievances. They demand their dues; they do not ask for alms; they are poor but they are faithful to the country. They ask for justice; they do not need charity. They need the following problems to be solved by the government. These are:

(a) Favourable prices for their output,

(b) Land rights over their land they cultivate
(c) Stoppage of imports when the country has more surplus of food grains or crops
(d) Removing government subsidies that are eaten away by government officials, industrialists and corporations
(e) Full rights over canal irrigation facility. The water in irrigation channel belongs to farmers not industrialists
(f) Waving out interest rate during calamities and
(g) Arranging national or international markets for sale of their commodities

The main reason for their rallies is that sale prices of rice and wheat must be much more than before. They deserve more prices for farm produce. They need that the government should hear their voices. They need income for family maintenance. This chapter includes farmers' agitations in USA, India, Tanzania and Germany to illustrate farmers in all countries feel suffocated by the state laws.

USA: **Black Farmers Rally on Capitol Hill**

John Boyd, a fourth generation farmer, wants it to be clear - his effort to secure Congressional funding for a discrimination settlement that Black farmers reached with the U.S. Department of Agriculture (USDA) is not the pursuit of "reparation."

John Boyd, the president of the National Black Farmers Association told Fox News, "It is (about) discrimination. It's about justice. Black farmers have not been getting justice."

Black farmers originally filed a lawsuit against USDA in 1997 and reached a settlement agreement in 1999. Even though thousands filed claims in the settlement, many more were unaware of the deadline. A second deadline was set for September of 2000 but only a small percentage of those farmers filing claims were declared eligible for payment. Now, nearly a decade later, Black farmers are still waiting for funding for the Black Farm bill. President Obama proposed adding $1.25 billion to settle the suit and the plaintiffs agreed. However, the money was to be allocated by Congress by March 31st, it was not.

Standing in solidarity beside the Black Farmers were members of the Congressional Black Caucus, including Rep. Sheila Jackson Lee (D-TX), CBC Chair Rep. Barbara Lee (D-CA), and former CBC Chair Rep. Maxine Waters (D-CA), who has been standing with the Black Farmers since the mid-1990s.

Maxine Waters said, "I was pleased to join my friend John Boyd of the National Black Farmers Association, and the many Black farmers and their families and friends...to urge the Senate to fund the $1.15 billion settlement owed to these hard working Americans.

I have been working on this issue for almost 15 years, as Chairwoman of the Congressional Black Caucus in the late '90s, I worked closely with my CBC colleagues to urge then-Attorney General Janet Reno to waive the statute of limitations so that farmers could redress decades of financial and racial discrimination with the Department of Justice. With support from the Obama Administration and with the funding already passed by the House, we now find ourselves waiting on the Senate, which is using procedure as an excuse to further delay and deny justice to these Black farmers. I firmly believe the Senate should make the Black farmers' settlement a legislative priority, and that they should not recess for mid-term elections until this issue is resolved. I therefore applaud Senator Kay Hagan and some of her colleagues' latest efforts to fast track this payment."

In a symbolic gesture to garner support for and bring attention to the Black Farmers Bill, Boyd recently led a peaceful march from the USDA headquarters to the U.S. Capitol atop an orange tractor he named "Justice". Prior to the march, Boyd drove "Justice" through the streets of Washington for a week. He has been calling on the Senate to pass funding for claims stemming from the class action lawsuit, known as "The Pig ford Case", in which Black farmers sued the USDA for denying them fair treatment when they applied for federal assistance. The case was settled in 1999 and the federal government paid out approximately $1 billion to claimants.

Approximately 80,000 black farmers missed the deadline for the 1999 settlement. In February 2010, the Obama Administration announced a $1.15 billion agreement to resolve the second round of claims, with the purpose of bringing "these long-ignored claims of African-American farmers to a rightful conclusion."

The funding has passed the House but has been stalled in the Senate, where it has been attached to several bills only to be scratched out.

Senators Kay Hagan (D-NC) and Blanche Lincoln (D-AR), chair of the Senate Agriculture Committee, also stood with Boyd, during the news conference to announce they are introducing a standalone bill with Sen. Mary Landrieu (D-LA) to fund the $1.15 billion settlement. Senator Hagan said:

We're working together to send this language to the President as quickly as possible because our Black farmers have waited too long. We want to ensure Black farmers in our country finally receive the justice they deserve. More than 4,000 African American farmers in North Carolina and over 75,000 nationwide have been discriminated against and denied just compensation for decades. Today, I join with my colleagues from Louisiana and Arkansas, Senators Landrieu and Lincoln, to introduce a bill to fund the settlement once and for all, and we are working to send this language to the President.

The news conference was the culmination of the mile long march, led by Boyd, which began at the steps of the Department of Agriculture and ended at the U.S. Capitol. Among the participants: John Bonner of Dinwiddie, Virginia, whose father passed away earlier this year but continues to have an outstanding claim. Mr. Waters said "At this late and critical stage of the process I was compelled to walk over to the Senate, stand up with my friends, and speak out for jobs, for justice, and for civil rights. I will continue to speak and work with John Boyd and the Black farmers to make sure that this issue is finally resolved in a swift and fair manner."[33]

Tanzania

J-K Agitates for cotton handlooms

VALUE addition through the manufacture of clothes using handlooms should be the top priority for Tanzanian cotton stakeholders -- growers, buyers and ginners, President Jakaya Kikwete has advised. "Most of the Indian clothes are actually done by families of cotton farmers," said President Kikwete, after visiting Al Adawi Company Limited's ginnery and cotton farms during his recent tour of Maswa District in Shinyanga Region. He implored local cotton growers to emulate their Indian counterparts, saying that exporting raw cotton was not profitable due to fluctuating commodity prices in the world market. Unlike unstable prices of unprocessed goods, finished products command higher and more stable prices.

"A kilo of cotton can produce two shirts that will fetch a much higher price on the market than the 460/- earned from selling raw cotton," the president said. 'Kilimo Kwanza,' the brainchild of President Kikwete, seeks to incorporate the private sector as a key

[33]National Black Farmers Association, October 7th, 2010

government partner in realizing a green revolution. President Kikwete pointed out that the private sector was an important agent towards the success of 'Kilimo Kwanza' program. Commending the Al Adawi Chairman and founder, Mr. Abdi Al Adawi, for taking the lead in implementing the 'Kilimo Kwanza' initiative, the president said that private companies are legal entities, which command a better chance to get bank loans for investment in agriculture projects.

During his tour of Maswa District, Mr. Kikwete, accompanied by First Lady Salma, handed over five Massey Furgerson tractors and 10 power tillers to smallholder cotton farmers in the district, courtesy of a loan facility by Al Adawi Company Limited. The loans are repaid in between three to seven years. Mr. Al Adawi said his company which bought a ginnery from the collapsed America agro firm, Cargill last year, plans to build the capacity of cotton farmers in Shinyanga Region, by providing them with modern farming skills, tractors, power tillers and farm inputs. Al Adawi said his company plans to supply farmers with 100 tractors by the end of next year, with funding from the Ministry of Agriculture and Food Security's Agro-Input Fund.

The firm also plans to install a thread making plant and provide handlooms on loan to farmers for cloth making, "We have initiated a 'Kilimo Kwanza' program because of the huge capacity of the factory," Al Adawi said. With capacity to process 600 bales of cotton a day, the factory plans to hire 500 workers during peak seasons annually. The company also has a five-hectare modern cotton growing demonstration farm that serves as training ground for smallholder farmers.[34]

[34]Tanzania Daily News, Dar Es Salaam — January 25, 2010

INDIA: **Farmer's movement in Punjab**

It was in Punjab that India's first farmers' movement emerged. The role played by Ghadar party led by Raja Mahendra Pratap, in the political awakening of India was an important step. The Sikhs of Punjab were the first to migrate to the United States and Canada in the 19th century. They financed and helped the formation of Ghadar party which when gave the call to Indians abroad to return home and fight British imperialism, had its call immediately heeded to. The majority of those who did return, 8000 of them comprised Punjab's Sikhs. Despite its apparent failure, the Ghadar Movement was to have a powerful impact on Punjab politics and especially on the peasants. It established a tradition of militant and secular anti-imperialism, enriched in subsequent years by social radicalism, which was to continue to inspire subsequent generations.

The peasant conferences were held in Lahore, Faislabad, Lyallpur and other places of West Punjab -- the most famous of them being 1938-39 Long March in Lahore when peasants from all over Punjab courted arrests for nine months in front of the assembly building. The slogan of "Hold your head high, O peasant" was first raised at a mass gathering in Lyallpur in 1907. Ten Thousand people -- the Hindus, the Muslims and the Sikhs alike -- attended this gathering.

Farmers' movements in Gujarat

Mahatma Gandhi had led two great revolts of communities of poor Indian farmers against the tyranny of the British government and allied landlords in Champaran (Bihar) and in Kheda (Gujarat). Both struggles had helped win the farmers economic and civil rights, and electrified India's people and became successful. In 1920, the India National Congress under Gandhi's leadership launched the Non-

Cooperation Movement. Millions of Indians revolted against the British, boycotting the courts, government services, schools and disavowing titles, pensions and British clothes and goods. The freedom fighters, known as *Satyagrahis*, peacefully protested authoritarian British laws, and called for India's independence. Many thousands were beaten, tortured and arrested.

Bardoli Satyagraha

Bardoli Satyagraha of 1925 in the state of Gujarat (India), during the British rule was a major episode of civil disobedience and revolt in the Indian Independence Movement. The Bardoli Taluk (revenue area) in Gujarat suffered from floods and famine, which hurt the crop produce, leaving farmers facing great financial troubles. However, the Government of the Bombay Presidency had raised the tax rate by 30 percent that year, and despite petitions from civic groups, refused to cancel the rise in face of the calamities. The situation for the farmers was grave enough, that they barely had enough property and crops to pay-off the tax, let alone for feeding themselves afterwards.

The Gujarati activists namely Narahari Parikh, Ravi Shankar Vyas and Mohan Lal Pandya talked to village chieftains and farmers, and solicited the help of Gujarat's most prominent freedom fighter, Vallabhbhai Patel, who had previously guided Gujarat's farmers during the Kheda struggle, and had served as Ahmadabad’s municipal president. He was widely respected by all people of Gujarat. Patel and Gandhi decided that the struggle be left entirely to the people of Bardoli taluka (Revenue area).

Governor of Bombay ignored the request made by Patel to reduce taxes but reciprocated by announcing the date of collection. Patel instructed all the farmers of Bardoli taluka to refuse payment of their taxes. Aided by Parikh, Vyas and Pandya, he divided Bardoli into several zones - each with a leader and volunteers specifically assigned. Patel also placed some Gujarati activists close to the government, to act as informers on the movements of government officials. Patel instructed the farmers to remain completely non-violent, and not respond physically to any incitements or aggressive actions from officials. He reassured them that the struggle would not end until not only the cancellation of all taxes for the year, but also when all the seized property and lands were returned to rightful owners.

The Government declared that it would crush the revolt. Along with tax inspectors, bands of Muslims were gathered from northwest India to forcibly seize the property of the villagers and terrorize them. The Muslims and the men of the collectors forced themselves into the houses, took all property, including cattle.

The government began to auction the houses and the lands. But not a single man from Gujarat or anywhere else in India came forward to buy them. Patel had appointed volunteers in every village to keep watch. As soon as he sighted the officials who were coming to auction the property, the volunteer would sound his bugle. The farmers would leave the village and hide in the jungles. The officials would find the entire village empty. They could never find out who owned a particular house.

Members of the legislative councils of Bombay and across India were angered by the terrible treatment of the protesting farmers. Indian members resigned their offices, and expressed open support of the farmers. Even many in the Raj's offices heavily criticized the Government.

In 1928, an agreement was finally brokered by a Parsi member of the Bombay government. The Government agreed to restore the confiscated lands and properties, as well as cancel revenue payment not only for the year, but cancel the 30% raise until after the succeeding year.

While Patel credited Gandhi's teachings and the farmers' undying resolve, people across the nation recognized his vital leadership. Gandhi and his fellow satyagrahis called him *Sardar* for the first time, which means *Chief* or *Leader*. It was after Bardoli, that Sardar Patel became the first home minister of free India and was known as the IRON MAN of India.

Farmers' movements in Rajasthan

Rajasthan is known as the land of kings and palaces and whose history is replete with encomium of their kings; the land known for 'Sati', the land known for its vast tracts of deserts was witness to a history in making, the successful agitation of farmers and peasants for their right to livelihood.

The twenty-two princely states of erstwhile Rajputana state did not form a common political collectivity which can be termed as a unified political action model. Each state had its own territorial area, which was exclusive politically in that it had its separate administration nag and army. Each state retained its cultural and linguistic distinctiveness. Political authority varied from ruler to ruler depending upon the terms of contract or covenant with the paramount power dating back to the period of subsidiary alliance of Lord Wellesley. Obviously in a state like this, the freedom movement was bound to be divided and segmented, depending upon the degree of unity and cohesiveness among political players in each state. The two states of Jaipur and Jodhpur provided differential patterns of political movements.

Justice Kan Singh Parihar, the retired Judge of High Court of Rajasthan, has written about exploitation of farmers by Jagiridars prior to Independence as under:

Everything that the Kisan[35] had, he never treated as his own. In Jagir areas all cultivators were really landless. There was no tenancy law and one could be thrown away from the land one cultivated at the pleasure of Jagirdar, his "malik". In most of the Jagirs a Jagirdar would in the first instance be taking fifty percent of the produce. This would be taken by actual division of the produce on the threshing floor or by appraisal of the standing crop. Then over and above the share of the produce the farmer had to pay numerous "lags" or taxes.

Kisans had to part with more than eighty percent of their produce. The findings of the Sukhdeonarain Committee in the years 1940-42 bear this out. If a Kisan had to marry his daughter he had to pay "Chavri Lag", if he held a dinner then a "Kansa Lag"; if members of the family separated then "Dhunwa Lag" and so on. If the Jagirdar had a guest then fodder for his mount had to be supplied. Moreover, there was forced labour for tilling the personal lands of the Jagirdar. The homestead in which the Kisan lived in the Abadi had to be vacated in case he ceased cultivating the land. He could not alienate the plot to anyone."

Mr. Kan Singh Parihar played a great role in drafting for enactment of Marwar Tenancy Act of 1949 and Marwar Land Revenue Act of 1949. His idea of fixing all tenants in cultivator's possession as Khatedars made all of them almost the proprietors of all their fields, wells etc. without paying any premium or compensation and further being relieved from paying any extra taxes. This Marwar Tenancy Act of 1949 and Marwar Land Revenue Act of 1949 became a role model for the Rajasthan Assembly in 1955 and similar laws were passed based on these Acts, thus greatly benefiting the farmers of Rajasthan.

---

[35]Note: Kisan or KIssan means farmer or peasant

Shekhawati farmers' movement

The farmers of the Sekhawati region are considered to be the most advanced in the state of Rajasthan. The Shekhawati region has the highest literacy in the state. The most dominating farmer community in the rural areas of Shekhawati is Jat (farming community). The Jats are politically and economically very sound. The major land holdings in the present times are with Jats. The Rajput community was the jagirdars before independence. The farmers of the region have done great struggle to come to the present status.

Before independence the conditions of the farmers were worst. The farmers of the Shekhawati region were exploited and oppressed by the Jagirdars during British Raj. They were deprived of fundamental rights. They were given inhuman treatment when the Jagirdars did not get cesses known as *lāg* (tax) or *begār* (unpaid work) in time, they were given hard punishments and their crop used to be destroyed. There were 37 kinds of *begārs* (work without pay) prevalent in Shekhawati. A newly married bride was forced to go first to Jagirdar.

The Shekhawati Jat farmers' movement had its genesis in the Jat Prajapati Maha-Yagna a socio-religious festival held in January, 1934. It lasted ten days and was the biggest of its kind in Rajputana. It facilitated a widespread involvement of Jats in a community festival. Each Jat household attending it was to contribute some cash and an unspecified quantity of ghee. A total of two hundred maunds of ghee were used in the sacrificial flame. The function concluded with a triumphal elephant ride hitherto prohibited by the rules of Sikar Thikana. The success of this movement encouraged the Jats to hold more meetings on local levels and print literature to glorify Jat history. The Yagna became a dominant symbol of folklore which glorified it as the beginning of an anti-feudal struggle. The peasants demanded remissions in taxes and finally a Jat- Sikar Thikana Agreement was signed on August 23, 1934, by which the Thikana authorities conceded to abolish various lags (taxes) and agreed to provide for a mobile dispensary. The following year, the Kisan Sabha formally came into existence and under its aegis the famous Sikar Andolan of 1935 was launched. With outside mediation efforts of Jamna Lal Bajaj, Sir Chhotu Ram - a renowned Jat leader of Punjab and Ratan Singh of All India Jat Mahasabha, a settlement was arrived at and the Jats were promised remissions of rent, abolition of internal taxes and an introduction of fixed rent tenure.

The Jats were also promised equal opportunities in Thikana administration and were permitted to ride elephants and horses and to construct schools for their children. The formation of a Jat Kisan Panchayat was officially sanctioned and the right to agitate for redressal of grievances in non-Khalsa areas was conceded. Much however, could not be made out of these agreements for two reasons. First, the subordinate Thikanedars of Sikar did not fully cooperate with Sikar authorities to ensure compliance with the terms of these agreements. Secondly, the beginning of settlement operations and reform of revenue administration was a time-consuming process which entailed enormous delay. This was interpreted by the Jats as a breach of agreement and hence, they indulged in acts of disorder and violence, which were perceived by Thikana authorities as signs of bad faith. In the meanwhile two un-savoury incidents led to a termination of agreements. The first occurred at Khudi village, where the sight of Jat bridegroom riding a horse incensed the local Rajputs and the two sides readied themselves for an armed combat. The state authorities asked the two parties to disperse but the Jats refused.

The state police charged and in the melee that followed, several people were injured. The second incident took place at Kudan village, where about one hundred armed Jats attacked Sikar revenue officials. The police fired upon the armed mob, which resulted in several casualties and injuries. A total of 104 Jats were arrested.

Farmers of the Shekhawati, mainly the Jats, united against oppression of Jagirdars by forming 'Sikar Jat-Kisan -Panchayat' and stopped giving "lags" or taxes to the Jagirdards. The 'Jaipur Praja-Mandal' also supported the Shekhawati farmers' movement against abolition of Jagirdari system. The leaders of 'Bijoria-Kisan-Movement' of 1922, 1931, and 1932 supported the movement of Shekhawati farmers. The Jagirdars tried to suppress the movement in many ways. Many farmers were killed and a large number were sent to jail. A Jat farmer was beaten to death in the market of Sikar town; his dead body was thrown and insulted. This movement got support from famous Kisan leaders like, Baldev Ram Mirdha, Nathuram mirdha and Kumbharam Arya. After a long struggle the farmers got rid of oppression and got the ownership right over the land they were cultivating.

The leading Jat farmers of Shekhawati region, who played important role in the movement for abolition of the Jagirdari system, were: Sardar Har Lal Singh, Mandasi, Iswar Singh Bhamu Bhairupura, Hari Singh Burdak and Hardeva Palthana, Prithvi Singh Gothra, Ganeshram Kudan, Panne Singh Bataranau, Goru Singh Katrathal, Deva Singh Bochalya, Chandrabhan Singh, Hardev Singh Nehra Harasawa.

Shekhawati farmers' movement against abolition of Jagirs got great support from outside Kisan leaders like Sir Chhotu Ram from Haryana, Kunwar Ratan Singh and Thakur Deshraj from Bharatpur, Kunwar Hukum Singh from Aangai.

Marwari farmers' movement

The farmers of the Marwar region are considered to be the most simple in the state of Rajasthan. The most dominating farmer community in the rural areas of Marwar is Jat. The Jats are politically and economically very sound. The major land holdings in the present times are with Jats.

Though the position of *Kisān* (farmer) in what was *Khālsā* (under the direct control of the state) was better in comparison to a Kisan of the Jagir areas, he was only a little above a beast of burden. In Jagir areas of Marwar state before independence all cultivators were really landless. There was no tenancy Law and one could be thrown away from the land one cultivated at the pleasure of Jagirdar, his "malik". In most of the Jagirs a Jagirdar would in the first instance be taking fifty percent of the produce. This would be taken by actual division of the produce on the thrashing floor or by appraisal of the standing crop (*kuntā*). The latter method proved at times more onerous as the appraisal depended on the whims of the *Kāmdār*. Then over and above the share of the produce the farmer had to pay numerous "lags" or taxes. There were 64 kinds of *begars* (work without pay) prevalent in Marwar. Then the bigger Jagirdars had judicial powers including magisterial powers. Further they had their own police force besides the revenue staff. This enabled them to keep their stronghold on the farmers. Over and above this policy of divide and rule was fully practiced. By offering the temptation of giving better land for cultivation one farmer would be set against another. There were no schools worth the name in rural areas and the masses were steeped in ignorance.

The oppression of the public by traditional (chiefs) and Jagirdars (feudatories) of Marwar state made their life difficult, which led to a class war. In urban areas, Jaynarayan Vyas started agitation against oppression, under the banner of "Marwar Lok Parishad" founded on 16 May 1938. This movement was supported by Indian National Congress.

The persons who played important role in "Marwar Lok Parishad" were: Shiv Dayal Dave and Jorawar Singh Oswal of Nagpur, Rajpurohit Manji Jagarwal, Kishanlal Sahu, Manak Chand Konari and Sari Mal , Tulsiram of Didwana, Srikishan Pandit of Kolia and Sukhdev Dipankar of Ladnu.

Rural masses of Marwar were united by Kisan Kesari- Baldev Ram Mirdha under the banner of "Marwar Kisan Sabha" founded in 1940. After the formation of Rajasthan, Baldev Ram Mirdha who had by then retired from Government service formed the "Rajathan Kisan Sabha" and unified the *Kisāns* of Rajasthan under its banner. He was its first president. Since the broad objectives of the *Kisān Sabhā* and the congress were identical the congress leaders approached Baldev Ram Mirdha to unite the Rajasthan *Kisān Sabhā* with the Congress. Baldev Ram Mirdha was a visionary and he realized that the two could not and should not remain separate. Therefore, he just made one demand from the national leaders that the Jagirs be abolished forthwith in Rajasthan. This was agreed to by the Congress high command with the result that the Jagirs were soon abolished. A tenancy law was passed and the cultivating farmers were made the owners of the land.

Peasant Movement TEVAGA in West Bengal

Just before Independence, 1946, farmers of Nandigram, Sutahata and Mahishadal of South Midnapore District revolted against Zamindari System. They demanded that the share croppers would get 2/3rd of the harvested crop and the landlord should get 1/3rd of the produce. This is known as TEVAGA movement. Bimala Majee, Ananta Majee and Bhupal Panda were the leaders of Tevaga movement in South Midnapore. Hindu and Muslim peasants fought united against Zaminders, Zotdars. Participation of Hindu and Muslim women were significant in Tevaga. The movement was successful and continued till 1949.[36]

The peasants of Nandigram were successful in another movement under the leadership of Ms. Mamata Banerjee. They could stop the establishment of a 'Car Industry' of the powerful TATA Company.

Gharsana (Rajasthan) movement:

The tehsil town of Gharsana and the neighbouring Raola in Sri Ganganagar district of Rajasthan is currently site of clashes between the police and the farmers agitating for irrigation water. The farmers, and their leaders who led the agitation under the banner of Kisan Mazdoor Vyapari Sangarsh Samiti, were either nursing their injured or in hiding. About 20 injured have been admitted to the Gharsana hospital and the district hospital in Sri Ganganagar. The authorities said curfew was clamped in Raola as a precautionary measure as in the previous agitation by the farmers on the same issue in October-November 2004.

Farmers of Gharsana, at Ganganagar in Rajasthan, are on path of confrontation with the Bharatiya Janata Party (BJP) government for the release of water from Pong Dam to the Phase I areas of Indira Gandhi Canal, the lifeline of farmers in the Gharsana-Raola agriculture belt. At a juncture when India is importing wheat from other countries, the state government is dissuading farmers in the region from cultivating wheat during the Rabi season. The farmers have been told to sow barley or mustard, rather than

---

[36]Wikipedia, the free Encyclopedia

wheat, which is a water-intensive crop. The movement has gained momentum with the Kisan Mazdoor Vyapari Sangharsh Samiti, the committee of farmers, labourers and agro-traders of the region deciding to go ahead with sowing wheat. The strife over water has seen the peasants and the state administration clash often in the past three years. Seven farmers were killed and many were injured when police fired at protesters in 2004.

Earlier in October 2004, defying prohibitory orders, hundreds of farmers had gheraoed the SDM's office at Gharsana town in Sri Ganganagar district, reviving their agitation for irrigation water after the October 27, 2005 police firing which claimed five lives. With a view to appeasing the agitating farmers, the Vasundhara Raje Government transferred the Divisional Commissioner of the region and Superintendent of Police, while two officers of the Rajasthan Administrative Service were placed under suspension. The farmers' agitation led the Government to impose curfew in July 2005 also.

Farmers organizations under attack in Punjab

The peasants' organizations in Punjab have been in the forefront in the struggle against the anti-people new economic policies of globalization, liberalization and privatization. They have fought for remunerative prices for agricultural produce, its procurement by state agencies, writing off farm loans, and against arrests of farmers due to non-payment of farm loans advanced by Cooperative Societies, attachments and sales of their lands at the instances of Commission Agents and money lenders etc.

They have also led glorious struggles against setting up of Special Economic Zones (SEZs) in the state, forcible acquisition of agricultural land for setting up giant industrial complexes, power projects, multi-lane roads etc. and against unbundling and ultimate privatization of the Punjab State Electricity Board (PSEB). Faced with stiff resistance from the farmers' organization, the Punjab Government was forced to abandon or curtail many projects. Irritated at this; the Akali-BJP Government in Punjab launched a massive offensive against the organizations of the farmers. A large number of leaders and activists of these organizations were implicated in false criminal cases. On September 8 2009, when Bharatiya Kisan Union Ekta (Ugrahan) held a massive demonstration at Chandigarh to oppose unbundling of the State Electricity Board, 4 FIRs were registered against all of its State Office-bearers. The leaders of Punjab Khet Mazdoor Union and Lok Morcha Punjab were also implicated in these cases.

Hundreds of farmers were injured in the brutal lathi-charge by the police. Their vehicles were badly damaged. As a result of the police brutalities, four persons lost their lives. The sacrifices of these farmers did not go in vain. Akali-BJP Government was forced to postpone the unbundling / corporatization of the PSEB, till mid-December.

Now as the day of reckoning is reaching near, and the farmers' organizations have started mobilizing the people against the privatization of the PSEB, the Akali-BJP Government has launched another attack. On November 17 2009, President of BKU (Krantikari), Mr. Surjit Singh Phul was arrested from the court premises when he had gone there to attend a hearing. The police would have kept him in illegal confinement and subjected to torture, but the democratic-minded advocates and farmer activists approached the Sub Divisional Judicial Magistrate (SDJM) and apprised him of the illegal act of the police. The SDJM immediately called the SHO of the concerned police station.

Fearing exposure, the police registered a case under Section 10, 13 of the Unlawful Activities (Prevention)

Act against Mr. Surjit Singh, branded him a member of the CPI (Maoist), planning to illegally overthrow the Government through armed struggle. He was immediately arrested in this case. Next day the police obtained his custody for 8 days by producing him before the Magistrate at his residence after court hours, and he was immediately sent to the infamous Joint Investigation Centre, Amritsar, which is Punjab's Guantanamo.

On November 26 2009, Mr. Surjit Singh was to be produced before the SDJM Phul for further remand. The police with a view to hoodwink his lawyers, made elaborate security arrangements at Phul Courts. Riot-police commandoes in full battle gear were deployed not only in and around the court-premises, but also on all entrances of the town, and at important road-junctions leading to this town throughout the district. But it was merely a drama.

In fact the police filed an application before the District and Sessions Judge Bathinda, expressing false and baseless apprehensions that people at Phul might take away Mr. Surjit Singh forcibly from the police, and obtained permission to produce him before the CJM at Bathinda. The real intention was to deprive Mr. Surjit Singh of any legal aid and exposure of the third degree methods adopted by the police. The police succeeded in obtaining his remand in its custody for another 8 days till December 3 2009.

As soon as this information reached his lawyers, who were camping at Phul Town, they immediately moved the court to obtain permission to meet Surjit Singh in police custody and for his interrogation only in the presence of his lawyers. The court allowed the lawyers to meet him on November 26 and 27, and informed the police about this order. But the police did not care about the Court's order and sent him to Joint Interrogation Centre, Amritsar again without informing the Court. When the lawyers tried to contact the Investigating Officer to fix the venue of the meeting, he switched off his mobile phone.

On November 27, the lawyers filed another application before the CJM Bathinda, seeking initiation of contempt of court proceedings against the police officials, and fixing new time and date for meeting with Surjit Singh. Acting on this application, the court granted permission to the lawyers, to meet Mr. Surjit Singh during his detention at Joint Interrogation Centre Amritsar, every day from 5 to 6 PM from November 30 onwards. The game-plan of the police has been foiled for the present, but its attack can be repulsed only by mobilizing masses against these anti-people, undemocratic, and repressive measures.

State offensive in Lalgarh

Statement from Lok Morcha Punjab

The Lok Morcha in Punjab strongly condemns the repression unleashed by the Indian State of Punjab on the struggling people of Lalgarh and has called upon the people of Punjab to raise their voice against it.

The tribal people of Lalgarh are fighting a glorious struggle to protect their lands, forests, natural resources, culture, lives, liberty and honor. After the land-mine blast on the caravan of West Bengal C.M. Budhdeb Bhattacharya and the then Union Steel & Mines Minister Ram Vilas Paswan, in November 2008, the West Bengal police launched a massive combing operation in the Lalgarh area, conducting mid-night raids; beating up, assaulting and dishonoring women and children, illegally detaining and torturing them in police camps.

The tribal people refused to take it lying down and took to the path of struggle against these repressive measures by organizing themselves in Committees for Resisting Police Repression, in numerous villages.

They held massive sit-down strikes and protest sieges before the police-camps and decided to socially boycott those police officials who perpetuated cruelties upon them. There was absolutely nothing "Maoist" in their 11-point charter of demands, which included public apology by policemen responsible for torturing & humiliating the people; an end to mid-night police raids; release of innocent persons detained without trial since 1998 on the suspicion of being 'Maoists'; removal of all police camps from various schools, hospitals & other public buildings in the area and compensation to the victims of police brutalities etc.

Although the authorities conceded these demands and promised to initiate action to implement these, but this announcement was a clever ploy to buy time. Shortly afterwards, the police raids restarted with increased vigor; police repression on the innocent people intensified & the police camps were re-established. Two leaders of the Committee for Resisting Police Repression, namely Nirmal Sardar & Hemadri Mahato were brutally murdered. CPI (M) goons are enacting a different type of 'Salwa Judam', openly firing upon struggling tribal people, killing & maiming many people.

Now a full scale offensive with a contingent of more than 5000 armed personnel is underway. Indian state is trying to overawe & crush simple tribal folks, by massive deployment of its security forces, armed with ultra-modern & sophisticated weapons, under the garb of flushing out the 'Maoists'.

The Santhal tribal people of Lalgarh have been deprived of the basic necessities of life, since decades. There is no electricity, irrigation facilities, motor-able roads etc. Facilities for education, health care, safe drinking water etc are scarce. For the last more than 5 years, the few existing school, hospital & other public buildings have been occupied by the security forces. Funds provided under various 'development schemes' such as NREGA, Indira Awas Yojna etc are cornered by Marxist-controlled Panchayats to benefit their own cadres. The Public Distribution System is being used for illegal enrichment of Depot Holders, who are members or sympathizers of CPI (M) & corrupt officials.

Now in the name of establishing Special Economic Zones, a wave of dispossession of tribal from their lands & forests has started to facilitate their exploitation by MNCs & their Indian agents. The CPI (M) which has remained entrenched in the Writers Building for more than three days on the strength of tribal votes has done nothing to ameliorate their lot. Rather it has worsened further due to anti-people neo-liberal policies being pursued by the West Bengal & Central Government. With the present armed offensive & extreme violent repression, the State may lull the movement temporarily. But the democratic revolutionary aspirations of Lalgarh people cannot be crushed. The movement will rebound with great vigor and increased strength, winning support & solidarity from the struggling people throughout India.[37]

Farmer's agitate for better prices for sugarcane

Farmers' agitation demanding better prices for sugar cane intensified in November 2009 with protestors blocking highways and disrupting train movement. The Samajwadi Party also stepped in and announced their support for the farmers' agitation, which saw protests spilling out on the streets at several places in western-UP. As per reports protesting farmers stopped the Shalimar Express, Delhi-Muzzafarnagar Express and a passenger train disrupting train timings. They also removed fishplates and damaged rail tracks in Baghpat. Cane farmers also came out on

---

[37] N.K. Jeet, "Farmers' organisations under attack in Punjab, Radical News, November 29, 2009

the streets and forced business establishments and shops to down shutter demanding that the government ensure better prices for cane.

At the Great-people's institution held recently farmers had given the government three days ultimatum that ended on Monday making the farmers takes to the streets. Three companies of PAC were deployed in these areas to control the protestors who have now resolved to shift their protests to New Delhi and the central government's move to implement Fair and Remunerative Price (FRP) for cane, from this year onwards.

Cane farmers said that the prices fixed by the government for cane this year was not economically viable for them and would hurt the interests of the farmers. They said that the SAP of 165 INR/quintal fixed by the Mayawati government was not acceptable to them and now the FRP regime brought by the central government proposes to give even lower rates at 130 INR/quintal which they cannot accept. They alleged that the government had played into the hands of the mill owners and threatened not to allow crushing of cane to begin in UP.

Farmers said that they would not sell cane to the mills at the rates fixed by the government and demanded prices as high as 215 INR/ quintal, in view of rising sugar prices and low cane production. Farmer leaders including Rashtriya Lok Dal chief and former union minister Ajit Singh have now decided to stage a protest near the parliament in New Delhi on November 19. Ajit Singh said that they would not let allow the parliament to approve the FRP legislation and formulate a joint strategy with other parties to oppose it.[38]

---

[38]The Economic Times, November 9, 2009

The farmers' agitation, which is currently being led, by Ajit Singh and Bhartiya Kisan Union saw the Samajwadi Party also jumping into the fray. Samajwadi Party President Mulayam Singh Yadav on Monday said that they would support the farmers' agitation and the party would stage a protest on November 16, 2009.

Farmers Agitation for higher Cane Prices Shows signs for Revival

The farmers' agitation for higher cane prices has again started showing signs of a revival. After the standoff between the millers and farmers was resolved last week with millers, goaded by the state government, agreeing to give an incentive of 25 INR/quintal over and above the SAP, most mills had opened to begin crushing.

But though the cane supply position has looked up, many mills are still finding it difficult to function at optimum levels due to erratic and short supply of cane. More than a dozen sugar mills out of about 130 operational mills in the state are yet to begin crushing due to the issue not being fully resolved in some districts. Many of those who have started crushing are yet to achieve the desired level of crushing per day due to shortage of supply.

Though most farmers under pressure to clear their fields for Rabi (winter) sowing have started selling cane to millers the demand for still higher prices has not died down completely.

Many farmers are still reluctant to sell cane at an incentive of 205 INR/quintal, which takes the effective price of cane 190 INR/quintal for the general variety and 195 INR/quintal for the early variety of cane.

With a sugar mill in Moradabad agreeing to purchase cane from farmers at the price of 205 INR/quintal the demand for this price to be made uniform across Uttar Pradesh has gained ground. Farmers argue that private mills would continue to make substantial profits even after purchasing cane at 205 INR/quintal and all mills in UP should agree to give this price to farmers.

Farmer leaders have now started threatening for another round of agitations and diverting their cane to neighbouring states like Haryana and Uttarakhand if the price of cane is not hiked to 220 INR/quintal. Rakesh Tikait of the Bhartiya Kisan Union, who is spearheading the campaign for higher prices, said that they have given the state government an ultimatum and if prices are not increased further they will resort to diverting cane to neighbouring states. Farmers are expected to regroup for another hike in prices once they get over with selling "ratoon" cane by December end. The "plant variety" of cane comes to the market only in January so farmers would have ample time between selling "ratoon" and "plant" variety of cane to negotiate with the mills for the second batch of supplies.[39]

Government Mulls Cotton Export Ban as Farmers Agitate

The government will take a decision on whether or not to ban cotton exports after assessing the domestic demand and supply situation. The Government is closely watching the price scenario in cotton. The current rise in cotton prices is in tune with an increase in the domestic demand. Domestic prices of cotton have been on the rise despite an increase in production expected this year. Several industry bodies have approached the government

[39] The Economic Times Dec 2, 2009

seeking a ban on cotton exports, saying the price rise is due to the increase in export of raw cotton.

Traders said despite good crop arrivals, prices of leading varieties had shot up 8 per cent primarily due to a surge in export demand. Cotton exports in October, including those of the most sought-after Gujarat Sankar variety, surged 300 per cent to about 116,000 bales from a month earlier, according to the Cotton Association of India. [40]

While the government remains keen on boosting its revenue through cotton exports as supplies have become scarce in the international market, farmer associations are up in arms against this policy.

Farmers agitate for Narmada water

Around 200 farmers from 20 villages around Halvad continued with their indefinite hunger strike at the mamlatdar's office on October 12, 2009. They're protesting the ban on water for irrigation from Narmada dam. The farmers are up in arms against Sardar Sarovar Narmada Nigam Ltd (SSNNL) for its decision to prevent them from pumping out water to irrigate their farms. They have decided to continue their strike till SSNNL allows them to avail water from the branch canal at Maliya village. Mr. Valji Patel, a farmer from Mangadh village said: We've had poor monsoon this year. Now, to add to our woes, SSNNL has clamped a ban on Narmada water. If the water is not released from Narmada canal, our crops will be completely ruined. Another farmer Mr. Vijay Patel, member of Halvad taluka panchayat said: **The hunger strike was inevitable as several representations made by us to resolve this issue fell on deaf ears. After issuing a memorandum to the district collector, we launched the strike on October 11, 2009.**

---

[40]Domain-b.com

The agitating farmers are from Tikar, Navaghatila, Mangadh, Miyani, Ajitgadh, Mayapuras, Prakashnagar, Ingorada, Isanpur, Kidi, Jogad and Janda villages.[41]

Cane farmers agitate for better prices

Around 100 sugarcane farmers from Solapur sat in protest against 15 sugar cooperatives in front of the sugar commissioner-ate on Tuesday. They alleged that for 2006-07, they are yet to receive the statutory minimum price (SMP) set by the government to be paid by the sugar cooperatives.

Babasaheb Lunshe of Mhada taluka said that the cooperatives were supposed to give us 900 INR per tonne, but farmers have been given only about 300 INR to 600 INR for that year. For a year now, we have been writing to the sugar cooperatives and the commissioner-ate but we are yet to receive the amount. In February 2007, the sugar cooperative collected his sugarcane from his farm, but he was paid only 560 INR per tonne.

Sugar commissioner Rajgopal Devra agreed that many farmers had not received the minimum price. He said that he would need to verify the complaints of these 100 farmers. If they are found to be true, then we will write to sugar cooperatives asking them to pay the balance. However, farmers alleged that letters to the sugar cooperatives in the past from the commissioner -ate have gone unanswered. [42]

Himachal Kissan Sabha agitate for Farmers' issue

Holding the state government responsible for being unable to provide fertilizers to the farming

---

[41]The Times of India –Rajkot, October 14, 2009

[42]Express India, Pune, August 27, 2008

community, the communist affiliated Himachal Kisan Sabha (HKS) has threatened to agitate by holding protest demonstrations throughout the state on Monday. Speaking to the media, Kuldeep Tanwar, president HKS said the sabha is going to protest demonstrations in over 3 dozen centers, which include district headquarters, sub-divisions and blocks over the government failure to timely meet the farmers demand for seed and fertilizers. A memorandum for the chief minister would also be handed over to officers where the demonstrations are held.

The vice-president of the Association informed that Initially the horticulture minister Narinder Bragta as well as the agriculture minister, who happens to be the state chief minister, had denied any shortage of seeds for the winter crop or any fertilizers but now they are trying to pass on the blame onto the central government. The government owes and explanation for attempting to hoodwink the people, and failing to make timely arrangements for meeting the demand. Unavailability of seeds has resulted in large tracts of farmlands not being sown.

Pointing out the hardships being faced by the farming community, the vice-president said that drought conditions had badly affected the last three crops, reducing productivity by as much as 70 percent of winter (winter) season and 80 percent of Rainy (rainy) season. Compounding their problems was shortages of seed and fertilizer, this season, he added. Reducing the ration quota from 35 Kg to 25 Kg through the public distribution system for the common man had severely brought down nutrition levels, they alleged.

Touching upon other issues, the organization has demanded that encroachment by small and marginal farmers needed to be regularized at the earliest as the BJP government had gone back on its commitment made in its previous term to do so for which it had even invited applications. Accusing the government of a partisan approach, he said that in the last decade, more than 10 thousand hectares of land has been handed over to big industries for opening private universities or constructing Hydel-projects. The century old timber distribution (TD) rights had been overturned to pave the way for forest mafia and richer sections to gain control of the natural resource, said the organization leaders. Implementation of the forest tribal and dwellers act that was being diluted needed to be ensured. Simian menace continues to haunt farmlands and the government has failed to act responsibly.[43]

Sanjay Chauhan, treasurer of the sabha said that the Kheti Bachao Sangarsh Samiti would organize a Jan Sansad 'Peoples Parliament' on 10th December and would hold protest demonstrations on 23rd December and on the other hand to stall privatization of the Gumma carton factory in Kotkahi, Fruits and Vegetable Producers Mahasangh would protest on 22nd December.

Farmers protest import of edible oils

Hundreds of farmers from across the State led by the Karnataka State Farmers Association (Rajya Raitha Sangha) blocked the main entrance of the New Mangalore Port on Monday in a symbolic protest against the Union Government's policy allowing the duty-free import of edible oils. Leaders of farmers from Kerala and Tamil Nadu also supported the agitation.

The agitation was timed just ahead of the seventh ministerial conference of the World Trade Organisation from November 30 to December 2 in Geneva, Switzerland. A strong lobby, led by the U.S.

[43] My Himachal, December 6, 2009

and other developed nations, is going to push for further relaxation of trade barriers, particularly in the farming sector, in developing countries such as India, explained the spokesman of the South India Coordination Committee of Farmers' Movements S. Kannaiyan.

Explaining why the protest was held outside the New Mangalore Port, the State president of the Kerala Coconut Farmers Association said that the Mangalore port was one of the major inlets for imported edible oil on the southwest coast. He said that 'the Kerala High Court had recently ordered a stay on the import of edible oil through the ports in Kerala. After this blockade was imposed, all the oil is being imported through the Mangalore port.

Pointing out that the Union Government had lifted all import duties on edible oils; KRRS State president said that the cheaply imported oil from countries such as Malaysia, the Philippines and Indonesia was ruining the livelihood of over 10 million farmers in 13 districts in the State.

Demanding that the State Government emulate the Kerala Government should term the Free Trade Agreement inked by the Union Government with other South East Asian countries for the import of edible oils unconstitutional. He pointed out that farming was a State subject and the Union Government could not take a unilateral decision on the subject. Farmers demand that the import duty on edible oil be raised to at least 150 per cent. The present policy of not charging any duty is not only absurd but also criminal. The Karnataka State Farmers Association also demanded that Chief Minister B.S. Yeddyurappa make a representation to the Union Government calling for the imposition of import duty on edible oil.

Mr. Chandrashekar announced that the KRRS would be participating in a meeting of the All India Farmers' Coordination Committee in Delhi in early December to chalk out a course of countrywide agitations against the Government's new liberal and pro-capitalist' agenda. He also expressed doubts over the possibility of any coordination with the Left parties for the upcoming agitation.

The Left parties had lost their credibility after the anti-people and pro-capitalist policies that they have been following in West Bengal. However, he said that in the best interests of the country's farming community, a decision on coordinated action would be discussed at the meeting in Delhi. The agitation on Monday had its tense moments after the port authorities tried to sneak out some transport vehicles even as the blockade was in place, drawing the ire of the protesters, who intensified their stir and physically blocked the exit of some vehicles.[44]

Farmers up: attack on sugarcane prices

Under a combined opposition attack that stalled the Lok Sabha, government promised to amend the controversial sugarcane ordinance against which growers from northern states converged here in protest. Outside parliament, thousands of farmers held a protest, paralyzing key Delhi roads and forcing the Prime Minister of India to review the pricing ordinance. The slogan-shouting farmers from Uttar Pradesh gathered in the capital, traffic on all roads leading to Jantar Mantar, the 17th century observatory in the heart of the capital, came to a standstill.

Farmers are protesting the government proposal to table an amendment that will raise the sugarcane prices from about 108 INR to 130 INR per quintal.

---

[44] The Hindu, Mangalore, Nov 23, 2009

They say this is insufficient compared to the rise in sugar prices. They demanded 280 INR per quintal for their produce.

Inside the Lok Sabha, all parliamentary work also came to standstill as opposition members raised slogans and demanded fair sugarcane price for farmers. Speaker Meira Kumar first adjourned the house till noon after a group of MPs led by Samajwadi Party's Mulayam Singh Yadav and former agriculture minister Ajit Singh (Rashtriya Lok Dal) gathered near her podium protesting the government's low sugarcane prices.

DMK, a key UPA ally, joined the demand for a review of the ordinance as the opposition stalled proceedings in the Lok Sabha on the issue leading to its adjournment on the first day of the winter session. With political temperatures rising on the issue, Prime Minister Manmohan Singh said suitable amendment would be made to the Ordinance if it went against interests of farmers. "We will not do anything that goes against the farmers. The government will look into the matter again and if it is in the interest of farmers the Ordinance will be suitably amended", Prime Minister told Rahul Gandhi who met him in the backdrop of a massive farmers' agitation here.

The government's response came as a determined opposition stepped up its agitation against the Ordinance brought by the Centre and to press for withdrawal of uniform price of sugarcane. As main opposition BJP, Samajwadi Party, Left parties, JD (U), JD (S), RJD and Rashtriya Lok Dal disrupted the proceedings of the Lok Sabha, DMK, too, voiced its opposition to the Ordinance. The Sugarcane Control (Amendment) Order 2009 Ordinance has changed the sugarcane pricing policy, fixing a uniform Fair and Remunerative Price (FRP), which would put the burden on states if they choose to pay more than FRP to farmers.

The Prime Minister's assurance came on a day of hectic consultations in the government that saw senior cabinet ministers P Chidambaram and M Veerapa Moily having detailed discussion with Food and Agriculture Minister Sharad Pawar on the issue. The Prime Minister is also believed to have a word with Pawar on the issue. To hammer out a solution, government has invited leaders of all political parties for a breakfast meeting on Monday ahead of the sitting of Parliament. The move by the government came close on the heels of the meeting of the Business Advisory Committee of the Lok Sabha.

The BAC meeting saw Deputy Leader of BJP Sushma Swaraj telling the government that her party has no objection to the ordinance brought out on the issue provided it is not used as a "pretext to deprive farmers of their due. We are open for discussion on all issues," Parliamentary Affairs Minister P K Bansal told reporters after the BAC meeting. Opposition leaders have meanwhile said they would continue to stall Parliament on the issue tomorrow, as the deadlock may not be resolved by that time.

Outside Parliament, hundreds of sugarcane farmers from western Uttar Pradesh today staged a demonstration here. Holding sugarcane stems and shouting slogans, the farmers marched from Ramlila grounds to Jantar Mantar, the sit-down-strike hotspot in the capital, this morning.[45]

Farmers threaten to agitate against Land Acquisition

President of Karnataka Pranta Raitha Sangha Maruti Manapade has threatened that the farmers would launch serious agitation against the state government, which is "contemplating acquisition of 200,000 acres of fertile land across the state to set

[45]Zeenews.com, February 27, 2010

up special economic zones (SEZ)". He has urged the state government to stop the process immediately.

Manpade accused chief minister B S Yeddyurappa of acting as a pawn in the hands of land mafia and selling the farmers' land to the capitalists in the guise of development. He alleged that the officials had tampered with land records to claim that the land under acquisition in Bellary and Davanagere were barren while actually the holdings were fertile. He pointed out that the farmers in Gurgaon and Punjab whose lands have been acquired for industrial purpose had been paid 15 million INR (Indian rupees) per acre and alleged that in Karnataka the government what the government paid was pittance. Instead of acquiring the land, the CM should convene a meeting of farmers to discuss and take up pro-farmer schemes, he said.

Expressing his displeasure at the quantum of compensation paid to the flood victims in North Karnataka and other places in the state, the leader said the total crop loss was to the tune of 300 billion INR but the state government has disbursed 800 INR per acre compensation and urged the government to enhance the compensation amount. He also sought amendments to the norms of payment for compensation under calamity relief fund (CRF).

Waiver of farmers' loans and proper supply of electricity to rural areas were his other demands. The farmers' leader met the members of his fraternity who have been lodged in Dharwad jail after being arrested in Davanagere during 'courting arrest' agitation.[46]

Indian Farmers Call off a Massive Planned Siege of New Delhi in 2011

[46]Business Standard, January 04, 2010

India's farmers' movements have been trying hard to get the attention of the Government. They have requested several appointments with no response from the PM. It is only after the farmers threatened to lay an indefinite siege of Delhi by cutting off all the major highways that connect Delhi with the rest of the country on March 9 2011 that the PM' office suddenly decided to grant them the much sought after appointment with top government officials following which the Delhi siege was called off. The farmers however were already prepared. It is a fact that about 12000 farmers who were already on their way reached Delhi from all across India while the majority were asked to cancel their plans to come to Delhi. Even the southern states of Karnataka and Tamil Nadu had sent about a thousand farmers. The farmers met the Ministers and officials of Government of India.

The worsening condition of the Indian agriculture sector has led to half a million farm suicides since 1995 - the largest recorded rate of suicides in human history. However the Indian government continues to formulate polices to favor the agri-business model of agriculture that increases food insecurity and dispossesses small farmers of their lands, seeds and productive resources including markets. Recently it is negotiating more than 30 FTAs, engaging in land grabs, reorienting the agricultural research establishment to the corporate agenda and setting up authorities to expedite GM crop entry, signing various deals between international seed companies and state governments among other things. It is to make specific demands to challenge these failing neo-liberal policies and to promote food sovereignty and the farming community's rights that the farmer movements had decided to block New Delhi. The PM finally did agree to some constructive things.

The first thing that the PMO has agreed to do is to organize a meeting with the farmers on the Land

Acquisition Act. This has been a long-standing demand of the farmers' movements. This is a colonial act from 1894 that has been misused by the government to gift peasants' lands at throwaway prices to companies for the development of townships, malls, Special Economic Zones or what the farmers' movements have called the "colonization of the countryside". All across India farmers have been mobilizing on the sites of land grabs not only for just compensation but also to stop unfair grabbing of fertile agricultural lands. The farmers' position is clear – agricultural land is for the peasant and cannot be used for any unproductive purposes. Furthermore farmers want the entire act to be scrapped – no amendments will do. They want a totally new act, which will address the land question and development in a holistic manner. They want a discussion and debate to take place on what is the meaning of "public purpose" - the clause in the outdated act that is being used by the government to grab land for private infrastructure projects (in the name of public purpose). Most importantly they want that decisions in this country are taken in a democratic fashion, and those whose lands are being grabbed are not just consulted but play a significant role in the decision-making and formulation of policies. Given the fact that the government did not make any effort to even address them until major agitations were launched in north India in August 2010 they have now managed to get a high level meeting with the Rural Development Minister and Prime Minister in the future to further discuss their demands for this act.

The second thing that the PM has promised is that he would organize a farmers meeting with the Finance and the Agriculture ministers to specifically discuss the issues raised by the farmers. He also told the delegation that every year before the budget; the government would bring out a white paper report on the state of Indian agriculture.

The main demands of the farmers were to improve farmers' incomes through more remunerative and scientifically calculated support prices, to provide health care to farm families, to scrap all agriculture deals in the various ongoing secret negotiations of bilateral F TAs and the WTO, to ban G MOs permanently since there is no need for them, to reduce the rate of farm loans. Farmers also stressed that there needs to be government support for a shift towards agro ecological models of farming. The government and the agricultural establishments should support pro farmer and not pro corporate research.

Farm incomes are an especially sensitive topic. The Indian government has increased the incomes of government employees by 4 or even more times in the last 15 years but the farmers income has only deteriorated. In fact even the lowest level government employee -the peon makes a monthly salary of 15000 INR (approximately 333 US $) for a 9 to 5 job along with other services like health. But the farming family that toils 24x7 made an average income of 2,115 INR (or US $ 50) in 2003-04 and the prices they receive are not even corrected for inflation. There is not even a body to fix their pay. See this article for a discussion on farmers' incomes –

The farmers have therefore been demanding that just like government employees their incomes need to be increased too and they too deserve health care. The solution to maintain the food security and sovereignty of India is to pay its farmers well not reduce the farm gate prices as is usually done to keep food prices low for consumers or for the industry. The prime minister was in agreement with the farmers despite the contradictory policies his government has promoted and stressed their full commitment to Indian farmers. Farmers have promised to carry on the pressure on the government and the PM to live up to the promises of the planned meetings.[47]

Agitating farmers try to block Rail traffic in UP

Tension prevailed at Bhatta village near here when agitating farmers tried to obstruct rail traffic after Uttar Pradesh Agriculture Minister Laxmi Narain allegedly failed to keep his promise to visit the dharna venue and look into their grievances. Angry farmers, who have been staging a sit-in in the village since January 17, demanding scrapping of the Land Acquisition Act and the right to sell their land directly to private developers, tried to obstruct rail traffic but heavy deployment of force foiled their attempt.

Around a thousand farmers then proceeded on foot to Dankore railway station but near Chuharpur canal they stopped, as on the other side there was heavy police and PAC deployment. They retracted fearing arrest of their leader Manvir Singh Tevatia. Alleging that the state government did not want to solve their problems, they said on Saturday peasants from Dankore, Jewar and Aligarh will meet and decide the future course of agitation.

They said they had lifted the hunger strike and agitation on the promise of UP Agriculture minister Laxmi Narain who had given an assurance to them to solve their problem by March 11. However, it appears that the minister could not satisfy UP Chief Minister Mayawati. Now state government is trying to divide the agitating farmers, they alleged.

District Magistrate Deepak Aggarwal said, "Farmers will not be allowed to resort to violence and disrupt rail or road traffic." On March 23 Baba Ram Dev is

---

[47]Secretariat La Via Campesina, South Asia, - March 10, 2011

likely to visit the strike site to extend support to agitating farmers.[48]

Krishna Tribunal Award

The farmers' outfits in Andhra Pradesh, with the support of political parties, are gearing up to launch an agitation against the Krishna Water Tribunal's Award, which they claim, will adversely affect them. An all-party meet has been convened here tomorrow to decide the future course of action on the Tribunal's award. Uniting under the banner of Krishna Delta Parirakshana Samithi, the political and farmer organisations discussed the pros and cons of the Tribunal here yesterday. The Samithi felt that the award, announced on December 30, is a boon for Karnataka and bane for Andhra Pradesh. Under the tribunal's award in the decades-old dispute related to sharing of Krishna waters, Andhra Pradesh will get the maximum share of water.

Share of Karnataka and Maharashtra, where Krishna originates, has also been enhanced. Now, Andhra Pradesh will get 1,001 TMC, Karnataka 911 TMC and Maharashtra 666 TMC of water from the river. Earlier allocation was 811 TMC for AP, 734 TMC for Karnataka and 585 TMC for Maharashtra. The tribunal also allowed increase in height of Almati Dam in Karnataka to 524 metres from earlier 519. The farmers' groups have opposed the increase in dam height, claiming it will lead to low flow of water in Krishna below the dam. If the dam height is raised, the fate of farmers in at least half a dozen AP districts will be in the hands of Karnataka Government, Samithi leaders said. "Karnataka will definitely restrict the flow of water to downstream of Almati to supply more water to its farmers. Unless, we fight for our rights, hundreds of thousands acres of land will become desert and the people of AP will face

[48] Yahoo News, March 11, 2011

starvation," they said, adding the State should move the Supreme Court.[49]

Cut in Import Duty

Will sound death knell for Sericulture Industry in Karnataka

The Union Government's move to reduce the duty on import of raw silk from 30 per cent to 5 per cent, as announced in 2011-12 Budget, has come as a rude shock for the State's sericulture farmers who are already agitated over the steep fall in cocoon prices.

Sericulture farmers and farmer leaders feel that the slash on the import duty would not only have a negative impact on the growth of the State's sericulture sector but also affect the very livelihood of hundreds of thousands of farmers and silk Reelers. At least 60 per cent of the farmers are likely to give up sericulture.

Karnataka is one of the major silk producers in the country and, an estimated 1.65 million people are into sericulture in the State. Mulberry is cultivated on an estimated 75,000 hectares of land, particularly in Chickballapur, Kolar, Bangalore Rural, Ramanagaram, Tumkur, Chamarajanagar and Mysore districts. Indeed, the Government Cocoon Markets in Ramanagaram, and Shidlaghatta in Chickballapur district are among the biggest cocoon markets in Asia and, together the two markets transact around Rs. 750 crore worth business annually.

According to Karnataka Rajya Raitha Sangha and Hasiru Sene State vice-president N. Venkata Reddy, with the reduction in the import duty, there would be huge arrival of imported silk, particularly from China. As a major section of the weaving industry was in favour of the imported silk, the demand for the local

[49]Press Trust of India – News, Vijay Wada, January 1, 2011

produce would come down. "Sericulture would be no longer lucrative and at least 60 per cent of the farmers would give up sericulture in the coming days," he opined. Dr. Reddy, who hails from the textile town of Doddaballapur in Bangalore Rural district, told The Hindu that "rich and influential weavers" had successfully lobbied in getting the import duty slashed. A team of weavers from Doddaballapur also had camped in New Delhi in this regard, he observed.

Progressive farmer Mallur Shivanna of Shidalghatta said that thousands of farmers from the erstwhile-undivided Kolar district were on the verge of committing suicide when the duty on silk imports was slashed in 2002. Farmers had thrown cocoons on roads and staged protests. Besides the increasing imports from China, what had affected farmers severely was the smuggling of 12 to 13 tonnes of silk yarn a year from other countries, he added. Sericulture farmers are of the view that the Centre should increase the duty on imports to safeguard the interests of farmers. It should ensure that the prices of cocoon did not drop below 350 INR/kg and silk yarn below 3,000 INR/kg.[50]

Protests of the Farmers

Farmers make Bonfire of GM seeds at Mumbai: On the eve of the World Food Day, hundreds of farmers belonging to the Kisan Swaraj Yatra organized by Kheti Virasat Mission made a bonfire of genetically modified seeds at Jalna on October 15, 2010 symbolically to oppose the corporate to be the owner of seeds and to encourage farmers to retain seed diversity. They assailed the Multinational Corporation Monsanto for aggressively capturing the seed market in India. They demanded such MNCs to quit Indian farming sector.

---

[50]K V. Subramanya, The Hindu March 4, 2011

Protests Against Submergence of Fertile Land: Protesting against the command area development (CAD) in respect of Indira Sagar and Omkareswar dams in Madhya Pradesh, prominent citizens wrote a letter to the Union Environment Minister Jairam Ramesh, informing the danger of the proposed canal system that it will destruct fertile agricultural and livelihoods rather than benefitting the same and demanded the government to take "immediate and clear decision" to stop work and exclude the irrigated region from the canal system and to prevent incalculable lifelong loss to the farming community, agrarian ecology and economy.

Assam Farmers Oppose Big Dams in Arunachal Pradesh: A farmer's organization Krishak Mukti Sangham Samiti (KMSS) opposed the proposed construction of 132 mega dams in the state, as they will have adverse impact in Assam. They also demanded to stop construction of 3 hydroelectric projects including the Lower Subsansiri Dam project.

Mizo Tribal people Protest against Repatriation: Due to ethnic clashes in Mizoram in 1997, 41,600 Renag Tribals have fled to Tripura and settled in 6 camps at Kanchanpur of North Tripura. Locally they are called Bru. They have been demanding an eight-point rehabilitation package including formation of autonomous district council in Mizoram besides reservation in government jobs and state assembly. They organized a rally in Oct. to protest the Mizoram government's inaction.

On Nov. 19 when 66 families tried to go back to Mizoram in accordance with the Tripura governments programme to relocate Renag tribal people, hundreds of other refugees put up a blockage on the Tripura - Mizoram highway protesting non-settlement of their eight-point demands. Police arrested 665 protesters and cleared the blockade.

Protests in Greece against Anti-People Policies: On the call given by the Greece Communist Party, protest marches were conducted on November 15 in cities of Athens, The solonica, Patros etc of Greece, protesting against the visit of Troika, representatives to Greece. They protested against the Greece government's anti-people policies implemented at the instance and behest of Troika and EU.

Protests in Haiti against Spread of Cholera:

Alleging that the U.N. Peace forces are the cause for spreading cholera in their country, the people of Haiti started protesting across the country against UN peace forces. They allege that for the past 100 years there was no cholera in their country and that with the entrance of UN peace forces, cholera entered in to their country and is spreading. Protester has barricaded against the vehicles of UN peace forces at Port of Prince the capital of Haiti. Police have tear-gassed the protesters. Nearly 1900 people died due to cholera and 84,000 people were infected.[51]

Religious Views on Peasants' War

There are many evil writings put forth of late which take occasion, on account of the assembling of the peasants, to cast scorn upon the gospel, saying: Is this the fruit of the new teaching, that no one should obey but all should everywhere rise in revolt and rush together to reform or perhaps destroy altogether the authorities, both ecclesiastic and lay? The articles below shall answer these godless and criminal faultfinders, and serve in the first place to remove the reproach from the word of God, and in the second place to give a Christian excuse for the disobedience or even the revolt of the entire Peasantry.

---

[51]Class Struggle Volume 2, Issue 12, December 2010

In the first place the Gospel is not the cause of revolt and disorder, since it is the message of Christ, the promised Messiah, the Word of Life, teaching only love, peace, patience and concord. Thus, all who believe in Christ should learn to be loving, peaceful, long-suffering and harmonious. This is the foundation of all the articles of the peasants (as Will be seen) who accept the Gospel and live according to it. How then can the evil reports declare the Gospel to be a cause of revolt and disobedience? That the authors of the evil reports and the enemies of the Gospel oppose themselves to these demands is due, not to the Gospel, but to the Devil, the worst enemy of the Gospel, who causes this opposition by raising doubts in the minds of his followers, and thus the word of God, which teaches love, peace and concord, is overcome.

In the second place, it is clear that the peasants demand that this Gospel be taught them as a guide in life and they ought not to be called disobedient or disorderly. Whether God grant the peasants (earnestly wishing to live according to His word) their requests or no, who shall find fault with the will of the Most High? Who shall meddle in His judgments or oppose his majesty? Did be not hear the children of Israel when they called upon Him and saved them out of the hands of Pharaoh? Can He not save His own today? Yes, He will save them and that speedily. Therefore, Christian reader read the following articles with care and then judge.

Here follow the articles:

The First Article — First, it is our humble petition and desire, as also our will and resolution, that in the future we should have power and authority so that each community should choose and appoint a pastor, and that we should have the right to depose him should he conduct himself improperly. The pastor thus chosen should teach us the Gospel pure and simple, without any addition, doctrine or ordinance of man. For to teach us continually the true faith will lead us to pray God that through His grace this faith may increase within us and become part of us. For if His grace works not within us we remain flesh and blood, which availed nothing; since the Scripture clearly teaches that only through true faith, can we come to God. Only through His mercy can we become holy. Hence such a guide and pastor is necessary and in this fashion grounded upon the Scriptures.

The Second Article — According as the just tithe is established by the Old Testament and fulfilled in the New, we are ready and willing to pay the fair tithe of grain. The word of God plainly provided that in giving according to right to God and distributing to His people the services of a pastor are required. We will that, for the future, our church provost, whomsoever the community may appoint, shall gather and receive this tithe. From this he shall give to the pastor, elected by the whole community, a decent and sufficient maintenance for him and his, as shall seem right to the whole community (or, with the knowledge of the community). What remains over shall be given to the poor of the place, as the circumstances and the general opinion demand. Should anything farther remain, let it be kept, lest anyone should have to leave the country from poverty. Provision should also be made from this surplus to avoid laying any land tax on the poor.

In case one or more villages themselves have sold their tithes on account of want, and each village has taken action as a whole, the buyer should not suffer loss, but we will that some proper agreement be reached with him for the repayment of the sum by the village with due interest. But those who have tithes which they have not purchased from a village, but which were appropriated by their ancestors, should not, and ought not, to be paid anything farther by the village which shall apply its tithes to the support of the pastors elected as above indicated, or to solace the poor as is taught by the Scriptures. The small tithes, whether ecclesiastical or lay, we will not pay at an, for the Lord God created cattle for the free use of man. We will not, therefore, pay farther an unseemly tithe, which is of man's invention.

The Third Article — It has been the custom hitherto for men to hold us as their own property, which is pitiable enough, considering that Christ has delivered and redeemed us all, without exception, by the shedding of His precious blood, the lowly as well as the great. Accordingly, it is consistent with Scripture that we should be free and wish to be so. Not that we would wish to be absolutely free and under no authority. God does not teach us that we should lead a disorderly life in the lusts of the flesh, but that we should love the Lord our God and our neighbor. We would gladly observe all this as God has commanded us in the celebration of the communion. He has not commanded us not to obey the authorities, but rather that we should be humble, not only towards those in authority, but also towards every one. We are thus ready to yield obedience according to God's law to our elected and regular authorities in all proper things becoming to a Christian. We, therefore, take it for granted that you will release us from serfdom as true Christians, unless it should be shown us from the Gospel that we are serfs.

The Fourth Article — In the fourth place it has been the custom heretofore, that no poor man should be allowed to catch venison or wild fowl or fish in flowing water, which seems to us quite unseemly and unbrotherly as well as selfish and not agreeable to the word of God. In some places the authorities preserve the game to our great annoyance and loss, recklessly permitting the unreasoning animals to destroy to no purpose our crops, which God suffers to grow for the use of man, and yet we must remain quiet. This is neither godly nor neighborly.

When God created man, He gave him dominion over all the animals, over the birds of the air and over the fish in the water. Accordingly it is our desire if a man holds possession of waters that he should prove from satisfactory documents that his right has been unwittingly acquired by purchase. We do not wish to take it from him by force, but his rights should be exercised in a Christian and brotherly fashion. But whosoever cannot produce such evidence should surrender his claim with good grace.

The Fifth Article — in the fifth place we are aggrieved in the matter of woodcutting, for the noble folk has appropriated all the woods by them. If a poor man requires wood he must pay double for it (or, perhaps, two pieces of money). It is our opinion in regard to wood, which has fallen into the hands of a lord whether spiritual or temporal, that unless it was duly purchased it should revert again to the community. It should, moreover, be free to every member of the community to help himself to such firewood, as he needs in his home. Also, if a man requires wood for carpenter's purposes he should have it free, but with the knowledge of a person appointed by the community for that purpose. Should, however, no such forest be at the disposal of the community let that which has been duly bought be administered in a brotherly and Christian manner. If the forest, although unfairly appropriated in the first instance, was later duly sold let the matter be adjusted in a friendly spirit and according to the Scriptures.

The Sixth Article — our sixth complaint is in regard the excessive services demanded of us, which are increase from day to day. We ask that this matter be properly looked into so that we shall not continue to be oppressed in this way, but that some gracious consideration is given to us, since our forefathers were required only to serve according to the word of God.

The Seventh Article — Seventh, we will not hereafter allow ourselves to be farther oppressed by our lords, but will let them demand only what is just and proper according to the word of the agreement between the lord and the peasant. The lord should no longer try to force more services or other dues from the peasant without payment, but permit the peasant to enjoy his holding in peace and quiet. The peasant should, however, help the lord when it is necessary, and at proper times when it will not be disadvantageous to the peasant and for a suitable payment.

The Eighth Article — in the eighth place, we are greatly burdened by holdings, which cannot support the rent exacted from them. The peasants suffer loss in this way and are ruined, and we ask that the lords may appoint persons of honour to inspect these holdings, and fix a rent in accordance with justice, so that the peasants shall not work for nothing, since the labourer is worthy of his hire.

The Ninth Article — in the ninth place, we are burdened with a great evil in the constant making of new laws. We are not judged according to the offense, but sometimes with great ill will, and sometimes much too leniently. In our opinion we should be judged according to the old written law so that the case shall be decided according to its merits, and not with partiality.

The Tenth Article — in the tenth place, we are aggrieved by the appropriation by individuals of meadows and fields, which at one time belonged to a community. These we will take again into our own hands. It may, however, happen that the land was rightfully purchased. When, however, the land has unfortunately been purchased in this way, some brotherly arrangement should be made according to circumstances.

The Eleventh Article — In the eleventh place we will entirely abolish the due called *Todfall* (that is, heriot) and will no longer endure it, nor allow widows and orphans to be thus shamefully robbed against God's will, and in violation of justice and right, as has been done in many places, and by those who should shield and protect them. These have disgraced and despoiled us, and although they had little authority they assumed it. God will suffer this no more, but it shall be wholly done away with, and for the future no man shall be bound to give little or much.

In short, in the twelfth place it is our conclusion and final resolution, that if any one or more of the articles here set forth should not be in agreement with the word of God, as we think they are, such article we will willingly recede from when it is proved really to be against the word of God by a clear explanation of the Scripture. Or if articles should now be conceded to us that are hereafter discovered to be unjust, from that hour they shall be dead and null and without force.

Likewise, if more complaints should be discovered which are based upon truth and the Scriptures and relate to offenses against God and our neighbor, we have determined to reserve the right to present these also, and to exercise ourselves in all Christian teaching. For this we shall pray God, since He can grant these, and He alone. The peace of Christ abides with us all.[52]

Conclusion

The government should fulfill the demands of farmers, if found justified. Normally the farmers cite a number of demands for the consideration of the government. The government can solve instantly a

[52] http://www.marxists.org/archive/marx/works/1850 /peasant-war-Germany /choe.htm

number of demands without budgetary provisions or adjustment in budget.

The government should constitute a 'Farmers' Commission' to deal with the problems and demands of the farmers. The Commission should study all demands of the farmers and suggest the government for necessary action. All commissions for the farmers should have at least five members and include one farmer, one agricultural economist, one administrator, one lawyer and a retired Judge, who would be the Chairman of the Commission.

The government should not follow 'foreign dictates' in developing countries straightway. The Government must consult with farmers' organizations and individual farmers on the issue and consult the specialists before finalizing the course of action.

Decisions taken by bureaucrats for agriculture often result in farmers' agitations because these policy makers belong to the upper echelon of Civil Services without practical knowledge on farming, poverty, sufferings or hunger.

Land should not be given away to the industrialists in thousands of acres and water in billions of cusecs. Big fish eats away small fish.

Government must have an open mind to help the poorest of the poor in the society by law and action. There should be a Senior Economist in the State Planning Board to study and report the new laws to be enacted by the Government. The politicians and Bureaucrats mislead the administration in policy matters. Each government must create and strengthen the Ministry of Agricultural Marketing supported by Secretary, Director, Agricultural Marketing specialists and extension workers to solve farmers' problems in the state. And, it is possible

Chapter IV

AGRICULTURAL MARKETING AND PRICES

We live in a world where 85 per cent of all farms are less than 2 hectares in size. In the developing world, many peasants own land as small as 0.25 hectares and 500 million-smallholder farms produce 80 per cent of the food consumed in the developing world. Rural women perform majority of agricultural work. In all patriarchal families women have no land rights. The farm youths are now migrating to the industrial areas for quest of employment. Agriculture has become a cursed profession as crop production has become a loss-bearing enterprise. Most of the farmers and farm labourers are happy with the yield, but they are unable to repay back their debts. They are born in debt, live in debt and die in debt. Farmers' suicides have become common news in all developing world.

The causes of all maladies of farmers, peasants, agricultural labourers, village artisans and sharecroppers need immediate solutions by awarding peace to the vast majority of population in all developing countries.

The present administrations in all developing countries run after foreign funding, infrastructure development, defense expenditure and awarding subsidy to food and agriculture. This policy of the government has created black money, corruption, unemployment, and disparity in income.

This has caused class struggle of yester years. The privileged group include: political leaders, bureaucrats, government employees, contractors, industrialists, business houses, traders and brokers, who lead royal life and pocket all benefits of planning process. The second group people are treated as poor people or 'Below Poverty Line' people or Beggars. They include farmers, peasants, sharecroppers, agricultural labourers, artisans, widows, tribal people and rural folk.

The government spends huge amount to ameliorate poverty of the people in different schemes, but it leads to massive corruption in government offices and government sponsored schemes. The budgeted amount never reaches the poor in full.

Former Prime Minister of India, Rajiv Gandhi expressed that hardly 16 percent of budgeted expenditure for the rural poor reaches them.

Unless the farming families organize their associations to express their demands to realize their dues, they cannot live in peace. How could the vast population of rural folk suffer silently till death?

The peasants know their duties but they are unable to achieve their rights. The privileged classes know their rights and they neglect in their duties.

(A). Agricultural Marketing

Asian Trauma

If the Doha Round of negotiations of the World Trade Organization (WTO) is stalemated, a great part of it is because of the resistance of small farmers, including those in Asia. One of the terrible truths of the 20th century is that it was blight on small farmers or peasants everywhere. Before looking at whether it needs protection from free trade, it is necessary to consider the historical background of Asia's peasantry, one that is shared by farmers in other parts of the South and in the North.

In both wealthy capitalist economies and in socialist countries, farmers have paid a heavy price. Asian industrialization also was carried out largely on the backs of the rural population as farm policies were manipulated in favour of industry. In advanced capitalist countries like the United States, a deadly combination of economies of scale, capital-intensive technology and the market led to large corporations cornering agricultural production and processing, thus reducing small and medium farms to a marginal role in production and a minuscule portion of the workforce.

The dynamics of the market in capitalist societies with its bias for big business has eliminated farmers as a class. In the Soviet Union, they were transformed into workers on collective farms. Expropriation of the peasants' surplus production was meant not only to feed the cities but also to serve as the source of `primitive accumulation' of capital for industrialization.

Professor Walden Bello of University of Philippines has studied in detail the miserable conditions of millions of small farmers engaged in agriculture in Asian countries. He has challenged the development planners, who are advocating industrialization as the growth model of countries, but it harms millions of farmers to realize their dues from the society. His arguments are so justified that his views would change the fate of millions of small farmers and peasants.

In Asia, government policies placed the burden of industrialization on the peasantry during the phase of so-called `development planners' industry-first policies. In Taiwan and South Korea, land reform first triggered prosperity in the countryside in the 1950s, stimulating industrialization. But with the shift to export-led industrialization in 1965, there was demand for low-wage industrial labour, so government policies deliberately depressed prices of agricultural goods. In this way, peasants subsidized the emergence of `Newly Industrializing Economies'. Peasant incomes declined relative to urban incomes, and the resulting stagnation of a once vibrant countryside led to massive migration to the cities and a steady supply of cheap labour for factories; this left farmers poor, ageing, and an increasingly small part of the national workforce.

In the Philippines and Thailand, industry-first strategies led to similar policies. In Thailand, for instance, a tax on rice exports insulated the domestic market from price movements in the international market, depressing the price of rice and reducing the wage costs of non-agricultural employers. A transfer of real wealth from the countryside to the city took place every year between 1962 and 1981, except for 1970. Not surprisingly, despite the image of Thailand as an agricultural superpower, a large percentage of the rural population remains poor.

In China, peasants died of starvation during the Great Leap Forward as the grain surplus was requisitioned to finance Mao Zedong's industrialization drive. The chaos of the Cultural Revolution allowed peasants to regain a degree of control over production because the government was in crisis and following the death of Mao in 1976; Deng Xiaoping introduced the `household contract responsibility system'. Each family was given a piece of land to farm, along with the right to sell what was left over after a fixed proportion of the produce was sold to the government at a state-determined price. This led to peasant prosperity that, as in Taiwan, stimulated industrial production to fulfill rural demand.

But, as in Taiwan, this golden age of the peasantry came to an end, and the cause was identical: the adoption of urban-centered, export-oriented industrialization. Primitive capital accumulation for industry took the form of requisitioning peasant surpluses via heavy taxation. Currently, the various tiers of the Chinese government foist a total of 269 different taxes on farmers, along with often-arbitrary administrative charges. Not surprisingly, in many places, taxes now eat up 15 per cent of farmers' income, three times the official national limit of 5 per cent. Not surprisingly, too, while the economy has been growing at 8-10 per cent a year, peasant income has stagnated, so that urban dwellers now have, on average, six times the income of peasants.

While policies that made peasants subsidize industrialization were harsh, they were at least mitigated by trade policies that barred agricultural imports that were cheaper than local commodities. In practically all-Asian countries with agricultural sectors, imports were tightly controlled via quotas and high tariffs. This protective shield, however, was severely eroded when countries signed the Agreement on Agriculture (AOA) and began joining the WTO in 1995.

The AOA forced open agricultural markets by banning quotas, converting these to tariffs and requiring governments to import a minimum volume of each agricultural commodity at a low tariff. At the same time, under the pretext of controlling the heavy subsidization of agriculture in developed countries, the AOA institutionalized the various channels through which subsidies flowed, such as export subsidies and direct cash payments to farming interests in the northern hemisphere.

The result was that in the first decade of the WTO, the level of subsidization of agriculture actually increased in developed countries. The total amount of agricultural subsidies provided by member-governments of the Organization for Economic Cooperation and Development (OECD) rose from $182 billion in 1995 to $280 billion in 1997, $315 billion in 2001, $318 billion in 2002, and almost $300 billion in 2005. The US and the EU were spending $9-10 billion more on subsidies in the early 2000s than they were a decade earlier. For every $100 of agro-exports from the US, government subsidies accounted for $20-30. In the case of the EU, the figure was $40-50. While unsubsidized smallholders in the developing world had to survive on less than $400 a year, American and European farmers were receiving, respectively, an average of $21,000 and $16,000 a year in subsidies.

With massive American and European subsidies distorting global prices in a downward direction, agriculture in developing countries became `non-competitive' under the conditions of the WTO-mandated trade liberalization. As the Food and Agricultural Organization (FAO) notes, instantaneous import surges following the adoption of the AOA in a number of developing countries led to 'consequential difficulties for import-competing industries' and `without adequate market protection, accompanied by development programs, many more domestic products would be displaced, or undermined sharply, leading to a transformation of domestic diets and to increased dependence on imported foods.

This historic shift to dependence on food imports was, needless to say, accompanied by the displacement of millions of peasants. Even before the AOA took effect, the World Bank was predicting that Indonesian farmers would be losers under the AOA regime. Indeed, since 1995, the marginalization of farmers `in rice and other basic commodities' has occurred while competitive pressures induced by trade liberalization led to the expansion of commercial plantations at the expense of smallholders.

In the Philippines, corn farmers, chicken farmers, cattle raisers and vegetable growers were driven to bankruptcy in huge numbers. In Mindanao, where corn is a staple crop, many were wiped out. `It is not an uncommon sight to see farmers there leaving their corn to rot in the fields as the domestic corn prices have dropped to levels [at which] they have not been able to compete.' With production stagnant, land devoted to corn across the country contracted from 3,149,300 hectares in 1995 to 2,150,300 ha in 2000.

In China, tens of thousands of farmers, including those growing soybeans and cotton, have been marginalized with China's entry into the WTO. Indeed, to maintain and increase access for its manufacturers to developed countries, the government has chosen to sacrifice its farmers. According to the Institute of International Economics, the challenge of managing the farm sector has grown with China's WTO commitments in agriculture, which are more far reaching than those of other developing countries and in certain respects exceed those of high-income countries. The Chinese government agreed to reduce tariffs and institute other policies that meaningfully increase market access; accepted tight restrictions on the use of agricultural subsidies; and pledged to eliminate all commitments on agricultural export subsidies that go far beyond those made by other participants in the Uruguay Round negotiations that led to the WTO's creation.

In Sri Lanka, thousands of small farmers staged street demonstrations against the import of chicken parts and eggs, claiming they were being driven out of business. The FAO concurred, noting that import surges on major food items like chilly, onion and potato made local production precarious, as reflected in the significant drop in areas of production.

In India, tariff liberalization, even ahead of the WTO commitments, has translated into a profound crisis in the countryside. Economist Utsa Patnaik has described the calamity as `a collapse in rural livelihoods and incomes' owing to the steep fall in the prices of farm products. Along with this has come a rapid decline in the consumption of food grain, with the average Indian family of four consuming 76 kg less in 2003 compared to 1998 and 88 kg less than a decade earlier. Andhra Pradesh, which has become a byword for agrarian distress owing to trade liberalization, saw a catastrophic rise in farmers' suicides from 233 in 1998 to over 2,600 in 2002. One estimate is that some 100,000 farmers in India have taken their lives owing to collapsing prices stemming from rising imports.

In 2004, a rural backlash against agrarian distress led to the unexpected defeat of the BJP - led ruling coalition that had campaigned on the vision of `India Shining'. India's rural electoral revolt was part of a global phenomenon that put governments on notice that the countryside would no longer accept policies that sacrifice farmer interests. In Asia, protests in the form of land occupations, hunger strikes, violent demonstrations, and symbolic suicides made rural distress a pressing issue.

In China, what the Ministry of Public Security calls `mass group incidents', or in other words, protest actions, increased from 8,700 in 1993 to 87,000 in 2005, most of them in the countryside. Moreover, the incidents are growing in average size, from 10 or fewer persons in the mid-1990s to 52 people per incident in 2004. Not surprisingly, the current leadership increasingly sees the countryside as a powder keg that needs to be defused.

The political consequences of what trade liberalization and other anti-agriculture policies brought to the countryside led to the formation of the Group of 20 and the Group of 33. The G-20 put the developed countries on notice that there would be no more concessions in terms of market access if no significant reductions were made in unfair domestic support for agriculture. The G-33 demanded that certain products considered vital to agricultural production and employment-special products (SP) - be exempted from tariff liberalization. They also wanted the right to raise tariffs and resort to other measures - special safeguard mechanisms (SSM) - to protect their products from surges of agricultural imports. When the EU and the US refused to compromise on these issues, the WTO's Fifth Ministerial Meeting in Cancun in 2003 collapsed.

The Ministerial Declaration of the Sixth Ministerial Meeting of the WTO in Hong Kong in December 2005 recognized the right of developing countries to designate SPs and institute SSMs. However, the US backtracking on this commitment and refusing to significantly reduce its domestic subsidies led to the collapse of the Doha Round of negotiations in July 2006. Developing countries simply could not provoke more discontent among their peasant populations by opening their markets even more in exchange for cosmetic reductions in the massive subsidies provided by the EU and the US to their agricultural sectors.

The suicide of the Korean farmer, Lee Kyung Hae, at the barricades in Cancun in September 2003 was a milestone in the development of farmers' resistance globally. Committed under a banner that read `WTO Kills Farmers', Lee's aim was to draw international attention to the number of suicides by farmers in countries subjected to liberalization. He succeeded only too well. The event shocked the WTO delegates, who observed a minute of silence in Lee's memory. By adding to what was already a charged atmosphere, it was certainly a key factor in the unraveling of the talks.

Farmers' International

In December 2005, invoking Lee's sacrifice, hundreds of Korean farmers tried to break through police lines in an effort to storm the Hong Kong Convention Centre. Some 900 protesters were arrested.

Lee and the Korean farmers protesting in Hong Kong were members of Via Campesina, an international federation of farmers that was established in the mid-1990s. Since its founding, Via Campesina, literally translated as the Peasants' Path, has become known as one of the most militant opponents of the WTO and bilateral and multilateral free trade agreements.

While there are other international farmers' networks, Via is distinguished by its position that small farmers must not only fight to survive in the current global system of corporate-dominated industrial farming, but also should lead the process to transform or replace the current system. Commenting on the vision of Jose Bove, the famous French activist who dismantled a MacDonald's restaurant in his hometown of Millau, France, and other Via leaders, one progressive journal has described the aim of the organization as the creation of a `Farmers' International' in much the same way that communist and social democratic groups sought to establish the Communist International and Socialist International to unite workers in the 20th century.

The main battle cry of Via Campesina, whose coordinating center is located in Indonesia, is `WTO out of Agriculture' and its alternative programme is `Food Sovereignty'. Food Sovereignty means first and foremost the immediate adoption of policies that favour small producers. This would include, according to Indonesian farmer Henry Saragih Via's coordinator, and Ahmad Ya'kub, deputy for Policy Studies of the Indonesian Peasant Union Federation (FSPI), `the protection of the domestic market from low-priced imports, remunerative prices for all farmers and fishers, abolition of all direct and indirect export subsidies, and the phasing out of domestic subsidies that promote unsustainable agriculture'.

Via's program, however, goes beyond the adoption of pro-smallholder trade policies. It also calls for an end to the Trade-Related Intellectual Property Rights regime, which allows corporations to patent plant seeds, thus appropriating for private profit what has evolved through the creative interaction of the natural world with human communities over eons. Seeds and all other plant genetic resources should be considered part of the common heritage of humanity, the group believes, and not subject to privatization.

Agrarian reform, long avoided by landed elites in countries like the Philippines, is a central element in Via's platform, as is sustainable, ecologically sensitive, organic or biodynamic farming by small peasant producers. The organization has set itself apart from both the `First Green Revolution', which was based on chemical-intensive agriculture, and the `Second Green Revolution', which is driven by genetic engineering (GE). The disastrous environmental side-effects of the first are well known, says Via which means all the more that the precautionary principle must be rigorously applied to the second, to avoid negative health and environmental outcomes.

The opposition to GE-based agriculture has created a powerful link between farmers and consumers who are angry at corporations for marketing genetically modified commodities without proper labeling, thus denying consumers a choice. In the European Union, a solid alliance of farmers, consumers and environmentalists prevented the import of GE-modified products from the US for several years. Although the EU has cautiously allowed in a few GE imports since 2004, 54 per cent of European consumers continue to think GE food is `dangerous'. Opposition to other harmful processes such as food irradiation has also contributed to the tightening of ties between farmers and consumers, large numbers of them now think that public health and environmental impact should be more important determinants of consumer behaviour than price.

More and more people are beginning to realize that local production and culinary traditions are intimately related. This relationship is now threatened by corporate control of food production, processing, marketing and consumption.

This is why Jose Bove's justification for dismantling a MacDonald's resonated widely in Asia: "When we said we would protest by dismantling the half-built McDonald's in our town, everybody understood why the symbolism was so strong. It was for proper food against *malbouffe* (awful standardized food) agricultural workers against multinationals. The extreme right and other nationalists tried to make out it was anti-Americanism, but the vast majority knew it was no such thing. It was a protest against a form of production that wants to dominate the world."

A Class for itself

Many economists, technocrats, policymakers and urban intellectuals have long viewed small farmers as a doomed class. Once regarded as passive objects to be manipulated by elites, they are now resisting the `development planners' paradigms that would consign them to ruin. They have become what Karl Marx described as a politically conscious `class-for-itself'. And even as peasants refuse to `go gently into that good night', to borrow a line from Dylan Thomas, developments in the 21st century are revealing traditional pro-development visions to be deeply flawed. The escalating protests of peasant groups such as Via Campesina are not a return to the past.

As environmental crises multiply and the social dysfunctions of urban-industrial life pile up, we realize that the farmers' movement has relevance not only to peasants, but to everyone who is threatened by the catastrophic consequences of obsolete modernist paradigms for organizing production, community and life.[53]

Trends in Cereal Supply, Demand, Trade and Stocks

Agricultural development in developing countries is a long-term proposition requiring large public investment in the rural sector and major commitment with respect to development strategy. Resource productivity will be higher if advantage is taken of international trade with consequent adjustment of domestic production according to international prices. The analysis of global cereal trends denotes that there exist longer-term price relationships with public investment decisions in agriculture.

First, developing countries in general can be expected to face rapidly increasing net imports of cereals. Because demand for food tends to increase more than domestic production as a result of development processes, increases in their net import position seem inevitable. That provides a relatively favorable

---

[53] Walden Bello (2007), 'Asian Trauma', Front Line, Volume 24, Issue 11, June 2 – 15, 2007, Indian National Magazine, The Hindu, Tamil Nadu, India

domestic price environment for developing countries that are net importers, as they price above international prices by their transfer costs. The developing country exporters, however, must compete in a market in which developed countries are generating increasing exports. At best, that will be a competitive environment requiring attention to reducing costs and taking maximum advantage of low-cost food to foster rapid growth in employment-increasing types of production.

Second, international prices are likely to be highly unstable, reflecting increasingly unstable production and a reluctance of the major exporters to hold larger stocks. Thus, at any given point in time, it will be difficult to judge the likely average international price. This also means that food security will be costly to achieve whether by domestic stock, domestic supplies, or foreign exchange. But Indonesia could achieve success in ensuring food security with an unstable global situation and that too at modest cost.

Third, in view of the strong growth in demand in developing countries, it is reasonable to expect pressure for real food prices to rise. With their production resources and greater adaptability to changes in output policy, developed country exporters can be expected to provide most of the response to this market demand. Thus exportable supplies will also grow rapidly over time. As only a small proportion of total food production moves in international trade, it is unreasonable to attempt to predict reliably the trend of cereal prices. But that should also warn us against trying to predict trend from sharp short-term movements one way or another.

Fourth, the market adjustment process for world grains involves various interacting forces, both economic and political, which affect world supply and demand. These include changes in output policies of the major exporting countries and in trade decisions of large grain importers, such as the USSR, that can alter market conditions considerably. The implications of these forces for the ability of developing countries to import cereals at prices they can afford can be very significant, particularly at a time when many countries have foreign exchange difficulties.

Finally, special concern needs to be given to the food situation of the world's poor and undernourished, as both developing and developed economies adjust their agricultural and trade policies to market changes. It is in the interest of developed countries as major exporters to use food aid to increase future markets. Food aid programs that increase consumption of low-income people beyond what they could otherwise afford is in line with those interests and facilitates development, food security for the poor and long-term prices that favor more resources devoted to agriculture than would otherwise be the case.[54]

Philippines

Rice Farmers Call for Trade Justice

In rural areas of the Philippines, poor rice farmers struggle to make a living, as they are forced to compete with cheap, subsidized imported rice. Half the population lives below the poverty line, and the poorest rely heavily on agriculture, particularly rice growing. Yet farmers find it hard to make a living, as they are forced to compete with cheap, subsidized imported rice.

---

[54]Leonardo A. Paulino (1988), "Trends in Cereal Supply, Demand, Trade and Stocks", Agricultural Price Policy for Developing Countries, International Food Policy Research Institute, The Johns Hopkins University Press, Baltimore and London.

If the WTO succeeds in forcing the Philippines government to further open their market to imported rice, the country will be flooded with cheap rice imports. The poorest farmers will be hit the hardest. The Philippines, and other developing countries, propose that they be allowed to protect those crops which are particularly important to poor farmers. But this plan is being resisted by rich countries within the WTO.

Rice is the staple food for 80 percent of Filipinos. It is the single most important agricultural crop in the Philippines. It is therefore a major source of income for millions of Filipino farmers.

Elizabeth Moteza is a director of a Social Action Centre in Zamboangadel Sur, Mindanao, which is supported by CAFOD. The centre works with small-scale rice farmers, assisting them with low interest loans, technology and training. Elizabeth also campaigns to encourage more small-scale and chemical-free processes, for the good of the economy, the community and the environment.

Elizabeth says, "The WTO is a big enemy for us, as WTO policies do not benefit poor people here. Because of liberalization there is an influx of products from countries like Vietnam and the US to the Philippines. This is driving the price down and making it impossible for small farmers to compete. Most consumers will choose cheap foreign rice over high quality local rice. Rice is my livelihood.

Rodrigo Costanilla, a father of seven, farms one hectare, rented from a land-owning family. Two-thirds of the land is used to grow rice, the rest for fruit trees, vegetables, pigs and fish ponds. Rodrigo says, "There is foreign rice in all the local markets and it's not helping small farmers to increase their income. It's cheaper and people are not buying our rice, which is higher quality and healthier. The good thing about small farms like mine is that the produce and income from the land is divided between lots of people, not just taken by one owner. Rice is my livelihood, and if it were taken away from me it is really the equivalent of death. Please continue to help."

Rodrigo's neighbour, 63-year-old Severino Saruna, also leases a hectare of land and grows rice. Saruna says, "The price we get for the rice has been going down. Last year we got 9.2 pesos per kilo and now it's just 8.8 pesos. The price of foreign rice is cheap compared to our organic rice... this is because the Government allows this rice to come in from abroad. To CAFOD supporters I'd like to say heartfelt thanks for supporting small scale farmers here in the Philippines. Please continue – your help and assistance is really appreciated."

CAFOD will be at the World Trade Organization meeting in December, along with partners from Kenya, South Africa, Cambodia and East Timor. We will be arguing the case for fairer trade rules, including allowing poor countries to protect special products which are important for reducing poverty among their people.

South Africa

A sugar farmer's story

David Dlamini, the father of seven, has been growing sugar cane in South Africa for 27 years. But the 66-year-old was forced to give up farming last year because he could no longer make ends meet. His sugar cane stands rotting in the fields north of Durban because he can't afford to harvest it.

David says, "It wasn't worth farming any more. You worked for months and when you looked at your expense, you found you never covered your costs". Although David's farm lays thousands of miles from Europe, decisions made by the European Union have a direct impact on his livelihood. The price of sugar fluctuates all the time. When it declines, it affects the farmer directly. If we got a higher price for sugar, it would help us a lot."

In 1975 when David first started farming, Europe imported most of its sugar. But today, because of subsidies, Europe is the world's second largest sugar exporter – producing more than 20 million tonnes of sugar every year and dumping around 5 million tonnes on the world market. The South African Sugar Association estimates that over the past decade the EU has depressed the world sugar price by 20 to 40 per cent, forcing small-scale farmers like David out of business. He says, "The price of sugar fluctuates all the time. When it declines, it affects the farmer directly. If we got a higher price for sugar, it would help us a lot".

Switzerland:
Farmers feel WTO Threat

Farmers from 53 countries, including Switzerland, have called on the World Trade Organization (WTO) not to give exporting nations the upper hand in agriculture.

The Swiss Farmers Association (SFA) warned that if markets are opened up to imports by cutting tariffs, farmers' livelihoods would be under threat in many countries. The association's director, Jacques Bourgeois, said on Wednesday that if a proposal made by the G20 group of the 20 biggest industrialized and emerging nations was accepted at WTO talks this week in Geneva, custom duties could be cut by up to 90 per cent in some cases. He added that this – along with reductions in subsidies - was more likely to benefit major agricultural producers rather than developing nations. According to Bourgeois, dropping tariffs would have "dramatic" consequences for farmers' families. The farmers' association reckons that accepting the G20 proposal would amount to cutting farming revenue in Switzerland by SFr 3 billion ($2.41 billion). Swiss farmers, who are among the most subsidized in the world according to a report released by the Organization for Economic Co-operation and Development last week, aren't the only ones, worried about the WTO talks.

Foreign allies

Farmers from the European Union are concerned about the outcome of the negotiations within the Doha round of trade talks. Rudolf Schwarzböck, president of the Committee of Professional Agricultural Organizations in the EU, said the G20 proposal was unacceptable. "We are ready to open our borders and give developing countries access to our markets," he said. "But we want a fair result that ensures a future for our agriculture and guarantees food supplies for each nation." Schwarzböck added that the United States among others should show the same flexibility as the EU during talks and be prepared to make some concessions. Farmers from non-EU states, Norway and Iceland, as well as from Japan, Korea, Indonesia, India and many developing nations are also worried about the outcome of the negotiations.

The SFA's president, Hansjörg Walter, said that his association's members weren't against trade talks. But he called for clear commercial rules that would allow family farms to survive. "Too much liberalization benefits first and foremost international corporations that can produce in bulk and save on costs," he added. The Swiss government has already planned to cut farm subsidies by SFr 600 million from SFr 14.1 billion to SFr 13.5 billion over the three-year period beginning in 2008. The SFA says this will mean a 20 per cent drop in farmers' revenues.

Negotiating: More than 60 ministers are expected in Geneva for the negotiations starting on Thursday to hammer out long-standing differences over opening up their markets to farm and manufacturing imports. Countries are supposed to outline by the end of July how they plan to implement binding aspects of a new global trade treaty. The Doha Round of trade talks, launched five years ago in the Qatari capital, aims to lift millions of people out of poverty through fairer trading conditions. But the complex negotiations, already two years behind schedule, have stalled as poorer countries demand the EU and United States offer greater cutbacks in support for American and European farmers. The US and EU in turn want major developing countries like Brazil and India to allow more foreign competition for their industrial and services sectors. The release of heavily contested negotiating texts last week underscored how far the WTO's 149 members are from consensus on setting precise formulas for slashing subsidies and reducing tariffs on farm and manufactured goods. But unless a blueprint is agreed this summer, diplomats say the whole process may have to be put on ice until after the French and US presidential elections.

The news agency reports: The 149 members of the WTO have been negotiating the latest round of talks on the liberalization of trade of goods and services since 2001. Switzerland has been defending its agricultural policies while pushing for liberalization of services and lower tariffs for industry. The WTO has asked the Swiss to lower farming subsidies and import tariffs on agricultural products. Over the past 15 years, 30,000 farms have disappeared in Switzerland; 120,000 people work in the agricultural sector n the 1960s; 420,000farmers demonstrated in the capital Bern last November 2005 against plans to cut subsidies and import tariffs.[55]

---

[55]Swiss Info, Ch, June 28, 2006

Sri Lanka

Top farmer left in poverty by unfair trade

In 1995, Mr. M. Dhanapla, a father-of-three from Anuradhapura, Sri Lanka, won a presidential award for the best paddy farmer. Now he has to take other jobs to make ends meet.

Mr. M. Dhanapla says, "I'm reduced to poverty. Paddy is now 18 rupees a kilo because it is after the harvest. But during the harvest it is 10 rupees a kilo. The price is so low because of the lack of government intervention. Merchants can charge whatever they like. Imported rice is one of the things which affect the price. Merchants can import cheap rice, forcing down the price of rice on the local markets. Meanwhile, production costs remain high. Due to the open economy, the merchants can buy at whatever price they want, and import cheap international rice."

Rice is Sri Lanka's largest food crop - and the staple food for most of its people. Around 1.8 million families grow rice, two-thirds of them farming plots smaller than one hectare. The government of Sri Lanka has traditionally used trade policy to protect basic foods from competition with imports. But the country has been undergoing liberalization; including making large cuts to the tariffs that protect local agricultural produce. Sri Lanka now has one of the most open economies in the region while, at the same time, there has been a lack of investment in agriculture for non-export produce, leaving the rice sector undeveloped. Small farmers have been badly hit by problems caused by increased rice imports from more competitive countries.

CAFOD trade policy analyst Matt Griffith says: "The remaining, much-reduced, rice tariff is of vital importance for Sri Lankan rice farmers. It is the central factor in determining domestic rice market prices – and hence the viability of their livelihoods. At the World Trade Organization, rich countries (notably the US) and more competitive developing countries are proposing tariff cuts that would force Sri Lanka to cut its agricultural tariffs even further. This would open the doors to a flood of cheap rice imports that would further undermine the livelihoods of poor Sri Lankan farmers.

Defending special products

The Sri Lankan government is part of a group of developing countries (the G 33) at the WTO trying to oppose this - by allowing poor countries to protect specific crops, such as rice, that are crucial to food security and poor people's livelihoods from further tariff cuts. They are supporting a proposal called 'Special Products' which will be further negotiated at Hong Kong. CAFOD will be at the World Trade Organization meeting in December, along with partners from Kenya, South Africa, Cambodia and East Timor. We will be arguing the case for fairer trade rules, including allowing poor countries to protect special products which are important for reducing poverty among their people.[56]

Public Stock Management

Countries that are regular importers or exporters of grain need to engage in little year-to-year storage of grains. Varying trade volumes is a more effective means of achieving domestic price stability than storage. Within a given marketing year, imports can be timed to arrive during the lean season or exports during the post-harvest season. This will lessen the seasonal price spread. If private traders are discouraged from engaging in sufficient storage by the low spread, the public food grains agency may have to procure and store domestic grain. This need not be costly, provided the price target is well defined

---

[56]CAFOD – Just One World

and realistic. The main function of public agencies in these countries should be to determine carefully the need for and level of working stocks and to establish a minimum reorder level that will assure adequate supplies.

Countries close to self-sufficiency usually acquire larger stocks than intended when they follow price policies dictated by considerations other than the balancing of domestic demand and supply. In such a circumstance, these countries must bear the higher storage costs, accept more price variability, or open up the food grain economy. The choice will depend on the policy objectives. Cost minimization objectives would tend to point toward a lessening of the government role in storage and a relaxation of its rules on trade.[57]

Canada

Changes in Canadian Agricultural Marketing and Trade Policy,

The Canada-United States Free Trade Agreement (CUSTA) and the subsequent North American Free Trade Agreement (NAFTA) have contributed to increasing concentration of agricultural trade between the United States and Canada. This has heightened bilateral trade tensions and trade conflicts for numbers of Canadian farm products. These conflicts, and the need to accommodate domestic marketing policies to the obligations of the General Agreement on Tariffs and Trade (GATT) and its successor, the World Trade Organization (WTO), have encouraged changes in Canadian agricultural marketing policies. Pressures to reduce government expenditures have also provided a compelling reinforcing impetus to changes in numbers of Canada's agricultural

---

[57]Stamwalla A. (1988)," Public Stock Management", Agricultural Price Policy for Developing Countries, International Food Policy Research Institute, The Jhons Hopkins University Press, Baltomore and London, 1988

marketing programs. However, despite some changes in the ways that the programs for the Canadian supply-managed farm products are organized and administered, there has been no reduction in the levels of policy-induced support provided to this group of producers.

Indeed, adjustments in marketing and trade policy for dairy, poultry and eggs have increased the levels of protection for these sectors. High levels of protection for supply-managed farm products reflect the strong influences of regional political pressures in Canada; this is an influence that is expected to continue in the future. In contrast to the supply-managed dairy and poultry sectors, major changes have been made in marketing programs for the export-oriented Canadian grains and red meats sectors in response to trade and budgetary pressures. These have involved the removal of longstanding rail freight subsidies for grains and the phasing down or termination of several stabilization and safety net programs.[58]

Tanzania

Agricultural Marketing and Supply Chain Management in Tanzania:

A Case Study

Policy Recommendations – The Way Forward

The government of Tanzania has made major changes in its policy to open the markets and to facilitate free trade in the country. Current agreements with the WTO allowing Tanzania to enjoy non-reciprocal preferential access to developed markets, such as the European Union (EU) under the very thing but Arms (EBA) agreement recent validation of the East African Community (EAC)

---

[58]Veeman Michele (1996), "Changes in Canadian Agricultural Marketing and Trade Policy", Review of Marketing and Agricultural Economics, Volume 64, No. 03, December, 1996

Customs Union, as well as membership at Southern African Development Community (SADC) are substantial changes into enlarging the market for the Tanzanian products. Also the national market has been enhanced and trade facilitated by continuing to streamline the national tax policies and remove legal barriers for entry.

Elina Eskola (2005)[59] has advocated that, however, changes at the top must be complemented with supporting policies at lower levels of administration to ensure that trade liberalization serves as a welfare increasing policy instrument. The government policy of trade liberalization has been successful in removing formal barriers for trade and increasing competition at all levels of the supply chain, but old attitudes and informal barriers still remain. Many traders still long for the good old days with practically no competition and government subsidies to the farmers guaranteeing low price of agricultural products at the farm gate. Even though the support of such marketing power and unsustainable subsidies that distort the markets are part of the past, attitudes change slowly. In order for trade liberalization to work for pro-poor growth, trade needs to be facilitated by active government policies. Improving road infrastructure has been on the government agenda for a long period of time but it has not received the emphasis and sense of necessity that it requires. Current level of road infrastructure fails to facilitate efficient trade leading to unnecessarily high transportation costs and long transportation times. It also decreases the size of the market by blocking more remote producers and potential consumers from the market giving market power to the few large-

---

[59]Elina Eskola (2005), "Agricultural Marketing and Supply Chain Management in Tanzania: A Case Study", ESRF Study on Globalization and East Africa Economies, Working Paper Series No. 16, Success under Duress: a Comparison of the Indigenous African and East African Asian Entrepreneurs

scale players who are able to meet the transaction costs. Investing especially in feeder roads is likely to bring about large welfare gains in terms of large volumes traded, which again brings more money into circulation and creates improved livelihood opportunities. Facilitating access not only to local village markets but also improving the regional markets by strengthening the national supply chain is vital in order to generate local growth centers and to allow poor rural households to benefit from the development by increasing their options for trading and income generation. On the whole, transportation costs are often hitting the poorest part of the population disproportionally hard for two main reasons. Firstly, the poorest groups are often living in geographically remote areas where transportation costs are higher. Secondly, the transportation costs comprise a proportionally more important part of the price of food crops than cash crops and the poorest groups usually spend largest part of their income on food. Thus decrease in transportation costs overall might well be considered as a pro-poor policy. Within Tanzania, several authorities are involved in the planning and management of road transport including Ministries of Transport, Works, Home Affairs, Regional Administration, and Local Government and Finance. However, currently the coordination between the authorities is poor, governance is weak due to corruption, and enforcement of agreed policies is insufficient (National Transport Policy 2003).

The government has recently acknowledged that achieving the general development targets set in the National Poverty Reduction Strategy Paper (PRSP), Vision 2025, and the Rural Development Strategy (RDP) requires enhancement of transport infrastructure with a view to speeding up the process in other productive sectors. In order to achieve the set targets for poverty reduction and to harmonies the existing policies, the government formulated a National Transport Policy in 2003, which outlines the measures to be taken in order to improve the infrastructure in the country. Ministry of Works has created a concrete plan for the road sector improvements, namely the Ten Year Road Sector Development Program that highlights the preferences of the Tanzanian Government in upgrading the existing road network, giving priority to important cash crop and food crop producing areas, areas with important mining or tourism sector, and areas with important international transit trade with neighbouring countries. The funding for this plan is expected to be divided between the donor community and the Tanzanian Government. However, under current financial setup of the road sector, the resources are insufficient even for the realization of the minimal work program consisting of "the indispensable actions in order to avert serious hindrances to a minimal growth of the national economy" (Ten Year Road Sector Development Program, Phase II, 2002). Financing the urgent infrastructure improvement is not a question of lacking resources, as the economy is already paying dearly for the poor road network in terms of higher vehicle operating costs and trade foregone, but a matter of giving the sector the priority it requires. As a rule of thumb every one US dollar of essential maintenance postponed, increases the cost of operating a vehicle in the current period by more than three dollars, which implies that road users could well afford to pay for maintenance if they can afford to own and operate a vehicle (Kruger et al. 2002)[60].

However, as investment in infrastructure at large-scale requires mobilization of large sums, donor community could consider increasing its role in

---

[60]Kruger, P; Wepener, D.A.; Botha, W.J. (2002) An Analysis of Financing of road Maintenance Based on a Cross-Section of African Countries, in *Proceedings for Year 2002 Annual Roads Convention (ARC2002)*, Dar es Salaam.

financing the readily designed Ten Year Road Sector Development Program.

If the road network would allow easy access even to more remote areas, processing facilities could be more easily based into rural areas where the surplus producers of perishable goods are. In absence of good storage facilities, goods processed close to their production site can then easily be shipped to larger markets and thus increase the effective demand and supply of these goods. Roads, processing, and storage facilities, as well as market infrastructure are all part of the necessary prerequisite for efficient trading. Currently the marketplaces are in poor condition, which presents a serious health risk to the traders and the consumers, and hinders the expansion of the market in terms of new customers and investors.

Yet another important part of infrastructure is the support for telecommunication infrastructure, which can serve an important role in disseminating market information. The mobile phones are becoming a more important part of trade and price negotiations also in Tanzanian agricultural trade, and the active involvement of competing private sector providers should be encouraged also in the future to ensure competitive pricing and reliable supply of the services. In addition to technical improvements, in order for market expansion to happen, the customer base must also be allowed to increase by encouraging non-farm rural employment opportunities and vocational 8 The maintenance cost per annum has been estimated at US$ 80 million whereas lack of maintenance is projected to cost the nation US $365 million annually mainly due to vehicle operating costs and loss of asset of the existing roads (Marmo et al. 1997).

These will ensure that the money stays in circulation in rural areas. Trade is only a part of a holistic development agenda aimed at improving people's welfare. Less costly but also less straightforward change needed to facilitate trade is the improvement of capacity base and institutions. The donor community alone cannot do this but the change needs to be homegrown in order to ensure ownership of and commitment to the changes at all levels of administration. At the grass root level providing more training in business skills, demonstration farms for more market based production, and other vocation training are likely to improve the income earning capacity of the small-scale producers and traders. Government institutions, on the other hand, need to tackle corruption as it currently forms a serious block at the market. Increased awareness and empowerment of the civil society, political will and improved training and incentive schemes for the police officers are means to tackle this problem. Also government efforts to stabilize and regulate the markets to facilitate trading between strangers are needed to shorten the supply chain and cut costs.

This would also facilitate the circulation of working capital, which is currently seen as a problem at every stage of the supply chain. Improved access to capital through loans is a desirable policy goal but the way in which such a policy is implemented is of crucial importance. Despite the burning need for loans credit schemes are unlikely to succeed unless they are properly followed up and complemented with training component in business skills and servicing the loan. On the other hand, in case demonstrated ability to save and commitment to enhancing the business has been raised at the grass root level, the capacity of the local government should be improved to facilitate such initiatives. Building capacity of the local government is also highly topical in light of the government plans to concentrate the channeling most of funds from the donors through the central and local governments.

Trade facilitation can be a powerful tool in poverty alleviation as it has the possibility of generating income earning opportunities for the rural farmers who currently have very little possibilities to earn income otherwise. However, for trade to be efficient and in order for the poorest farmers to be able to gain from trade, mere changes at the national level are not sufficient. Active policy measures are needed to empower farmers to negotiate the prices, access the larger markets and to move people up the supply chain from the village markets to regional and national markets by removing the informal barriers of entry. As discussed above, based on the findings of this study, the following areas should gain priority in the government policy:

(a) Increased funding for physical infrastructure (trunk and feeder roads, telecommunications, market infrastructure) both from national and international sources
(b) Emphasis on rural non-farm employment and intra-regional market development
(c) Large-scale capacity building in business skills and market orientation
(d) Improved access to credit and better management of credit schemes
(e) Empowerment of civil society to form representative bodies to improve their bargaining power and to facilitate fight against corruption
(f) Enforcement of existing laws, and formalization of contracts to diminish risk of trading

Improved dissemination of market information:

The President's Office has already launched a Business Environment strengthening for Tanzania (BEST) Programme that aims at facilitating the transformation of the governance and regulation to provide businesses and traders an enabling environment to expand. BEST, Agricultural Marketing Policy, Anti-Corruption Policy, Agricultural Sector Development Policy, and Micro Finance Policy are all examples of political commitment to improve the agricultural marketing environment in Tanzania along the same lines as outlined in this study. However, it is not the lack of policies at the macro level but the weak implementation of existing policies at the micro level that currently hinders trade and economic growth. Active policy measures that allow people who currently have very few possibilities to benefit from trade to participate with equal terms are likely to lead to welfare improvements that can greatly improve the living standard of the poor.

This has also a strong gender implication as women are currently unequally represented in the supply chain and usually only fulfill the role of a small-scale retailer of perishable goods. Production, processing and trading tasks are clearly segregated between the sexes disfavoring women's placement at the powerful positions in trade. The Agricultural Marketing Policy sets a clear vision "to have an agricultural marketing system that is efficient, effective and equitable by 2015". The major challenge for the years to come is the effective and timely implementation of this policy so that agricultural trade could realize its potential as a tool in the fight against poverty.[61]

(B)Agricultural Prices

Pricing Principles and Public Intervention in Domestic Markets:

World cereals prices have become more variable since the early 1970s, which has led to corresponding increases in the variability of domestic 6. Even though the prices of different cereals have become

---

[61] Marmo, F., Kimambo, I.N., Andreski, A. (1997) Road Financing for Sustainable Development, in *Proceedings from the Annual Roads Convention on Road Transport: The Key to Development,* Dar es Salaam

more closely correlated, they still do not move in perfect unison. Thus there is still scope for changes in relative prices to favor one crop over another. Farm gate prices in some of the major cereal-exporting countries. However, many countries have successfully buffered their domestic prices from the increased volatility of world markets, and some have even been able to reduce the variability of domestic prices.

There is a surprising lack of collinearity between domestic and world cereal prices in many countries. Countries that buffer their domestic market prices apparently also shield their farmers from directional changes in world market prices. There does not appear to have been any significant change in these patterns of collinearity since the early 1970s.

On the other hand, a dramatic increase in the collinearity of world cereal prices between crops has been reflected in an increase in the correlation of domestic farm gate prices between crops, both within and among countries. The growth in world cereal production from 1960/61 to 1982/83, largely due to improved yields, was accompanied by a more than proportional increase in the standard deviation of production. Increases in yield variances and a simultaneous loss in offsetting patterns of variation in yields between crops and countries were the overwhelming sources of the increase in production variability. More research is required before firm conclusions can be drawn about the cause of these changes in yields. An important factor may have been that the increased use of improved seed and fertilizer-intensive technologies since the 1960s has led to more variable and synchronized patterns of input use across crops and regions in response to changing prices. This effect may have been amplified by the sharp increase in the variability of world cereal prices since the early 1970s, and particularly by the increase in price correlations between crops. It does not appear that any inherently higher sensitivity of new technologies to environmental stress has been a significant cause.

Continued high levels of variability in world cereal prices seem likely. The United States is unlikely to return to its stockpiling policies of earlier years, and cereal imports by the USSR remain unpredictable. The levels of production variability now established would also affect world prices. These factors, together with a continuing trend towards more input- intensive technologies, suggest that world cereal production and prices are likely to continue to become more variable in the years ahead.

A country pursuing a positive price policy and intervening in markets can do the job better by adopting proper principles for determining domestic producer and consumer prices and implementing them with consistent and well-designed measures of intervention. The principle of cost of production, widely used in developing countries, is not a socially optimal guide for determination of producer price. However, it is a useful basis for discussion in the political process of determining prices that involves both social and private gains and monitoring technological transformation in agriculture.

Use of world prices complex and imprecise (as they are, as a reference for producer prices) is socially optimal in the sense that the principle is consistent with the maximization of growth potential. Setting domestic price in reference to world price does not mean setting it at par with world price. Instead, it implies an alignment of the domestic toward the world price trend so that the impact of world price fluctuations can be minimized and short-run constraints associated with the principle can be accommodated through selective interventions. These interventions are primarily related to price stabilization and consumer subsidy.

The extent of consumer subsidy depends on the level of subsidized price and the coverage of the subsidy program. The level of subsidized price is determined by a complex set of factors involving political and humanitarian considerations. But a low consumer price is likely to involve a high subsidy and an implicit taxation on producers through a reduced producer price. Similarly, coverage of a subsidy program has to be restricted to target groups to keep the subsidy down. After all, the subsidy implies a lost opportunity for investment, perhaps in infrastructure development. If such a dual mechanism, involving markets as well as special subsidy programs, is not effective because of widespread poverty and political infeasibility, a low producer price in markets becomes unavoidable. The critical factor, however, is avoidance of the instability that occasionally causes a spurt in food prices. If instability can be contained, the pressure for food subsidy will be minimal and the subsidy can be kept down and even eliminated as the economy grows and the incidence of absolute poverty diminishes.

Such fine-tuned management of producer and consumer prices depends, of course, on an institutionalized analytical input in policy formulation. Governments use various forms of direct and indirect interventions in the domestic market to maintain higher producer and lower consumer prices in a stable manner. Often these measures are undertaken without a correct appreciation of the functions of the domestic market. Implementation of a measure may also falter because of inadequate skilled administrative and professional management and infrastructure facilities. In such a case, instead of spatial and inter-temporal price spreads being narrower, these faulty measures tend to impose additional transaction costs in the market and widen the price spread. Transmittal of price signals in the market channel gets blurred. This is particularly evident in Africa.

The longer-run solution to this problem lies in infrastructure development and correction of market imperfections. Market imperfection can be corrected by development of financial institutions, creation of institutions for gathering market information, standardization of grades and weights, strengthening of the legal framework for enforcement of contracts, and minimization of uncertainty arising from haphazard public intervention and natural factors. Infrastructure development contributes crucially, albeit indirectly, to the growth of market institutions and the elimination of imperfections. Achievement of long-run goals, particularly in Africa, may have to be gradual. Introduction of unencumbered private trade (or elimination of public monopoly) should be given a priority. This should be followed by liberalization of regulatory measures (for example, movement restriction, licensing, etc.) and adoption of positive measures for improving the structure and conduct of markets. Public marketing should be limited to certain strategically important areas such as management of security stocks and supporting prices, if necessary, in infrastructure-backward areas and for accelerating diffusion of a technology in its initial stages. Determining when and where such support measures are necessary should be based on case-by-case analyses of price variability. Price rather than quantity should be the target for price stabilization.[62]

Risk and Uncertainty in Domestic Production and Prices

Risk has significant effects on the welfare of farmers and low-income people. It can also lead to distortions

---

[62]Ahmed R. (1988). "Pricing Principles and Public Intervention in Domestic Markets", Agricultural Price Policy for Developing Countries, International Food Policy Research Institute, The Johns Hopkins University Press, Baltimore and London, 1988

in resource allocation that are costly to the national economy.

Governments may have an important role to play in reducing risk for farmers. Some public investments, such as irrigation, can reduce yield risks while also enlarging average production. This risk-reducing aspect may enhance the value of such investments in cost-benefit analysis.

Risk-pooling schemes such as crop insurance can also reduce the cost of yield risk to farmers and allow them to allocate their resources more efficiently. But such schemes should only be implemented when their benefits are commensurate with their costs. The government has subsidized many crop insurance schemes heavily.

Price risks are often as important as yield risks in agriculture. If prices are negatively correlated with yields, the correlation has a stabilizing effect on income over time, and policies that stabilize yields or prices alone would act to destabilize farm incomes. The appropriate intervention in this case is to stabilize both prices and yields or not to stabilize either. Where the correlation is zero or positive, stabilizing either prices or yields will suffice to help stabilize incomes.

Price stabilization schemes based on buffer stocks are likely to be too expensive in terms of the benefits they generate. More realistic policies to reduce price risks are minimum support prices. These can be achieved through deficiency payments or where the commodity is traded internationally, through variable levies and tariffs.

An additional advantage of reducing price variability is that it helps farmers to forecast prices more accurately when committing their resources. However, market and resource allocate-efficiency still depends on farmers' holding rational price expectations, such as the unit revenue forecast, so as to take account of any nonzero correlations between prices and yields. Where alternative and less efficient price forecasting prevails, significant improvements in resource productivity might be attained by introducing or improving market information services for farmers.

Such programs might range from assistance to farmers in recording and calculating weighted averages of past revenues and yields to more elaborate intelligence services that provide timely and detailed information throughout the year on prices, weather, sown areas, and the like.

Finally, the government may also have an important role to play in protecting low-income people from fluctuating food prices. Again, buffer stock schemes to stabilize prices would seem to be too expensive. Emergency food stocks might prudently be carried as insurance against major catastrophes in production, but emergency ration schemes, food subsidies, and food-for-work programs can also be useful.[63]

Relative Prices in the People's Republic of China:

Rural Taxation through Public Monopsony

Unlike the countries depicted as successful models of economic development, which are reputed to have financed industrialization by squeezing agriculture, the People's Republic of China was unable to extract resources from the agricultural sector through deliberate policy without serious consequences for the

---

63 Peter B R Hazell (1988), "Risk and Uncertainty in Domestic Production and Prices", Agricultural Price Policy for Developing Countries, International Food Policy Research Institute, The Johns Hopkins University Press, Baltimore and London, 1988

rate of overall economic growth and the destruction of agriculture's other developmental functions. This was the case despite very effective rural institutions for mobilizing savings, a substantial increase in labor application per hectare, and an active rural response to rural industrialization and technical transformation of agriculture though the real values are lower due to generalized price inflation.

China is clearly relying on local investment in agriculture to make up for the drift in central expenditures. One of its primary mechanisms is a rebate to counties and townships for taxation of their industries, one-quarter of which is supposed to be spent in support of agricultural production. This could be an important source of agricultural development financing, but, like the loans to communes and brigades, it is not clear what proportions of these funds are actually spent to support growth in crop productivity. With the exception of a few large projects, state expenditures on water control have dropped substantially. Again, local efforts are supposed to take up the slack, financed by water fees imposed on farmers. This transition, however, is not likely to be easy.

This conclusion is reminiscent of Ellman's (1975) findings for the Soviet Union in the 1930s and is of some relevance to a large number of developing countries whose attempts to squeeze agriculture have failed to extract a surplus of much quantitative importance to national capital formation in the short run while leading to disastrous implications for the longer run.

As in many other developing countries, an immediate policy emphasis on cheap urban food in the PRC, without sufficient state investment in all requisite aspects of agriculture's technical transformation, set up a contradiction between the short-term and long-term fulfillment of the sector's role as a source of savings and food for the development of other sectors.

Increasing market control for various farm inputs and outputs and rural organizational efforts to resolve the contradiction also focused on short-term gains at the expense of long-term deterioration in resource allocate- efficiency and perhaps in the quality and intensity of applied agricultural labor. These are the elements that combined to depress the returns to Chinese agriculture's incomplete technical transformation. And thus relative prices, no longer far out of line internationally, still proved a critical limitation.

But it is important to note that it was not price increases alone that resolved the problem. What did prove effective was the combination of massive provision of nitrogen, revival of gains from regional and occupational specialization, resolution of imbalanced allocation patterns limiting resource productivity within farming areas, and reestablishment of the link between effort and reward underwritten by the positive shock of price increases—all these added to a firm base, developed over decades, of improved seed technology, relative agronomic sophistication, and water control.

Finally, during the three decades in which an urban, capital-intensive strategy increasingly constrained agriculture's ability to provide food and savings for the dynamic development of other sectors, agriculture's other developmental functions—as a source of labor and foreign exchange and as a domestic market for goods and services of other sectors—were seriously curtailed. All in all, it is not yet evident how, in China's case, a sufficient state investment in agriculture to allow balanced growth would have been consistent with a sizable net outflow of resources from the sector for a large part of the People's Republic period.

Yet China is now at a crossroads. Substantial resolution of the constraints, which have inhibited the acceleration of farm production of a considerably transformed agricultural sector, now provides an unprecedented opportunity for agriculture to fulfill several of its theoretical functions as a pivotal sector in the rapid development of the entire economy. What remains to be determined is whether the struggle to deal with the short-term difficulties associated with the unfamiliar chaos of China's current economic revolution will lead the country to return to more familiar inertial states of urban and industrial orientation and restriction of growth in order to achieve a measure of control, or whether China will succeed in forging ahead with the second half of the program aimed at rebalancing the economy.

This would call for an employment-intensive development of the rural nonagricultural sector, bolstered by infrastructure investment as a counterpart to sustained commitment to agricultural expansion and a link to the capital-intensive urban sector. In all of this, the role of price, as China's markets for food, inputs, and consumer goods are decreasingly controlled by government, may be neither the most critical instrument for achieving this development nor even an appropriate one, but rather an indicator of sectoral performance.[64]

India: **Price Fixation of Agricultural Commodities**

The Commission for Agricultural Costs and Prices (CACP) fixes procurement prices of all notified commodities for a Marketing year (such as October

---

[64]Bruce Stone (1988), "Relative Prices in the People's Republic of China: Rural Taxation through Public Monopsony", Agricultural Price Policy for Developing Countries, International Food Policy Research Institute, The Johns Hopkins University Press, Baltimore and London

2010 to September 2011). The CACP believes that it does justice to the farming community. It fixes prices with the following objectives.[65]

Along with the thrust on strategies for accelerated growth of food production, there should be greater focus on research efforts and the requisite research – extension - farmer linkages for achieving higher yields per hectare as well as efficient use of the available resources.

The Government should on priority carry out a review of the state of procurement operations in the non-traditional areas of the country aimed at initiating corrective measures. Associating various appropriate agencies available in the States other than the usually enlisted organizations (ex: cooperative organizations, SHGs) for procurement operations needs to be given serious consideration.

The Government should consider providing food items for daily use including coarse grains, through authorized outlets at reasonable prices along with the traditional public distribution system, so that their availability across the country is assured to the public and price rise could be kept under check.

Any sound strategy for agriculture development should have an integral component for adaptation to the impact of climatic change through action plans in areas such as agricultural research to evolve varieties that are climate resilient as well as cope with the likely increase in water stress.

The plan priorities and related schemes / programs for irrigation development should follow a balanced approach, with greater thrust on micro irrigation and

---

[65] Commission for Agricultural Costs and Prices, Report on Price Policy for Kharif Crops of 2010- 2011 Season - Recommendations

enhanced efficiency in water utilization as well as limited extraction of groundwater in over-exploited regions along with its increased utilization in under-exploited regions.

The Government should follow a two-pronged strategy in the seeds sector: increase SRR to the advisable levels in respect of various crops, and lay equal emphasis on the production of quality/hybrid seeds.

Along with the thrust on increased availability of farm credit, there should be emphasis on the greater inclusion of new farmers, especially small and marginal, under institutional coverage as well as the increased outreach of cooperative credit societies.

The monitoring and evaluation aspects of NREGA have to be adequately strengthened with greater role for social audit, and the implementation may be focussed towards off-season times when the agricultural operations are not in peak, laying emphasis on agriculture-related activities, with appropriate regional variations, through requisite amendments in the operational guidelines, so that the usual agricultural work in the areas may not face problems in obtaining sufficient farm labour.

Urgent steps are to be taken to notify the rules that are pending under the new/amended statutes pertaining to agricultural markets as well as bring in or improve the basic infrastructure and facilities in these markets, so that the market yards facilitate and not frustrate the production and other related activities on the farm front.

Greater emphasis should be laid on the post-harvest management of agricultural commodities through development of appropriate technologies and facilities as well as development of small and medium scale food processing units.

Concerted efforts have to be made through effective extension services for immediately spreading about the pulses varieties and technologies developed in the research organizations to the farmers' field.

In order to bring level-playing field for the benefit of farmers and also domestic oil sector, Government needs to review the present import duty structure on edible oils.

Keeping in view the urgent need to augment domestic availability of edible oils, the productivity of all the oilseed crops especially of oil palm and tree borne oilseeds should be given special attention by replacing the existing Integrated Scheme of Oilseeds, Pulses, Oil palm and Maize (ISOPOM) to a newly constituted Technology Mission for Oilseeds.

Ministry of Textiles should look into the limitations in the capacity expansion of the domestic textile mills with a view to increasing the export of value added cotton products like yarn, fabrics and textiles.

Ministry of Textiles may look into the grievance of the Cotton Industry regarding low priority being given to by-products of cotton, which suffer from faulty processing, traditional crushing techniques, lack of extension education etc. and may take appropriate remedial measures, either through a new scheme or through the existing Technology Mission on Cotton.

DES and Tobacco Board need to sort out the discrepancy in the cost of cultivation data collected by Directorate of Tobacco Development and Central Tobacco Research Institute and consider extension of coverage for collection of cost of cultivation data to Karnataka also.

Procurement Prices: The Commission fixes the procurement prices (Minimum Support Prices per Quintal of agricultural commodities) for each marketing year (October to September). The procurement prices for agricultural commodities for crop season 2010 – 11 were as follows:

(a) Paddy (Rice + Husk) FAQ at 1000 INR (Indian Rupees),
(b) Paddy Grade 1 at 1030 INR,
(c) Jowar Hybrid - 880 INR,
(d) Bazra - 880 INR, Maize - 880 INR,
(e) Ragi – 965 INR
(f) Arhar – 2800 INR,
(g) Moong – 3170,
(h) Urad – 2900,
(i) Ground Nut –in shell – 2300 INR
(j) Soybean Black – 1400 INR,
(k) Soybean yellow – 1440 INR,
(l) Sunflower seed – 2350 INR,
(m) Sesamum – 2900 INR,
(n) Niger Seed – 2450 INR,
(o) Cotton 2500 INR to 3000 INR

INDIA:

Determination of Administered Prices of Food grains

Incentive prices in the form of minimum support prices are essential to the success of agricultural production programs based on high-yielding-varieties technology. At the same time, undue reliance cannot be placed on high prices alone as an incentive for increasing production of food grains, especially when shortages are widespread. Effective implementation of price support policies requires adequate institutional arrangements for the purchase of quantities offered for sale at that price. At the same time, the Alternatives to large buffer stocks such as foreign exchange buffer funds and/or option forward dealings are often suggested. Food grain consumption needs of the vulnerable sections of the population have to be met through appropriate public distribution systems. These supplies may have to be sold at prices below the economic cost. This implies subsidization.

Procurement and public distribution are in fact two sides of the same coin. A public distribution system can be effectively maintained through domestic procurement of grain at reasonable prices. Quantities procured through price support operations find an outlet through the public distribution system. To even out the supplies between good and bad years and ensure price stability, buffer stock policies are essential to prudent food management. Imports do not provide a complete answer in bad crop years, particularly in countries with severe foreign exchange constraints. Although large buffer stocks are expensive to operate, these costs must be weighed against the gains to society from mitigation of the hardships caused by supply and price instabilities.[66]

In India, the Agricultural Prices Commission and the Food Corporation of India provide institutional support for implementation of price policy. The former plays an advisory role to the government in price determination. The latter assists in coordinated implementation of procurement, distribution, and buffer stock policies and functions in a manner somewhat similar to that of BULOG in Indonesia. Both the Indian and Indonesian experiences suggest that public intervention in the food grains market requires considerable administrative resources and analytical support.

---

[66]Sarma S. (1988), "Determination of Administered Prices of Food grains in India", Agricultural Price Policy for Developing Countries, International Food Policy Research Institute, the Johns Hopkins University Press, Baltimore and London.

Consumers' welfare

Food Subsidies: Consumer Welfare and Producer Incentives

Per Pinstrvp- Andersen[67] has analyzed the economics of food subsidy and its impact of consumer welfare and producer incentive. The researcher opines that policies to strengthen incentives to expand food production through higher food prices are likely to result in short-run reductions in real incomes of food consumers.

Since a large share of the income of the poor is generally spent on food, higher food prices may cause severe hardships to those who do not derive their incomes from food production either directly as producers or farm workers or indirectly as providers of inputs and consumption goods to farmers.[68]

But not only will the poor be adversely affected. Food expenditures of the better-off consumers also will rise as food prices increase. Although the poor will have a larger loss relative to current incomes, their absolute loss will be smaller.

Although increased food prices may contribute to long-run economic growth and food self-sufficiency goals, the short-run economic, welfare, and political implications may be untenable. Reactions by urban

---

[67]Per Pinstrvp – Andersen (1988), "Food Subsidies: Consumer Welfare and Producer Incentives", Agricultural Price Policy for developing Countries, The International Food Policy Research Institute, The Johns Hopkins University Press, Baltimore and London

[68]Gray (1982) estimated that the poorest 30 percent of the Brazilian population spent 59 percent of total income on food, as compared to 16 percent for the 20 percent with the highest incomes. Mellor (1978) found that the poorest 20 percent of the Indian population spent 54 percent of income on food grains alone, as compared to 15 percent for the richest 5 percent.

consumers to recent attempts to increase food prices in a number of countries have clearly demonstrated the political implications. Furthermore, a number of studies have shown that food price increases may cause serious hardships for the poor, including deterioration of an already precarious nutritional situation.

There is no easy solution or general policy that would be applicable to all countries. The choice and design of policies for each country must be based on its particular mix of economic, social, and political considerations, including the characteristics of low-income population groups. Options available to governments for dealing with food price issues based on the experience from various countries and the results from studies are presented below.

General Food Policies and Subsidies

Many countries follow cheap food policies enforced through various combinations of exchange rate manipulations, domestic price fixing, forced food procurement, export taxes, and government monopolies in foreign and/or domestic food trade. Combined with similar measures for nonfood agricultural commodities, these policies have resulted in the extraction of economic surplus from agriculture for use in promoting growth in nonagricultural public and private sectors, thereby reducing investment and production incentives in agriculture.

The impact of cheap food policies on the real income of the poor cannot be measured easily. Different groups may be affected differently. The most obvious distinction is whether a group depends on food production for its income. Furthermore, the immediate impact may be quite different than the intermediate and longer-run effects.

The immediate impact of an increase in food prices on poor wage earners who do not derive their income from food production would be negative. The longer-run impact depends on whether higher food prices lead to higher wages and whether upward adjustment in food prices improves the efficiency of resource allocation and utilization and thus generates economic growth and increased employment. In a study of Argentina, Cavallo and Mundlak (1982) found that trade liberalization and exchange rate management would accelerate economic growth while causing agricultural prices to increase faster than nonagricultural wage rates, thus reducing real wages in terms of food. They further demonstrated that compensation could be paid to consumers in the form of subsidies, which would keep food wages constant, at an economic cost considerably less than the economic gains resulting from trade liberalization and exchange rate management.

Thus, although, under the assumptions of their model, the rate of economic growth would be lower if food wages were kept constant, it was shown that policies reflecting long-term economic efficiency goals would be feasible without adverse effects on food wages.

The extent to which consumers capture benefits from food price subsidies rather than passed on in the form of lower wages varies among countries, and empirical evidence is scarce. The period of adjustment of wage rates is also likely to vary depending on institutional and other aspects.

Pending additional empirical evidence, it may be concluded only that while the effect of food price increases on real incomes of poor wage-earners who do not derive their income from food production is likely to be negative in the short run, it may eventually become positive in the longer run. However, long-run effects may be of little or no interest to the poor who are adversely affected in the short run. The subjective discount rate for the poor is likely to be very high, and uncertain future gains may be insufficient to compensate for immediate losses. Thus food price increases may be politically difficult or impossible unless compensation is made for short-run losses.

The impact of food price increases on the poor who derive their incomes from food production would be expected to be positive provided that the price increase is reflected in farm-gate prices. Higher prices would add to revenues from marketable surpluses, and labor demand in food production would be expected to increase. However, total demand for rural labor need not increase if the food price increases cause substitution of less labor-intensive for more labor-intensive commodities, for example, substitution of rice for jute in Bangladesh (Ahmed 1981).

Food price increases often may be much less favorable for the rural poor than expected. Many of the rural poor derive only a small share of their incomes from wage labor in food production or from the sale of food. Results from a study of the implications of increasing domestic rice prices in Thailand show that the rural poor would not benefit greatly from such increases. Even though many of the poor are rice producers, the marketable surplus is often small, and large proportions are a net buyer of rice. Although these findings may not have general application, it is clear that food price increases will create short-run hardships among many rural poor, particularly those in the informal sector. Thus compensatory measures may be needed in both urban and rural areas. In the somewhat longer run, increasing demand for rural services is likely to result in increased incomes among the same groups of rural poor.

A variety of compensatory measures are available, including increases in wages in the public sector and in minimum wages in the private sector. While the poor non-wage-earners—for example, the large number of people working in the informal sectors—would be affected in roughly the same way as wage earners, compensation through wage manipulations would obviously not be possible. Other compensatory measures are discussed later.

Explicit General Subsidies

Some countries have used subsidies to shield consumers from the effects of increasing food prices (whether the increase is in real or nominal terms) in order to maintain political stability, avoid negative impact on the poor, and maintain low wages. The fiscal costs of a publicly financed wedge between consumer and producer or import prices can be very high, depending on the size of the subsidy, the marketing costs if borne by the public sector, and the amount of food to which the subsidy is applied. The size of the subsidy depends on the source and price of the food available to governments and the desired consumer price levels. The wedge may be large, as illustrated by domestic consumer prices fixed by the government for wheat, sugar, and beans in Egypt, which were 28, 29, and 35 percent, respectively, of the international prices in 1980 (von Braun and de Haen 1983).

The size of the subsidy may change considerably over time, either to insulate domestic consumers from price fluctuations in the international markets or because of a widening gap between international and domestic price trends. Because of its traditionally large price fluctuations, the sugar market provides a good illustration of the former. Domestic sugar prices to Egyptian consumers varied from 22 percent of the international prices in 1974, to approximately parity in 1977, to 144 percent in 1978, and back to 29 percent in 1980. One of the principal reasons for a widening gap between international and domestic price trends in some countries is a desire to maintain constant or near-constant nominal prices for basic food staples in the face of increasing general price levels. It is reported that consumer prices of wheat and rationed sugar, rice, and lentils in Egypt were virtually unchanged in nominal terms during 1971-81. Unless the subsidized quantity is reduced, a larger publicly financed price wedge results in higher fiscal costs. If no targeting or rationing is attempted, costs may be high. The fiscal costs of the wheat subsidies in Egypt, which are neither targeted nor rationed, increased from E£ 21 million in 1970/71 to E£ 511 million in 1980/81, or the equivalent of 0.05 to 3.5 percent of GDP (Alderman, von Braun and Sakr 1982]). Rationing of the quantities subsidized without targeting does not assure low fiscal costs. Although smaller than those of the wheat subsidies, which are not rationed, the fiscal cost of subsidies on rationed foods in Egypt is high.

Large public expenditures on food subsidies may have significant macroeconomic effects. On the assumption that the explicit Egyptian food subsidy program is financed through deficit spending at the margin, that is, that changes in the fiscal costs of subsidies would be reflected in similar changes in deficit spending, it was estimated that a 10 percent change in subsidy expenditures would result in a change in the rate of inflation of 5 percent in the same direction. In other words, increasing subsidy costs would fuel inflation. They would also cause an increase in foreign liabilities and a devaluation of the free market exchange rate for Egyptian currency.

Import demand for food in Egypt was found to be very inelastic. This is in large measure caused by the subsidy program, the high priority on Food Subsidies maintaining stable and relatively low food prices for Egyptian consumers, and the government monopoly on food imports, which makes it easier for government to control imports. As a consequence, changes in either the price of imported food or the supply of foreign exchange are likely to be reflected primarily in the importation of industrial goods. It was estimated that a fall of one dollar in foreign exchange would reduce imports of food and other consumer goods by only sixteen cents, while imports of industrial raw material, fuel, and chemicals would fall by forty cents and capital goods by thirty-four cents. This has important implications for real output and investment in the industrial sector. The study estimates that a fall of 10 percent in foreign exchange supplies reduces real industrial output by 4 percent and investment by 6 percent. Similarly, a 10 percent rise in the cost of imported food will result in a fall of 1 to 2 percent in industrial output, as imports of raw materials are reduced to provide more foreign exchange for food imports.

Rapidly increasing fiscal costs occurred for the Sri Lankan food ration shop scheme through the first half of the 1970s, reaching Rs 1,000 million in 1975, or around 15 percent of total government expenditures. Changes in the subsidy program during the second half of the 1970s, including a shift to food stamps with a fixed nominal value, rapidly increasing food prices, and exclusion of about one-half of the population from the program reduced the fiscal costs of the Sri Lankan food subsidies dramatically to the current level of about 3.5 percent of total government expenditures. These reductions have been attained by targeting as well as drastic reduction in the real value of the subsidy to the poor target groups.

Targeted Food Price Subsidies

Because of the high fiscal costs of maintaining general food price subsidies, efforts have been and are currently being made to target food subsidies to groups of households expected to be particularly vulnerable to high and increasing food prices and to limit the subsidies to specific foods or rations. If the sole goal of food subsidies is to increase or sustain the ability of the poor to purchase enough food to meet nutritional requirements and other basic necessities, the goal could be reached and cost reduced by targeting, provided that it is politically and logistically feasible.

The cost-effectiveness of explicit subsidies, that is, the cost to government of improving the ability of food-deficient households to acquire a certain amount of food, is positively correlated with the degree of targeting up to a certain level. This is because targeting excludes some or all non-deficit households from the benefits of the subsidies. However, the administrative costs of operating a food price subsidy program go up as the degree of Per Pinstrup-Andersen targeting increases. Thus there is a point beyond which increases in administrative costs exceed savings from further reducing benefit leakages to non-deficit households.

Targeting implies restriction of eligibility or participation. It may imply rationing of the quantity of food that can be obtained under the subsidy program or it may limit subsidies to particular periods of the year, for example, to the months when seasonal fluctuations in food supplies or purchasing power are a major cause of malnutrition. Targeting may be based on other criteria, the most obvious of which would be household income, whether total or per person. While this is used as a criterion in certain programs, for example, Sri Lankan food stamp scheme, it is usually difficult, to obtain a reasonably accurate estimate of individual household incomes.

Another criterion relates to the location of outlets for subsidized foods: they may be placed in neighborhoods with a high proportion of poor households. A third approach used in a number of integrated health and nutrition programs—for example, the rural health clinics in Costa Rica and the recently terminated food stamp program in Colombia—is to select malnourished individuals at existing health clinics. Targeting may also result in cases where the customers desiring to purchase subsidized foods must wait in line for a long time. Whether intentional or merely a result of inefficient operation, a long wait may discourage participation by higher income groups. Of course, if the subsidy is sufficiently large, those with higher incomes may hire persons to wait in line for them.

Targeting can also be accomplished by offering lower-quality products that are considered undesirable by higher-income groups. Distribution of subsidized wheat flour perceived to be of low quality in ration shops in Pakistan is a case in point. In a study of wheat flour consumption in Rawalpindi City, Khan (1982) found that poor households purchased more than 30 kg/month of subsidized wheat flour from ration shops, compared with around 20 kg/month for the highest-income households. Purchase of non-subsidized wheat flour from the open market was about 16 kg /month for the poor and 58 kg/month for the highest-income group. A study for Bangladesh concluded that distribution of sorghum through the ration shops in Bangladesh would be more cost-effective than the distribution of rice and wheat because almost exclusively the poor would acquire sorghum.

Targeted or rationed food price subsidy programs may be implemented in various ways. Food may be distributed in public ration shops, as in India, Bangladesh, and Pakistan, through private shops, or through a combination of the two, as in Egypt. Target households may be issued ration cards that specify the amount of food that can be obtained under subsidy. Although food price subsidy policies have been implemented with reasonable success in many urban areas, their success has been limited in rural areas except for Egypt, Sri Lanka, and parts of India. Limited success in rural areas may be due to lack of rural infrastructure or government priorities.

Implementation of targeted food price with subsidy programs may be difficult. It is difficult to identify the target groups. As a result, a large proportion of the subsidized food may actually go to non-targeted households while administrative costs run high.

Obtaining food for a subsidy program presents difficult problems. These include the most appropriate way of procuring food domestically to avoid disincentives in production and negative effects on incomes of poor producers and the proper combination of foreign food aid, commercial imports, and domestic procurement. Frequently, certain commodities are available on concession-terms under foreign food aid programs. Use of these commodities would greatly reduce government costs of a subsidy program.

Furthermore, it might reduce the need for procurement from domestic producers at prices below the market. However, great care should be taken to avoid extensive use of food aid commodities that are not readily produced within the country. Consumer preferences may be generated that may be difficult to meet out of domestic production at a later time. The implications of heavy dependence on foreign food aid should be carefully considered in view of the uncertainty of future supplies of food under concession- terms.

Procurement schemes that include producer prices below market prices may be hard to enforce and may involve not only large administrative costs but also large economic costs and disincentives for the agricultural sector. Rice subsidies in Egypt provide an illustration. The greater part of the difference between consumer and producer /import prices for most foods is financed by the government, that is, the subsidy is mostly *explicit.* However, the rice subsidy is borne by the producers through depressed prices and is basically *implicit.* The low prices are enforced by a combination of forced procurement and export taxes. The procurement price varied from 11 percent of international prices in 1974, to 50 percent in 1972, to 42 percent in 1980. These variations reflected a relatively constant and low procurement price in the face of wide fluctuations in the international market. Losses to the producer sector were equal to about 20 percent of explicit food subsidies. However "because it is financed mainly by the farmers it does not appear in the government's accounts and the public awareness of it is small". Insufficient recognition by the government of the costs of implicit subsidies is a common problem, even when the cost is borne by the public sector. Unfortunately, it appears that revenues foregone by government generally receive much less attention than government expenditures in the deliberations about fiscal budgets and deficit spending.

Effectiveness of Subsidy Programs in Reaching the Poor

According to a number of studies, food subsidies have increased incomes and improved the nutritional status among the poor, particularly the urban poor. A study of the past Sri Lankan food ration shop scheme "indicates that the scheme contributed to a better standard of living among low income groups and a more even pattern of consumption throughout the society. At its peak, the ration subsidy contributed the equivalent of 16 percent of the purchasing power of low-income families in Sri Lanka". Research on food ration shops in Kerala, India, shows that about one-half of the total income of low-income families was accounted for by ration income. The researcher concludes "the removal of rationing would have a very serious impact on these low-income consumers" (George 1979). Kumar (1979) found that rations supplied the bulk of rice eaten by low-income groups and that the subsidy scheme "greatly improved the distribution of income." She further concludes that the "subsidy program was effective in raising nutrition and consumption levels of the poorest households and was more effective than other forms of direct resource transfers."

In a study of the food ration shop scheme in Bangladesh, Ahmed (1979) concludes that "rationing has aided the urban poor quite successfully since without it the consumption levels of the poorest 15 percent of the urban population would have been 15 to 25 percent lower in 1973-74 than they were. A strong urban bias was found in food subsidies in Bangladesh. Most of the poor people reside in rural areas, but two-thirds of the subsidized grains were distributed to urban areas." Yet the study concludes that expanding the rationing program in rural areas would be extremely expensive and would, if based on external food aid, cause strong downward pressures on domestic food prices and disincentives to domestic producers.

The Egyptian food subsidy policies accounts for 6 percent to 7 percent of average consumer incomes. Since the absolute value of the subsidy is virtually constant among income groups, the poor receive a much larger percentage of total income from subsidies than the rich. The poorest people account for 16 percent of the food subsidy. Contrary to common belief prior to the study, no urban bias was found for the food price policies as a whole. However, due to higher consumption of wheat bread in the urban areas, some urban bias was found in the explicit wheat subsidy. This bias was offset by a higher rural consumption of explicitly and implicitly subsidized wheat flour. The relative bias was less than the difference between rural and urban incomes, with the subsidies contributing 7 percent of rural and 6 percent of urban incomes. If other agricultural price distortions, such as the protection of animal production, are included, the rural sector received considerably larger net benefits.

Further insights into the short-run welfare and nutritional implications of food subsidies were provided by studies for Brazil, Sudan, and Mexico. In the Brazil study, it was found that a shift of existing explicit subsidies on wheat to rice would greatly enhance the impact on calorie consumption by calorie-deficient population groups without changing government outlays (Gray 1982). Similar analyses aimed at the estimation of the short-run nutritional effects of reducing or removing existing wheat subsidies among urban households in Sudan found that poor and calorie-deficient households would make relatively large adjustments in calorie consumption in response to changes in bread prices (Pinstrup-Andersen et al. 1983). Thus, a 50 percent increase in the bread price would increase calorie deficiencies among the poorest 12.5 percent of the population by about one-third. The decrease in real incomes would be positively correlated with income level if measured in absolute terms, and negatively if expressed in percent of current income level.

While the above studies used household food consumption as a proxy for nutritional impact, a study of the Mexican milk subsidies analyzed the impact of a subsidy program on individual household members (Kennedy 1983). Preliminary results indicate that, while the subsidy caused an increase in milk consumption by preschool children, their total calorie consumption did not increase. Thus it appears that the program caused commodity substitution in the diet of the children. Their protein intakes increased and their calorie intakes held constant. Furthermore, calorie intakes by other household members increased.

Alternative Measures

In addition to food price subsidies, tied or untied cash transfers and food transfers provide another set of policy measures by which governments may increase the purchasing power of the poor and compensate for losses in real incomes caused by higher general food prices. Untied cash transfers tend to be less palatable politically than transfers linked to food such as food stamps, targeted food price subsidies, or food supplementation schemes. Political resistance to programs directly aimed at reducing starvation and malnutrition is likely to be much less than to cash transfers, even when the former results in transfer of real income that is partially or fully interchangeable, as in most food stamp programs. Cash transfer programs are very difficult to implement, and the cost of control measures to avoid excessive leakage to non-target groups and fraud is likely to be high. Self-targeting, which may be possible if food subsidies are aimed at less desired foods, is not possible in cash transfers.

Another argument in favor of food-related transfers is that they contribute to substitution of food for nonfoods by reducing food prices relative to other commodity prices. However, food price subsidies and direct feeding schemes are frequently limited to quantities of food that are less than what would be purchased in the absence of subsidies. Thus food does not become cheaper at the margin.

There is some evidence that the marginal propensity to consume food is higher for real income originating from food subsidy programs or direct feeding schemes than from cash (Kumar 1978). The reason is probably to be found in differences in preferences of household members and the relationship between source of income and intra-household control of budget.

Finally, in comparing the pros and cons of cash vs. food transfer schemes, it should be recognized that food might be available from foreign aid at a cost to governments considerably below its market value, thus making food-related transfer less expensive. If food aid donors permit cash payment of the food aid, this advantage disappears.

Some countries have attempted to reduce leakages to non-target households and to focus more sharply on improved nutrition by supplementation of food or direct feeding of individuals deficient in calories and protein. These usually are children and pregnant and lactating women. School lunch programs and feeding of preschool children in health and nutrition clinics are examples of direct feeding. Such programs may assure that leakages to non-targeted households are small. However, intra-household leakages will still occur through adjustments in the allocation of food to target individuals. Households also may reduce food acquisition from other sources.

In a review of over two hundred reports of past food distribution programs for young children, Beaton and Ghassemi (1979) found that the net increase in food intake by the target recipients was 45-70 percent of the food distributed. Thus, leakage varled between one-half and one-third of the food provided. But such leakage benefited other household members through added real household income and possibly improved nutrition.

The leakage merely reflects household preferences regarding expenditure and consumption patterns. These programs have generally not improved the nutritional status of target individuals over and above the effect operating through transfer of real income to households except in cases where they were effectively integrated with nutrition education or primary health care. Furthermore, administrative costs tend to be large relative to other income transfer programs.

Other policy measures are available for increasing the ability of the poor to acquire food, such as food-for-work programs and policies aimed at reducing unit costs in food production and marketing.

In short, efforts to develop the most appropriate food price policies for a given country involve complex economic, social, and political considerations. Considerations of their impact on consumers were the focus of this chapter. The remarks are as follows:

Changes in food prices have important implications for low-income urban and certain groups of rural consumers. Failure to consider these in efforts to provide incentive pricing to farmers may result in severe hardships for the poor, at least in the short run. The political reactions may be untenable for the government unless compensatory measures are introduced.

Before such measures are designed it is important to clarify which consumer groups the government wishes to compensate and whether such compensation will meet welfare goals as well as dissipate political opposition. Opposition to food price increases may not be most effectively expressed by those most adversely affected.

Depending on the extent to which food price changes are reflected in wages, the benefits of consumer food price subsidies may be passed on to employers in the form of lower wage rates. In some cases, food price subsidies are closely linked with public sector wage levels, and removal of the subsidies is likely to result in equal or close to equal wage increases.

General food price subsidies may be very costly either for the government, in the case of explicit subsidies, or for the agricultural sector, in the case of implicit subsidies. Irrespective of the source of financing, food subsidies are likely to have implications for economic growth.

A move away from general to targeted food price subsidies may greatly reduce both fiscal and economic costs without reducing the effectiveness of the subsidy to reach welfare goals, provided the target households can be identified. Identifying households below a specified income level is one of the most challenging and difficult tasks facing governments in efforts to improve the cost-effectiveness of subsidy programs.

In addition to targeted food price subsidies, a number of alternative measures are available to governments for alleviating hardships experienced by poor consumers due to high or increased food prices. These measures include tied or untied cash transfers as well as food transfers and food-for-work programs.

The focus on subsidies and transfer programs in this chapter should not be interpreted to imply that they are necessarily the most effective way of dealing with the conflict between high producer and low consumer prices of food. Long-term self-sustaining solutions should be sought in policies and development strategies, which generate and expand the income-earning capacities of the poor while improving the efficiency and reducing the unit costs of food production and marketing. However, for a long time to come, consumer subsidies and/or transfer programs will be needed in many developing countries to achieve welfare goals.

Fulfilling the Promise

The announcement in the budget of providing fertilizer and fuel subsides through cash transfer, if successfully implemented, can effectively reach the poor and reduce the burden of subsidies. There are, however, skeptics who question if this can be effectively implemented. The old-age pension and widows' pension schemes that involve cash transfer are, according to some, the least effective schemes in reaching the intended beneficiaries. Also, questions are raised whether cash transfer can work when many poor are illiterate and do not have bank accounts. It is also suggested that cash would be easier to siphon off. These are misplaced concerns.

Often when a new policy or measure is suggested, people point out all that can go wrong and say it is not perfect. However, the question that should be asked is whether it is substantially better than present policy or not.

Let's look at how the present policy performs. A number of studies have shown that between one third to half of kerosene supplied through the public distribution system (PDS) gets diverted to adulterate diesel and does not reach the intended persons. Also, as per the National Sample Survey data for 2004-05, among rural households that get any kerosene from PDS, the bottom 90 percent of the households get around three litres per household per month. Some 25 percent of the rural households in all docile groups do not get any kerosene at all. Thus, 25 percent of the poor are excluded and nearly 75 percent of the rich are included. If we consider that 50 percent are poor, then only half of the 66 percent kerosene distributed through PDS reaches the poor. Thus, the poor today get only 33 percent of the subsidy expenditure by the government.

If all the poor households were to get kerosene - five litres instead of three - it would require around 75 percent of the kerosene that is currently supplied to the PDS system. The subsidy burden of kerosene would come down by 25 percent.

An effective targeting scheme, which is the key to this, can be based on Aadhaar, the Unique ID Card. Aadhaar is a smart card that carries finger prints and iris scan data. A person with the card can go to a shop and put his fingers on a small device that transmits the data to the Aadhaar computer system, which confirms within five seconds if the person is the same one as the card holder. It is thus not possible for anyone else to claim the entitlement associated with the card. The cards can be charged with their entitlement. The poor can go to any shop, buy kerosene at market price, pay the ration price in cash and the difference between market price and ration price is electronically transferred from the government's account to the trader's account. This way, there will be only one price of kerosene in the market and traders will have no incentive to divert it. Direct cash transfer would require a bank account for each family, while what is proposed here, just giving the entitlement through Aadhaar card, does not.

The key element in the scheme's success is identification of the poor. How do we ensure that this is done correctly? If the poor are identified in an open village meeting, the errors of exclusion of the poor as well as erroneous inclusion of the rich can be minimized.

Can illiterate persons manage smart cards? Illiterate does not mean dumb. People manage their ration cards even today. A smart card is no different. Also, by now families without at least one literate person would be very few.

Finally, should kerosene or LPG subsidy be given as entitlement or as cash transfer that the consumer is free to use for anything? LPG is a clean cooking fuel and is a merit good that we want everybody to use. Cooking with firewood and dung causes indoor air pollution with significant adverse impact on health. The social cost of it has been estimated to be much more than the cost of subsidizing LPG for the poor. When cash is provided, the poor may not spend it on LPG, especially if a man - rather than a woman - takes the decision on spending in the household as the burden of smoke from firewood is largely borne by women. In such a case, it is better to provide subsidy as an entitlement rather than as cash. One can argue that even when given as entitlement, the poor can sell it and convert it into cash. While this is possible, it would involve a transaction cost which would discourage people from selling it. If cash is to be given, it should at least be given to the woman of the household.

Thus, the announcement by the finance minister in the budget to give subsidy for kerosene, LPG and fertilizer in the form of cash transfer is to be welcomed if it is based on a mechanism that leads to effective targeting, empowers women and eliminates dual pricing. I prefer entitlement to cash transfer at least for merit goods where there are externalities. We are generally averse to experimenting with new solutions. Why not implement this for Aadhaar card holders (a card for poor people) and test whether they are better off than ration card holders? In two to three years, we could be ready to implement a superior scheme nationally.[69]

Power to the People

There has been a change of guard at the power ministry and Jyotiraditya Scindia, the new man in charge, has described his task as daunting. To simplify the many complexities, it's worth keeping in mind an adage that's particularly apt for rural India: Nothing is more expensive than no power.

---

[69]Kirit S Parikh (2011), " Fulfilling the Promise", The Times of India, Bhubaneswar, March 9, 2011, P 16

While on one hand there are thousands of villages that still remain to be electrified, on the other even the ones that have been electrified, get power for a mere four to five hours per day, and that too mostly at night time.

The stark reality is that due to the short-sightedness of our policymakers and the political class, we are unable to mobilize the national consensus needed to do away with subsidized power to the agricultural sector. The decision-makers fail to realize that more than subsidies; it is round-the-clock and quality power supply that holds the potential to completely transform life in rural India.

It is worthwhile to mention here that agriculture, which accounts for over 25 percent of the electricity consumption, contributes to a mere 5 percent of the revenue. Inadequate tariffs on one hand and high technical and commercial losses on the other have completely destroyed the financial health of all state utilities.

Aggregate loss in the year 2012 is estimated at a whopping 1.2 trillion INR (1.5 percent of GDP). This poor financial health has resulted in inadequate investment in the entire generation, transmission, distribution value chain - which in turn has impacted the overall quality and reliability of the supply.

Recent back-to-back grid failures leading to a complete blackout of the entire northern half of the country, affecting over 600 million people, is as much due to lack of investment in capacity-building and modernization as it is due to excess drawls by the states. And very often, we find that cash constrained state electricity boards prefer selling power outside the state to paying customers rather than supply to non-paying farmers.

While it is laudable that the government is investing huge amounts in electrifying villages under the Rajiv Gandhi Village Electrification Plan, the question is: Are the financially distressed distribution utilities in a position to supply power to these villages at zero net realization after accounting for cash expenses? With the average cost of supply at over 5 INR per unit, every 10 percent increase in agricultural supply will add 75 billion INR (Indian rupees) to the deficit.

Where will it come from? With the combined (central/state) budget deficit in the region of 9 percent of GDP, the government's hands too are tied; clearly, it is not in a position to fund any subsidy, or for that matter, loss.

It is time that we take cognizance of the fact that this subsidy does not help anyone. First and foremost, instead of four to five hours of subsidized power every day, our farmers need round-the-clock quality supply, even if it comes at a higher cost. This need is evidenced not only in high demand for power from micro-generating units selling to clusters of villages at over Rs 6 per unit, but also in our rural folks often using diesel generator sets, which cost a staggering 14 INR per unit. Besides, low and fluctuating voltage combined with imbalances in three-phase supply not only significantly reduces operating efficiency of pumps but also leads to frequent motor burnout.

It is surprising that in this 21stcentury world of science and technological advancements, rural India is still starved of basic necessities like electricity and roads. It is even more surprising that our planners and policymakers have failed to realize this. They also need to realize that free or subsidized power encourages excessive and wasteful use of pumps and has led to rapid depletion of water tables, jeopardizing the future cultivability of vast tracts of land. This is a serious issue that needs urgent attention. Affordable power can be better achieved by removing the bottlenecks in domestic coal production. This can be done by either improving Coal India's productivity or involving private players in coal production. By following these methods, allowing us to do away with costly coal imports, power costs can be brought down by over 25% on an average from current levels. Further, affordable power in the medium term will also come from AT&C loss (theft) reduction initiatives. It is unfortunate that the slogan 'Free power to farmers' has ended up as 'No power to farmers'. There is no debating the fact that round-the-clock power availability in rural pockets will transform our villages and will be the single most important step towards enabling inclusive growth, a concept very dear to all of us. There is urgent need to evolve national consensus in this direction within the political class and among policymakers.[70]

Conclusion

Food price subsidy (rice or wheat), government-sponsored programs like food for work, free midday meals in schools and fair price shops create problems than solutions. Government announces different pro-poor programs to attract people's support. But these programs encourage corruption at all levels. Most of the programs are limited to government files only. It creates 'no work culture' and it is detrimental to the economy of the country.

For example, government of India is implementing subsidy in kerosene, petrol, rice and wheat. People do not produce kerosene and petrol, so there is some justification in subsidy in these two essential commodities. But subsidy in petrol helps only to the rich, who owns vehicle. Subsidy in diesel helps to all members of the society in varying proportions

[70]Lalit Jalan (2012), " Power to People" Times of India, October 31, 2012

because it is necessary for buses and trucks, which carries passengers and goods. But subsidy in rice and wheat would dislocate the entire agricultural economy of the country. The farm labourer's wage has been increased and the availability of cheap rice and wheat has been increased. As a result, agricultural labourers are not available for agricultural operations. Rice and wheat is sold in Fair Prices Shops at the rate of 2 INR per kilogram and labour charge is 200 INR per day. So with one day's labour, a labourer is able to meet enough rice and wheat to meet the requirement for a month. The government also spends huge subsidy on production, storage, transportation and distribution of cereals, but fixes procurement prices less than the cost of production of cereals.

Who would produce cereals, if farmers bear loss in agriculture? Why the government would force the peasants and sharecroppers to sell paddy or wheat at prices fixed by the government? Why the government procures cereals from other countries on reduced prices? Why the government exports onion when there is scarcity of onion in the local market? Why the government offers subsidy to fertilizer companies to reduce the prices of fertilizer? Why the government offers subsidy for purchase of power tiller? The government awards subsidies in seeds and insecticides to companies. So it results in corruption in inputs, outputs, storage, and management.

It would be better if the government announces higher prices for grains to encourage the farmers to earn profit in agriculture? It should be fixed on parity prices or Index number with a base period, (say 1961 or 1971, or 2001 and so on). The argument is that the price is / was fixed by market mechanism always. Because the availability and price of cereals need to be uniform for most part of the year, the government declares price for a year. The government would also purchase rice and wheat for that year as buffer stock to control market mechanism. The government should also dispose of all stocks before the new arrivals to the market. The market would determine the availability and prices of rice and wheat. There should not be any subsidy in agriculture. If there is no subsidy, corruption could be controlled or stopped in agriculture.

Market forces should determine open market prices of cereals; subsidized sale of cereals should be stopped and subsidies to all institutions must be scrapped to make agriculture competitive and profitable. The quantum of money spent by the government for agricultural purposes should be paid to the vulnerable people, such as farmers, peasants, share-croppers, agricultural labourers, widows and poor people through bank accounts as pension, insurance policies and natural disaster policies. If farmers get profit in agriculture, food security is possible without assistance of new institutions or foreign governments.

Subsidies in agriculture should be scrapped, but the government must fix procurement prices of rice and wheat to procure some quantities of rice and wheat for emergency purposes. The procurement prices should be based on parity prices or index number with a base period. If general price trend increases by 10 percent per year, the price of cereals is increased by 10 percent. The volume of money circulation in the country must be taken into account to fix agricultural prices, at least for rice and wheat.

We find that the government continuously keeps price of rice or wheat at the lowest bottom to gain popularity among the people. But this attitude of the governments has created uproar among the farmers in all countries. Now the farmers, which were peace-loving people in all countries, are turning to be violent. It is time to award justice to them. The government should find the following variables in a country in a year /month during a Base Period, say

1961 or 1971 (or a long period of time) and the current price (2011 price). Then it could be easily calculated what should be the present procurement price of rice or wheat. These are:

(a) Pay + DA of an employee in Government service per month,
(b) Price of gold per 10 grams
(c) Procurement price of rice or wheat per Quintal

If the pay+ DA of a Government employee' increases by (X) times and gold prices increase by (Y) times during 1961–2011, procurement prices of rice or wheat should be increased by (X + Y)/2 times (of both the variables). It is not being practiced because of political reasons. And, farmers are committing suicides each year.

The agricultural markets are not developed and are managed by corrupt administrators; there is no space for storage of paddy (un-husked Rice) or Wheat during post harvest season. The traders' associations generally make whimsical decisions to stop trading to control market prices.

The government should try that agricultural labourers should stick to farming. As agriculture has become a loss bearing profession; even farmers feel suffocated in farming. The government cannot allow all rural youths to settle in towns and cities. So farming should be a profit generating profession that could employ all youths living in rural areas.

It is time to think for these real peace workers (farmers), which are working for us throughout their life without justice or honour. They are hungry but they are loyal to the government and the country. If vast majority of people was food secured and lives in peace, the country would boast that the government is of the people, by the people and for the people. And there prevails peace in the country.

Chapter V

FARMERS' ORGANIZATIONS

Agriculture is highly labour-intensive enterprise in all the developing countries. About 80 percent of farmers are small farmers or peasants with less than 2 hectares of land. They are satisfied that they are the owners of land and they are able to meet their daily needs through farming. But they do not consider that most parts of farm income is derived because of family labour, bullock power, utilization of own land, own capital, family management, compost and farm yard manure and farmer's own labour that are utilized in raising crops. Moreover, he stores the grains in his house till it is disposed off. They are happy to see bumper crop, better yield, but the saleable grains never get remunerative prices. The bureaucracy, the trade practices of traders, state laws, and political party's populist measures are acting as barriers to their profit and happiness.

The governments of developing countries are wedded to announce daily some favors to the hungry and poor people to strengthen their political mileage. But these governments have made the farmers poor and alms–hungry people. The governments award them subsidies in fertilizer, seeds, pesticides, power tillers, free farm kits, low-interest bank loan, and construct village roads, ponds and allow their children for free mid-day meals, free school books, free dresses for all pupils and false consolation to improve their livelihood capacity. The political parties assist them with free non-vegetarian meals during election days,

But the farmers commit suicides; they do not get the rights over the land, which they cultivate. They do not get the right prices of their saleable commodities. Let us consider the example of India with some questions?

(a)Why the government would sell rice or wheat at 2 or 3 INR (Indian rupees) per kilo? Is it for the benefit of the farmers, which constitutes more than 60 percent of population in country?

(b)Does the government award right prices and parity prices for paddy (rice + husk) or wheat, cotton, or sugarcane or pulses?

(c)Why the government procures food grains or oil from other countries, which could be made available in the country itself?

(d)Has the government studied the cost of cultivation of cereals, fruits or pulses in the government or university or research farms?

(e)Why the governments of low-income countries or heavily populated countries are more interested for industrialization of the country without the consent of poor and hungry people residing countryside?

(f)Why the government undertakes eviction of tribal people, farmers, poor and landless people for gifting the vast acreage of fertile land to the industrialists?
(g)Why the government allows subsidy to the industrialists, government institutions, and financial institutions for development and increase of agricultural production?

(h)Why the government borrows millions of dollars for construction of buildings, roads, and institutions for a long-term of 40 – 50 years?

(i)Why agriculture budget accounts for less than 3 percent of budget when farmers constitute more than 60 percent of population in all developing countries?

Irrigation is a factor of production in agriculture along with a number of other factors like ownership of land, quality of land, family labour, availability of hired labour, seeds, fertilizers, manures, pesticides, technical know-how, management, risk and uncertainty, climate, rainfall, choice of crop and price behaviour in markets, government procurement policy, import-export policy and so on. But irrigation expenditure is always more than all factors combined. Why it is so? It is because corruption is deep-rooted among the engineers and politicians. It is because the engineers have the capacity to revise the budgets each year for the same project even for 25 times as in a project of Keonjar district. It is because corruption through foreign funding and construction work could escape audits easily as everyone in administration could be purchased. In Orissa state (India), there are 150 engineering colleges but there are only two agriculture colleges. And each week witnesses a farmer commits suicide for crop loss and inability to pay crop loan.

All governments know fully-well that people's memory is short-lived and the farmers, peasants and the poor could be purchased at least during the election process. So the time has come that the farmers of each country should be united to demand for justice for them and to guide the government to follow the right path of governance. The farmers should be a part of the policy-making bodies, governance, and evaluation committees.

Need for Farmers' Organization

Rashid Pertey has analyzed the need for 'Farmers' Organization' in all farm communities.

Fundamental Concepts: when farmers are not strong, many political people are ready not only to tell the farmers what they should do, but even worse, to speak on their behalf. Most ministries, political parties, associations, promotional, non-governmental organizations as well as development agencies and even experts have indeed committed this sin. Indeed, many a political party has set up campaign sub-committees to get farmers' votes. Many a non-governmental organization, from the north or the south, but with no mandate from farmers, have stood up in international meetings to voice, in often fascinating detail, the farmers' plight. The farmers only grumble and non-farmers speak on their behalf. When they speak; they speak of a 'problem'. It is because these NGOs get schemes from the international organizations through convincing the donors, but they simply grab the funds for their private gains.

Irrespective of its desirability, the lack of an effective farmers' voice is indeed an impediment to agricultural and rural development. Whether it is the development of agriculture or of rural society or the protection of environment, farmers play a vital role. A two-way dialogue therefore needs to be established between farmers, and other actors, which determine the political, economic, and legal as well as technological framework within which farmers operate.

In short, an effective farmers' voice is not only the basis of mutual respect and democracy, but it is also the true basis for agricultural and rural development.

Importance of Farmers' Organizations:

Farmers' voice cannot be obtained without farmers' organizations. In the world, for instance, there are hundreds of millions of farmers. To engage in any sensible dialogue with the rest of society, farmers need their representative organizations, the farmers' organizations, structured from grassroots to the international level, as their legitimate voice. This is why farmers' movement gives a lot of importance to farmers' organizations as an important pillar of today's society.

Farmers' Organizations and the Non-Governmental Sector: For many decades, farmers' organizations have made persistent calls to underline the importance of nongovernmental organizations and the importance of their participation in the process of development. Now this principle is widely accepted and applled. In this context, farmers' organizations should strongly maintain that the time is ripe for making the difference between farmers' organizations and NGOs. The farmers should assume the responsibility of 'Farmers Organization'.

Structures of Farmers' Organization:

In January 1992, the Mediterranean farmers' organizations have set up an IFAP Committee of Mediterranean Farmers to provide them with an opportunity to meet and cooperate as partners in order to promote the economic and social condition of farmers. The objectives of the Committee include: Establishing and strengthening ties between farmers and various research and development bodies in the region, The Committee also aims at the provision of information and encouragement of actions in the field of technical or economic co-operation among farmers' organizations, including in the area of training and extension. During its Cairo Session last April, the Committee confirmed its objectives with regard to the solution of Mediterranean agricultural problems as a whole, particularly through productive diversification, qualitative improvements, more judicious use of water resources and closer collaboration with research activities.

The Committee also underlined its objective of changing the existing relations in the fields of agriculture and research. Particularly, agriculture should not merely be the target of scientific, economic and technological choices adopted within the confines of research institutions but should ensure that research can comply more adequately with its productive and qualitative requirements so as to protect farmers' incomes more effectively. The IFAP African Regional Committee launched an important initiative of strengthening links between farmers and researchers in November 1991, when the Committee had its First African Farmers – Researchers Consultative Conference at Ibadan, Nigeria.[71]

International Federation of Agricultural Producers (IFAP) is a world organization of farmers, grouping together 82 national level farmers' organizations from 57 countries, representing over 500 million family farmers.

---

[71]Note: The Nairobi Regional Working Session followed this initiative between African NARS and African farmers' organizations in December 1992. It caused to the recent IRRI-IFAP Consultation in Los Baños, Philippines, in October 1993.

Hence, farmers' organizations would be benefited as follows:

(a) Research, Extension and Farmers: The importance of establishing a triangular (and not a linear) relationship between farmers, extension specialists and researchers;
(b) That this triangular relationship be repeated at all levels, from the local level to the international level.
(c) The objectives of Farmers' organization could be fulfilled only through the active involvement of the farmers.

Now, there is renewed consensus on the need to support smallholder farmers in their efforts to overcome poverty, cope with climate change and contribute to mitigating its effects. Stronger organizations of smallholder farmers, fishers and pastoralists are essential if we are to seize the opportunities that arise from today's challenges. Rural producers have stronger bargaining power when they unite and work together to achieve a common goal to influence policies and development programs.

There will be no effective response to the challenges of food security for all, eradication of extreme poverty and mitigation of climate change without more and better investment in their farms and more supportive policies for rural development.

Investment in agriculture is essential to make farming profitable for the young women and men in the fields of developing countries who will feed the world tomorrow.

National governments, development partners and the private sector must join hands in building their capacities, in providing them with the technologies they need, the rural infrastructures, the financial institutions, the market information and linkages that are essential ingredients of the transformation from subsistence to small agro-business entrepreneurs. Invest in rural youth today who are farmers of tomorrow.

In short, IFAP suggests, there should farmers' organizations that would establish coordination with the researchers and agricultural scientists for development in agriculture. These organizations should join hands with international partners, and funding partners.[72]

Attending seminars by few influential and educated people would not produce any result at the farm level. The farmers would be benefited provided there is pressure on the government to make agriculture a profitable venture. This is possible by the State Farmers' Organization.

Foreign funding in agriculture would cause cancerous growth in state budget, but it won't assist the peasants and might increase number of farmers' suicides.[73]

Sustainable Agriculture and Rural Development:
Policy Briefs on Farmers' Organizations

Farmers' Organizations (FOs) are essential institutions for the empowerment, poverty alleviation and advancement of farmers and the rural poor. Governments and development agencies can create more appropriate and sustainable agriculture and rural development policies and programmes, to identify and benefit small and poor farmers more

---

[72]IFAD/16/2010; Press Release

[73]Rashid Pertey, "The Role of Farmers and Farmers' Organizations, Mediterranean Committee of the International Federation of Agricultural Producers (IFAP), Paris (France)

effectively, by working with, supporting and involving FOs in the planning, design and implementation of agricultural and rural policies and programs, and by supporting them in implementing farmers' own agendas.

In rural areas, farmers' organizations (FOs) are the nearest and often only institutions providing essential goods and services to the rural poor and helping them break from the poverty cycle.

Small farmers' income tends to fluctuate seasonally and this can easily tip them into poverty. By providing financial services, Farmers' organizations reduce the risk of individual farmers, which face during seasonal shocks. Farmers Organizations also help mobilize capital and contribute to the growth of the local economy.

Although figures are hard to come by, one type of farmers' organization provides an estimate of scale: globally there were about 569 000 agricultural cooperatives in 2002, with more than 800 million farmer members, making it the largest cooperative sector in the world. In 1994 agricultural cooperatives in Canada and in Brazil each produced an output of US $12 billion, whilst China and India's agricultural cooperatives each generated an output of US $9 billion.

A number of governments and regions, such as Mali and Mercosur, have already adopted processes of consultation with Farmers' organizations resulting in new policies and legislative frameworks.

Duties of Farmers' Organizations:

1. A range of agricultural and rural services in developing countries, including supply of inputs, transportation and marketing of agricultural goods as well as research and extension were provided by the

public sector; many were privatized under Structural Adjustment Programs (SAPs). However, in several countries the private sector did not replace public provision, and where it did, it often did not reach the poor. FOs can be effective alternatives where private and public provisions of agricultural services have failed, but they require support and freedom to operate.

2. Mainstream agricultural research and development does not benefit from the full participation of farmers. Limited dialogue with individual farmers exists at the field level, but there are too few institutional mechanisms for farmers to be included at higher levels of decision-making. FOs can be an effective channel to communicate farmers' needs and priorities to higher levels in national and international research bodies.

3. Individual small farmers are weak players in the market, by organizing into larger groups and FOs, they can increase their bargaining power, reduce their transaction costs for accessing inputs and transportation, facilitate processing and marketing of agricultural products, thereby enhancing their earnings.

4. As conventional financial institutions rarely reach small farmers, they often turn to moneylenders who offer a limited range of financial services, the cost of which may be high. Farmer Organizations (FOs) can play an instrumental role in reducing the cost of financial services to small farmers, either by providing credit and loans, offering insurance and a safe place for savings, or by linking farmers to the formal financial sector.

5. Farmers' opinions, needs and suggestions are not sufficiently heard nor taken into account in national global policy and decision making processes related to world agricultural trade rules, poverty reduction

strategies and agricultural and rural development policies, all of which profoundly affect the livelihoods of millions of farmers. To define locally appropriate, democratic, pro-poor and sustainable policies programs and investments, FOs must be effectively included throughout these policy and program formulation processes.

The policy goals:

(a) Ensure farmers to join freely and participate democratically in the multiple forms of FOs that help them improve their livelihoods.
(b) Enact appropriate legislation and regulatory frameworks to ensure FOs enjoy the right and freedom to operate independently and manage them.
(c) Institutionalize mechanisms to effectively involve FOs in agricultural and rural policy making, implementation, and assessment as well as in agricultural research and development.
(d) Support the development and improvement of FOs through capacity-building assistance and financial services.

The policy issues:

(a)**Benefits of organization:** Organization is a tool for empowerment and equitable development. Through FOs, farmers can improve their political power as a group, increasing the likelihood that policy makers and the public hear their needs and opinions. There is a wide range of formal and informal FOs, most tend to be based on several, and in some cases all, of the cooperative principles. Cooperatives are one type of profit oriented FO that strive to meet common economic, social and cultural needs and aspirations through a jointly owned and democratically controlled enterprise. Informal organizations include self-help groups, committees and networks, among others. The size, function, organizational requirements and appropriate approaches for different FOs depend upon their objectives and needs at any given time. No single organizational model can address all the issues and capabilities small producers face. FOs developed through self-organization often demonstrates self-reliance and strong and lasting solidarity; although they are sometimes limited in scale and in the diversity of activities they can undertake. F Os that are supported by external parties are often easier for outsiders to work with because members can usually access more resources and carry out more activities. However, they are often less stable over time and run the risk of losing their focus on member priorities, as well as their autonomy and effectiveness.

(b)**Organization for marketing:** FOs can help farmers gain skills, access inputs, form enterprises, process and market their products more effectively to generate higher incomes. By organizing, farmers can access information needed to produce, add value, market their commodities and develop effective linkages with input agencies such as financial service providers, as well as output markets. FOs can achieve economies of scale, thereby lowering costs and facilitating the processing and marketing of agricultural commodities for individual farmers. Marketing-oriented FOs can assist their members purchase inputs, equipment, meet quality standards and manage the drying, storage, grading, cleaning, processing, packing, branding, collection and transportation of produce. In this way FOs provide a more reliable supply to buyers and sell larger quantities at higher prices. Organized farmers have greater bargaining power than individuals and are better able to negotiate with other more powerful market players to ultimately increase the profits that accrue to farmers rather than intermediaries and buyers.

(c) **Bias against the term 'cooperative':** In several developing countries, governments used to finance agricultural cooperatives to deliver essential agricultural services. Such cooperatives were important but they were quasi-government agencies that controlled rather than empowered farmers. They were neither ruled nor managed by farmers, were sometimes misused and often benefited the middle class and not the rural poor. As a result, the term cooperative acquired a negative connotation.

(d)**Difficulty combining member control and competitiveness:** Remaining member -owned and member-run, retaining their democratic identity and keeping touch with their members and local roots is sometimes a challenge for FOs, including cooperatives that are striving to be economically viable and competitive. Nevertheless, doing so is critical if the poorest members are to be included and market power concentration prevented. Instead of opening up to external investment and becoming hybrid businesses, FOs need to ensure that some funding comes from member contributions and income generating activities, as these stimulate commitment and guarantee financial independence and autonomy. Developing synergies through networks, partnerships and federations at the local, national, regional and international levels can strengthen both member control and competitiveness, for example through computerization, internet and other information technologies.

(e)**Farmers' and rural producers' organizations**: Farmers' and rural producers' organizations (FOs) refer to independent, non-governmental, membership-based rural organizations of part or fulltime self-employed smallholders and family farmers, pastoralists, artisans fishers, landless people, women, small entrepreneurs and indigenous peoples. They range from formal groups covered by national legislation, such as cooperatives and national farmers unions, to looser self-help groupings and associations.

(f)**Elite capture in farmers' organizations**: Large farmers' organizations and federations, which have links to government and industry, have the ability to influence policymaking. However, such organizations are often dominated by the interests of a few, large, powerful farmers. Small producers, family farmers and women farmers are sometimes excluded from such organizations, because of expensive membership fees and other reasons. Even when they are members, their needs and interests are often sidelined and not fully represented by the organizations' leaders, who are usually men, better educated, wealthier, and more able to advocate for the larger farmers in their constituency. Therefore, governments and development agencies should identify or create spaces in which representatives of small farmers' and women's organizations can directly represent their own needs and perspectives, so that these are taken into account and addressed more effectively in agricultural and rural policy making.

What are the policy options?

Freedom of association: In recognition of Article 20 of the Universal Declaration of Human Rights, which states that everyone has the right to freedom of peaceful assembly and association, as well as the ILO Conventions 87 and 88 on freedom of association, the right to organize and collective bargaining, all governments should recognize by law the right of farmers to organize and act collectively. This includes ensuring companies, corporations and competition laws do not limit the freedom of association of farmer workers. When the civil and political rights of farmers are violated, the legal system should effectively enforce their rights and protect and defend farmers.

Favourable legislation: In several countries legal and regulatory frameworks place barriers to the free and efficient operation of FOs through complicated administrative and bureaucratic procedures. FOs often lack support and recognition or are discriminated against and excluded by the government and powerful elements in society. ILO's Recommendation 193 provides advice on the formulation of a supportive legal and regulatory framework for the promotion of cooperatives, which includes simplifying administrative procedures and allowing easy, affordable and rapid registration, decentralizing administrative and legal procedures to regional or local levels, facilitating the development of autonomous financial services, and gathering statistics and disseminating information on the cooperative movement. These recommendations are also applicable to other forms of FOs. Countries with restrictive, intrusive or discriminatory regulations on FOs, including cooperatives, should review and modify them. Governments and civil servants must recognize the full operational autonomy and private nature of FOs and acknowledge their positive contributions to rural and national development. Mechanisms must be institutionalized at all levels of government for the inclusion and participation of FOs in agricultural, rural development, and agrarian reform policies and programmes.

Capacity building: Development agencies, governments, employers, and workers, as well as cooperative organizations can assist FOs with capacity-building efforts to train their members and representatives in business skills, accounting and financial administration, information technology, planning and management as well as organizational leadership to represent their FOs in various policy forums. Training could tackle other areas needing improvement including transparency, democracy and accountability. Funds could be provided for this purpose, but the identification of training needs and the farmer- members themselves must do definition of the training program's content.

Provision of financial services: Often FOs aim to provide financial services to their members such as credit, loans, insurance and savings. Any development assistance or government project extending financial services to the rural poor must first analyze and understand the local formal and informal lending institutions that have been established by the poor themselves. These organizations have an expert knowledge of seasonal cash needs and are based on trust and reciprocity, often using reputation as a form of collateral and achieving good repayment rates and low default numbers. FOs can link with local financial service providers and thereby reduce their operational burden of maintaining loan and repayment records and managing risks of the loan portfolio. New financial services must not affect or undermine the functioning of local financial organizations and instead must work with and improve them to extend their reach.

Agricultural research and development: Improved linkages and coordination between farmers, via FOs, agricultural research agencies and extension services are needed at all levels and not only at the farm level. This can be facilitated through periodic consultations among these key stakeholders. FOs should participate in planning meetings and, where possible, serve on the boards of research agencies to have a greater say in the research agenda and to ensure that trials are designed to address the needs of small-scale farmers. Knowledge, information and technologies can reach farmers at the grassroots level more effectively if agricultural research and extension institutions proactively involve FOs.[74]

---

[74]Sustainable Agriculture and Rural Development Policy Briefs on Farmers' Organizations (2007) - This report was

Basic Principles of Farmers' Organization

Farmers' Associations or organization should be governed by the following basic principles:

(a)Professionalism: that is, only agricultural producers, such as livestock farmers, foresters, fishermen, etc. can be represented by these organizations

(b)Universality: anyone or any organization with a legal status satisfying the criteria set forth by statutes on agricultural producers is automatically a member of the association.

(c)Representation of all categories of farmers: each category of farmers in the different production systems must be represented and can express its point of view, to be taken into account in analyzing problems and agricultural policy proposals. This principle leads to the establishment of colleges corresponding to categories of farmers. You might have a college for women for example, for shepherds or for any other category.

(d)Autonomy: the freedom of farmers' associations to choose their development goals, their action programs, and the management of their resources, without external interference.

(e)Decentralization: the whole system of representation and decision-making process must come from below. This decentralization is the necessary condition for the effective participation of farmers and for the consideration of local realities. The decentralization of farmers' associations does not mean they should be dispersed. The institutional set-up for representation should be conceived as a set of

---

prepared by Sofia Naranjo with members of FAO, roppa, Agricore, ILO and IFAD

decentralized structures, a national network, which facilitates exchanges and cooperation between them and reinforces the whole system of representation vis-à-vis public and private partners.

(f)Incompatibility between representation mission and commercial activity: farmers' associations should in no circumstances carry out commercial transactions with member farmers.

Functions of Farmers' Associations:

The basic mission of farmers' associations is to represent farmers, in order to ensure their participation in the formulation and implementation of policies and agricultural development actions. The accomplishment of this mission is based on three principal functions:

(a) Consultation
(b) Information and training of farmers
(c) Support for professional organization of farmers

Although recognized by law as the official interlocutors of the government, farmers associations do not have a monopoly of this function; other actors can carry out these functions. The role of farmers' associations in this case is to facilitate dialogue between all those who exercise these functions on behalf of farmers.

Consultation Function

Consultation consists of, on the one hand, communicating farmers' view of their situation and that of the agricultural sector, and on the other, participating in the formulation of agricultural policy and the options to be considered in rural development.

This function is exercised first in relation to the state: it is to inform the government of the situation of different categories of farmers, of their assessment of economic measures taken by the government. It should give farmers' associations the right to sit in all decision-making bodies examining agricultural questions, from the local to the national level. It should also make it compulsory to consult them before making any decision on equipment, programs, land development, and industry location, in order to protect farming land and natural resources. To properly exercise this function, farmers' associations should have the capacity to have:

(a) Obtain up-to-date information on production channels, the different categories of farmers, and to analyze the micro and macroeconomic factors which determine their activities;
(b) Formulate, with the participation of farmers, proposals to improve the condition of different categories of farmers, and production channels;
(c) Communicate and assert the point of view and proposals of farmers in all bodies and at all levels, to the government and its partners in other professions.

Information Function

The information function of farmers' associations is directed to three types of public, the aim being to facilitate the integration of farmers into markets, the improvement of the quality of life of rural areas, and to ensure a better balance between towns and the countryside.

In this spirit, it is aimed first of all at farmers, to enable them to direct their activities according the requirements of markets, and adapt them to the current economic and regulatory context. At the same time it must be able to aid farmers to improve their managerial and organizational capacity (to make better production and investment choices), and to make them more competitive on the market. It must also improve the know-how of farmers beyond training provided by specialized institutions. To this end, farmers' associations should have data banks on agro-climatic, economic, technical, commercial, and regulatory conditions, constantly updated and easily accessible to farmers and technicians who advise them. Their contents must relate to local agricultural activity and must be widely disseminated, using all the verbal, written and audiovisual means currently available, and communicated in a way that responds to the requirements of each category of farmers.

On a broader level, the information function is aimed at rural populations, through the most accessible media for them. Rural radio stations should be launched, which farmers' associations should launch and manage with the participation of different groups, adapting programs to each group's specificity.

It is also aimed at the government, and economic partners of farmers in the public and private sectors, and especially professional organizations of other sectors, like the Chamber of Commerce, and Artisan Associations. The objective is to inform them about the condition of the rural sector, about its problems and priorities, on its wishes and proposals, so that they can take actions favorable to the agricultural sector. This type of information is meant to facilitate the integration of agricultural activities with those of other economic sectors, and a better balance between towns and rural areas. For this purpose, all existing media must be used, with priority given to inter-professional informational and consultation meetings, and to meetings devoted to the study of topical issues in agriculture.

Professional Organization of Farmers:
Support Function

It is incumbent on farmers to create their organizations themselves, and to contribute thus to the professionalism of agriculture, the basis for their participation in development and perfect integration into the market economy.

It is recognized that professional farmers' organizations are important civil society actors and that their development contributes toward it's strengthening. On this basis, they acquire an important role in the privatization process by providing institutional formulae, which are decentralized and adapted to the specificity of the agricultural milieu, and which require the participation of farmers.

The Farmers' Organizations should follow and analyze the situation of agricultural organizations, and propose political and legislative measures in favor of the development of their activities. It also gets them the advice they need by mobilizing the necessary support from existing public and private institutions. This function and the information and training function go hand in hand. Both functions seek to extend and reinforce structuring at all levels of the agricultural world, and to aid farmers, especially younger farmers and women to create a framework suitable for the improvement of their activities.

The organization of farmers' associations comprises two types of structures:

(a)Elected organs which represent farmers and which are solely entitled to speak on their behalf. They have responsibility for institutional type of activity that they assume with the support of technical and operational organs. They have all decision-making powers with regard to the management of associations, the choice of goals and action programs, use of funds, policy and agricultural development proposals to fight for, in dealing with the government and private partners.

Elected organs are defined in the laws creating farmers' associations. Their characteristics, their powers, the rules governing their operations are the same for all associations. Their composition could depend on the composition of farmer populations in any region.

(b) The technical and operational organs are under the authority of the elected organs. Their mission is to assist the latter in the realization of their objectives, activity programs, in the management of their funds, and in preparing agricultural development policy proposals.

The technical and operational organs are the techno-administrative structure of the associations. They might have similar structures for tasks that are the same among all associations, like financial management and making information available to farmers. They could have different structures, unequal means, depending on regional characteristics.

General Set-up

The farmers' association is composed of all farmers and their organizations. The sovereign and constituent organs of a farmers' association are formed by their elected members (grass-roots elections), and represent different categories of farmers and professional organizations of the jurisdiction.

To defend the point of view and interests of farmers, farmers' associations must be present at the regional or provincial level, and at the national level, since both are strategic decision-making levels. The general set-up is: decentralized and autonomous farmers' associations constituting a lively network, and a federation of regional associations managing activities at the national level.

Forming Regional Farmers' Associations:

For compatibility with decentralization and to reflect the diversity of local agriculture, regional farmers' associations have several tiers: local, intermediate and national. At the local level, each grassroots unit (the village, normally) meets as a grass-roots assembly of farmers. This assembly designates three representatives for each of the existing colleges. Each college corresponds to a sector of activity: grain farming, livestock rearing, forestry, fishing, etc., or to a category of production. These colleges are determined along agro-ecological zones, and a classification done at grass-roots level with the participation of farmers, to reflect their diversity.

At the intermediate level, all the grass-roots representatives from the assembly of the intermediate level, which is between the local level and the regional or provincial level. At the regional or provincial level, all of the delegates from the Assembly of the Regional Farmers' Association, which also comprises the elected representatives of professional agricultural organizations (cooperatives or trade unions) of different levels, credit and agricultural insurance mutual funds. The assembly elects the executive board, the president and vice-president of the regional farmers' association. These officers represent farmers, speak on their behalf, and manage the regional farmers association, to realize its objectives. The management of the regional farmers' association is under the control of the assembly, which adopts the activity programs and budgets, translates the point of view of farmers on important questions that concern them, after consultations at grass-roots level, and evaluates the management accomplishments of the executive board.

The network is institutionalized in the form of a National Federation of Farmers' Associations, responsible for coordinating and running the activities of the network at national level. Its existence in no way impinges upon the decentralized and autonomous nature of the Regional Associations, from which it is derived, and over which it has no supervisory powers to the extent that it is the regional associations that determine its activities and finance its operations.

The federation has a light structure consisting of an executive board, the presidents of the regional farmers' associations, who elect a president and vice-presidents. On the basis of the synthesis of points of view expressed by regional associations, the board formulates the common position to be defended at national level, within decision-making bodies, and with the government and other public and private partners of farmers. Also, it manages the federation and the actions or common projects of several regional associations. To remain close to their grass-roots organizations, the executives of the federation continue to carry out their responsibilities as presidents of regional associations. The federation has an important information role, first toward farmers, informing them on their national and international economic environment, then toward the government, apprising it of farmers' point of view, and finally toward external partners, to develop cooperation with agricultural professions of other countries. In this regard, all actions are coordinated with actions of regional associations. The federation must use all existing means, making an effort to arrange frequent meetings with farmers.[75]

---

[75]Food and Agriculture Organization and the United Nations – Contact: Jean Bonnel

INDIA: **All India Peasants Organization**

The All India Kisan Sabha (AIKS) or the All India Peasants Organization was formally established on April 13, 1936, it had not been built in a day. The peasant movements in different parts of the country had existed for the past century. Many of the peasant struggles fought in those days were spontaneous in character, lacked proper direction and in many cases were badly organised. Still they played a role in raising the consciousness of the peasantry to fight against oppression and in defence of their rights.

The first half of the nineteenth century witnessed uninterrupted anti-colonial activity on the part of the peasantry, and tribesmen led by feudal lords who had lost their privileges. The feudal lords in the Northern *Sarkars* had been strongly resisting British domination ever since the beginning of the nineteenth century. In 1807 the whole Delhi regime took up arms in 1814 at Tuppan of Muneer (near Varanasi). Rajput peasants secured the abolition of the sale of land by public auction of a large village community to a stranger. In 1817 the peasants of Orissa led by local feudal lords, rose up in protest against the introduction of taxation of their rent free service lands. Poona district witnessed the uprising of the peasantry from 1826 to 1829 when the authorities were obliged to cede to them holding subject to low revenue charges. In 1830-31 British troops were sent to suppress a peasant uprising in Bedsore district of Mysore State against the tax increase. In 1835-37 there was an uprising in Gumsur in Madras Presidency. In 1842 an uprising flared up in Sagar. In 1846-47 the peasants in Karnal rose up in revolt. In 1848 Rohillas in Nagpur took up arms. In 1844 in the Kolhapur and Santavadi State bordering Bombay Presidency, there was a large-scale revolt in protest against the British decisions increasing the land revenue to pay the princes' tribute. The peasants of

Khandeth in Bombay Presidency rose up in protest against the land settlement, which resulted in the increase of land tax.

There were also innumerable uprisings of tribal people in this period – of the Bhils in 1818-1831 and Kolis in 1824 in Bombay Presidency, unrest in Kutch in 1815 and 1832 and revolt in Kittur in 1824-1829. In 1820, there was an uprising of the Mers in Rajputana and of the Hos tribe in Chote Nagpur in 1831-32. In 1846 the Khonds rose up in Orissa and 1855 witnessed the Santhal revolt in Bihar. There was also unrest in the Indian towns usually resulting from the introduction of new taxes, which generally took the form of strikes. These heroic struggles culminated in the First War of Independence of 1857, when Sepys (soldiers) took up the leadership of the movement.

Peasantry in Action for National Liberation

In northern India the Gurudwara Reforms Movement, which started with the Nankana Massacre, brought the vast Sikh peasant masses into action against British rule, thus making it a part of the liberation movement. In UP had begun the Eka Movement of tenants who were fighting against the extortions and oppression of the landlords. In the south there was the Moplah Rebellion in Malabar (Kerala) an uprising tenants against the oppression of *jenmies* (landlord).

The main slogan of the Gurudwara Reforms Movement was the liberation of Gurudwaras from the control of Mahants who had the patronage of the British imperialists. Bringing the Sikh peasantry into the national mainstream, it soon took the form of an anti-imperialist movement. The Eka Movement was also widespread and militant. It raised the demands of fixed rents, receipts for payments, and stoppage of *beggar* for the landlord, free use of water from ponds, and the freedom to graze cattle in the jungles. It was a revolt of the tenants against the unbearable oppression of the landlord.

The Moplah rebellion, again essentially an uprising of the tenants in Malabar, began on August 20 1921. The tenants were Muslims while the *jenmies* were Hindus. The main targets of the attack of the rebellion were the police, military, landlords and moneylenders. The police and military suppressed the rebellion with brutal violence in which 3,266 Moplahs were killed.

The period also witnessed big working class actions- in the textile and jute Mills in Calcutta, Bombay, Madras; in the North Western and Eastern Railway, the coal-fields of Jharia, the P & T Department of Bombay; plantations of Assam; tramways of Calcutta, etc.

This organisation was a forerunner of the Workers and Peasants Party. On February 6-7, 1926 the Second Session of the All Bengal Kisan Conference was held in Krishna Nagar (Nadia District). It decided to organise a peasants and Workers Party called the Bengal Peasants and Workers Party.

While the basic demand mentioned that the ultimate ownership of land would vest in a self-contained autonomous village community, it put forward the following immediate demands:

(a) Fixity of rates in relation to the rents payable by the tenants: the interest charged on arrears of rent to be equal to the rate of interest charged by the Imperial Bank.
(b) Cultivator's undivided ownership should be recognised on the land he tills.
(c) Permanency of tenure in land (which the cultivator tills) banning of evictions.
(d) Stopping of all unjust and illegal cesses.

(e) Right freely to transfer the land to another without payment of *salami*.
(f) Right to cut the trees, to dig wells and cut canals and build a house on his land without paying any
(g) *Salami.*
(h) Fixing conditions for catching fish in the ponds on the land.
(i) The highest rate of interest to be charged by the mahajan (money lender) to be fixed at a rate not more than 12 per cent.
(j) Establishing cooperative agricultural banks to give credit to the peasant and thus to release him from the grip of the greedy and professional moneylender.
(k) Machinery needed for cultivation etc. to be sold outright to the peasant or to be given to him on rent for use, and the price of the same or the rent amount thereof to be recovered from peasant in easy instalments.
(l) To make arrangement for the wholesale sale of jute or other commercial crops so that a just profits rate is guaranteed to the peasant.

In formulating the economic demands it is proposed:

The abolition of indirect taxation and the introduction of graded income tax on all income exceeding Rupees 250 per month.

(a) Nationalisation of land wherein Government will lease all cultivable land to cultivator.
(b) Nationalisation of means of production, distribution and exchange.
(c) Rent of land holding not to be excessive.
(d) Establishment by the government of State-aided cooperative banks controlled by local organisations for the provision of credit to peasants, at a rate of interest not exceeding seven per cent.

Agrarian Program

The formation of the All India Workers and Peasants Party and the subsequent historic Meerut Trial, helped in popularising the agrarian programme among the Indian masses. The Meerut Trial went on for more than four years. The persons involved in the trial in their statements advocated the programme of the Communists in relation to the working class, peasantry and other toiling sections of the Indian population, along with their unflinching opposition to imperialist rule in the country.

This was the period when the economic crisis of the 30s had engulfed the world. India was the worst hit during this crisis and in 1931 the Central Banking Enquiry Committee registered the general conviction that "Indebtedness leads ultimately to the transfer of land holdings from the agricultural class to the non-agricultural money-lenders leading to the creation of the landless proletariat with a reduced economic status. The result is said to be loss of agricultural efficiency as the moneylenders sub-let at a rate which leaves the cultivators with a reduced incentive."

(Enquiry Committee Report P. 59)

The 1931 Census report reached the conclusion that "It is likely that a concentration of the land in the hands of the non-cultivating owners is taking place."

(*Census of India,* 1931, Vol. 1)

Similarly, the extent of the collapse in prices of agricultural commodities was such that whereas in 1928-29 the value of agricultural crops, taken at an average harvest price, was about 10. 340 billion INR (Indian Rupees), in 1933-34 it was only 4.730 billion INR a fall of 55 per cent.

In the United Provinces, the number of tenants abandoning their land because they could not pay rent, reached as high as 71 440 in 1931. The burden of debt doubled. Peasants were groaning under their heavy indebtedness, their lands were passing into the hands of moneylenders and they were being forced to live the life of paupers.

The peasant organisations emerging in various States now had a clear-cut programme not only for immediate relief but also directed against the system of landlordism. The peasants had realised the necessity of organising themselves as a class which was numerically not only strong but also the worst exploited under the triple attack of the imperialists landlords and moneylenders and traders. The Indian National Congress was desirous of mobilising them in the struggle for independence since without them it was not possible to bring pressure to bear on the imperialists but it did not want the peasantry to emerge as a class conscious of its rights and determined to put an end to the rule of the landlords.

The Congress started the Civil Disobedience movement but its 11-point charter of demands did not contain any demands of the working class and peasantry against the capitalists and the landlords.

The resolution of the Karachi Session of the Congress where fundamental rights were mentioned in relation to the peasant demands it did not stipulate more than a substantial reduction of land revenue and rent, and total exemption only for the necessary period in the case of uneconomic holdings. There was no reference to abolition of landlordism or even the annulment of at least a portion of the rural debt. It was clear that that Indian National congress did not want to rouse the peasantry against feudal oppression.

Gandhi's hopes for a compromise were shattered at the Round Table Conference and he had again to continue the movement, which lasted up to 1934, drawing into its fold huge masses. Once again the movement was withdrawn without achieving its aim, and Gandhi withdrew from the Congress exercising his influence from outside.

Formation of All-India Kisan Sabha (All India Farmers' Association)

The Communist Party was banned in 1934 but continued to exercise its influence on the working class and on the Left in the Congress. The ideas of Socialism wee becoming very popular and left dements in the Congress, becoming disillusioned with Gandhi formed the Congress Socialist Party, in order to give the Congress a Left orientation. Coming to realise that the vast masses of the peasantry could be brought into the struggle for independence only by taking up the anti-feudal struggle and their immediate demands they were also realising the necessity of organisation the peasantry as a class. They had already come to the conclusion that the struggle for real political freedom could not be separated from the struggle of the peasantry for an end to landlordism and for radical restructuring of rural society. The Communists were already trying to develop class organisations and had popularised the ideas of independent class organisations of the working class peasants and other sections of the toiling people. Thus It was the Left Congressmen, Congress Socialists and Communists who took the initiative in organising the All India Kisan Sabha (Farmers' conference).

The First Session was held in 1936, Lucknow to coincide with the holding of the Session of the Indian National congress. The idea was to project the kisan movement as a part of the national movement though maintaining its separate identity as a class organisation.

The participants of the first All India Kisan Sabha Session were EMS Namboodiripad, Dinkar Mehta, Kamal Sarkar, Sohan Singh Josh, Lal Bahadur

Shastri, K D Malaviya, Mohan Lal Gautam, B Sampooranand, Jayaprakash Narain, Swami Sahajanand, Dr. Harekrishna Mahtab, Naba Krishna Choudhury, N G Ranga, Indulal Yajnik, R K Khadilkar, Bishnuram Medhi, Sarat Chandra Sinha, Annie Besant, Raja Mohinder Pratap, Maulana Mohammed Barkatullah, Pabitra Mohan Pradhan and Maulana Obeidullah Sindhi.

Many of them became prominent national and state-level personalities in subsequent years. It also suggests how broad-based the Kisan Sabha was from the very beginning and how it tried to attack people of varying political views to join together in defence of the democratic rights of the kisans.

A meeting in Meerut in January 1936 preceded the formation of the AIKS, where the necessary preparations were made. A clear decision was taken to launch the organisation with a broad-based programme and membership to link it closely with the national movement for independence and to view the fight against imperialism as an integral part of the fight against the feudal social order since the former patronised and provided state support to the latter.

Today with the benefit of hindsight one is struck by the simplicity and directness with which the very first session set out its tasks in the main resolution. To quote:

(a)The objective of the Kisan movement is to secure compete freedom from economic exploitation and the achievement of full economic and political power for the peasants and workers and all the other exploited classes.

(b)The main task of the Kisan movement shall-be the organisation of peasants to fight for their immediate political and economic demands in order to prepare them for their emancipation from every from of exploitation.

(c)The Kisan movement stands for the achievements of ultimate economic and political power for the producing masses through its active participation in the national struggle for winning complete independence.

(d)It their indicted the zamindari system, "supported by the British government in India", as "iniquitous unjust, burdensome, and oppressive to the Kisans", and declared that "all such system of landlordism shall be abolished and all the rights over such lands be vested in the cultivators."

This was the essence of what the kisan movement stood for at the time of the launching of the AIKS. The other issues covered by resolutions included questions of rent, irrigation rates and prices of inputs, prices of marketed agricultural products, indebtedness, forced labour and illegal exactions from the tenants by the landlords and the distribution of landlords land to the landless poor peasants as also the vesting of waste land and grazing land in the village level organisation (panchayats). The AIKS also demanded minimum wages for the regulating their unionisation. Any one reading those resolutions will immediately notice that many of the issues raised by the conference of the AIKS in its first session have remained unresolved till today.

Part of the National Movement

The Bombay session of the Central Kisan Sabha Council (CKC) held in August 1936 further elaborated many of the points raised in the founding session. It categorically stated that, since the kisans constituted more than four-fifths of the population, "no political or economic programme which has the audacity to ignore their needs and demands can by any stretch of imagination, be labelled as a national programme", and called upon the Indian National Congress to make "the solution of the problems of the peasantry the chief plank of its political and economic policy." At the same time the CKC felt the need for a political movement, which draws "its main strength and inspiration from the peasantry."

These two struggles - the kisan movement and the national movement were seen as "inter-dependent, the strength of the one adding to the other."

Agrarian Policies of Congress

In the post-independent period the bourgeoisie continued its alliance with the landlords and the balance sheet of bourgeois agrarian policy is explained in the Programme of the CPI (M), in Para 34.

"In no field is the utter failure of the bourgeois-landlord government's policies so nakedly revealed as in the case of the agrarian question. Nearly two decades of Congress rule has proved beyond any shadow of doubt that the aim and direction of its agrarian policies is not to smash the feudal and semi-feudal fetters on our land relations, and thus liberate the peasantry from age-old bondage, but to transform the feudal landlords into capitalist landlords and develop a stratum of rich peasants. They want to depend upon the landlord and rich peasant section to produce the surplus of agricultural products to meet the requirements of capitalist development. They also want to make these sections the main political base of the ruling class in the countryside."

Although these measures did not bring the desired resulted of making the tiller of the soil the owner of the land it made certain changes in the agrarian relations. Under the impact of the agrarian movement intermediary tenures like Zamindari, jagirs, imams, etc., which prevailed over quite a large area of the country were abolished in the early 50s and more than 20 million tenants were brought into direct relation with the State. It was these occupancy tenants who directly benefited from the land reforms to become owners of the land they tilled. These rich and middle peasants were no longer interested in radical land reforms. This has been shown by the subsequent developments also.

The overall result has been that even after four decades of independence the pro-landlord, anti-peasant policies of the Government have resulted in the further deepening of the agrarian crisis, which manifests itself in growing landlessness increase in disparities both inter-regional and inter-sectional in the same region, an extremely low level of consumption of food-grains despite increasing production and bourgeoning stocks held by the Government growing poverty and unemployment despite all the poverty alleviation schemes and growing indebtedness which finds partial reflection in the growth of overdue in institutional credit supplied to the agricultural sector and so on.

In spite of two rounds of Land Ceiling legislations in the 1950s and 1970s only 7.2 million acres have been declared surplus out of which 5.6 million acres have been taken over and 4.4 million acres actually distributed. This is about seven per cent of the surplus estimated i.e., 63 million acres by the Mahalanobis Committee after the first round of ceiling laws were enacted and one fifth of the surplus estimated on the basis of date made available by the NSS 26th Round.

Even if we take into consideration the 1981 Agricultural Census land concentration continues. As compared to three per cent land holders holding 10 acres and above and operating a total of 26 per cent of the land in 1976-77 in 1981-82, 2.4 per cent of land holders held 22.8 per cent of the land. The Planning Commission that has estimated that even now, if a 20-acre ceiling is imposed and all loopholes in ceiling laws plugged about 23 million acres of land can be made available for distribution. But the Seventh Plan makes no mention of amending the ceiling laws or about breaking the land monopoly. And typically the Central Government took more than five years to give Presidential assent to the West Bengal Land Reforms Legislation, which seeks only to plug certain loopholes.

Peasant Movement after Independence

In the first six years of the post independence period the peasant movement again had to face severe repression at the hands of the Government Afraid of the tempo of the growing revolutionary movement, it unleashed repression making the functioning of various units impossible. The All India Kisan Sabha was not able to hold any session till April 1953. But in spite of this the Kisan Sabha was busy organising the resistance of the peasantry especially on the question of evictions, and militant fights were put up in many States. Subsequently various Congress Government were forced to take measures of land reforms such as ceiling legislations security of tenure and rent reduction, consolidation of holdings, etc., but all failed to fulfil the declared objectives. On the other hand the period witnessed a large-scale eviction offensive throwing millions of tenants into the ranks of agricultural workers.

In the late fifties the Kisan Sabha fought many struggles on the issues of land fair prices for peasants produce, debt relief, in defence of the rights of tribal people and on the issue of the burden of heavy taxation. The most important of these struggles was the heroic struggle of the Punjab peasantry against the imposition of the betterment levy tax in the beginning of 1959. This was the most important struggle fought under the flag of the Kisan Sabha after the epoch-making Telengana struggle. The peasants defied firings, lathi-charges, beating and all types of repression. The all in peasant unity forged during the struggle was unparalleled, when peasant united irrespective of their political affiliations. The movement ultimately forced the Government to withdraw the tax amounting to 1360 million INR.

The agrarian crisis further aggravated in the 1960s. By the mid-1960 stagnation in agriculture and the consequent food crisis worsened. The bourgeois-landlord classes began losing their hold over the mass of the peasantry with the result that in the 1967 elections the Congress monopoly of power was broken in eight States with West Bengal and Kerala giving victory to the Left and democratic force among which the CPI (M) played an important role. Powerful peasant struggle took place in different States on different issues. In Kerala and West Bengal these struggles were most widespread and became intimately connected with political issues.

The United Front Government of West Bengal and Kerala made a big impact on the masses, not only in those States but also in the rest of the country. When the Central Government dismissed these governments hundreds of thousands of peasants actually joined the struggle for democracy in West Bengal combining this with the struggle for defending heir land and crops.

Mid-term elections gave a bigger victory to the United Front in West Bengal and the peasant movement attained wider sweep. Millions of peasants all over the State unleashed an unprecedented struggle with the backing of the United Front Government, for recovering benami (ownership in another's name) land for possession and distribution of surplus lands, for loans in kind and for checking hoarding and black-marketing. In this period more than three hundred thousand acres of land were located; taken over and distributed among the landless through village level committees. Many peasants lost their lives in the battles fought on this issue, but it gave a big impetus to the kisan (peasant) movement and the AIKS spread to all districts.

These struggles achieved important gains and helped in raising the political consciousness of the peasantry. It was because of this that the Kisan Sabha was able to face the semi-fascist terror of 1917 to 1977, fight back the repression and defend their interests though working in semi-legal conditions.

In Kerala, the peasants conducted a state wide movement for agrarian legislation and debt relief legislation for the rights on Government lands against threat of central intervention. As a result of the campaign, one hundred thousand pattas (government orders of land right) were distributed to erstwhile-unauthorised occupants of the land. The ceiling was revised downwards and made family-based many exemptions were withdrawn and hutment dwellers were given rights on land on which they lived. Tens of thousands of agricultural labourers conducted powerful and successful struggle for better wages and living conditions.

The discontent found powerful expression in other parts of Indian also. In Maharashtra, Andhra Pradesh, Uttar Pradesh, Bihar, Assam, Tripura, etc., widespread struggles took place for occupation of forest or government lands and against eviction from these lands. In Punjab and UP widespread agitations took place on the question of sugarcane prices. Struggle took place against increased taxation on the question of food and relief rent reduction and against unjust levies. Militant struggles of agricultural labourers took place in Tamil Nadu and Andhra Pradesh.

This period also witnessed two splits in the AIKS one from the Right and other from the Left. While they did a lot of harm to the Kisan Sabha, it not only survived these attacks but also advanced further. At the same time it also failed to properly understand the changes in the agrarian structure and work out the appropriate tasks on that basis. By 1978-79 it was able to give a new orientation to its policy, which led to its big advance. Membership of the Kisan Sabha (Farmers' Organization), which had never gone beyond one million till 1968-69 after 1978-79 jumped by millions and now stands at 8.4 million.

In other states also the kisan sabha has grown through struggles. Kisan Sabha units in different States have taken up different issues depending on the concrete situation in each state. In Bihar the question of eviction of sharecroppers has remained very acute and struggle fought over it; in some, states against rise in taxation and on remunerative prices in most of the states. The first half of 80s witnessed a tremendous upsurge among the peasantry where even the Congress base was drawn into struggles. This shows the tremendous possibilities for building the peasants movement.[76]

India achieved her independence on August 15, 1947 but the farmers of the country have not yet achieved all the demands that were raised in the nineteenth century. Till today, the price policy goes against the farmers. The peasants have no voice in policy formulation committee of the government. They are ill treated even by the revenue inspectors. The police constable arrests even an innocent peasant with false grounds. A farmer is treated as a under-rated citizen of the country. He dies without medicines, sleeps

---

[76]Harkishan Singh Surjeet (1986), "Fifty Years of Organised Peasant Movement", the Marxist, Volume 4, No. 2, April-June 1986. This is an abridged form of original article.

without food, and sends his child to work as a daily labourer in a kiln.

Even today, the governments are allotting land to industrialists in thousands of acres from the poor peasants with help of police force. The governments treat the industrialists as son-in-laws in lie of hard cash.

U.S.A.

Farmers, the Populist Party, and Mississippi

(1870-1900)

In the late 1800s, the United States experienced a tremendous growth in industrialization. Led by oil, steel, and other manufacturing industries, the United States had become the world's leading producer of manufactured goods by 1900. The value of American exports tripled from 1870 to 1900 as America went from a debtor to a creditor nation. National wealth and national income skyrocketed. It was the age that amassed fortunes for John D. Rockefeller, Andrew Carnegie, Commodore Vanderbilt, Jay Gould, James B. Duke, and E. H. Harriman, to name a few. Before 1860 there were few millionaires in the United States, but by 1900 there were more than four thousand. Yet in the midst of all this industrial growth and production of wealth, almost ten million Americans, or about one out of eight people, lived in poverty.

Among the Americans left out of the prosperity were the farmers who experienced difficult economic times. An article in the April 28, 1887, edition of the *Progressive Farmer* magazine accurately summed up the attitude of farmers:

There is something radically wrong in our industrial system. There is a screw loose. The wheels have dropped out of balance. The railroads have never been so prosperous, and yet agriculture languishes. The banks have never done a better or more profitable business, and yet agriculture languishes.

Manufacturing enterprises never made more money or were in a more flourishing condition, and yet agriculture languishes. Towns and cities flourish and 'boom' and grow and 'boom,' and yet agriculture languishes. Salaries and fees were never so temptingly high and desirable, and yet agriculture languishes.

Farmers opine that their economic demise results from the low prices, which they receive for their produce.

Statistics validate their belief as the price of agricultural produce did fall drastically during the closing decades of the 19th century. According to the U.S. Department of Agriculture, from 1870 to 1897, wheat prices fell from $1.06 a bushel to 63¢ a bushel, corn from 43¢ to 30¢ a bushel, and cotton from 15¢ a pound to 6¢ a pound. Most of the time farmers received even less for their produce.

Farmers refused to admit it, but the primary cause of their problem was overproduction caused by increases in acreage of farmland and increased yields per acre due to improved farming methods generated by newly created agricultural colleges. Thus, farmers produced more than consumer demand, and prices fell to a point that farmers barely made a profit. Farmers, however, came to believe that their chief problem was not the market dynamics of supply and demand but that they sold goods in a free market and purchased goods in a protected and monopolistic market. They primarily zeroed in on two villains – banks and railroads. In their view banks charged outrageous interest rates, and monopolistic railroads not only charged outrageous rates but their rates were unfair and arbitrary in that the railroads charged farmers higher rates than they charged fellow industrialists.

Farmers' organizations

In an attempt to improve their condition, farmers in the 1870s decided to organize. They created numerous organizations including the Patrons of Husbandry or Grange, the National Farmers' Alliance, the National Farmers' Alliance and Industrial Union, and the Southern Alliance. Working within existing political parties, farmers attempted to bring about political change. They managed to gain control of several state legislatures and to enact state laws, which regulated railroads. At first the U. S. Supreme Court in *Munn v. Illinois* upheld these laws of railroad regulation, but in the late 1880s the court reversed it and either declared state regulatory laws unconstitutional or took most of the starch out of them.

Frustrated by the reversal of the court and their inability to get either major political party to adopt their agenda, farmers in 1890 decided to field candidates for state and national offices under diverse party labels. Farm leaders surprised themselves by gaining partial or complete control of twelve state legislatures and by electing six governors, three senators, and approximately fifty congressmen.

Populist Party is created

Elated over their success, the agrarian leaders decided it was time to create a national farm and labor party. Accordingly in July 1892, they held a convention in Omaha, Nebraska. The agrarians created the People's or Populist Party, drafted a platform, and nominated James B. Weaver for president and James G. Field for vice president. The Omaha platform of 1892 concisely documented the grievances and demands of farmers. It was also one of the most radical platforms to this point in American history. Among other things, it called for government ownership and operation of the railroad, telephone, and telegraph systems.

Third parties have never won national elections and the Populist Party was no exception. Grover Cleveland, the Democratic candidate in 1892, won the presidency, but Weaver did poll more than a million popular votes and twenty-two electoral votes. In the 1896 presidential election, the Democratic Party nominated William Jennings Bryan and adopted a platform that included several planks from the 1892 Populist platform. After much discussion, Populist leaders decided to support Bryan and in so doing, signed the death warrant of the Populist Party. Bryan lost three presidential elections as the nominee of the Democratic Party.

Mississippi farmers blame Bourbons

Like the rest of the nation, Mississippi farmers languished in economic distress during the late 1800s. Many of them joined and supported the Grange and the Farmers' Alliance. Like their national counterparts, Mississippi farmers believed that railroads, banks, large lumber companies, corporations, and the middleman were the major causes of their economic plight. After the overthrow of Radical Republican governments in 1875, Mississippi virtually became a one-party state for the next hundred years. After 1875, a political machine emerged to control the Democratic Party. Led by James Z. George, L. Q. C. Lamar, Edward C. Walthall, John M. Stone, and Robert Lowry, this machine controlled politics in Mississippi for the next two decades. Labeled "Bourbons" (called Redeemers by some) by their opponents, the leaders' championed railroad and corporate interests, and, in the eyes of farmers, favored the industrialization of Mississippi at the expense of agriculture.

Mississippi farmers blamed the Bourbon leaders for their economic problems, and in the 1880s they believed that in order to improve their economic plight, they needed to gain control of the Democratic Party by electing candidates who reflected their interests rather than attempting to create a third party. Like other farmers in the South, Mississippi farmers feared that a third party would endanger white supremacy.

One candidate farmers supported in the 1880s was Ethelbert Barksdale, editor of the Jackson *Clarion*. A Democrat and one of the leaders of the overthrow of Republican rule in Mississippi, he nevertheless supported regulation of railroads and other programs championed by farmers. Barksdale, however, failed in his bid for the United States Senate in 1880, and again in 1891 when he attempted to defeat incumbent Senator James Z. George. Farmers also supported Putnam Darden, head of the state Grange, in an unsuccessful bid for the governorship in 1885. While farm candidates did win some elections, they never won a major one and never came close to gaining control of the Democratic Party. They failed, in part, because parties selected nominees in county, district, and state conventions, which were easily controlled by a political organization and not by a vote of the people.

In the 1880s there was much support in Mississippi for a constitutional convention to draft a new constitution. While the main driving force for the convention was to legally disfranchise African-Americans, there were other issues including apportionment of the state legislature, ending the convict-lease system, regulation of railroad and corporations, electing the state judiciary, and equalization of the school fund. Bourbon leaders were divided in their support for a new constitution. Among Bourbon leaders, Senator George was the driving force for a constitutional convention, while Senator

Edward C. Walthall was the main spokesman for the opposition. Walthall argued that it was impossible to disfranchise blacks without also disfranchising thousands of white voters.

Frank Burkitt says:

Agrarian leaders generally supported a constitution convention to draft a new constitution. Newspaper editor Frank Burkitt and the Farmers' Alliance were among the earliest supporters of a constitutional convention. In 1888 the Mississippi Legislature passed a bill for a constitutional convention, but Governor Robert Lowry vetoed it. In 1890 the legislature again passed a similar bill and the new governor, John M. Stone, signed it.

One hundred and thirty-four delegates met in Jackson in August 1890 to draft a new constitution. After much bitter debate, a new constitution emerged.. Among its most far-reaching provisions were the disfranchisement of black voters through the literacy clause and poll tax, the reapportionment of the state legislature, and the abolition of the convict-lease system. In addition, railroad companies were placed under state laws.

A new constitution did not bring an end to the farmers' economic ills. Cotton prices continued to fall and dropped to 7.5¢ a pound by 1892, or about the cost of production. Efforts by farmers to bring economic and political change within the Bourbon-controlled Democratic Party seemed hopeless. This led Mississippi farmers to turn to and support the newly created Populist Party.

Frank Burkitt, editor of the Okolona *Chickasaw Messenger*, led the movement to unseat what he described as the "putrid, putrescent, putrifying political moribund carcass of bourbon democracy." In the 1892 elections, Mississippi Populists ran candidates in all congressional districts except one. All of them lost. Burkitt, who ran in a northeast Mississippi congressional district, made the best showing winning 39 percent of the vote. Weaver, the presidential candidate, won 19 percent of the state vote.

Populist Party fades away

Nevertheless, in their eyes Populists had made a good showing and thus believed they would ultimately triumph. However, Populist results at the polls in elections from 1892 to 1898 were, at best, terribly disappointing. In 1898 cotton prices fell below the cost of production, yet in the congressional elections that year, Populist candidates received fewer votes than in previous elections. In 1900 William McKinley, the Republican candidate for president, received more votes than Wharton Barker, the Populist candidate. For all practical purposes, Populism had died.

In the late 19th century, the Populist Party arose out of agrarian economic and political protest, was short lived, and passed into history. Yet, in time, it achieved most of its platform. At the national level, the presidential administration of Woodrow Wilson (1913-1921) and the New Deal of Franklin D. Roosevelt (1933-1945) enacted most of the Populist demands into law. [77]

In Mississippi, the state legislature passed the direct primary law in 1903 which led to the election of pro-farmer Democratic governors like James K. Vardaman (1904-1908) and Theodore G. Bilbo (1916-1920 and 1928-1932) whose administrations passed into law many of the demands of the Mississippi farmers.

---

[77]Kenneth G. McCarty (2003), "Farmers, the Populist Party, and Mississippi, Mississippi History Now, A quarterly Journal of Mississippi History, July 2003

Thus, like most third parties in America, the Populists failed to win elections, but in time achieved many of their goals.

USA: **National Black Farmers Association (N B F A)**

In the spring of 1995, as a result of mounting frustration with the U.S. Department of Agriculture's (USDA) apparent discrimination on racial grounds concerning disbursement of loans to farmers, Virginia poultry farmer John Boyd Jr. began galvanizing efforts for massive protests on behalf of a dying breed of black farmers in the United States. Initially his efforts consisted of making phone calls of inquiry to USDA officials using his name alone; but after adopting the name National Black Farmers Association (NBFA), his calls and appeals were at least acknowledged. Boyd quickly picked up steam from kindred black farmers whose complaints and concerns mirrored and oftentimes exceeded his own, arguing undue process regarding bank foreclosures and subsequent auctioning of land. After unearthing what was identified as years-old backlogs on discrimination and muscling by the USDA of black landowners, NBFA set out to bring attention to such grievances through high profile, direct action. Through its ten year history, NBFA has successfully provided leadership and activism that led to the largest class action suit in the nation's history and remained at the forefront of struggle with the intent of salvaging a future for the endangered constituency represented by the organization.

"We Have Our Mule, Now We're Looking for Our 40 Acres" was the slogan adopted by sixty black farmers led by Boyd who trekked to Washington, D.C. on December 12, 1996, to the White House in support of raising the stakes and of having their pleas heard at the highest level of governance in the land. Their monumental work from 1996 to 1998 produced results and concrete outcomes, igniting intervention activity through presidential roundtables, agricultural secretarial treatise, and federal senatorial advocacy. Indeed, sessions with President Bill Clinton resulted in the establishment of a federal advisory committee on civil rights designed to essentially keep the USDA intricately posted on legislation changes regarding the $500 million operating budget for small farmers. Secretary of Agriculture Dan Glickman vowed to clean up the mess created by USDA's catastrophic malice by transforming the engrained traditional practices of what he called "the last plantation." Considerable campaigning from Virginia senator Charles Robb also proved valuable in addressing the copious retribution claims made by black farmers.

The analogy of life being a marathon and not a sprint aptly fits the NBFA movement because the obstacles faced and red tape applied for black farmers to receive their respective share of USDA's $2.3 billion settlement for class-action discrimination has meandered at a snail's pace. A 1999 report produced by NBFA and the Environmental Working Group claims that the administration of George Bush was in violation of obstructing justice. Accordingly, they provided evidence from Mississippi and Alabama to show how stifling policy steeped in bureaucratic loopholes hindered 19,000 out of 19,269 Mississippi late-filing applicants and 14,268 out of 14,562 in Alabama. Regardless of the settlement from six years prior, evidence produced suggests that most claims were simply being ignored, and black and other minority farmers' issues remained dormant at the federal level. Despite apparent setbacks, NBFA efforts never waned, and the plight perforated international arenas as well. The United Nations was the natural body to appeal to, and unanimous support from leading civil rights organizations such as the National Association for the Advancement of Colored People (NAACP), the National Urban League, and the Southern Christian Leadership Conference (SCLC) championed the cause. According to Akwasi Evans in the New York Daily Challenge, SCLC's Joseph Lowery emphatically charged "you do not deserve to lose 13 million acres of land in half a century just because you are black."

International ties for NBFA did not stop with just appeals. Program implementation with foreign nations to help black farmers with direct ties and contractual work has been sought, too. Of historical consequence is the export deal brokered by NAACP's Kweisi Mfume with the Cuban government in 2003. The United States adopted an over forty-year embargo on Cuba, and devastated the economy of Cuba, but ultimately the USA accepted trade relationship with Cuba and this represents a tremendous upside for Cuba. As sanctions have been slightly loosened in recent years, the current policy limits all transactions to cash-and-carry only. Nevertheless, NBFA began selling corn, wheat, rice, soybeans, and chicken through coastal outposts directly to Cuba. The benefit of such a program stems from the fact that NBFA was able to negotiate a more equitable agreement from cutting out expensive middlemen. Cited corporate diminishment of black farm-produced goods includes erroneous claims of impurities and the subsequent taxation on the open market. The historical implications must be considered as consistent practices by the Fidel Castro-led Cuban government, who has deliberately supported Third World infrastructures and likened the scenario of ostracized black farmers in America in similar fashion.

John Boyd has remained relentless in his work on behalf of NBFA up to the moment. In an interview with Lou Dobbs, Boyd made it clear of his outrage at Mexican president Vicente Fox's disparaging remarks about black farmers in the United States where it was implied that illegal immigrant Mexican workers were better. It was because conflict turned into resolution. Thus, he began pushing for Jackson's assistance and

Fox's openness to forging partnerships where NBFA could secure contracts with the Mexican government modeled after the ones established in Cuba. Currently, arrangements for Boyd's travel to Mexico are in negotiation, and the NBFA claims 66,000 members throughout the United States.[78]

Conclusion

The Farmers' Organizations in all countries should act on the principle **'United we stand, divided we fall'.** The farmers should follow peaceful paths to achieve their rights. Each farmer is so busy that he does not find time to take part in deliberations. So there should be regional farmers' committees to express their grievances. The farmers should take up crops, which can be sold in the markets with profit.

The farmers should create agricultural markets in each cluster of villages or in each village for easy sale of agricultural produce. No organization should collect market fees in these markets. It would create more labour days and can create more traders and would connect the village to the national markets without any investment.

The Farmers' organizations should arrange facilities for training of farmers and must gather information on farmers' problems and solution thereof. It could distribute research results, future market prices, and invite specialists for expert opinion on agriculture.All organizations putting hurdles in farmers' activities would automatically cooperate with the farmers.

All cooperative organizations that are corrupt or facing losses must be closed immediately. Similarly Fair Price Shops, free midday meals, subsidized seeds, and subsidized fertilizers, subsidized pump sets, guaranteed employment policy, Self Help

---

[78] Maxizip Com

Groups, NGOs working on money lending, private money lending, money circulation practices by unregistered firms and non-working institutions must be closed immediately. These government policies create corruption, unemployment, and no-work culture in rural villages. High indebtedness of small farmers causes farmers' suicides.

The Farmers' organizations should claim for higher procurement prices for cereals, pulses, cotton and sugarcane for the benefits of all farmers. They should demand not to import food grains to the country in normal years. The government must ensure that the country is self-sufficient in food grains.

This should be done peacefully. The farmers' organizations should claim for family pension-benefits. It should be at least one-tenth of pension paid to the highest government employees.

If the Farmers' organizations fail in achieving the Farmers' Rights; all farmers could form a political party at the country level to enter into the Parliament or the highest policy making institution to make laws for the vast majority of people in a peace process.

Ballot Is more powerful than Bullet.

It is overdue that the farmers of India should form a political party to safeguard their interest and the country.

+++++

Chapter – VI

INTERNATIONAL ORGANIZATIONS FOR FARMERS

Land, agriculture and farmer give us food. The credit goes to our forefathers, which discovered that agriculture could be practiced in land to produce food for all time for all people. But agriculture has become a loss bearing profession and enterprise. Land is continuously depleted and converted into non-agricultural uses such as houses or roads or industrial uses. The farmers are shifting to non-farm sector for higher income. But growth of population is emerging as the great challenge to the governments. All international institutions are scared of the future. It is estimated that by 2050, there would be more than nine billion of people on this earth. Food security would emerge as the greatest challenge to the farm scientists, administrators and politicians to check outflow of agricultural workers into the cities or towns. It could be possible through higher income to farmers, providing modern amenities in rural areas such schools, hospitals and communication facility. The demands of rural folk could be fulfilled through farmers' organizations. Their activities and achievements could spread nationally and internationally with clean persons.

In this chapter topics like 'The First World Food Conference, Third Global Meeting of the Farmers' Forum, The State of Food Insecurity in the World, Millions More Food-insecure, MORE AND BETTER, IFAD, The USAID Program, Current Farmer to Farmer Program, Roots of Peace: Restores Agriculture in Afghanistan, Institute for Agricultural Trade Policy, Supporting Small- scale farmers, The food movement, International Federation of Agricultural Producers, are discussed and Conclusions have been drawn for a meaningful policy options.

The first World Food Conference

In fighting to set the agenda of meeting the world's needs for food, and each nation's right to food self-sufficiency, we will find useful the history of the origins of the Food and Agriculture Organization. The FAO came directly from the mind of Franklin Delano Roosevelt (FDR), the President of United States and the historic proclamations of principle, which he composed with the Atlantic Charter (1941) and the Four Freedoms (1942). In 1943, with an eye to the fact that the Allies were on the verge of winning the war, FDR took the initiative of founding a United Nations organization based on these principles. The first of those was the FAO.

FDR convened a United Nations Conference on Food and Agriculture in Hot Springs, Virginia on May 18, 1943. Representatives of 44 nations participated, and hammered out an agreement calling for the establishment of an Interim Commission, entrusted with formulating "a specific plan for a permanent organization in the field of food and agriculture." The

Conference was successful, and completed its work on June 3, 1943. The opening sentence of the Declaration the Conference adopted said:

"This Conference, meeting in the midst of the greatest war ever waged, and in full confidence of victory, has considered world problems of food and agriculture and declares its belief that the goal of freedom from want of food, suitable and adequate for the health and strength of all peoples, can be achieved."

On June 7, FDR invited the participants to a gathering in the East Room of the White House, and addressed them for 14 minutes. The speech is available on the FAO history site in audio only, so I summarize here.

FDR said the meeting was "epoch-mocking," in that it was the first conference of the "United Nations." He noted that the conference was based on the ideas of the Atlantic Charter. He endorsed the Declaration's statement that the principle responsibility of each nation is to see that its people have food, but added that for each nation to do this, it requires working with other nations. He formally accepted the declaration as head of the United States.

At the launching of the first World Food Conference, President **Franklin D. Roosevelt** declared:

Freedom from want and freedom from fear go hand in hand, and that is true even today.

After some discussion of the issues of agriculture per se, he concluded by restating the goals:

(a)To build for all men, a world where each individual human being can live in peace, work productively, take care of his family, choose his own friends, and die in the knowledge that his children will have the same opportunity he did.

(b)Freedom from want and freedom from fear go hand in hand. And the world's nations should go forward "united in the war against fear and want."

The Interim Commission was set up in Washington, where it worked on issues of production and consumption. **Lester Pearson** of Canada chaired it until the FAO was formally established in the Chateau Frontenac at Quebec, in October 1945.

President **John F. Kennedy** played a major role in attempting to revive FDR's original outlook for the FAO. He addressed the World Food Congress on June 4, 1963, the 20th anniversary of the founding, as follows:

We rededicate ourselves to the objectives: that all nations, all people, all inhabitants of this planet have all the food they need, all the food that they deserve as human beings. We are here to renew a worldwide commitment to banish hunger and outlaw it. [79]

Third Global Meeting of the Farmers' Forum

The third global meeting of the Farmers' Forum took place on 15 and 16 February 2010 in conjunction with the Thirty-third session of IFAD's Governing Council. The forum brought together more than 70 farmers' leaders from around the world, representing millions of smallholders and rural producers from all over the world who will interact with IFAD staff and selected partners. The President of IFAD, Kanayo Nwanze, opened the Forum.

The 2010 edition of the Forum gave more space to operational matters. To this end, the two working group sessions focused on country and regional dimensions. The forum promotes women's leadership

---

[79] Food for Peace, Schiller – Institute, May 2008

in farmers' and rural producers' organizations, Operational collaboration between IFAD and farmers, food security, small farmers value chain, policies and investment in agriculture. IFAD achieved at least 30 per cent of women farm leaders participating in the Forum.

Crises and new opportunities

Over the past two years, the interrelated food and energy crises have been exacerbated by the financial crisis and a global recession. The sobering consequences of this conjunction of crises were brought cruelly to the forefront by FAO's announcement that the number of hungry people had surpassed one billion in 2009. And many more people have seen their livelihood and purchasing power significantly worsened. Furthermore, agriculture – the livelihood of the vast majority of poor people in developing countries – is increasingly being affected by climate change, desertification, loss of biodiversity and a growing competition over land and water as the world's population runs towards 9 billion.

The international community reacts

Faced with this situation, last year the international community demonstrated a growing political and financial commitment to food security and agriculture. In L'Aquila, 26 countries and 14 multilateral agencies agreed on a coordinated Food Security Initiative. Last November, in Rome, the participants in the World Summit on Food Security reiterated their commitment to intensify national and international support to agricultural development and food security, in particular to smallholder farmers. As 2015, the target year of the Millennium Development Goals, is approaching, a renewed consensus is emerging to support poor rural women and men in their effort to overcome poverty, achieve their right to food, and adapt to and contribute to mitigating climate change.

Stronger organizations of smallholder farmers, fishers and pastoralists are essential to face these challenges and seize opportunities. Cooperation among rural producers improves their access to markets and knowledge. It allows for economies of scale and stronger bargaining power in value chains. It increases small farmers' capacity to manage resources and infrastructure and to influence policy and development programs.

IFAD's response

IFAD is facing these challenges with a sense of urgency and responsibility. Its membership agreed upon an unprecedented level of replenishment. Over the last two years the Fund has committed more than US $1.2 billion to finance 69 rural and agricultural investment projects of its member countries. National or local farmers' organizations participated in the design of 70 per cent of these projects and were involved in most of IFAD's country strategies formulated during the biennium. Direct grant financing to farmers' organizations for capacity building more than doubled compared to the previous biennium.

As world agriculture is at a crossroads and as IFAD begins to implement its eighth replenishment, the third global meeting of the Farmers' Forum is a unique opportunity to take stock of a "partnership in progress" and to reflect with farmer leaders on ways and means to further increase our development effectiveness and to strengthen the capacity of 500 million small farms worldwide to overcome poverty and hunger.

IFAD and farmers' organizations: Partnerships in progress

The report " Partnerships in Progress 2008-2009" is based on a survey of all IFAD Country Program Managers, 12 directors of IFAD funded projects and leaders of 24 farmers' organizations involved in the design and implementation of development projects or country strategies.

Key partners in IFAD operations

The survey shows that the positive trends observed in the previous biennium have been confirmed over 2008-2009: IFAD's overall commitment to involve farmers' organizations in the formulation of country strategic opportunities programs (COSOPs) and in project design and implementation has been maintained throughout the last biennium and improved in terms of quality and intensity of collaboration. Farmers' organizations were involved in 86 per cent of new COSOP formulations in 2008-2009, and in the majority of cases (61 per cent) the involvement went far beyond a simple consultation: farmers' organizations were full members of Country Program Management Teams or special workshops were organized with them. In the design of investment projects, farmers' organizations were consulted in 70 per cent of the new projects over the period. Both IFAD and borrowing countries were satisfied in the progress. The involvement increased from 34 per cent of new projects in 2006-2007 to 55 percent in 2008-2009.

Increased direct support

Furthermore direct support to farmers' organizations through grant financing has increased dramatically since the beginning of the Farmers' Forum process, from US $2.4 million per biennium in 2004-2005 to over US $12.0 million in 2008-2009.

Another positive trend has been the evolution towards fewer large grants supporting various national farmers' organizations through their regional networks or federations. It reduces IFAD's transaction costs for the design, approval and supervision of grants, contributes to the strengthening of regional groupings and fosters stronger coherence in overall partnerships with farmers' organizations.

Support to policy dialogue

IFAD continued to support the participation of farmers' organizations in policy dialogue at country, regional and international levels, including in recent global conferences and at the World Summit on Food Security.

In Latin America, the regional network of farmers' organizations (COPROFAM) has been supported to engage in the MERCOSUR Specialized Commission of Family Agriculture. In Central America, farmers' organizations have been supported to identify common interests and jointly engage in the discussion on the Central America Agricultural Policy. In sub-Saharan Africa, IFAD and the European Commission are jointly financing a large program on institutional development and support to policy engagement at national, sub-regional and Pan-African levels. Partnership between farmers' organizations, IFAD and governments has brought significant advantages in areas, which is the key to further improving IFAD's development effectiveness. It improves understanding of rural poverty and helps to better identify the target groups of projects. The contribution of farmers' organizations has ensured a stronger focus on small and poorer farmers.[80]

It has also given access to a wealth of local and indigenous knowledge and experience, which has enhanced project relevance. And it has contributed to increase project sustainability and local ownership.

---

[80] IFAD: Enabling poor Rural People to Overcome Poverty

The State of Food Insecurity in the World

World hunger is increasing: The World Food Summit (WFS) goal of halving the number of undernourished people in the world by 2015 is becoming more difficult to reach for many countries. FAO's most recent estimates put the number of hungry people at 923 million in 2007, an increase of more than 80 million since the 1990–92 base period. Long-term estimates (available up to 2003–05) show that some countries were well on track towards reaching the WFS and Millennium Development Goal (MDG) targets before the period of high food prices; however, even these countries may have suffered setbacks.

High food prices share much of the blame: The most rapid increase in chronic hunger experienced in recent years occurred between 2003–05 and 2007. FAO's provisional estimates show that, in 2007, 75 million more people were added to the total number of undernourished relative to 2003–05. While several factors are responsible, high food prices are driving millions of people into food insecurity, worsening conditions for many who were already food-insecure, and threatening long-term global food security.

The poorest, landless and female-headed households are the hardest hit: The vast majority of urban and rural households in the developing world relies on food purchases for most of their food and stands to lose from high food prices. High food prices reduce real income and worsen the prevalence of food insecurity and malnutrition among the poor by reducing the quantity and quality of food consumed.

Initial governmental policy responses have had limited effect: To contain the negative effects of high food prices, governments have introduced various measures, such as price controls and export restrictions. While understandable from an immediate social welfare perspective, many of these actions have been ad hoc and are likely to be ineffective and unsustainable. Some have had damaging effects on world price levels and stability.

High food prices are also an opportunity: In the long run, high food prices represent an opportunity for agriculture (including smallholder farmers) throughout the developing world, but they will have to be accompanied by the provision of essential public goods. Smallholder gains could fuel broader economic and rural development. Farming households can see immediate gains; other rural households may benefit in the longer run if higher prices turn into opportunities for increasing output and creating employment.

A comprehensive twin-track approach is required: Governments, donors, the United Nations, non- governmental organizations, civil society and the private sector must immediately combine their efforts in a strategic, twin-track approach to address the impact of high food prices on hunger. This should include:

(a) Measures to enable the agriculture sector, especially smallholders in developing countries, to respond to the high prices; and
(b) Carefully targeted safety nets and social protection programs for the most food-insecure and vulnerable

This is a global challenge requiring a global response.[81]

Millions more food-insecure

Urgent action and substantial investments needed

Soaring food prices have triggered worldwide concern about threats to global food security, shaking the unjustified complacency created by many years of

---

[81]The State of Food Insecurity in the World 2008, FAO, Rome

low commodity prices. From 3 to 5 June 2008, representatives of 180 countries plus the European Union, including many Heads of State and Government, met in Rome to express their conviction "that the international community needs to take urgent and coordinated action to combat the negative impacts of soaring food prices on the world's most vulnerable countries and populations". At the G8 Summit in Japan in July 2008, the leaders of the world's most industrialized nations voiced their deep concern "that the steep rise in global food prices, coupled with availability problems in a number of developing countries, is threatening global food security".

Moving away from hunger reduction goals

The concerns of the international community are well founded. For the first time since FAO started monitoring undernourishment trends, the number of chronically hungry people is higher in the most recent period relative to the base period. FAO estimates that, mainly as a result of high food prices, the number of chronically hungry people in the world rose by 75 million in 2007 to reach 923 million. The devastating effects of high food prices on the number of hungry people compound already worrisome long-term trends. Our analysis shows that in 2003–05, before the recent rise in food prices, there were 6 million more chronically hungry people in the world than in 1990–92, the progress towards the World Food Summit and Millennium Summit hunger reduction targets is measured. Early gains in hunger reduction achieved in a number of developing regions by the mid-1990s have not been sustained.

Hunger has increased, as the world has grown richer and produced more food than ever in the last decade. As this report has pointed out many times, this disappointing outcome reflects the lack of concerted action to combat hunger despite global commitments.

Soaring food prices have reversed some of the gains and successes in hunger reduction, making the mission of achieving the internationally agreed goals on hunger reduction more difficult. The task of reducing the number of hungry people by 500 million in the remaining seven years to 2015 will require an enormous and resolute global effort and concrete actions.

Poorest and most vulnerable worst hit

Food price increases have exacerbated the situation for many countries already in need of emergency interventions and food assistance due to other factors such as severe weather and conflict. Countries already afflicted by emergencies have to deal with the added burden of high food prices on food security, while others become more vulnerable to food insecurity because of high prices. Developing countries, especially the poorest, face difficult choices between maintaining macro-economic stability and putting in place policies and programme to deal with the negative impact of high food and fuel prices on their people.

Riots and civil disturbances, which have taken place in many low and middle income developing countries, signal the desperation caused by soaring food and fuel prices for millions of poor and also middleclass households. Analysis in this report shows that high food prices have a particularly devastating effect on the poorest in both urban and rural areas, the landless and female-headed households. Unless urgent measures are taken, high food prices may have detrimental long-term effects on human development as households, in their effort to deal with rising food bills, either reduce the quantity and quality of food consumed, cut expenditure on health and education or sell productive assets. Children, pregnant women and lactating mothers are at highest risk. Past experience with high food prices fully justifies such fears.

A strategic response: the twin-track approach

The food crisis brought about by soaring food prices in many developing countries needs an urgent and concrete response. At the same time, it should be recognized that high food prices are the result of a delicate balance between food supply and demand. These two facts show that, more than ever before, the twin-track approach to hunger reduction advocated by FAO and its development partners is key to addressing not only the threats to food security caused by high food prices but also the opportunities that arise. In the immediate term, carefully targeted safety nets and social protection programs are urgently required in order to ensure that everyone is able to access the food they need for a healthy life. In parallel, the focus should be on helping producers, especially small scale farmers, to boost food production, mainly by facilitating The State of Food Insecurity in the World 2008 their access to seeds, fertilizers, animal feed and other inputs.

This should improve food supplies and lower prices in local markets. In the medium-to-long term, the focus should be on strengthening the agriculture sectors of developing countries to enable them to respond to growth in demand. Expanding food production in poor countries through enhanced productivity must constitute the cornerstone of policies, strategies and programs seeking to attain a sustainable solution for food security. High food prices and the incentives they provide can be harnessed to re-launch agriculture in the developing world. This is essential not only to face the current crisis, but also to respond to the increasing demand for food, feed and bio-fuel production and to prevent the recurrence of such crises in the future. Re-launching agriculture in developing countries is also critical for the achievement of meaningful results in poverty and hunger reduction and to reverse the current worrisome trends.

This will entail empowering large numbers of small-scale farmers worldwide to expand agricultural output. If we consider, agricultural growth as an engine for poverty reduction, we have address the structural constraints facing agriculture, particularly for the millions of smallholder producers in agriculture-based economies. Therefore, the public sector should expand public investment in rural infrastructure and essential services – in roads, irrigation facilities, water harvesting, and storage, slaughterhouses, fishing ports and credit, as well as electricity, schools and health services – in order to create favourable conditions for private investment in rural areas. At the same time, increased resources must be devoted to more sustainable technologies that support more-intensive agriculture and that assist farmers to increase the resilience of their food production systems and to cope with climate change.

A coherent and coordinated strategy is vital

Many developing countries have taken unilateral action in efforts to contain the negative effects of high food prices, including the imposition of price controls and export restrictions. Such responses may not be sustainable and would actually contribute to further rises in world price levels and instability. To face threats and exploit opportunities posed by high food prices effectively and efficiently, strategies must be based on a comprehensive and coordinated multilateral response.

Urgent, broad-based and large-scale investments are needed in order to address in a sustainable manner the growing food-insecurity problems affecting the poor and hungry. No single country or institution will be able to resolve this crisis on its own. Governments of developing and developed countries, the UN agencies, international institutions, civil society, donors and the private sector all have important roles to play in the global fight against hunger. It is vital that the international community share a common vision of how best to assist governments in eradicating chronic hunger and that all parties work together to translate this vision into reality on the scale required. The situation cannot wait any longer.

The resolve of world leaders at the June 2008 Summit on World Food Security in Rome and the fact that the G8 Summit placed concerns surrounding high food and fuel prices at the top of its agenda demonstrates a growing political will to address hunger. Moreover, substantial commitments have been made for increased financial support to developing countries to address the food security threats caused by high food prices. Nevertheless, unless this political will and donor pledges are turned into urgent and real actions, millions more will fall into deep poverty and chronic hunger. The need for concerted action to combat hunger and malnutrition has never been stronger. I am hopeful that the global community will rise to the challenge.[82]

MORE AND BETTER

MORE AND BETTER is an international campaign for food, agriculture and rural development aid to eradicate hunger and poverty.

The world has the resources and know-how to eliminate hunger and poverty. It is totally unacceptable that 30 000 people die of hunger each day, that 850 million people are severely hungry, and that 1,3 billion people live in extreme poverty.

---

[82]Jacques Diouf, FAO Director-General

MORE AND BETTER has been established to support and be a part of the fight to eradicate hunger and poverty. The campaign will advocate for increases to both the quantity and quality of aid for agriculture, rural development and food as an important part of eradicating extreme poverty and hunger. This goal links closely to the first Millennium Development Goal, which provides an important milestone for this campaign.

MORE AND BETTER is an independent campaign comprising social movements, civil society and nongovernmental organizations. Our shared goals:

(a) A world without hunger and poverty: Under the banner of MORE AND BETTER the campaign will lobby for vital changes in national and international policies geared towards:
(b) A substantial decrease in the number of hungry and undernourished people and people living in poverty
(c) A major increase in development aid for agriculture, rural development and food in the developing countries and
(d) Significant improvements in the quality of aid for agriculture, rural development and food security

Focus on agriculture and rural development:

The majority of the undernourished people live in poverty in rural areas of developing countries, often in drought prone and marginalized areas. The majority are farmers or others whose livelihoods are closely linked to the land.

To eradicate hunger and poverty, aid must be targeted to these people and focus on agriculture and rural development, which creates livelihoods that are truly sustainable for generations to come. The causes of hunger and poverty are complex and manifold. Food production and rural development in developing countries are impacted by global, national and local policies, economies and power structures; trade rules and trading practices, ownership of land and land reforms, the quality and quantity of agricultural research, possibilities and terms for credit, tax policies etc.

MORE AND BETTER recognizes that increasing the quantity and quality of aid for agriculture and rural development addresses one component of global hunger. It is complementary to other campaigns also fighting to end hunger and poverty.

Reversing the trend!

Aid for agriculture and rural development has dropped dramatically in recent years. According to the Rural Poverty Report 2001 by the International Fund for Agricultural Development (IFAD), support for agriculture collapsed – decreasing by two-thirds, between 1987 and 1998. The total external assistance to agriculture and rural development has fallen from US $ 21.8 billion in 1988 to US $ 11.9 billion in 2000 (1995 US $). Today, only 12 percent of total Official Development Assistance (ODA) goes to agriculture as opposed to 20 percent in the late 1980s.

The trend needs to be reversed!

The support for agriculture and rural development must increase dramatically. The quality of aid is important. The quality of aid and support for agriculture and rural development is as important as the quantity. There are as many examples of good aid as there are of ineffective and inappropriate aid and support.

MORE AND BETTER is concerned about the quality of aid that is delivered to developing countries. We will evaluate the aid and support, find out what is good and bad, work out guidelines, promote good examples and influence governments, organizations and agencies to increase the quality of aid and support.

Common principles

The climatic, natural, political, cultural and economic situations of countries are diverse and often unique. However, there are several common principles, which could improve the quality of aid targeted for agriculture, fisheries and rural development:

Aid should support the programs and policies developed by the recipient communities and countries

Aid should be provided in a manner that does not disrupt local production and markets. It should support long-term development and respond to the expressed needs of local communities. Local and national food security should be a top priority for aid. Aid should lead to greater autonomy and self-reliance of the recipient countries with regard to food production and availability of food for all. AId should strengthen the local control of resources and reach the intended beneficiaries in rural areas.

Working with local communities and social organizations:

Better aid supports local communities, community-based organizations and social organisations particularly in building: political empowerment; the capacity of people to articulate their views; implementation their own development models; and meaningful participation in development processes.

It recognizes that the needs and realities of rural communities are at the core of solutions to solve hunger and poverty. Development aid should give priority to strengthening small-scale production sector to ensure realization of sustainable livelihoods for the majority.

Building on local culture and knowledge: Knowledge held by communities is based on generations of people interacting with their unique surroundings. Better aid should build on the wealth of local culture and knowledge held by communities, supporting processes that facilitate appropriate technological solutions.

Promote diversity: Aid should promote diversities - human, cultural, biological, environmental, and in production methods.

A culture of participation: Better aid generates inclusive dialogue and engagement among different development actors. Implementation of agricultural, pastorals', fisheries, forestry and rural development must be based on democratic consultations and meaningful ongoing community participation. Aid should contribute towards reducing existing inequalities.

Gender is a factor: Women play a major role in agricultural production and in local food security. Better Aid facilitates the empowerment of women, recognizing the fundamental importance they hold in providing food for their families and for the community.

Sustainability: Livelihoods are sustainable when they can cope with and recover from stresses and shocks that threaten food security without undermining their natural resource base. Building local capital, social systems, financial capital and the natural resources on which they depend is critical.

Better aid should be guided by a clear development paradigm supportive of the principles of social, economic and environmental sustainability and intergenerational equity.

Coherence and linkages: Efforts should foster linkages between the local, national and global, opportunities for learning and knowledge sharing. Better Aid should provide platforms for the exchange of experience globally, provide nationally coherent programs for delivery of Aid, and should foster linkages among local efforts. It should address problematic structures and mechanisms that limit the effectiveness of aid in reaching the poor and hungry people in the world.

Changes in delivery and focus of aid: New policies and practices for agriculture, pastorals', fisheries and global food trade are needed to end hunger and poverty, and to promote sustainable development. Changes in the delivery and focus of aid are needed to achieve this. To support such new policies and practices aid should:

(a) Facilitate provision of sufficient, safe, nutritious food (food security),
(b) Put emphasis on income strategies, peoples' livelihoods, local production systems, local markets, fair trade, fair and good distribution systems, protection of markets where needed to enhance national and local food security, and avoid the use of food aid where it will threatened the marked for local products
(c) Support realization of land reform, water rights and unrestricted access to genetic resources for food and agriculture and wider agricultural biodiversity for smallholder farmers; exclusive fishing zones for artisan fisher-folks; grazing rights for pastoralists; improved common property resource management;

(d) Support sustainable, farmer-led, smallholder / family / community agricultural systems (e.g. agro-ecology, sustainable agriculture, organic agriculture).
(e) To achieve this requires improved education and public awareness not only for how to implement this but also how to avoid problems cause by poorly conceived aid.

The campaign: MORE AND BETTER is an independent campaign comprising more than 50 countries and a core of unified national campaigns. The campaign is closely linked to the purposes of the Food and Agriculture Organization of the United Nation's International Alliance against Hunger (IAAH) and the achievement of the Millennium Development Goal to reduce hunger and poverty.

The MORE AND BETTER also recognizes and cooperates with the International Planning Committee for Food Sovereignty, which is established by social movements and nongovernmental organizations. Participants have joined hands to mobilize political will to increase both the quantity and quality of aid for agricultural and rural development. This is the thread that binds the participants in common cause. The causes of hunger and poverty are complex and manifold. Each organization and campaign focuses on those that it sees are the most important and the decline of aid to agriculture and rural development and have agreed to join together to reverse this trend and improve the quality of this aid.

MORE AND BETTER will seek to increase the level and quality of development assistance directed towards food, agriculture and rural development to eradicate hunger and poverty. The organizations and campaigns in developing countries will play the major role in defining better aid. They will also work to increase the level and quality of support from their own governments and donors for agriculture and rural development.

Organizations and campaigns in the OECD /donor countries will lobby their own governments for MORE AND BETTER aid for agriculture and rural development, based on the overall goals of the campaign and the particular policies chosen at the national levels that best address these goals.

The international campaign will approach international institutions on issues of common concerns to the national campaigns, facilitate cooperation, exchanging of experiences and viewpoints.

The international coordinating committee:

Representatives from the following organizations are members of the international coordinating committee of 'More and Better':

(a) IFAP /FIPA; International Federation of Agricultural Producers
(b) ROPPA; Network of Peasant Organizations and Producers in West Africa
(c) MAELA; The Agro-ecological Movement of Latin-America
(d) Action Aid International,
(e) Green Movement of Sri Lanka,
(f) IRDF; Integrated Rural Development Foundation (the Philippines)
(g) CENESTA; Center for Sustainable Development & Environment (Iran) / APNEK; Association for the protection of Nature and the Environment, Kairouan (Tunisia)
(h) CRDA; Christian Relief and Development Association (Ethiopia)
(i) Kenyan Federation of Agricultural Producers (Kenya)

(j) CIPRES; the Centre for research, promotion, rural and social development (Nicaragua)
(k) Canadian Food grains bank (Canada)
(l) Bread for the World Institute (USA)
(m) UK Food Group (United Kingdom)
(n) Italian Food Sovereignty Campaign (Italy)
(o) Development Fund (Norway)

Some definitions in this document:

Aid in this document is synonymous with 'development assistance' and other similar terms. Different terms are used in different languages and by different organizations.

'Agriculture, Pastorals' and Fisheries' includes cropping, livestock husbandry, pastorals, fisheries, forestry and other natural resource use for food production and food gathering, which is dispersed throughout rural, urban and semi - urban areas.

'Farmers, Herders and Fisher-folk' in this document refer to smallholder peasant / family crop and livestock farmers, herders/ pastoralists, fisher-folk, landless farmers and indigenous peoples, among other users of natural resources for food production.

'Natural Resources' include land, water, coastal commons, forests, genetic resources / agricultural biodiversity, Farmers, fisher-folks, herders, pastoralists, indigenous peoples and agricultural workers

We encourage all organizations and networks, which support the goals of the MORE AND BETTER.

More and Better has been established to support and be a part of the fight to eradicate hunger and poverty. This objective is closely linked to the first Millennium Development Goal which provides an important milestone for this campaign. More and

Better will advocate for the increase of both the quantity and quality of support to agriculture, rural development and food.

A world free of hunger and poverty:

The world has got enough resources to feed the planet but still 923 million people go to bed hungry every night (FAO 2008). This is totally unacceptable. Under the banner of MORE and BETTER the campaign will lobby for vital changes in national and international policies geared towards:

(a) A substantial decrease in the number of hungry and undernourished people and people living in poverty;
(b) A major increase in development aid for agriculture, rural development and food in the developing countries;
(c) Significant improvements in the quality of aid for agriculture, rural development and food.

Why focus on agriculture and rural development?

The majority of the undernourished people live in poverty in rural areas of developing countries, often in drought-prone and marginalized areas. The majority are farmers or others whose livelihoods are closely linked to the land. To eradicate hunger and poverty, aid must be targeted to these people and focus on agriculture and rural development which creates livelihoods that are truly sustainable for generations to come. The causes of hunger and poverty are complex and manifold. Food production and rural development in developing countries are impacted by global, national and local policies, economies and power structures; trade rules and trading practices, ownership of land and land reforms, the quality and quantity of agricultural research, possibilities and terms for credit, tax policies etc.

More and Better recognizes that increasing the quantity and quality of aid for agriculture and rural development addresses one component of global hunger.

The quality of aid is important:

The quality of aid and support for agriculture and rural development is as important as the quantity. There are as many examples of good aid as there are of ineffective and inappropriate aid and support. More and Better is concerned about the quality of aid that is delivered to developing countries. We will evaluate the aid and support, find out what is good and bad, work out guidelines, promote good examples and influence governments, organizations and agencies to increase the quality of aid and support.

Participants have joined hands to mobilize political will to increase both the quantity and quality of aid for agricultural and rural development. This is the thread that binds the participants in a common cause. The causes of hunger and poverty are complex and manifold. Each organization and campaign focuses on those that it sees are the most important and will determine its own goals and priorities. But, we are all concerned by the decline of aid to agriculture and rural development and have agreed to join together to reverse this trend and improve the quality of this aid.

The organizations and campaigns in developing countries will play the major role in defining better aid. They will also work to increase the level and quality of support from their own governments and donors for agriculture and rural development.

Organizations and campaigns in the OECD/donor countries will lobby their own governments for More and Better aid for agriculture and rural development, based on the overall goals of the campaign and the particular policies chosen at the national levels that best address these goals.

The international campaign will approach international institutions on issues of common concerns to the national campaigns, facilitate co-operation, exchanging of experiences and viewpoints.

The More and Better cooperates, among the others, with the International Alliance Against Hunger (IAAH) and the International Planning Committee for Food Sovereignty (IPC) which is established by social movements and non-governmental organizations.[83]

IFAD

The International Fund for Agricultural Development (IFAD) announced that it will raise **$1.5 billion** in new contributions to support the agency's efforts to boost the living conditions of rural poor across the developing world.

In a Press release, IFAD stated that across the world, 2 billion rural people depended on 500 million smallholder farms in developing countries which inspired it to focus its efforts on the areas of food and Income securIty. "ThIs sIgnIfIcant support from IFAD's member states, especially during these challenging global economic times, demonstrates extraordinary resolve and political will to give agriculture a major boost and help the world's small farmers find their way out of poverty," IFAD's president Mr. Kanayo F. Nwanze said.

The injection of new funds will fuel IFAD's role in building international development architecture for

[83]More and Better – An International network for support of food, agriculture and rural development to eradicate hunger and poverty, C/o Terra Nuova, Rome, Italy, www. More and Better Org

the world's poorest people, the agency said in a press release. Some 40 to 50 per cent of the financing is expected to be redirected to development projects across Sub-Saharan Africa. The resources that IFAD provides as loans and grants to developing countries are replenished by member states during a consultation period at the agency headquarters in Rome. The agency leverages the contributions in an effort to mobilize greater funding through project co-financing with national governments, international donors and the private sector.[84]

The USAID Program

For more than 50 years, the Food for Peace program has brought hope and nourishment to the hungry corners of the world. Approximately 3 billion people in 150 countries have benefited directly from our food. The secret of Food for Peace's success lies in the unique combination of American compassion together with the unmatched efficiency of our nation's farmers. It is less a triumph of government than of working Americans, for in its essence, Food for Peace is the work of farmers, businessmen, grain elevator operators, truckers, bargemen, freight forwarders, port operations, private voluntary organizations, and government officials. Together they form an unbroken chain of humanity stretching from this country's fertile fields to hungry families half a world away.

In the end, hope is what America has promised, and hope is what Food for Peace delivers around the world every day.

Upon reaching its destination, the food is used in a variety of ways, and always for the people most vulnerable to the effects of hunger: children under

---

[84]Anjali Sharma (2011), "$1.5 billion to be raised for rural poor", The Statesman, December 20, 2011

age 5, pregnant women, the elderly, and the poorest families in a community. During an emergency in which people face threat of imminent starvation, food - wheat, sorghum, corn and other commodities are distributed to save their lives. If the symptoms of extreme malnutrition have already appeared, a nutritionally fortified ration with blended, fortified, and processed food is provided. In less dire circumstances, food can be used to compensate people for work, such as building roads or repairing water and irrigation systems. In turn, these projects help protect communities from future hunger by providing them access to local markets for their produce, keeping them healthy, and improving their harvests.

Other methods of using food aid include:

(a) Working with farmers to identify better ways to sow and tend their fields or providing improved seed, thus improving their harvest by linking them with American know-how
(b) Improving women's education about nutrition, resulting in healthier babies and children
(c) Encouraging the production of higher value commodities that could earn money in local markets
(d) Providing micronutrients, such as vitamin A, iodine, zinc, and iron, that hungry children often lack
(e) Feeding children at school to encourage attendance and improve academic performance

Though there are many ways of providing food aid, Food for Peace's goal remains constant: to minimize hunger in the world so that people everywhere can enjoy active and productive lives and, ultimately, to ensure that one day no one needs food aid.

Farmer-to-Farmer Program (FTF):

SAID has awarded cooperative agreements to four institutions for implementation of the core FTF volunteer programs for international agricultural development for fiscal years 2009 - 2013. The program will provide services to 20 core countries, providing nearly 3,000 volunteer technical assistance assignments averaging three and a half weeks each. An additional Special Program Support project funds volunteer activities with new implementing organizations and special activities in about 10 countries. The four FTF Program implementing organizations will work closely with overseas USAID Missions and local partner organizations, supporting a variety of development programs aimed at reducing poverty and stimulating sustainable and broad-based economic growth. The core FTF program agreements allow USAID country programs to provide additional funding for agricultural development projects using FTF volunteers.

FTF places increased emphasis on economic impact and measurable results by concentrating volunteer assignments in specific geographical areas, commodities programs, and service sectors. New programs go beyond simply placing volunteers on an individual basis and focus on developing specific market chains for which over-all impact can be evaluated.

Programs build institutions and transfer technology and management expertise to link small farmers with markets that make use of comparative advantages in production, processing, and marketing. Volunteers typically work with medium and small agro-enterprises, cooperatives, individual producers, agricultural extension and research agencies, and financial institutions.

Current Farmer-to-Farmer Program:

The implementing agencies and country activities are listed below:

Countries	**Country Projects**
Egypt:	Dairy, Horticulture
Lebanon:	Ruminants, Horticulture
Ghana:	Horticulture, Staple foods
Mali:	Staple Foods, Small ruminants
Nigeria:	Staple Foods, Apiculture
Kenya:	Oil Seed, Grain Crops
Tanzania:	Legumes, Horticulture, and Grain Crops
Uganda:	Oil seed, Grain Crops
Georgia:	Dairy, fruit and Vegetable, Hazelnuts
Moldova:	Dairy, Fruit and Vegetable
Uzbekistan;	TDB
Tajikistan:	Dairy and Livestock
Angola:	Horticulture, Legume
Malawi:	Groundnuts, Horticulture, and Soya Beans
Dominican Republic:	Tree Crops, Horticulture
Guyana:	Non-traditional Horticulture, Aquaculture
Haiti:	Horticulture, Small LIvestock, and Apiculture
Nicaragua:	Dairy
El Salvador:	Horticulture, Dairy
Bangladesh:	Potato, Maize, Fisheries and Livestock
Ethiopia:	TBD, Cambodia: TBD
Kenya:	Avian Influenza (Partnerships with Kenya)
South Africa:	Grapes, Fish and Agricultural Education
Senegal:	Millet and Moringa species
Niger:	Millet and Moringa Species
Latin America:	Fair Trade Coffee
Africa, Asia:	Fair Trade Coffee

Dominic, Grenada, St Kitts and Nevis:	Food Security
Ethiopia:	Sesame
Peru and	SME Competitiveness
Honduras:	SME Competitiveness
Mexico:	Aquaculture Development
India:	Aquaculture Development
Bangladesh:	Aquaculture Development
Trinidad:	Aquaculture Development
Tobago:	Aquaculture Development
Indonesia:	Aquaculture Development
Liberia:	Animal Healthcare Training

In short, major areas of program focus are: horticulture, dairy and livestock, staple food crops, producer organization development, financial services, marketing and processing, and natural resources management.[85]

Afghanistan

Roots of Peace:

Restores Agriculture in Afghanistan

Roots of Peace (RoP), a California-based non-profit organization, has successfully implemented agricultural programs helping more than 100,000 farmers to rebuild their farm enterprises, growing food crops to feed their families and for export. Director of Horticulture for the Afghan Ministry of Agriculture, Irrigation and Livestock says that 'Roots of Peace' is the premier international horticultural specialist working with us in Afghanistan. We would like to see their effective programs replicated throughout our 32 provinces across Afghanistan.

R-o-P, which initiated its Afghanistan programs in 2001, receives funding from the United States Agency for International Development (USAID), U.S. Department of Agriculture (USDA), U.S. Department

---

[85]USAID Program Report

of State, the Asian Development Bank, the European Union, and the World Bank to remove minefields and restore vineyards and orchards in this nation once known as "The Garden of Central Asia." R-o-P has partnered with the University of California Davis and other international agricultural experts to bring modern but simple agricultural practices to Afghan farmers. Its successful programs are now being replicated by other international organizations in a collective effort to increase farm income in a country where 80 percent of the population is dependent on small-scale farming for their livelihoods. Roots- of - Peace has a program, the ROP Penny Campaign, which has raised over 25 million American pennies to build schools and soccer fields in Afghanistan.

Grapes: R-o-P assists grape producers with the simple but forgotten practice of trellising their vineyards, which lifts the grapes off the ground and into the sun. Knowing that farmers who invest their own money in a project are more likely to succeed, RoP has targeted farmers who are willing to pay a portion of the cost of installing trellises on their vineyards. The response to the program has been tremendous. In the first year, only ten farmers participated in the program. In the second year, more than a thousand signed up to participate; exceeding the number RoP could serve. The second year USAID put $100,000 into the program. Follow these successes, the World Bank is putting $1,000,000 and the US Department of Defense is putting $800,000 into trellising programs modeled after RoP's. Farmers easily see that trellising greatly increases the amount of high-quality table grapes they can produce per acre. With the right conditions, many farmers have doubled their income the year after installing the trellises, making significantly more money per hectare than they can with any other crop including poppies.

Orchards: R-o-P is importing over 50,000 orange saplings from California as a first step in rebuilding the Eastern Afghan citrus orchards destroyed during decades of war. This is part of more than 7,000 acres of new fruit and nut orchards being established in Eastern Afghanistan by small-scale farmers with help from USAID, funneled through RoP. In Northeast Afghanistan, R-o-P and local farmers have established 93 nurseries and 1,098 small-scale commercial orchards since 2007. This gift will continue supplying high-quality, highly productive trees to support the expansion of Afghanistan's tree crops for years to come.

Women and Walnuts: Thanks to a USAID-funded program implemented by R-o-P in 2006-2008, women in a small community in Afghanistan's northeastern province of Badakhshan are finding part-time employment processing walnuts in a new walnut purchasing and processing center built partially with U.S. funds and partially with funds invested by a Kabul business. This is probably the first outside-the-home job most of these women have ever had, adding to their families' incomes and increasing the value of the walnuts produced on their family's trees. This and other marketing efforts provide the monetary incentives for the families of these women and their neighbors to plant the improved-performance walnut, apricot, almond and cherry trees that local tree nurseries are producing with assistance from R-o-P. More than 80,000 trees were planted in 2008 with another 80,000 ready for planting in 2009. The combination of production and marketing efforts will assure the sustainable development of this tree-based industry.

Fruit / Nut Processing, Packaging and Marketing: R-o-P established the first cold chain in Afghanistan in 2005 to maintain the shelf life of fresh grapes, melons and pomegranates exported to neighboring countries India and Pakistan and began testing trade routes to Dubai, Germany, Russia and Ukraine. In the initial year of export trials (2005), 100 metric tons of chilled grapes were exported. RoP looks forward to continuing its work in Afghanistan, promoting good relations between America and the Afghan people.

As the USDA and USAID International Food Aid Conference convenes in the "breadbasket" of America today, Roots of Peace, a California based humanitarian NGO, announced the award of a major grant for 12,500 metric tons of wheat flour estimated at $4 million. The bounty they shared between Afghan farmers through this USDA/ROP program given in the form of wheat flour will be directly donated and sold to fund local development projects —a resource providing food security and horticultural programs to fund the creation of 5,000 new orchards and grape vineyards in the challenging war-torn South Central Afghan provinces of Ghazni, Wardak and Logar.

Speaker Nancy Pelosi who attended the "launch" of Roots of Peace over a decade ago and joined with Founder & CEO Heidi Kuhn at the U.S. Embassy in Kabul, Afghanistan on February 21, 2009, stated, "Through Mines to Vines™, Roots of Peace brings hope to the people of Afghanistan by replacing the scourge of landmines with bountiful agricultural fields. Their work is an outstanding example of how an organization committed to improving the lives of the Afghan people can bring about positive change."

Since 2001, Roots of Peace has removed over 100,000 landmines to create fertile grounds for peace and trained over 120,000 Afghan farmers to grow alternative agricultural crops to poppies. Through innovative programs such as MINES TO VINES™ and POPPIES TO POMEGRANATES, the funding from USAID and other international agencies has created successful export markets for Afghan farmers- often doubling their income through sustainable horticultural programs to teach the next generation.

"Farming is an act of hope. This is 'why' nothing could be more important to an American wheat producer than knowing they can make a difference in an Afghan farmers' life by sharing a bountiful harvest—providing sustainable alternative agricultural crops to poppies by empowering families to heal the wounds of war and ultimately 'breaking bread' with neighbors again. The Dari word for wheat is 'naan' and we aspire for the bread of life to rise again," says Heidi Kuhn, Founder and CEO.[86]

Institute for Agricultural Trade Policy
Where Global and Local meet sustainably

In 1986, leaders of rural and farm movements from around the world gathered in Geneva to discuss the deepening farm crisis that was forcing farmers off the land and devastating rural communities. It quickly became clear that many of the obstacles facing farmers in the U.S. were the same challenges facing farmers in Europe, Asia and Africa, and international trade agreements were deeply affecting local rural communities across the globe. At the conclusion of the Geneva meeting, a small group of rural and farm leaders—who now comprise IATP's board of directors—identified the need for a new organization to examine the links between global policy and local communities.

Mark Ritchie, then a trade policy analyst for the state of Minnesota, returned from the Geneva meeting to the United States and incorporated the Institute for Agriculture and Trade Policy as a non-profit, tax-exempt organization, with the mission of fostering

---

[86]Roots of Peace, Heidi Kuhn, USA / Dr. Zach Lea, Kabul, January 16, 2009 / April 7, 2009—Kansas City, Missouri

sustainable rural communities and regions. In 1987, IATP began to organize and report on the newly launched round of international trade negotiations being conducted by the General Agreement on Tariffs and Trade or GATT—which eventually became the World Trade Organization. The rules of agricultural trade set in the GATT and implemented at the WTO have deeply influenced national and local farm policies around the globe over the last two decades. Since its founding, IATP has played a unique role in analyzing international trade policy and summarizing the ramifications of these policies on local communities, both in the U.S. and abroad.

In the 1990s, IATP expanded beyond its initial focus on international policymaking institutions like the WTO to include the promotion of positive alternatives to economically, socially and environmentally destructive agricultural and trade practices. This wider focus gave IATP the opportunity to work with a much larger audience of partners. For example, with the Center for Agriculture and the Environment in the Netherlands, IATP developed tools to help U.S. farmers increase their income by reducing on-farm pollution. We tackled major health concerns of rural communities by organizing campaigns to stop the contamination of farmland by toxic waste incinerators.

We helped launch international efforts to promote certified sustainable farming, fishing and forestry and sustainable consumption, including fair trade for farmers and fair wages for everyone working to put food on our tables. We put our ideas into action to demonstrate the viability of fair trade by founding Trans-fair USA, an international fair trade certification organization, and starting Peace Coffee, now a nationally consumed fair trade coffee brand.[87]

---

[87] Institute for Agricultural Trade Policy website

With offices and staff in the U.S. and Switzerland, IATP continues to expand international partnerships, adapting ideas, strategies and experiences from the global community to the challenges facing local communities.

Supporting small-scale farmers:
(Sweden 2011)

Development support for small-scale farmers must be based on both the enforcement of basic human rights and a pro-poor development of markets. This was the conclusion of a seminar on "Rights-based versus market-based development: a false dichotomy for small-scale farmers" held in Stockholm, Sweden in 2011.

The seminar, part of a series of 'provocations' initiated by IIED and Hivos and hosted by The Swedish International Agriculture network Initiative (SIANI), The Swedish Cooperative Centre (SCC) and the Swedish International Development-cooperation Agency (SIDA), was attended by 90 policymakers, academics and practitioners working at the interface between small-scale production, markets and development.

A quick show of hands at the seminar's start suggested that almost all the participants believed that development approaches for small-scale farmers should be based on human rights first, and markets second.

Rights alone are not enough

There are many reasons why development policy should focus on the most vulnerable, clearly define their entitlements (as well as the duty-holders of those entitlements) and emphasize non-discrimination. "Rebalancing food systems so they can work more equitably is absolutely key to combating hunger in the world today", said Olivier de Schutter, UN special rapporteur on the right to food. The extreme poverty of small-scale food producers — 500 million farmers, fishers and herders are food insecure — is caused not by a lack of economic growth but by unequal power relations, according to Ngolia Kimanzu of the Swedish Cooperative Centre. "You can only address that with a rights-based approach to development," he said.

But if the room was behind Kimanzu's thinking, it was soon clear that emphasizing rights alone is not enough to lift small-scale farmers out of poverty.

In practice, rights-based policies are difficult to implement and generally do not avoid problems of power and embedded advantage. "Many low income groups...would not trust the courts or the legal system to deliver for them and would feel excluded from that sort of discourse", explained IIED researcher Diana Mitlin. "Court outcomes often clearly favour the most powerful social groups," she added.

Rights-based approaches present a simplistic package of measures to tackle what are very diverse and complex problems on the ground. And they are not easily separated from markets — markets depend on rights and the way in which rights are constituted has profound implications for the way in which markets function, said Mitlin.

And let's not forget the proven power of markets. One participant from Sweden's Ministry of Foreign Affairs provided a reminder of just how much we already owe to market-led development: "Before we chuck out standard market-based approaches... can I remind people that the big story of development over the past three decades is that millions of entrepreneurs in Asia have lifted hundreds of millions of people out of poverty and, in the process, put a number of countries on course to achieving the first Millennium Development Goal".

Combinations in practice

Instead of opting for rights or markets, it seems we need both. But how do we blend the two in practice? There was no shortage of examples in the room.

Many were based on governments tilting markets so that they favour small-scale farmers. André Gonçalves, from the Centro Ecologico in Brazil, talked about the Brazilian Food Acquisition Programme, where the government buys products directly from smallholders and distributes them to a network of daycare centres, hospitals and other food insecure groups. Gonçalves also described Brazilian legislation, brought in in 2009, to guarantee at least one-third of the annual budget from the National Programme of Schools Meals — around US$500 million — to be used in buying food from family farmers.

Brazil is not alone in focusing on school meal programmes to support smallholders. "There are many examples of countries that have built entire industries on these types of initiatives," said Katarina Eriksson, from the Tetra Laval group. "Thailand, for example, has built its whole dairy industry on school milk and Iran is doing the same thing".

Other examples were based, not on state procurement, but on supporting organizations to integrate smallholders into industrial value chains. "We support [efforts] to build systems whereby you can treat a lot of small farmers as a larger entity," said Eriksson. This includes working with 'dairy hubs' in developing countries to link small dairy herders to global value chains.

Kimanzu echoed the need to support producer organizations as the most effective way of giving farmers a voice in markets. He talked about a program in Costa Rica run by nongovernmental organization Sedeco that, by supporting an organic farmers association, has enabled small-scale farmers to compete with big multinationals such as Monsanto and penetrate the country's organic production sector.

Kimanzu's comments seemed to strike a chord. Indeed, when asked by Lasse Krantz from Sida what the implications of a right-based approach to market development would be for donors, all the speakers stressed the importance of supporting grassroots farmers' organizations as the best way to give farmers a stronger voice and more bargaining power in policy negotiations. Rights-based and market-based approaches to development for small-scale farmers may be promoted separately in theory but, as the breadth of examples showed, they are often more effective when taken together. The overwhelming message from last week's seminar is that it is a false dichotomy.[88]

The Food Movement:
Its Power and Possibilities

The number of hungry people has soared to nearly 1 billion, despite strong global harvests. And for even more people, sustenance has become a health hazard—with the US diet implicated in four out of our top ten deadly diseases. Power over soil, seeds and food sales is ever more tightly held, and farmland in the global South is being snatched away from indigenous people by speculators set to profit on climbing food prices. Just four companies control at least three-quarters of international grain trade; and in the United States, by 2000, just ten corporations—with boards totaling only 138 people—had come to

[88]International Institute for Environment and Development, 4 end sleigh Street, London, 2011

account for half of US food and beverage sales. Conditions for American farm workers remain so horrific that seven Florida growers have been convicted of slavery involving more than 1,000 workers. Life expectancy of US farm workers is forty-nine years.

That's one current. It's antidemocratic and deadly.

There is, however, another current, which is democratizing power and aligning farming with nature's genius. Many call it simply "the global food movement." In the United States it's building on the courage of truth tellers from Upton Sinclair to Rachel Carson, and worldwide it has been gaining energy and breadth for at least four decades.

Some Americans see the food movement as "nice" but peripheral—a middle-class preoccupation with farmers' markets, community gardens and healthy school lunches. But no, I'll argue here. It is at heart revolutionary, with some of the world's poorest people in the lead, from Florida farm workers to Indian villagers. It has the potential to transform not just the way we eat but the way we understand our world, including ourselves. And that vast power is just beginning to erupt.

Work

In a farm worker camp in Ohio, a young mother sat on her bed. She was dying of cancer, but with no bitterness she asked me a simple question: **"We provide food to people —why don't they respect our work?"** That was 1984. She had no protection from pesticides, or even the right to safe drinking water in the field.

Twenty-five years later, in Immokalee, Florida, I walked through a grungy, sweltering 300-foot trailer, home to eight tomato pickers, but what struck me most was a sense of possibility in the workers themselves.

They are among the 4,000 mainly Latino, Mayan Indian and Haitian members of the Coalition of Immokalee Workers, formed in 1993—more than two decades after Cesar Chavez's United Farm Workers' victorious five-year grape strike and national boycott. In the 1990s, CIW's struggle over five years, including a 230-mile walk and hunger strike, achieved the first industry wide pay increase in twenty years. Still, it only brought real wages back to pre-1980 levels. So in 2001, CIW launched its Campaign for Fair Food. Dogged organizing forced four huge fast-food companies—McDonald's, Taco Bell, Burger King and Subway—to agree to pay a penny more per pound and adhere to a code of conduct protecting workers. Four large food-service providers, including Sodexo, were also brought on board. Beginning this fall, CIW will start implementing these changes at 90 percent of Florida tomato farms—improving the lives of 30,000 tomato pickers. Now the campaign is focused on supermarkets such as Trader Joe's, Stop & Shop and Giant.

Land: In Brazil, almost 400,000 farm worker families have not only found their voices but gained access to land, joining the roughly half-billion small farms worldwide that produce 70 percent of the world's food.

Elsewhere, calls for more equitable access to land in recent decades have generally gone nowhere—despite evidence that smallholders are typically more productive and better resource guardians than big operators.

So what happened in Brazil?

With the end of dictatorship in 1984 came the birth of arguably the largest social movement in the hemisphere: the Landless Workers Movement, known by its Portuguese acronym MST. Less than 4 percent of Brazil's landowners control about half the land often gained illegally. MST's goal is land reform, and in 1988 Brazil's new Constitution gave the movement legal grounding: Article 5 states that "property shall fulfill its social function," and Article 184 affirms the government's power to "expropriate...for purposes of agrarian reform, rural property" that fails to meet this requirement. Well-organized occupations of unused land, under the cover of night, had been MST's early tactic; after 1988 the same approach helped compel the government to uphold the Constitution.

Because of the courage of these landless workers, a million people are building new lives on roughly 35 million acres, creating several thousand farming communities with schools serving 150,000 kids, along with hundreds of cooperative and other enterprises.

Nevertheless, MST co-founder João Pedro Stédile said early this year that the global financial crisis has led "international capitalists" to try to "protect their funds" by investing in Brazilian "land and energy projects"—driving renewed land concentration.

Let us discuss about the United States. The largest 9 percent of farms produce more than 60 percent of output. But small farmers still control more than half our farmland, and the growing market for healthy fresh food has helped smallholders grow: their numbers went up by 18,467 between 2002 and 2007. To support them, last winter the Community Food Security Coalition held community "listening sessions," attended by 700 people, to sharpen citizen goals for the 2012 farm bill.

Seed: Just as dramatic is the struggle for the seed. More than 1,000 independent seed companies were swallowed up by multinationals in the past four decades, so today just three—Monsanto, DuPont and

Syngenta—control about half the proprietary seed market worldwide.

Fueling the consolidation were three Supreme Court rulings since 1980—including one in 2002, with an opinion written by former Monsanto attorney Clarence Thomas—making it possible to patent life forms, including seeds. And in 1992 the Food and Drug Administration released its policy on genetically modified organisms, claiming that "the agency is not aware of any information showing that [GMO] foods...differ from other foods in any meaningful or uniform way."

The government's green light fueled the rapid spread of GMOs and monopolies—so now most US corn and soybeans are GMO, with genes patented largely by one company: Monsanto. The FDA position helped make GMOs' spread so invisible that most Americans still don't believe they've ever eaten them—even though the grocery industry says they could be in 75 percent of processed food.

Even fewer Americans are aware that in 1999 attorney Steven Druker reported that in 40,000 pages of FDA files secured via a lawsuit, he found "memorandum after memorandum contain[ing] warnings about the unique hazards of genetically engineered food," including the possibility that they could contain "unexpected toxins, carcinogens or allergens."

Yet at the same time, public education campaigns have succeeded in confining almost 80 percent of GMO planting to just three countries: the United States, Brazil and Argentina. In more than two dozen countries and in the European Union they've helped pass mandatory GMO labeling. Even China requires it.

In Europe, the anti-GMO tipping point came in 1999. Jeffrey Smith, author of Seeds of Deception, expects that the same shift will happen here, as more Americans than ever actively oppose GMOs. This year the "non-GMO" label is the third-fastest-growing new health claim on food packaging. Smith is also encouraged that milk products produced with the genetically modified drug BGH "have been kicked out of Wal-Mart, Starbucks, Yoplait, Dannon, and most American dairies."

Around the world, millions are saying no to seed patenting as well. In homes and village seed banks, small farmers and gardeners are saving, sharing and protecting tens of thousands of seed varieties.

In the United States, the Seed Savers Exchange in Decorah, Iowa, estimates that since 1975 members have shared roughly a million samples of rare garden seeds.

In the Indian state of Andhra Pradesh—known as the pesticide capital of the world—a women-led village movement, the Deccan Development Society, puts seed-saving at the heart of its work. After the crushing failure of GMO cotton and ill health linked to pesticides, the movement has helped 125 villages convert to more nutritious, traditional crop mixes, feeding 50,000 people.

On a larger scale, Vandana Shiva's organization, Navdanya, has helped to free 500,000 farmers from chemical dependency and to save indigenous seeds—the group's learning and research center protects 3,000 varieties of rice, plus other crops.

Agriculture: In all these ways and more, the global food movement challenges a failing frame: one that defines successful agriculture and the solution to hunger as better technologies increasing yields of specific crops.

Its near obsession with the yield of a monoculture is anti-ecological. It not only pollutes, diminishes and disrupts nature; it misses ecology's first lesson: relationships. Higher Productivity isolates agriculture from its relational context—from its culture.

The International Assessment of Agricultural Knowledge, Science and Technology for Development" (known simply as IAASTD) in 2008, explained that solutions to poverty, hunger and the climate crisis require agriculture that promotes producers' livelihoods, knowledge, resiliency, health and equitable gender relations, while enriching the natural environment and helping to balance the carbon cycle. Painstakingly developed over four years by 400 experts, the report has gained the support of more than fifty-nine governments, and the World Bank.

IAASTD furthers an emerging understanding that agriculture can serve life only if it is regarded as a culture of healthy relationships, both in the field—among soil organisms, insects, animals, plants, water, sun—and in the human communities it supports: a vision lived by many indigenous people and captured in 1981 by Wendell Berry in The Gift of Good Land and twenty years later by Jules Pretty in Agriculture: Reconnecting People, Land and Nature.

The global food movement is furthering agriculture by uniting diverse actors and fostering democratic relationships. A leader is La via Campesina, founded in 1993 when small farmers and rural laborers gathered from four continents in Belgium. Its goal is "food sovereignty"—a term carefully chosen to situate "those who produce, distribute, and consume food at the heart of food systems and policies, rather than the demands of markets and corporations," says the declaration closing the group's 2007 global gathering in Nyeleni, Mali. La via Campesina connects 150 local and national organizations, and 200 million small farmers, in seventy countries. In 2009 it was included among civil society players on the UN Committee on Food Security.

Today, more and more Americans are getting their hands in the dirt—motivated increasingly by a desire to cut "food miles" and greenhouse gases. Moreover, 41 million Americans take up gardening in 2009 alone. As neighbors join neighbors, community gardens are blooming. From only a handful in 1970, there are 18,000 community gardens today. In Britain community gardens are in such demand—with 100,000 Brits on waiting lists for a plot—that the mayor of London promised 2,012 new ones by 2012.

And in 2009 the Slow Food movement, with 100,000 members in 153 countries, created 300 "eat-ins"—shared meals in public space—to launch its US "Time for Lunch" campaign, with a goal of delicious healthy school meals for the 31 million kids eating them every day.

Economics of Agriculture

Agriculture's unity of healthy farming ecology and social ecology transforms the market itself: from the anonymous, amoral selling and buying within a market structured to concentrate power to a market shaped by shared human values structured to ensure fairness and co-responsibility.

In 1965 British Oxfam created the first fair-trade organization, called Helping-by-Selling, in response to calls from poor countries for "trade, not aid." Today more than 800 products are fair-trade certified, directly benefiting 6 million people. Last year the US fair-trade market passed $1.5 billion.

The Real Food Challenge, launched by young people in 2007, is working to jump-start a US swing to "real food"—defined as that respecting "human dignity and health, animal welfare, social justice and environmental sustainability." Student teams are mobilizing to persuade campus decision-makers to commit themselves to making a minimum of 20 percent of their college or university food "real" by 2020. With more than 350 schools already on board, the Challenge founders have set an ambitious goal: to shift $1 billion to real food purchases in ten years.

Farmers' markets, the direct exchange between farmer and eater, are also creating a fairer agriculture. So rare before the mid-'90s that the USDA didn't even bother to track them, more than 7,000 farmers' markets dot the country in 2011, a more than fourfold increase in seventeen years.

Other democratic economic models are also gaining ground:

In 1985 an irrepressible Massachusetts farmer named Robyn Van En helped create the first US Community Supported Agriculture (CSA) program, in which eaters are no longer just purchasers but partners, helping to shoulder the farmer's risk by prepaying for a share of the harvest before the planting season. On weekends, "my" CSA—Waltham Fields, near Boston—is alive as families pick and chat, and kids learn how to spot the yummiest strawberries. Now there are 2,500 CSAs across the country, while more than 12,500 farms informally use this prepay, partnership approach.

The cooperative model is spreading too, replacing one dollar, one vote—the corporate form—with one person, one vote. In the 1970s, US food cooperatives took off. Today there are 160 nationwide, and co-op veteran Annie Hoy in Ashland, Oregon, sees a new upsurge.

Funky storefronts of the 1970s, famous for limp organic carrots, have morphed into mouthwatering community hubs. Beginning as a food-buying club of fifteen families in 1953, Seattle's PCC Natural Markets has nine stores and almost 46,000 members, making it the largest US food cooperative. Its sales more than doubled in a decade.

Producer co-ops have also made huge gains. In 1988 a handful of worried farmers, watching profits flow to middlemen, not to them, launched the Organic Valley Family of Farms. Today Organic Valley's more than 1,600 farmer owners span thirty-two states, generating sales of more than $500 million in 2008.

Rules: The global food system reflects societies' rules—often un-codified—that determine who eats and how our earth fares. In the United States, rules increasingly reflect our nation's slide into "privately held government." But in rule-setting, too, energy is hardly unidirectional.

In 1999, on the streets of Seattle, 65,000 environmentalists, labor and other activists made history, blunting the antidemocratic agenda of the World Trade Organization. In 2008 more citizens than ever engaged in shaping the farm bill, resulting in rules encouraging organic production. The movement has also established 100 "food policy councils"—new local-to-state, multi-stakeholder coordinating bodies. And this year, eighty-three plaintiffs joined the Public Patent Foundation in suing Monsanto, challenging its GMO seeds' "usefulness" (required for patenting) as well as the company's right to patent seeds to begin with.

Even small changes in the rules can create huge possibilities. Consider, for example, the ripples from a 2009 Brazilian law requiring at least 30 percent of school meals to consist of food from local family farms.

Rules governing rights are the human community's foundational guarantees to one another—and the

1948 Universal Declaration of Human Rights gave access to food that status. Since then, nearly two dozen nations have planted the right to food in their constitutions. If you wonder whether it matters, note that when Brazil undertook a multifaceted "zero hunger" campaign, framing food as a right, the country slashed its infant death rate by about a third in seven years.

Food Power: Only Connect

This rising global food movement taps universal human sensibilities—expressed in Hindu farmers in India saving seeds, Muslim farmers in Niger turning back the desert and Christian farmers in the United States practicing biblically inspired Creation Care. In these movements lies the revolutionary power of the food movement: its capacity to upend a life-destroying belief system that has brought us power-concentrating corporatism.

Corporatism, after all, depends on our belief in the fairy tale that market "magic" (Ronald Reagan's unforgettable term) works on its own without us.

Food can break that spell. For the food movement's power is that it can shift our sense of self: from passive, disconnected consumers in a magical market to active, richly connected co-producers in societies we are creating—as share owners in a CSA farm or purchasers of fair-trade products or actors in public life shaping the next farm bill. The food movement's power is connection itself. Corporatism distances us from one another, from the earth—and even from our own bodies, tricking them to crave that which destroys them—while the food movement celebrates our reconnection.

At its best, this movement encourages us to "think like an ecosystem," enabling us to see a place for ourselves connected to all others, for in ecological systems "there are no parts, only participants," German physicist Hans Peter Duerr reminds us. With an "eco-mind" we can see through the productivity fixation that inexorably concentrates power, generating scarcity for some, no matter how much we produce. We're freed from the premise of lack and the fear it feeds. Aligning food and farming with nature's genius, we realize there's more than enough for all.

As the food movement stirs, as well as meets, deep human needs for connection, power and fairness, let's shed any notion that it's simply "nice" and seize its true potential to break the spell of our disempowerment.[89]

International Federation of Agricultural Producers (I F A P)

Representing Farmers' organizations globally

IFAP was established in 1946 to bring together nationally representative farmers' organizations (FOs) to ensure the security of the world's food supply. IFAP seeks to develop the capacity of farmers, mostly from developing countries, to influence decisions affecting them—at both the domestic and international levels. To facilitate this development, IFAP acts as an international forum where issues of common interest to farmers are highlighted and coordinated plans to address these issues are formulated.[90]

---

[89]Frances Moore Lappé, "The Food Movement: Its Power and Possibilities", The Nation, collected from Daily Good. Org

[90] This case study was prepared by a team comprising Prof. Deepti Bhatnagar and Ankita Dewan at the IIT (Ahmedabad) and Magui Moreno Torres and Parameeta Kanungo at the World Bank (Washington DC)

Farmers are represented through regional committees that act as permanent bodies where FOs meet and work together. Meetings, conferences, workshops, and training seminars focusing on capacity building needs as expressed by FOs are held on a regular basis. A "Standing Committee of Women in Agriculture" facilitates the participation of women farmers in international conferences and workshops. Periodicals, reports, and newsletters provide regular updates on activities undertaken by member organizations as well as disseminate information on diverse topics such as agricultural policy, trade issues, and commodity market trends.

Due to the efforts of IFAP, the 1995 U.N. World Summit for Social Development recognized farmers and FOs as essential elements of civil society. Nevertheless; it is critical that government policies regarding farming be coherent and stable and facilitates the development of agriculture.

Background:

A large number of farmers living in developing countries comprise some of the poorest sections of society. Mostly unorganized and vulnerable, their voices often go unheard. They have inadequate access to agriculture extension services, reliable input supplies, or marketing services. Lack of information and education further weakens their position. National research agendas and agricultural development policies hardly reflect farmers' real needs. This situation poses a serious threat to long-term sustainable agriculture systems and in turn to world food security.

Headquartered in Paris, IFAP works to improve the economic and social status of all who live by and on the land, from both developing and developed countries. In pursuit of these goals, IFAP seeks to:

(a)Promote the creation and strengthening of independent, representative organizations of farmers throughout the world.

(b)Serve as a forum in which leaders of national FOs can meet to: highlight mutual interests and take coordinated action to further such interest, develop an understanding of world problems and exchange information, experiences, and ideas.

(c)Act as a recognized spokesperson for the world's farmers, bringing concerns of agricultural producers to the attention of international meetings of governments and other bodies. Some of these bodies include the United Nations Food and Agricultural Organization (UNFAO), the Organization for Economic Co-operation and Development (OECD), the World Trade Organization (WTO), and the World Bank.

(d)Keep member organizations informed about international events of concern.

IFAP is financed by voluntary contributions from its member organizations. Any organization that substantially represents farmers at the national level is eligible for membership. Approximately 100 national Farmers' Organizations from 71 countries across the globe constitute IFAP's present membership. In addition, IFAP also maintains a working relationship with a number of FOs at various stages of development that are not presently members of IFAP.

Farmers' Organizations are represented in four regional committees, namely: African Farmers, Asian Farmers, Mediterranean Farmers, and Farmers from Central America, the Andean Region, and the Caribbean. The Development Cooperation Committee (DCC) is IFAP's main instrument for building alliances with specialized development agencies to strengthen Farmers' Organizations in developing countries. IFAP promotes the status and position of women farmers through the Standing Committee of Women in Agriculture. This committee is the only worldwide body of women farmers' representatives.

IFAP works in partnership with governmental and nongovernmental international organizations, along with several agricultural agencies and civil society organizations. Some of these international bodies are the International Cooperative Association (ICA), the International Labour Organization (ILO), the Rodale Institute (U.S.), the Food and Agriculture Organization (FAO), the International Fund for Agriculture Development (IFAD), the International Bank for Reconstruction and Development (IBRD), the United Nations Conference on Trade and Development (UNCTAD), the General Agreement on Tariffs and Trade, and the EEC Commission.

Impact/Results

The participation and representation of farmers at international events and conferences concerning issues such as water management, agriculture research, rural development, and education, to name a few, has increased. IFAP has aided in the international recognition of farmers as important contributors to the global economy. During the 1995 U.N. World Summit for Social Development in Copenhagen (Denmark), as a result of IFAP's efforts, the world's governments recognized farmers—particularly family farmers and small landholders, both men and women, along with Farmers' Organizations — as essential elements of civil society. The summit officially marked the end of top-down agriculture and the beginning of people-centered development.

In order to strengthen the links between FOs and research institutes, IFAP organized a series of consultations starting in 1989. By the end of 2001, 12 agricultural agencies had confirmed their interest in the coordination of their efforts for the support of farmer organizations in developing countries, and their partnership within the Development Coordination Committee. Projects linking FOs and research institutes have been implemented in Burkina Faso, Kenya, Zambia, and Zimbabwe. IFAP has also supported country-level projects and initiatives for organizational strengthening.

A few such examples are listed below.

The Philippines National Peasant Caucus (PNPC) was established in October 1996, grouping together the main FOs of the Philippines.

In June 1997, Sanduguan (Small Farmers' Supreme Council) in the Philippines finalized the conversion of 30 grassroots farmers' associations into full-fledged cooperatives.

In January 1997, farmers in Burkina Faso re-launched the second phase of their project for consolidating their national-level organization.

Through IFAP, the views and interests of women farmers have been reflected in important intergovernmental documents, such as the Beijing Platform for Action and the FAO/WHO International Conference on Nutrition and The World Food Summit Declaration and Plan of Action for Food Security, to name a few. IFAP was instrumental in the setting up of the annual IFAD (International Fund for Agricultural Development)/NGOs Consultation, where women's issues are regularly discussed. Due to the joint efforts of IFAP and other international bodies, many countries recognize October 15 as World Rural Women's Day across the globe. The day contributes greatly to the promotion of women farmers and to the dissemination of information on their leading role in society.

In order to address the issue of small farmers and land rights, IFAP initiated work on a policy document titled "Land Issues and Property Rights" in 1999. Issues such as property rights, security of tenure and compulsory land takeovers are expected to be addressed through a number of reform measures.

In 2000, IFAP entered into a collaborative program with the Global Forum for Agricultural Research (GFAR). The program is designed to increase the participation of farmers and Farmers' Organizations in agricultural research for development through requisite capacity-building activities for FOs. In March 2003, the DCC started formulation of the "Capacity Building for Trade," a four-year project designed to strengthen the capacity of farmers' organizations in developing countries in the area of trade.

Key Elements of Empowerment:

Information: The IFAP maintains an up-to-date collection of directories of agricultural information sources. The IFAP Documentation and Information Service receives and analyses more than 300 international periodicals from member organizations and other sources covering such diverse topics as agricultural policy, trade issues, commodity market trends and statistics, rural economy and sociology, farming systems, cooperatives, and rural development issues. This keeps the member FOs up-to-date on the latest developments in the field of agriculture at a global level.

In addition, IFAP publishes the following periodicals and reports for improved access of FOs:

IFAP Newsletter presents a quarterly summary and update on the activities undertaken by IFAP and its member organizations.

Magazine of the World Farmers Times Foundation in Zurich edited by IFAP outlines and reviews agricultural issues worldwide.

World Sugar Farmer News, the specialized newsletter of the World Association of Sugar Beet and Cane Growers

Since 1984, IFAP has circulated a development publication series—reference bulletins outlining a basic strategy for FOs based on papers and discussions at IFAP seminars. These publications provide valuable information on development projects, national agricultural pricing policies, commodity marketing, sustainable farming systems, services of farmers' organizations, and many other topics.

On World Rural Women's Day, information on the contribution of women farmers is disseminated to the public and rural women themselves through the following mechanisms:

Some of the reform measures include:

(a) Increasing access of member organizations to relevant information, skills, and experience on land reform
(b) Enabling exchange of experiences and know-how among member and contract organizations
(c) In cases of an ongoing land reform process, exploring possibilities for establishing pilot projects, based on increasing the role of farmers' organizations in the successful conclusion of such processes.
(d) Workshops and dialogues with regional and national leaders based on gender and democratization issues, cultural and traditional problems, and the like.

(e) Experience-sharing through visits to schools, for instance, to give insight into the role of women in agriculture and in society
(f) Posters on the work and lives of rural women
(g) Agricultural fairs where women exhibit their products and skills.

These outreach activities facilitate better understanding and more accurate perception of rural women in society.

Inclusion/Participation: The governing and operational structure of IFAP incorporates mechanisms to facilitate the active involvement and participation of member organizations that represent farmers at the grassroots level. They are listed as follows:

(a)The Regional Committees act as a permanent forum where FOs in developing countries meet and work together on a regular basis.

(b)The participation of women farmers is facilitated through international events, training sessions, workshops, and conferences.

(c)IFAP's Development Program is carried out through regular consultative and training seminars, action-research, regional and country projects, and international coordination of farmers' development efforts and publications. The meetings and workshops focus on priorities for capacity building as expressed by the participating FOs.

(d)The World Farmers Congress—the General Conference of IFAP—brings together the representatives of member organizations every two years. Among other things, the conference enables member farmers to identify common problems and seek joint solutions to these problems.

(e)IFAP organizes meetings every six months where members come together to work on one major issue, such as strengthening links between farmers; agricultural research and extension services; farming for sustainable development; and the like.

Local Organizational Capacity: IFAP has been instrumental in bringing together farmers' organizations from many developing countries and increasing their representation in international events. Issues concerning farmers have been effectively raised and have garnered support from various international bodies. In order to enhance the capacity of farmers to participate and influence decisions at international levels, some of the following capacity building exercises have been or are in the process of being conducted by IFAP:

(a) Organizing farmer-to-farmer exchanges on technology of farming, biotechnology, development alternatives, quality of produce, best practices, and farmers' success stories
(b) Developing and managing trade operations and other income-generating activities
(c) Using information technology in all its applications, including organization, management, accountancy, and human resources
(d) Follow-up and monitoring of agricultural markets of specific commodities (including prices, trading, and quality standards)
(e) Dynamic organizational development, federation building, profiling, membership, and organizational strengthening and staff training

Issues and Lessons

Challenges: Through its Standing Committee of Women in Agriculture, IFAP has encouraged FOs to undertake steps to integrate rural women into their institutional operations and agricultural development policies. However, progress in this direction has been slow.

Technical education and training programs for capacity building among farmers have been relatively lower for women. Training strategies intended specifically for rural women need to be designed and effectively implemented.

Initiatives and programs undertaken by FOs to reduce poverty levels have encountered the following problems:

(a)Illiteracy, low levels of education, and technical training Inability to reach remote rural areas due to lack of infrastructure facilities

(b) Low access to financial resources. Lending institutions like banks require that farmers have land tenure (or similar collateral) to secure credit. Most rural farmers do not have such resources.

(c) Warfare, political and social instabilities causing mass migration and loss of resources.

(d) Bureaucratic and inefficient government policies. One such example concerns the Grenada Cane Farmers' Association (GCFA), a member organization of IFAP. The association built a cane mill on land that was originally leased from the previous government. And although the present government agreed to transfer the land title over to the GCFA, the agreement was never implemented, and the government has not to respond to requests to resolve the issue.

Key Factors for Success:

It is critical that government policy be coherent and stable, and facilitates the development of agriculture. When the economic and political environments are degrading, capacity building becomes difficult for FOs. In this context, problems such as political interference, social and political instability, and warfare need to be effectively addressed. Easy access to roads, irrigation systems, and market opportunities, public funding for research and development and farmer-driven taxation and land-credit policies should also be ensured.

FOs needs to be strengthened not only at the grassroots, but also at the local, district, regional, and global levels. Approaches that merely focus on strengthening grassroots farmers' groups are bound to fail when farmers have no influence on higher-level decisions. The farmers themselves best articulate the problems of farmers through their representative organizations.

It is essential to maintain the initial momentum generated by the World Rural Women's Day Worldwide Information and Awareness Campaign. Attempts should be made to forge partnerships with the media so as to communicate views and international recognition of farmers as important contributors to the global economy.

Conclusion

The governments and funding institutions may examine the following suggestions to protect the interests of the farmers:

The international community should work for Farmers' Rights. The farmers are in need of justice, sustainable living and prestige for their profession.

The farmers are producing food materials for the people of the world. They are the real peace workers for all ages.

Agricultural Scientists have contributed significantly towards higher yield in crops.

The world community has not honored a single farmer in a world forum till date.

The farmers are not awarded National Lotus Awards (Padma shree, Padma Bhushan, Padma Bibhusan and Bharat Ratna) in India. It is a fact that cricket players, singers, cine actors or sand artists and others are honoured with Lotus Awards in India.

The farmers of the world should not be treated as beggars, a burden, and a dependant class and should not be looked down upon by the elites.

There should be regional, national and international Farmers' Organizations to fight for:

- **(a) Right Prices of agricultural commodities;**
- **(b) Farmers' Pensions after 60 years of age; and**
- **(c) Right approaches for Food Security to all.**

All national and international awards must include few farmers to boost the morale of the farmers' community. They have been neglected since time immemorial and should not be neglected further.

The world organizations, developed countries and top economists have failed in their approaches to solve the problems of the farmers; on the other hand, millions of farmers are being dragged into poverty each year.

All subsidies in agriculture should be withdrawn as it encourages management problems and corruption. The percentage of budgetary allotment for subsidy should be deposited in their (farmers') bank accounts with a formula as decided by the respective governments.

Chapter VII

WORLD PEACE IS POSSIBLE

Food is strength, and food is peace, and food is freedom, and food is a helping hand to people around the world whose good will and friendship we want. - John Fitzgerald Kennedy
In a speech in South Dakota Speech in 1960

orld peace is not a utopian thought. It is possible through farmers' involvement. Majority of world population long for world peace, but the political leaders, military rulers, smugglers, corrupt bureaucracy, fundamentalists, and law manipulators disturb the peace environment of the world. These people run after money, power, privileges and recognition. They forget that peoples' power could throw them into the Pacific Ocean once they understand their right to live in peace. There exists super power, the Omnipotent God, which has created this world and all living beings, plants, animals, air, water, soil and even sunlight. But do we have the power to punish the ill motivated people? Yes, we do have.

Gresham's Law clearly defines that bad coins drive away the good coins out of circulation. The Judicial Laws provide that all are equal in the eyes of Law. So the culprits could be punished and their illegal activities could be mended and/ or they could be identified. Cannot the national and international laws stop their anti-human activities? It is also possible.

Vast majority of people in this planet are poor, hungry, and are devoid of natural justice. They are shy, innocent, and oppressed. They reside in rural areas; they suffer from mental torture; they cry and quarrel among family members; they hide their feelings; they put too much loyalty to God and powerful people; they are aggrieved; they are not united; yet there is possibility that they would live in peace. They are the peasants, small farmers, farmers, sharecroppers, agricultural labourers, nomads and poor people, who are scattered throughout the nook and corners of this world. They work for the nations to safeguard the country as soldiers, supply food to the civilized world to make the rich healthy and as workers in industries for profit of the industrialists, and pay grand ovation to the politicians in scorching rays in summer. These peasants revolt for others. But the 21st century would not neglect them forever. It is time for the peasants of the world to roar for justice. Let us hope that all people live together in a world of peace, brotherhood and plenty.

The World Needs its Small Farmers

World Food Day, commemorated on October 16, has become more of an exercise in expiation of sins than a renewal of a serious commitment to end hunger. Throughout the world, the press decries the latest Food and Agriculture Organization (FAO) statistics: 852 million people lack adequate food, 13 percent of the world's population is "food insecure." Hunger and famine exist on every continent.

Forums are held to discuss the problem. Experts opine on proposals that have been debated for decades. But it's unlikely that much real progress will result from the day's soul-searching. The proposals fill pages of print but have been consistently ineffective in actually filling bellies.

The war on hunger declared after World War II has largely been abandoned. With the advent of the "market fixes all" philosophy of recent decades, the structural causes of hunger have been ignored in favor of free market philosophy, technological fixes, and charity-based interventions.

Global trade liberalization separates the food we eat from the land we inhabit, and the communities we live in. While international trade in food products is both inevitable and to some degree desirable, the drastic deregulation of a distorted market has led to a breakdown in communities, productive chains, and ecosystems.

In many countries, the guarantors of food supplies—small farmers—are being driven out of production by agricultural imports from the United States and other developed countries under free trade agreements.

Promotion of high-yield crops has increased the volume of food production in some regions, but has also created greater vulnerability and eroded agricultural biodiversity by supplanting native varieties that are often better adapted to local dietary needs and ecosystems.

In the midst of this crisis, the FAO's slogan this year: "Investing in agriculture for food security—the whole world will profit" is off the mark. No doubt the countryside requires more investment to produce food and feed its own inhabitants. The FAO points out that foreign aid to agriculture have fallen from $9 billion per year in the early 1980s to less than $5 billion in the late 1990s. Except in countries like Argentina, where large-scale soy production has exploded, most countries are seeing a decrease in investment, employment, and income generation in their rural sectors. The irony that 70 percent of the world's hungry live in rural areas is proof that the world's farmers need help—and fast.

But investment in agriculture, not surprisingly, tends to flow to sectors that generate profit. In developing countries, structural adjustment programs have decimated public funding for the rural sector, and both private and public investment is overwhelmingly oriented toward agri-business for export.

The profit motive will not solve hunger because that is not its purpose. In fact, it has done much to skew both production and distribution of the world's food supply. Its capacity to provide a long-term solution is even more doubtful, since the high-yield models promoted by transnational seed, biotech, and agricultural trading companies (often the same conglomerates) decrease the ability of the soil to produce the food we need in the future. Mono-cropping, chemical use, and intensive natural resource use and contamination, produce food and profits while generating costs passed on to the next generation.

The profit ends up benefiting not "the whole world" but a very narrow group of large producers and traders. In both developed and developing countries, the model has led to a sharp divide between a small group of industrial farmers and millions of small farmers on the verge of economic collapse. As they collapse, their land either goes out of food production or is gobbled up by large landowners. The rate of land re-concentration is turning the clock back on hard-won struggles for social justice throughout Latin America. The threat posed by a free trade agricultural model can be seen in Mexico, the classic example of a developing nation plunged head-first into a market economy. There the price of corn paid the nearly 3 million corn farmers fell 50 percent between 1999 and 2004, as massive U.S. imports flooded the Mexican market. This in turn led to a massive conversion of farmers to migrants.

Did economic integration in agriculture enable the nation to import cheap food and solve hunger? Let's look at the statistics. The price of tortillas to consumers rose 380 percent since NAFTA went into effect. Mexico recently reported that more than one million children under five, or 12.7 percent, are chronically malnourished. In the countryside, where food is grown, the percentage is nearly double.

At the same time, and often in the same regions, obesity has risen at a rate unparalleled anywhere else in the world. The percentage of obese or overweight adults increased from 35.5 percent in 1988 to 70 percent in 2006. Changes in diet due to importation of processed foods and immigration's cultural impact are among the prime culprits.

The world as a whole now faces this dual crisis of malnutrition and obesity, which has resulted from economic polarization, cultural changes, and a decline in the quality of our food supply.

A concept of **food security** posits that it doesn't matter if food is imported or grown at home is highly compatible with globalization but it ignores both the plight and potential of small farmers. Without protecting their livelihoods, they will remain in poverty and constitute the ranks of the hungry. Without recognizing the contributions they make to society—not only in food production but also in ecosystem conservation, social cohesion, traditional knowledge, and cultural diversity—we stand to lose irredeemable public goods. In contrast to the food security paradigm, many grassroots farmers' organizations have adopted the term **food sovereignty** to describe the right of people or nation to produce and consume its own food. They call for government and global policies that enable small farmers to continue to farm.

The FAO is not proposing that small farmers be driven from agriculture or that investment flow only to large competitive interests. However, it's unfortunate slogan not only does nothing to correct this situation, it reinforces the concepts at the heart of the current crisis. An increase in investment without a serious critique of the current model of agriculture could actually exacerbate rather than resolve the problem.

The results of the market-based, large-scale, hi-tech approach have not only been inadequate; they have been downright counterproductive in rural areas throughout the world.

There can be no solution to hunger that doesn't have small farmers at its center. Peasant and indigenous farmers in developing countries cannot peacefully coexist with industrialized, monopolized agriculture without regulations and policies in their favor. Even though they sell for consumption in local markets they are forced to compete with imports while saddled with disadvantages that include their small scale, lack of capital, and U.S. farm subsidies.

Hunger is a disease whose "cure" is in prevention. Up to now, few proposals that would support small-scale agriculture have made headway with policymakers. It's time for the FAO, other international agencies, and national governments to restore the emphasis where it should be—on the small farmers.

The peasants must be protected by law and the state. They are poor because they are neglected for generations. The problems of peasants, agricultural labourers, unemployed youths and no-income families and women headed families in low-income counties must be solved to award peace to all.[91]

Rising Global Interest in Farmland

Juergen Voegele (2011) has opined that land has become the most important factor in agriculture in the twenty-first century. Its importance would increase further as world population increases at a faster rate.

Interest in farmland is rising. And, given commodity price volatility, growing human and environmental pressures, and worries about food security, this interest will increase, especially in the developing world.

Many countries have suitable land available that is either not cultivated or produces well below its potential. This was a development challenge even before the food price rise of 2008. Seventy-five percent of the world's poor are rural, and most are engaged in farming.

The need for more and better investment in agriculture to reduce poverty, increase economic growth, and promote environmental sustainability was already clear when there were "only" 830 million hungry people before the food price rise. The case is even clearer today when, for the first time in human history, over a billion people go to bed hungry each night.

One of the highest development priorities in the world must be to improve smallholder agricultural productivity, especially in Africa. Smallholder

---

[91] Laura Carlsen, IRC , "The World Needs its Small Farmers", October 25, 2006, World hunger Org / Americas irc online org /am / 3641

productivity is essential for reducing poverty and hunger, and more and better investment in agricultural technology, infrastructure, and market access for poor farmers is urgently needed. When done right, larger-scale farming systems can also have a place as one of many tools to promote sustainable agricultural and rural development, and can directly support smallholder productivity, for example, throughout grower programs. However, recent press and other reports about actual or proposed large farmland acquisition by big investors have raised serious concerns about the danger of neglecting local rights and other problems. They have also raised questions about the extent to which such transactions can provide long-term benefits to local populations and contribute to poverty reduction and sustainable development.

Although these reports are worrying, the lack of reliable information has made it difficult to understand what has been actually happening. Against this backdrop, the World Bank, under the leadership of Managing Director Ngozi Okonjo-Iweala, along with other development partners, has highlighted the need for good empirical evidence to inform decision makers, especially in developing countries. The report on **"Rising Global Interest in Farmland: Can It Yield Sustainable and Equitable Benefits?"** clearly explains the present situations prevailing worldwide.

To prepare the report, a multidisciplinary team was tasked with carrying out a multi-country study on large-scale agricultural land acquisition and investment. While this task proved to be less straightforward than originally anticipated, the effort has produced some striking results.

First, the demand for land has been enormous. Compared to an average annual expansion of global agricultural land of less than 4 million hectares before

2008, approximately 56 million hectares worth of large-scale farmland deals were announced even before the end of 2009. More than 70 percent of such demand has been in Africa; countries such as Ethiopia, Mozambique, and Sudan have transferred millions of hectares to investors in recent years.

At the same time, in many cases the announced deals have never been implemented. Risks are often large. Plans are scaled back due to a variety of reasons including unrealistic objectives, price changes, and inadequate infrastructure, technology, and institutions. For example, we found that actual farming has so far only started on 21 percent of the announced deals. Moreover, case-studies demonstrate that even some of the profitable projects do not generate satisfactory local benefits, while, of course, none of the unprofitable or non-operational ones do.

Institutional gaps at the country level can be immense. Too often, they have included a lack of documented rights claimed by local people and weak consultation processes that have led to uncompensated loss of land rights, especially by vulnerable groups; a limited capacity to assess a proposed project's technical and economic viability; and a limited capacity to assess or enforce environmental and social safeguards.

Such problems are not due to a lack of potential. For example, although deforestation associated with the expansion of the agricultural frontier has been a serious problem (and one of the world's largest contributors to greenhouse gas emissions), our analysis shows that the projected increase in the demand for agricultural commodities over the next decade could be met, without cutting down forests, by increasing productivity and farmland expansion in non-forested areas. In particular, none of the Sub-Saharan African countries of most interest to investors is now achieving more than 30 percent of the potential yield on currently cultivated areas. So, increasing productivity on existing farmland would have a much bigger impact than simply expanding the land area at current yields.

There is also considerable scope for a South-South exchange of good practice. Again, when done right, larger-scale farming can provide opportunities for poor countries with large agricultural sectors and ample endowments of land. To make the most of these opportunities, however, countries will need to better secure local land rights and improve land governance. Adopting an open and proactive approach to dealing with investors is also needed to ensure that investment contributes to broader development objectives. Experience in Asia and in Latin America and the Caribbean can provide lessons for Sub-Saharan African countries that have confronted these issues more recently.

A major conclusion of the report is that access to a basic set of good information is essential for all stakeholders. Good public information can help governments formulate policies, identify gaps in implementation, and perform essential regulatory functions. Good public information can help civil society educate local communities about their rights and the potential uses and value of their land, assist in specific negotiations, and monitor agreements so they are indeed adhered to. And good public information can help investors effectively design and implement projects that respect local rights, are profitable, and generate local benefits.

Helping countries reduce poverty and hunger by increasing agricultural productivity is at the core of the World Bank's agenda. In collaboration with partners, the World Bank is ready to contribute to this important agenda by providing information and analysis, helping countries build their institutional and regulatory capacity, and supporting more and better investment in agriculture, especially smallholder agriculture, so that the rising global interest in farmland contributes to results that are sustainable and equitable.[92]

Uzbekistan's Troubled Farm Reforms

Farmers say a switch to a new more commercial system leaves them burdened with debt and tied up in Soviet-style regulations.

Agricultural reforms currently under way in Uzbekistan are supposed to make farmers richer and the land more productive. But agriculture experts and farmers themselves say the changes are unimpressive, because the rural economy is still weighed down by Soviet-style controls and production quotas. Some analysts believe the basic obstacle is the government's reluctance to cede its ownership of all land. However much the farms are re-organized, they remain leaseholders beholden to a powerful and intrusive state.

The reforms, which are supposed to be finished, next year, involve turning large agricultural enterprises known as shirkat (literally "company") into private farming units. The shirkats are the successors to the collective and state farms of the Soviet era, and like them have proved inefficient despite the economies of scale.

A third form of business exists on the margins of the bigger farms – the "dehkan" ("peasant") unit which usually consists of one family working a small plot of

---

[92] Juergen Voegele (2011), "Rising Global Interest in Farmland: can it Yield sustainable and suitable benefits – The Preface" Director, Agriculture and Rural Development Department, The World Bank

land of two hectares or less, but despite their small size they still tend to be much more productive in relative terms than the larger units.

All in all, these different kinds of farm account for half of Uzbekistan's working population according to official statistics, and it is generally recognized that reform of the sector is crucial to future economic growth.

The shirkat is a cooperative business whose members both work in it and hold shares. But local government at district level in practice continued to direct the shirkats' activities so as to ensure that the set production quota – which is often unrealistically high - is met. Uzbek-style market economics means that if a shirkat has not fulfilled the "plan", its members do not get paid – but they are not allowed to opt out of the system and seek their own customers.

Turning shirkats into the new-style private farms – called "ferma" after the English word – is intended to give those who work there greater control over how they are run. But the persistence of a rigidly top-down bureaucratic system geared to mass production for the state is greatly diluting the effect of any liberalization, sector-al experts say. The central obstacle is the continuation of the "state order" – a procurement system under which farmers are required to grow particular crops, generally cotton or wheat, to the exclusion of others, and sell it to monopoly state buyers at prices well below the world market rates for these commodities. The government effectively pockets the difference.

Ranging between 10 and 50 hectares, the private farms are smaller than the shirkats, and since the reform was instituted in 1999 they have grown into an important part of the rural economy. The new farms are said to be a lot more effective than the shirkats, and according to official figures were responsible for 70 per cent of the grain and cotton grown in Uzbekistan last year. But some of those involved in the farming sector cast doubt on these figures, saying the they are being massaged in order to show the Uzbek leadership how well the transformation is going. Even thought they are supposed to be independent businesses, the private farms are still subject to government sanctions for poor performance.

A staff member of the regional government in Andijan, in the Fergana valley of eastern Uzbekistan says that the private farmers are forced to fulfill the state plan, and they are held to account for doing to a much greater extent than the shirkat chairmen. At most, a shirkat head who failed to fulfill the plan can be dismissed, but the private farmer can lose his leasehold.

This sanction can be applied even when a farm underperforms for reasons beyond its control, such as bad weather or the state's failure to provide it in good time with the seeds, fertilizer and water it needs.

Another private farmer in Andijan said, "I do not feel free; I can't use the land as I wish. Things have got so bad that last year, the district government chief banned people from gathering in the harvest until the cotton had fully ripened. The cotton on my field ripened early and I urgently needed to pick it but I had to wait for permission to be given. Then it rained, so I had to sell all my cotton to the state at a reduced price as the rain had spoiled it."

However the land is managed, it remains in the hands of the state, and some local analysts say little will change until farmers have the incentive of actually ownership instead of the leaseholds of 30 to 50 years they have been given. The private farms are tax-exempt for the first two years. But according to a local agriculture expert, they still face near-impossible conditions as they inherit any debts left by the shirkat whose land they take over.

In addition, they have to fulfill the same cotton and wheat plan that was set for the [previous] shirkat for a ten-year period. And those quotas were always set too high.

A farmer affected by inherited debts and obligations of the shirkat says, "We acquired the land of a loss-making shirkat which had debts. After its assets were sold off, the rest of the debt was transferred to those who got the land.... I have three years to pay it off."The farmer added, "This year I'll have to fulfill the wheat delivery plan as my contract states that the terms of the shirkat contract extend to my farm."

Contradictory legislation means that even though the law on private farms says they are free to choose which crops to grown, this right is nullified by a government decree according to which the farmer's lease contract stipulates the crops grown and the size of the harvest. Failure to deliver on these requirements, says the agriculture expert, constitutes breach of contract which can result in loss of leasehold.

Because the farmers remain trapped in a web of controls, they adopt the same defense mechanisms as their Soviet forebears - massaging production figures upwards. "The private farmers are obliged to use every kind of truth and untruth to fulfill the plan and show high rates for property," said the Andijan official.

The agriculture expert explained that "the government needs to show the private farms are highly profitable in order to demonstrate that agricultural reforms are taking place." But are things actually getting better? Not really, says this expert. Every year the official statistics say the private farms are a great deal more profitable than other kinds of rural business.

However, just look at the facts: the 130,000 private farms across the republic now account for 3.65 million hectares, in other words 80 per cent of all irrigated land. Yet the position of rural peasants is not improving. An army of unemployed people, many thousands strong, are leaving their home villages in search of work. You can see it at any of the mardikar (hired day-labour) markets that have sprouted like mushrooms in recent times.

The bulk of the new rural unemployed are people left out in the cold after the shirkats are broken up. The Andijan official said there should have been a plan to place these people in work to ease the transition. He says the one measure that was introduced – requiring new private farmers to take on some of the spare manual labourers – has been a failure, "It hasn't solved the problem. Everyone agrees to these [contractual] terms in order to acquire land, but once they get it they immediately begin sacking them [workers] so as not to assume the burden of wages and social security payments – a young private farm just cannot afford those costs. At best they keep the jobs open but pay only minimal wages." His conclusion is that "the creation of private farms does not solve the social problems of the countryside; instead, it lays them bare".

Some farmers complain that the procedure for acquiring a landholding is itself unfair. The shirkat is divided up into parcels of land by local "liquidation commissions", and then holds a tender in which anyone can take part. Applicants have to supply documents including a business plan and letters of recommendation. We then award points out of ten to each applicant. The highest scorer gets the land. If there's a tie, preference goes to the one who's a member of the shirkat that is being restructured.

One man who lost out in the process says he was treated unfairly. After 14 years in the local shirkat, and five years in a Soviet state farm before that, he thought he must be in with a good chance, arguing, "Who knows how to work this piece of land better than me?" In the event the land was awarded to a younger man from outside the village. The farmer complained but was told everything was above board.

The commission member insists the procedures are fair, "The tendering system is perfect. It's practically impossible to exert external influence on it.... There are people who have doubts about the transparency of tenders, but that's understandable as losing bidders will always think it isn't fair.

But the Andijan local government staffer disagrees, saying some of the criteria used in the tender are necessarily subjective and are thus open to manipulation. "It's mostly rich people who have acquired land," he said. "In some places they kept the local peasants from complaining by the cunning ploy of promising them verbally to give them a sub-lease on half the land they [wealthy bidders] acquired. That's impossible as subletting land is illegal." [93]

Many rural people have been left disillusioned by the process. "I didn't even take part in the tender," said a young man from Pakhtaabad in Andijan. "I worked for three years on a shirkat and I didn't even get a new (traditional and inexpensive) skullcap in that time," he said. "Rather than bribe someone to get the right to work on my own land, and still end up with the same rights as a shirkat employee, I'm going off to work in Kazakstan. No matter what – as a porter or manual labourer – I'll be able earn a living, however hard it is."

---

[93] WPR staff – Central Asia, RCA Issue 433, February 4, 2006

FAO Conference on Farmers' Rights

Conference resolutions

1989 marks a breakthrough for the negotiations on Farmers' Rights in the FAO. The FAO Conference adopted two resolutions on Farmers' Rights, one of which should provide an important basis for all further negotiations.

In April 1989, the Commission on Genetic Resources held its Third Regular Session, which prepared the ground for the adoption of two resolutions on agreed interpretations of the International Undertaking at the Twenty-fifth Session of the Conference of FAO in November 1989.

Two draft resolutions were presented to and welcomed by the Conference. According to the Conference Report (paragraph 105), the first draft resolution, presented by the Delegation of Spain, was based on the text prepared by the Commission for an agreed interpretation of the International Undertaking. The second one was prepared by the Commission and concerned Farmers' Rights. The draft resolutions, preserving the principle of unrestricted availability of germ-plasm, recognized the rights of both donors of technologies and donors of germ-plasm to be compensated for their contributions through the simultaneous recognition of plant breeders' and Farmers' Rights. The Conference recognized that both resolutions were intended to lay the foundations for an equitable and lasting global system for sharing the costs and benefits of the world's plant genetic resources for present and future generations.

During the ensuing debate on the two resolutions, a few countries made specific proposals for amendments, but it was recognized that such changes needed further detailed review before they could be considered. Several countries expressed their intention to join the Undertaking or to withdraw their reservations should the resolutions be adopted (paragraph 106). Finally, the Conference recognized that these resolutions were the end-result of wide-ranging and intensive discussions and negotiations among many countries, including a non-member of FAO, some non-members of the Commission and some that did not adhere to the Undertaking, and expressed its satisfaction with the draft resolutions (paragraph 107). The two resolutions were adopted by consensus at 29 November 1989 as Resolution 4/89 'Agreed Interpretation of the International Undertaking' and Resolution 5/89 'Farmers' Rights' (paragraph 108), and the Conference decided that they were to be annexed to the International Undertaking (paragraph 109).

Resolution 4/89 endorses that the agreed interpretation is intended to provide the basis for an equitable and therefore solid and lasting global system, and thereby to facilitate the withdrawal of reservations, which countries have made with regard to the International Undertaking, and to secure the adherence of others. The Resolution presents the rationale behind the agreed interpretation, before listing its components (paragraph 108):

1. Plant Breeders' Rights as provided for under UPOV (International Union for the Protection of New Varieties of Plant) are not incompatible with the International Undertaking.

2. A state may impose only such minimum restrictions on the free exchange of materials covered by Article 2.1 (a) of the International Undertaking as are necessary for it to conform to its national and international obligations.

3. States adhering to the Undertaking recognize the enormous contribution that farmers of all regions have made to the conservation and development of

plant genetic resources, which constitute the basis of plant production throughout the world, and which form the basis for the concept of Farmers' Rights.

4. The adhering states consider that the best way to implement the concept of Farmers' Rights is to ensure the conservation, management and use of plant genetic resources for the benefit of present and future generations of farmers. This could be achieved through appropriate means, monitored by the Commission on Plant Genetic Resources, including in particular the International Fund for Plant Genetic Resources, already established by FAO. To reflect the responsibility of those countries, which have benefited most from the use of germ-plasm, the Fund would benefit from being supplemented by further contributions from adhering governments, on a basis to be agreed upon, in order to ensure for the Fund a sound and recurring basis. The International Fund should be used to support plant genetic conservation, management and utilization programs, particularly within developing countries, and those, which are important sources of plant genetic material. Special priority should be placed on intensified educational programs for biotechnology specialists, and strengthening the capabilities of developing countries in genetic resource conservation and management, as well as the improvement of plant breeding and seed production."

The recognition of Farmers' Rights was clearly motivated by the need to create acceptance for the formulations on plant breeders' rights, particularly among developing countries. Nevertheless, opponents of plant breeders' rights gained recognition of Farmers' Rights in exchange for something that already existed, i.e. plant breeders' rights. As such, this can be seen as a breakthrough for the proponents of Farmers' Rights.

The resolution on Farmers' Rights (paragraph 108, Resolution 5/89) represents a milestone in international negotiations on this topic, as it seeks to outline the contents and implications of this concept. It is therefore quoted in full.

The Conference recognized that:

(a) Plant genetic resources are a common heritage of mankind to be preserved, and to be freely available for use, for the benefit of present and future generations,

(b) Full advantage can be derived from plant genetic resources through an effective program of plant breeding, and that, while most such resources, in the form of wild plants and old landraces, are to be found in developing countries, training and facilities for plant survey and identification, and plant breeding, are insufficient, or even not available in many of those countries,

(c) Plant genetic resources are indispensable for the genetic improvement of cultivated plants, but have been insufficiently explored, and are in danger of erosion and loss,

Considered that:

(a) In the history of mankind, unnumbered generations of farmers have conserved, improved and made available plant genetic resources,
(b) The majority of these plant genetic resources come from developing countries, the contribution of whose farmers has not been sufficiently recognized or rewarded,
(c) The farmers, especially those in developing countries, should benefit fully from the improved and increased use of the natural resources they have preserved,

(d) There is a need to continue the conservation (in situ and ex situ), development and use of the plant genetic resources in all countries, and to strengthen the capabilities of developing countries in these areas,

Endorses: the concept of Farmers' Rights (Farmers' Rights mean rights arising from the past, present and future contributions of farmers in conserving, improving, and making available plant genetic resources, particularly those in the centers of origin/diversity. These rights are vested in the International Community, as trustee for present and future generations of farmers, for the purpose of ensuring full benefits to farmers, and supporting the continuation of their contributions, as well as the attainment of the overall purposes of the International Undertaking) in order to:

1. Ensure that the need for conservation is globally recognized and that sufficient funds for these purposes will be available,

2. Assist farmers and farming communities, in all regions of the world, but especially in the areas of origin/diversity of plant genetic resources, in the protection and conservation of their plant genetic resources, and of the natural biosphere,

3. Allow farmers, their communities, and countries in all regions, to participate fully in the benefits derived, at present and in the future, from the improved use of plant genetic resources, through plant breeding and other scientific methods."

Though this resolution was a milestone, it was not legally binding, nor was the way in which it was to be implemented delineated. Furthermore, the 'definition' did not actually define the concept. It stated where the concept had arisen and the purpose of Farmers' Rights. What they were rights to, who the rights holders were, and how the rights were to be maintained - these issues were not clarified. Thus we may say that the resolution marked an important beginning, but the actual realization of Farmers' Rights would require a lot of further conceptualization and operation. "Farmers' Rights will be implemented through an international fund on plant genetic resources which will support plant genetic conservation and utilization programs, particularly, but not exclusively, in the developing countries." This fund was to be operated by the donors of genetic resources, funds and technology through the Commission on Plant Genetic Resources. The fund, however, never materialized.[94]

[94]FAO – Report of the Conference of FAO, Twenty-fifth Session, Rome, 11-12 November 1989, C 1989/REP

In 1991 a new annex to the International Undertaking was adopted (C 1991/REP, Conference Resolution 3/91). This time, the FAO Conference stated that the concept of genetic resources being the heritage of mankind, as applied in the Undertaking, was subject to the sovereignty of the States (ibid, paragraph a). This principle of international law was reaffirmed by the Commission on Genetic Resources already at its first meeting in 1985, in an effort to attract further countries to adhere to the International Undertaking: 'With regard to Article 1 and 5 of the Undertaking, the commission agreed that the sovereignty of governments over their plant genetic resources should be respected and that reciprocity in the exchange process was included in the substance of the Undertaking' (CPGR/85/REP, paragraph 9). With the new formulations in Resolution 3/91, the FAO members also felt it necessary to state that the conditions for access to plant genetic resources required further clarification (C 1991/REP, Conference Resolution 3/91, paragraph d). This was a highly controversial issue, which caused heated debate. To balance between proponents and opponents and reach to a consensus decision, the Conference again adopted provisions on Farmers' Rights. Building on the negotiations in 1987 and the 1989 resolutions, the Conference decided (ibid, paragraph 3):

The Right to Land: What does FAO do?

The right of land is a social justice. It's a real no-brainer to say that farmers need land to grow crops. But it's a sad fact that millions of farmers don't have any secure rights to the land. And it's not just about land. It's about everything that comes with it: the water, the trees, the wildlife, and all the things rural people need to grow food, earn a living and survive.

In many countries, especially in Asia and Latin America, a relatively small number of wealthy people own a lot of land, while millions of landless farmers struggle to make a living and feed their families. Lacking secure land rights, they are often denied their right to food. What's more, without property, poor farmers are often denied basic public services like sanitation and electricity. They are treated as second-class citizens.

This isn't just bad for people; it's bad for the planet. When farmers have no secure rights to their land, they have little reason to care whether their farming methods are "sustainable". Working to protect the land for future generations makes little sense. After all, they won't be able to pass the land on to their children. If the fertility of their fields becomes degraded, they move on and clear more of someone else's land.

Some people might like for FAO to play Robin Hood and force governments to take the land from the rich and give it to the poor. To these people, we can only repeat that FAO wasn't established by its Members so that it could boss them around. What FAO does is help countries, once they have decided to undertake land reforms, find the solutions that are right for their particular situation. FAO works to makes sure that land reforms bring real benefits and security to poor and hungry farmers and boost the country's overall agricultural production. A central part of this work involves setting up procedures for the peaceful resolution of conflicts over land rights.

But there's a whole lot more to the issue of land rights than dealing with unequal land ownership. What about places where no one owns the land? Get this: in Africa more than 90 percent of land remains outside the formal legal system. Fields, forests and pastures are often communally held, and rights to who can use them are determined by local customs.

But times and traditions are changing. African countries, looking to reduce hunger and poverty, are encouraging rural people, many of whom only grow food for their own families, to become commercial farmers. But commercial farming requires a more formal system for land rights. Also, under traditional systems, women often don't have the same rights to land as men. This inequality is not just a violation of women's rights; it also contributes to hunger and poverty. FAO helps governments and local communities find acceptable ways of modifying traditional land rights so that they don't hinder local economic development and don't discriminate against women.

And hey, let's not forget about thc former communist countries of Eastern Europe and central Asia. Under communism, state-controlled agricultural collectives owned much of the farmland. When the communist system collapsed, so did the collectives. These countries are now in the process of privatizing the land. But it's not an easy job. FAO is helping these countries set up agricultural real estate markets that are fair to local farmers and good for agriculture and the environment. The issue of land rights is extremely complex. But there are some principles that are constant. Here's one: successful reforms of land rights are not imposed; they are negotiated.

The people who depend directly on land, water and forests for their livelihoods need to participate in the land reform process. The participation of women farmers is especially important. Women produce about half of the world's food but they own only about two percent of all land. Land reforms can do a lot to redress this imbalance. But if rural women are not included in the reform process, there is a risk that the changes can end up doing them more harm than good.

FAO has a team of experts specifically dedicated to helping countries increase the participation of rural men and women in all aspects of rural development, including the reform of land rights. One way the poor have pushed for their rights and made their voices heard is by organizing themselves. FAO helps rural communities, especially those that are poor and vulnerable, to set up self-help groups, including rural women's associations, youth clubs and farmers cooperatives.[95]

Farmers' Rights and the FAO:

Thorough analysis of the documentation shows that the concept of Farmers' Rights was first brought up in international negotiations in FAO in 1986. However, various considerations and practical solutions were suggested already at this point in 1987, and these were more or less reflected in later discussions, in the literature and in the final recognition of Farmers' Rights in the International Treaty. The negotiations in 1987 can be said to form the foundation for all further negotiations on Farmers' Rights, and provided substantial input to the framing of our current understanding of the concept.

The International Undertaking on Plant Genetic Resources was formed in 1983 to act as the supreme

---

[95]The Food and Agriculture Organization, The UN

governing body of the organization. The objectives were to ensure that plant genetic resources for food and agriculture would be explored, preserved, evaluated and made available for plant breeding and scientific purposes. The Undertaking was based on 'the universally accepted principle that plant genetic resources are a heritage of mankind and consequently should be available without restriction' (Article 1). This formulation, and other articles were to form the basis for controversies with regard to intellectual property and plant breeders' rights, as they had already emerged in the negotiations leading up to the International Undertaking. In turn, these controversies came to provide the background for the introduction of 'Farmers' Rights' as a political concept, as we shall see. In 1983, there was, however, as yet no documented mention of Farmers' Rights.

At the same Conference Session, the Commission on Plant Genetic Resources was established (Resolution 9/83, Twenty-second Session of the FAO Conference, Rome, 1983), to deal with issues related to plant genetic resources, including monitoring the operation of the international arrangements provided for in the International Undertaking.

The Commission was later to become an important arena for discussions on Farmers' Rights. Later on, in 1995, the mandate of the Commission was broadened to cover all components of agro-biodiversity of relevance to food and agriculture (Resolution 3/95, Twenty-eighth Session of the FAO Conference, Rome, 1995). It was then renamed the Commission on Genetic Resources for Food and Agriculture (CGRFA).

A number of conferences have been held in the FAO to decide the owner of seeds. What are rights of the farmers? Till today it has not been decided.

The working Group emphasized that, in addition to the recognition of plant breeders' rights, the breeders originated seeds should make specific mention of the rights of the farmers of the countries where the materials used. These materials were the result of the work of many generations and were a basic part of the national wealth. FAO should study this subject with a view to formulating a constructive solution.

The Working Group agreed that the three major items that should be negotiated by the Contact Group were: Breeders' Rights or Farmers' Rights or the free exchange of genetic material.

The Commission also discussed the establishment of an International Fund for Plant Genetic Resources, and the topic of Farmers' Rights was brought up:

It was pointed out that such a fund should serve mainly to increase support for the improved conservation and utilization of plant genetic resources in developing countries. In this way, the fund would provide a mechanism, which would help to realize the Farmers' Rights to benefit directly from increased agricultural production through improvement of varieties.

The Council noted with satisfaction the Commission's decision to initiate negotiations through its Working Group to achieve an agreed interpretation of the controversial parts of the international Undertaking on Plant Genetic Resources, and to include in this interpretation clarification and recognition of plant breeders' rights and Farmers' Rights.

In short, the world forums could not decide to whom seeds belong? In other words, the United Nations Organization, member countries and plant breeders have overlooked the rights of farmers.[96]

---

[96]FAO Meetings of 1983, 1985, 1986, 1987 and 1995

The Valley of 1000 Hills Declaration

We the participants of the Conference on Community Rights held at The Valley Trust, 1000 Hills, Kwa Zulu Natal, South Africa, between 1 - 8 March 2002, who came from Africa, Asia, Latin America, North America and Europe, discussed the rights of local communities, and make the following declaration.

These are:

Human beings are an integral part of the community of life on Earth. Human welfare is derived from and depends on the health of this community. Accordingly, we must ensure that human actions do not destroy the web of mutually enhancing relationships that create the earth community.

The human species is social and the individual cannot live a solitary existence. We, therefore, believe that the local community is essential for the survival of the human species, and local communities create and use knowledge in partnership with other life forms to meet society's basic needs of food, health, clothing and shelter.

The Industrial system has alienated us from the rest of the earth community and is increasingly privatizing biological, land and water resources. This privatization is destroying rural local communities and their natural resource base.

Many local communities have maintained an intimate relationship with the ecosystems on which they depend and have shared timeless connectedness with all life. It is, therefore, fitting that the local community is humanity's best manager of land, water and biodiversity. Privatization and so-called free trade destroy this connectedness. By allowing the destruction of our local communities, we condemn other living organisms to accelerating extinction and further impoverish local communities.

The most potent instrument in this destruction is the patenting of living organisms. The Convention on Biological Diversity recognizes the rights of local communities and their role in generating agricultural biodiversity out of wild land biodiversity. Yet corporations are patenting living things and increasingly controlling agricultural production systems. We condemn this act as violence both to humans and to other living things.

The rights of Local Communities are being threatened by genetic engineering of crops - a dangerous technology that comes with corporate control, dependence on external inputs, and the undermining of regenerative systems of agriculture and sustainable use of biodiversity. We oppose the introduction of genetically modified organisms in agriculture and the increasing corporate control over Africa's agriculture and biodiversity.

The world adopted the Cartagena Protocol on Bio-safety and the precautionary principle. Because of genetic engineering negative effects we are concerned about the pollution of food and agriculture through genetic engineering and the way the biotechnology industry inevitably pursues its interests at the expense of the public good. This has led to the disastrous adventurism in Mexico, where the immensely valuable diversity of maize, developed by local communities over thousands of years, has been polluted with unintended genes from genetically engineered maize, some of which have not even been approved for human consumption. The food-base of the world's communities must be protected from such adventurism. We call upon all governments to provide this protection.

Local communities have the inalienable right and responsibility to nurture, manage, exchange and further improve the biodiversity on which their livelihoods are based - for the benefit of themselves, ecosystems and of future generations. This is the basis of community rights, which cannot be made subservient to any other right or responsibility, and includes the right to life, food, land, water, healthy environment and a decent livelihood.

Community rights over biodiversity and indigenous knowledge are collective in nature, and therefore cannot be privatized or individualized. Current systems of intellectual property rights applied to biodiversity and traditional knowledge are private and monopolistic in nature and therefore incompatible with community rights.

In that context, the initiative of the World Intellectual Property Organization (WIPO) to develop systems for the protection of traditional knowledge is highly inappropriate. WIPO should work to stop bio-piracy that occurs because of biodiversity patents, and not to define the rights of communities, which should be done by the communities themselves.

Access to water is a natural and fundamental right. It is not to be treated as a commodity traded for profit. People should have the right to freedom from thirst and should have adequate access to safe water for their needs.

We call on the global community to urge governments to acknowledge the community rights to land, water and biodiversity, protect them globally and initiate internationally legally binding frameworks for such protection. Communities over millennia evolved equitable and sustainable ways of gathering, producing and sharing food based on cooperation and partnership, to meet their food needs. The present thrust towards corporate management of food production and distribution systems threatens the co-operative nature of communities, jeopardizes their ability to meet their food needs through culturally appropriate and equitable ways and thus destroys their sovereign right to food security.

The African Model Law for the Protection of the Rights of Local Communities, Farmers and Breeders, and for the Regulation of Access to Biological Resources has been endorsed by the OAU Summit of Heads of State and Government in May 1998 in Ouagadougou and re-endorsed in July 2001 in Lusaka. It represents the African position on the protection of local community rights, farmers and breeders' rights and the regulation of access to biological resources. We support this position and strongly urge all African governments to take steps to implement it at the national level.

We, therefore, urge the global community to support the implementation of the African Model Law for the Protection of the Rights of Local Communities, Farmers and Breeders, and for the Regulation of Access to Biological Resources and desist from any activities or policies that directly or indirectly undermine its adoption and operation by African countries. [97]

Farmers' Rights on Seeds

Farmers' Rights are a precondition for the maintenance of crop genetic diversity, which is the basis of all food and agriculture production in the world. Basically, realizing Farmers' Rights means enabling farmers to maintain and develop crop genetic resources as they have done since the dawn of agriculture, and recognizing and rewarding them for this indispensable contribution to the global pool of genetic resources.

---

[97] Africa Policy E –Journal April 2002, Dated this 7th Day of March 2002

Plant genetic diversity is probably more important for farming than any other environmental factor, simply because it is the factor that enables adaptation to changing environmental conditions such as plant diseases and climate change. Thus, as a precondition for the maintenance of this diversity, Farmers' Rights are crucial for ensuring present and future food security in general, and in the fight against rural poverty in particular.

This website is about Farmers' Rights as they are addressed in the International Treaty on Plant Genetic Resources for Food and Agriculture. The Treaty recognizes the enormous contributions made by farmers worldwide in conserving and developing crop genetic resources, and it provides for measures to protect and promote these rights.

Definition of Farmers' Rights: The International Treaty does, however, not define Farmers' Rights. The following is a working definition developed on the basis of the research of the Farmers' Rights Projects and can be seen as a lowest common denominator of all stakeholders consulted and all documents and literature surveyed:

Farmers' Rights consist of the customary rights of farmers to save, use, exchange and sell farm-saved seed and propagating material, their rights to be recognized, rewarded and supported for their contribution to the global pool of genetic resources as well as to the development of commercial varieties of plants, and to participate in decision making on issues related to crop genetic resources.

State of Farmers' Rights: Despite the huge challenges ahead, efforts are already underway with regard to all measures highlighted in the provisions on Farmers' Rights in the International Treaty on Plant Genetic Resources for Food and Agriculture.

Progress is being made with regard to the protection of traditional knowledge, equitable benefit sharing, the participation in decision making and Farmers' Rights to save, use, exchange and sell farm-saved seed (Article 9.3). This indicates that there exists an opportunity for learning and for deriving models.

However, there are many and substantial barriers to the realization of Farmers' Rights, particularly with regard to legislation and incentive structures. Analyzing these barriers together with the progress made in many countries, allows us to derive options for the realization of Farmers' Rights.

How to realize Farmers' Rights at the national level: How can you proceed to realize Farmers' Rights in your country, according to the provisions in the International Treaty on Plant Genetic Resources for Food and Agriculture? What are the steps required? Taking the Treaty as point of departure, and based on the research carried out in the Farmers' Rights Project, we here offer a framework for implementation of Farmers' Rights at the national level with seven steps. Within this framework different avenues are possible, dependent on the needs and priorities in your country.

The first four steps are about how to design a constructive and fruitful implementation process, particularly with Farmers' Rights, which involve and affect so many stakeholders, the process is crucial to ensuring good and lasting results. The last four steps are about the contents of Farmers' Rights, as derived from the International Treaty, and how they can be realized in practice. They start out with options on how to assess and improve the legislation and regulations in the country with regard to the legal space for farmers to conserve and sustainably use crop genetic diversity. The next steps are about ensuring the protection of traditional knowledge, the participation in equitable benefit sharing and farmers' participation in decision making with regard to genetic resources. A workshop module comprising these elements is offered for free use. It is aimed at bringing stakeholders together, broadening their understanding of the topic, framing a fruitful dialogue, identifying required measures, and providing inspiration for joint action.

Farmers Rights: Around the world much is happening with regard to Farmers' Rights. There is increasing interest around the issue, and despite negative trends there are many examples of projects, legislation and policies, which contribute to Farmers' Rights actually being realized. Best practices from a range of countries are presented here to draw attention to some of the very important work being done in this area, and to communicate the possibilities that exist for succeeding with efforts targeted at the realization of Farmers' Rights. The success stories collected here represent only some of the work being done to implement the International Treaty on Plant Genetic Resources for Food and Agriculture, and it is our hope that this collection will grow as more stories are brought to our attention.

A success story is defined here as a project or activity that has resulted in substantial achievements with regard to one or more of the suggestions for the realization of Farmers' Rights addressed in the International Treaty. The chosen examples are not necessarily perfect; the main criterion is that significant achievements have been made and that they can provide inspiration for others. The success stories are sorted into four categories of achievements: success stories from the realization of Farmers' Rights to save, use, exchange and sell farm-saved seed; success stories on traditional knowledge related to agro-biodiversity; success stories on benefit sharing; and success stories on participation in decision-making. In the presentation of these stories, the main successes are highlighted together with the explanations for success and the lessons to be learned. The success stories in this collection tell about achievements in different areas related to Farmers' Rights, but common features may be discerned. Farmer-scientist collaboration, capacity building, community based approaches and participatory approaches are all elements that have proved to be central. A comparison of the stories also suggests that NGOs play an important role and that networking can be very valuable. Last, but not least, the link between Farmers' Rights and development is noted, and the importance of protecting these rights in order to maintain what is left of agro-biodiversity and to ensure the livelihoods of farmers throughout the world.

Thus, Farmers' Rights are critical to ensuring the conservation and sustainable use of genetic resources for food and agriculture and consequently for food security – today and in the future. Farmers' Rights are also a central means in the fight against rural poverty in developing countries.

Implementing Farmers' Rights internationally:

The extent to which Farmers' Rights can be implemented in a country is not only dependent on the needs and priorities within the country. Often it is also subject to the obligations that the country has towards various international and regional agreements. Thus, harmonization of Farmers' Rights is not only important at the national, but also at the international level.

Among the most important international agreements are – aside from the Internal Treaty itself – the Convention on Biological Diversity (CBD), the Agreement on Trade-related Aspects of Intellectual Property Rights (TRIPS) of the World Trade Organization (WTO), the Convention of the Union for the Protection of New Varieties of Plants (UPOV) and

World Intellectual Property Organization (WIPO) of the United Nations (UN). These international agreements are interlinked and they interact in various ways with regard to Farmers' Rights.

Here the international agreements and their interaction will be analyzed with regard to effects for Farmers' Rights, and options for harmonization in this regard will be presented. Also regional agreements will be addressed.

Resources: The substantial and increasing body of literature on farmers' rights provides a valuable source of insights in the potentials for, and possible pitfalls in, the realization of farmers' rights. Although the authors differ in their points of departure, emphasis and perspectives, their contributions are largely compatible. We will seek to draw a synthesis here.

In this section you will find a selection of literature on Farmers' Rights. Please help us to keep the section updated, and contact us if you have information about new, important publications in this field.

The Farmers' Rights Project: The Farmers' Rights Project is aimed at supporting the implementation of Farmers' Rights as they are recognized in the International Treaty on Plant Genetic Resources for Food and Agriculture. Starting in 2005, it is a long term project with many different components, comprising research and surveys as well as more operational activities such as this website.

What are Farmers' Rights?: Farmers' Rights are basically about enabling farmers to continue their work as stewards and innovators of agricultural biodiversity, and about recognizing and rewarding them for their contribution to the global pool of genetic resources. Farmers' Rights are addressed in the International Treaty on Plant Genetic Resources for Food and Agriculture, but are not defined there. However, measures to protect and promote these rights are suggested, including the protection of traditional knowledge relevant to crop genetic resources, the right of farmers to equitably participate in the sharing of benefits arising from the utilization of crop genetic resources, and the right to participate in decision making processes at the national level on matters related to the conservation and sustainable use of these resources. Farmers' Rights to save, use, exchange and sell farm-saved seed and propagating material are also addressed.

The concept of Farmers' Rights: The idea of Farmers' Rights came up in the early 1980s as a countermove to the increased demand for plant breeders' rights, as voiced in international negotiations. The purpose was to draw attention to the unremunerated innovations of farmers that were seen as the foundation of all modern plant breeding. The concept was first brought up in international negotiations in 1986.[98]

Why are Farmers' Rights important?

Farmers' Rights are a precondition for the maintenance of crop genetic diversity, which is the basis of all food and agriculture production in the world. Genetic diversity of agricultural plants is the very basis of farming. It provides the pool from which plant traits can be found which meet the challenges of crop pests and diseases, of marginal soils, and - not least - of changing climate conditions. Genetic diversity is also vital for spreading risks for smallholder farmers. Plant genetic diversity is probably more important for farming than any other single environmental factor, simply because it is the

---

[98] Regime Andersen, Governing Agro–biodiversity: Plant Genetics and Developing Countries '(published August 2008).

factor that enables adaptation to changing environmental conditions. As farmers are custodians and developers of crop genetic resources, their rights in this regard are crucial for enabling them to maintain this vital role for local and global food security. The realization of Farmers' Rights is therefore also a central means to achieving UN Millennium Development Goal 1 on eradicating extreme hunger and poverty.

What is (P. G. R. F A)?

The term agricultural biodiversity (also called agro-biodiversity) refers to the diversity of plants and animals used for food and agriculture production.

PGRFA (plant genetic resources for food and agriculture) is defined in the International Treaty on Plant Genetic Resources for Food and Agriculture as any genetic material of plant origin of actual or potential value for food and agriculture. This means that the genetic material of all the various crops grown around the world today, as well as any genetic material that may prove to be of value to food production and agriculture, are encompassed by the term.

Genetic material

Genetic material is defined in the International Treaty as any material of plant origin, including reproductive and vegetative propagating material, containing functional units of heredity. Seeds and propagating material are genetic material. It is both ex-situ conservation and in-situ conservation.

Ex-situ conservation means conservation of plant genetic resources for food and agriculture outside their natural habitats. This often means conservation of seeds and propagating material in gene banks. In- situ conservation means the conservation of ecosystems and natural habitats and the maintenance and recovery of viable populations of species in their natural surroundings and, in the case of domesticated or cultivated plant species, in the surroundings where they have developed their distinctive properties. For domesticated plants for food and agriculture, this means in farmers' fields and in gardens.[99]

INDIA:
Farmers' Rights for Protection of Plant Varieties

India is among the first countries in the world to have passed legislation granting Farmers' Rights in the form of the Protection of Plant Varieties and Farmers' Rights Act, 2001. India's experience is important due to its international contribution to negotiations on Farmers' Rights, its position as a center of biodiversity, and the complexities of agriculture in India within which the country is attempting to implement these rights. India's law is unique not only because of its far-reaching rights for farmers, but also in that it simultaneously aims to protect both breeders and farmers. This attempt to evolve a multiple rights system could, however, pose several obstacles to the utilization and exchange of plant genetic resources among farmers. India has framed a unique legislation, but still faces the task of implementation. This should serve as a signal internationally that establishing legislation is insufficient to effectively promote Farmers' Rights.

Failing to implement Farmers' Rights in India would be a heavy loss for all the farmers who need Farmers' Rights to protect their livelihoods, secure their access to resources, protect their rights to seeds, and, above all, lift them out of poverty.

---

[99] Dr. Regime Andersons, farmers Rights Project, fridtjof Nansen Institute, PO Box No. 326, 1326 Lysaker, Norway

The International Treaty on Plant Genetic Resources for Food and Agriculture recognizes Farmers' Rights and obliges the countries being Parties to the Treaty to protect and promote these rights. Countries, however, have not yet been able to evolve any consensus on how to define or implement Farmers' Rights. International coordination in this regard is also lacking. These are serious drawbacks that could prevent Farmers' Rights from becoming a realistic and workable mechanism. This report attempts to evolve options for the practical implementation of Farmers' Rights through a case study of India. Over forty stakeholders, including farmers, NGOs, industry and government representatives in India have been interviewed to explore methods to realize Farmers' Rights.

India is among the first countries in the world to have passed legislation granting Farmers' Rights in the form of the Protection of Plant Varieties and Farmers' Rights Act, 2001 (PPVFR). India's law is unique in that it simultaneously aims to protect both breeders and farmers. The Indian case assumes immense importance due to the country's lead in establishing a legal framework on Farmers' Rights, its international contribution to negotiations on Farmers' Rights, and the complexities of agriculture in India within which the country is attempting to implement these rights. India's case is also significant as the Indian gene center is recognized for its native wealth of plant genetic resources.

Agriculture plays a key role in India's economy both from the point of view of employment generation as well as its share in GDP. A recent economic survey expressed concern with the decline in the share of the agricultural sector's capital formation in GDP. The dismal situation in which many farmers find themselves in India today was reflected in a study sponsored by the Government of India, known as the 'Situation Assessment Survey of Farmers' (SAS), which for the first time assessed the situation of farmers in 2003. An alarming trend has been witnessed in India in recent years with rising rates of farmers committing suicide. Newspapers echoing the 'crisis in Indian agriculture' continue to report daily incidents of suicides in various parts of the country. Several different reasons have been put forward as the cause of suicides including: mounting debt of farmers, crop failures due to overuse of pesticides, imbalances of international trade, or social and psychological factors.

Agriculture was generally excluded from intellectual property protection in India and there was no legal system of Plant Breeders' Rights or Farmers' Rights for decades. The Seed Association of India, formed in 1985, has actively promoted the need for plant breeders' rights in the country. With the adoption of the WTO Agreement on Trade Related Aspects of Intellectual Property Rights (TRIPs), bilateral and multilateral pressure was also exerted on India to establish intellectual property rights in agriculture. There was enormous protest against implementing TRIPs by non-governmental organizations and farmers' lobbies in the country. The Protection of Plant Varieties and Farmers Rights Act (PPVFR), 2001 arose amidst this controversy. The PPVFR Act initially emerged as a result of the demands of the seed industry for breeder's rights. A chapter on Farmers' Rights was added to the Act due to pressure by NGOs.

India's PPVFR Act not only upholds farmers' rights to save, use and exchange seeds and propagating material but also attempts to enable farmers to claim special forms of intellectual property rights over their varieties. The Act grants plant variety protection on new varieties (largely modeled on UPOV), extant varieties and essentially derived varieties. Extant varieties include farmers' varieties, varieties in the public domain and varieties about which there is common knowledge. Nine rights can be said to have been given to farmers under the Act including: the rights to save, exchange and (to a limited extent) sell seeds and propagating material, to register varieties, to recognition and reward for conservation of varieties, to benefit sharing, to information about expected performance of a variety, compensation for failure of variety to perform, availability of seeds of registered variety, free services for registration, conducting tests on varieties, legal claims under the Act, and protection from infringement.

The National Biodiversity Act, 2002, based on the Convention on Biological Diversity, regulates access to and use of genetic resources in India. This Act also focuses on benefit sharing, protection of traditional knowledge and prior informed consent. The Geographical Indications Act, the Patents Amendments Act and the Seed Bill also have implications for Farmers' Rights in India. The Seed Bill could restrict farmers' right to sell their seeds, and the Patent Amendment Acts could pave the way for further extensions of patent-ability in agriculture that may restrict farmers' rights to save, use or exchange seeds. The Geographical Indications Act may enable farmers to claim rights for agricultural goods originating in a specific region, or it could restrict access of farmers to the protected goods depending on the way it is implemented.

A large number of diverse stakeholders influence India's policy on Farmers' Rights. The views of various stakeholders on the importance, barriers and options for implementing Farmers' Rights were compiled and analyzed in this study. Forty-two interviews were conducted among representatives from NGOs and farmer's lobbies, the government, the seed industry, experts and among farmers. Interviews were conducted in various parts of India: New Delhi, Chennai, Hyderabad, Bangalore, Pune and Uruli Kanchan.

Stakeholders across various categories acknowledge the importance of Farmers' Rights nationally and globally. A majority of the respondents expressed that Farmers' Rights must incorporate rights beyond the farmer's right to save, use and exchange seeds. Various issues were addressed as important rights for farmers, such as support for inputs, access to technology and farmer's participation in decision-making. While some favoured the government as the main agency to facilitate benefit sharing, others pointed to the need for NGOs or for an independent agency to promote benefit sharing. The stakeholders place a great deal of responsibility on the Authority established to implement Farmers' Rights in India to overcome the barriers. In addition, stakeholders are looking to the Governing Body of the International Treaty to provide guidance and direction for the implementation of Farmers' Rights.

India's case holds some lessons for developing countries. Two broad approaches to defining Farmers' Rights in India reflect the options facing developing countries: 1) Farmers' Rights as a form of intellectual property rights 2) Farmers' Rights as a development right. The first approach poses Farmers' Rights as a counter to Plant Breeder's Rights and argues that if commercial breeders can acquire intellectual property over their inventions, then farmers' innovations must also be recognized and rewarded. The second encompasses a range of concerns including food security, livelihood rights, social justice and access to resources. India's policy largely adopts the first approach, but also acknowledges the second view. Many respondents to the survey felt that Farmers' Rights should move beyond ownership rights to incorporate development rights. Yet, even among NGOs, farmer leaders, and individual farmers, there were differences regarding the nature of development rights to be addressed. NGOs focused on conservation and access to seeds, while individual farmers pointed to guaranteed prices, electricity, low interest credit and reducing the role of middlemen.

The approach of defining Farmers' Rights as intellectual property rights may provide political rather than economic benefits for developing countries, whereas defining Farmers' Rights as development rights may ensure greater economic/social advantages. While defining Farmers' Rights as a kind of intellectual property rights could provide a tool for negotiating at the global level, it may not be of great utility in ensuring rights for farmers in developing countries. Legal and economic costs of establishing the system, the difficulties of legally claiming rights for farmers, and the limited returns from plant variety protection itself are some of the reasons why IPR-based Farmers' Rights approaches are unlikely to provide significant economic returns to farmers.

In addition, developing countries may not gain much from seeking royalty payments for ownership of germplasm and may gain more from effectively utilizing genetic resources. Domestically, there is a need to gradually incorporate more development-oriented rights within the Farmers' Rights framework. Developing countries could attempt to forge a strategy that takes advantage of both approaches by utilizing the IPR type approach as a strategic tool to argue for Farmers' Rights globally, while domestically incorporating greater development oriented rights.

Another important lesson in defining Farmers' Rights is the need to avoid an 'anti-commons tragedy'. An 'anti-commons tragedy' arises when governments grant too many people rights over a resource with no one having an effective privilege of use. India's PPVFR Act is an attempt to evolve a multiple rights system that could pose several obstacles to useful utilization and exchange of resources. Developing countries need to evolve mechanisms to ensure exchange of agricultural resources as part of Farmers' Rights.

India and other developing countries could explore options to further develop the International Treaty's Multilateral System approach. The International Treaty on Plant Genetic Resources establishes a specified list of crops on which there are agreed rules for access and benefit sharing. In a sense, the Treaty attempts to redefine the principle of common heritage. India could not only support this initiative by making more crops available on the terms and conditions of the Multilateral System, but could also explore the option of developing a parallel national system which includes crops significant for India's food security. Such systems could provide the means for promoting farmers' and breeders' access to resources.

India's ability to be one of the first countries in the world to forge a national legislation on Farmers' Rights is a significant landmark. India has evolved a unique legislation, but still faces the task of implementation. This process is likely to be fraught with difficulties not only in balancing intellectual property rights with Farmers' Rights, but also in ensuring coordination between various legislations such as the PPVFR and the National Biodiversity Act. It is also evident from the study that no clear agreement exists among the various stakeholders in terms of how to implement the Act. This should serve as a signal internationally that establishing legislations is insufficient to effectively promote Farmers' Rights.

The Governing Body of the International Treaty must now take up the task of establishing clear guidelines for defining and implementing Farmers' Rights. An international movement for Farmers' Rights would have to tread carefully to respect the sovereignty of nations while promoting global cooperation. However,

Farmers' Rights must be promoted at the international level and cannot be left only to national governments to design. If each country, under Farmers' Rights, sets up barriers to access of genetic resources, limits exchange of resources, and competes to stake claims over innovations, the implications would be severe for farmers.

The Farmers' Rights movement has witnessed a long and chequered (checkered) history. An international mechanism is urgently required to promote some level of consensus on defining and implementing these vital rights. If the global community does not face up to the challenge of unambiguously articulating Farmers' Rights, what has been achieved so far in the battle to establish these rights may be lost. Such a loss would be heavy for farmers in India and other developing countries that need Farmers' Rights to protect their livelihoods, secure their access to resources, protect their rights to seed, and, above all, lift them out of poverty.[100]

Farmers' Rights in India

India is among the first countries in the world to have passed legislation granting. Farmers' Rights in the form of the Protection of Plant Varieties and Farmers' Rights Act, 2001. India's experience is important due to its international contribution to negotiations on Farmers' Rights, its position as a center of biodiversity, and the complexities of agriculture in India within which the country is attempting to implement these rights. This case study provides an overview of the state of Farmers' Rights, and opinions of over forty stakeholders in India including farmers, NGOs, industry and government representatives, on the prospects for the further realization of Farmers' Rights. India's law is unique in that it simultaneously

---

[100]Anitha Ramanna (2006), "The Farmers' Rights", Background Study 4: FNI Report 6/2006, 52 pages

aims to protect both breeders and farmers. The study analyses the achievements, barriers and limitations of India's approach. One of the findings is that the attempt to evolve a multiple rights system could pose several obstacles to the utilization and exchange of plant genetic resources among farmers.

India has framed a unique legislation, but still faces the task of implementation, without any clear consensus among the various stakeholders on how to achieve these rights. This should serve as a signal internationally that establishing legislation is insufficient to effectively promote Farmers' Rights. An international mechanism is urgently required to promote some level of consensus on defining and implementing these vital rights. If the global community does not face up to the challenge of unambiguously articulating Farmers' Rights, what has been achieved so far in the battle to establish these rights may be lost. Such a loss would be heavy for farmers in India and other developing countries who need Farmers' Rights to protect their livelihoods, secure their access.

The Farmers' Rights movement has witnessed a long and chequered history. That it has taken years to establish a binding agreement may be disheartening, but the fact the momentum was not lost and the Treaty finally emerged, should be a source of inspiration. India's ability to be one of the first countries in the world to forge a national legislation on Farmers' Rights is a significant landmark. The Indian case provides important lessons for other countries in establishing Farmers' Rights, and demonstrates the complex and contentious issues that must be tackled to implement Farmers' Rights. The fact that agreement on defining and implementing Farmers' Rights has not emerged in India, even after establishing a law on Farmers'

Rights, should serve as a signal internationally that establishing legislations is insufficient. [101]

A global mechanism is urgently required to promote some level of consensus on defining and implementing Farmers' Rights. Attention must now turn to the brass tacks of how to achieve Farmers' Rights. The political and strategic gains of defining Farmers' Rights as IPR type rights must be accompanied by measures to ensure economic benefits by focusing on Farmers' Rights as development rights. Farmers' Rights must also incorporate mechanisms to promote access and sharing of resources rather than only ownership rights.

Farmers themselves must be seen as important stakeholders in policy making. If the global community does not face up to the challenge of unambiguously articulating Farmers' Rights, what has been achieved so far in the battle to establish Farmers' Rights may be lost. The nuts and bolts on the machinery for driving Farmers' Rights forward must now be fitted. Without proper direction, the Farmers' Rights movement itself may come to a grinding halt.

A Charter of Farmers' Rights

A Charter of Farmers' Rights was drawn up by leaders of farmers' organizations as well as environmental, health and consumer groups participating in a consultation workshop on Biodiversity, Farmers' Rights and Intellectual Property Rights. The following is the text of this important document.

1. **The right to land:** Farmers across the country are being displaced to give way to factories, mines, dams

---

[101] Anita Ramanna (2006), Farmers' Rights in India, FNI Report, May 2006

etc. Under the new liberalization regimes of the Structural Adjustment Program, the Land Acquisition Act is being used to appropriate land from farmers and transfer it to multinational corporations. Farmers have a fundamental right to land. Prime farmland should be protected for social and environmental reasons and not be acquired for non- agricultural purposes. No agricultural land should be acquired without the farmer's consent and no agricultural land should be made available to multinational corporations.

2. **The right to conserve, reproduces, and modifies seed and plant material:** Third World farmers are the original donors and custodians of most genetic resources which are the first link in the cycle of food production. Both patents and sui generis systems create production, distribution and import monopolies. Every time such a monopoly is created, a part of India is handed over to monopolies/business conglomerates. There are few safeguards against monopolies in either the patents or the sui generis systems. In both, the rights of business have been protected over all else. Article 19 of the Indian Constitution gives every citizen the freedom to practice his/her occupation.

This freedom entails the right to shape one's means of production. Since the seed is the primary tool of agricultural production _ the 'occupation' of farmers, the Article ensures the rights of farmers to produce, reproduce, modify and sell seed. Any changes resulting from IPR regimes as proposed by Dunkel would deny farmers their right to freedom of occupation as protected in Article 19 of the Indian Constitution. We reaffirm our faith in the Indian Patents Act, 1970 which exempts horticulture and agriculture from patentability. We also affirm that farmers' right to protect biodiversity on their farms and to reproduce and modify seed freely is non-negotiable.

3. **The right to feed and save the country:** Farmer has the right to ensure the food security of the country. Structural adjustment is undermining the very basis of food security in India, a process that will be further aggravated by GATT's proposed policies. Countries like those in Sub-Saharan Africa that have neglected the capacity to feed themselves and have depended on purely export-oriented agriculture today face the specter of famine and starvation. The Bengal famine, which killed 3 million people, was a product of the policy of 'free trade' in agriculture of the colonial regime. These famines are not 'natural disasters'.

4. **The right to just agricultural prices and public support for sustainable agriculture:** The terms of trade in agriculture in India are rapidly declining. The debts of farmers have been artificial creations of the various development strategies. The farmers of India are not debtors and owe nothing to any of the financial institutions. The rural sector in India is negatively subsidized to the extent of 2 percent. There is a need for scientifically calculated parity prices for agriculture according to the price index, taking 1967 as the base year. Export does not bring the Southern peasants assured markets or incomes. The trends in the recent past have shown that Third World farmers have to export larger volumes at lower prices due to structural adjustment programs and global market fluctuations.

Farmers also need public support to make a transition to sustainable agriculture with changes in credits and prices to reflect the real environmental costs of production. Chapter 14 of Agenda 21, to which the Government of India was a signatory, requires that financial and policy support be given to ensure a transition to sustainable agriculture. Not all subsidies are undesirable. Subsidies that ensure the transition to sustainability and equity are in fact a social and political imperative.

5. **The right to information:** The Government's negotiations vis-à-vis GATT and the Dunkel Draft text has taken place in secrecy - excluding the parties who will be affected by them. Farmers have a right to be informed, at every stage, of any developments that will affect the agricultural sector, whether the Government feels that the impact will be adverse or not. Democracy requires that the farmers be informed of all developments in the agricultural sector at the local, national and global levels.

6. **The right to participatory research:** Farmers have been the original agricultural innovators and have a right to continue this age-old tradition. GATT will rob them of this right and will also accelerate the existing tendencies towards the privatization of research and the dismantling of public sector research. Current public sector agricultural research has thus far not treated farmers as partners in research. Farmers have a basic right to innovate, create and participate in all research pertaining to agriculture. Democratization of research is necessary for the implementation of this right.

7. **The right to natural resources:** Farmers have a right to local natural resources. Local resources have to be managed on the principle of local sovereignty, wherein the natural resources of the village belong to the village. The local management of natural resources for agriculture has been accepted in Agenda 21 of the United Nations Conference on Environment and Development (UNCED 1992) which has been endorsed by the Government of India and which the government and international agencies need to implement. Article 14(17) of Agenda 21 requires governments to ensure 'equitable access of rural people, particularly women, small farmers, landless and indigenous people to land, water and forest resources' and it also requires governments to 'strengthen and develop the management and internal capacities of rural peoples' organisations and

extension services and to decentralize decision-making to the lowest community level'.

8. **The right to safety and health:** The application of fertilizers, pesticides and insecticides in agriculture has occurred since the Green Revolution days. This has not been matched with a concomitant effort to protect the farmer or the consumer from associated hazards. Farmers and consumers have a right to health and environmental safety standards. [102]

A cruel joke on farmers

This Budget is in line with the policy framework that India adopted in 1991: imaginary carrots to peasantry, cake to service classes.

A man with only 10 flowers is given a challenge to decorate his room in the best possible way. He juggles with his kitty, toys with new permutations, and finally settles down with one.

I felt finance minister Mr. Pranab Mukherjee was akin to that man, who, while reading out the Union Budget on Friday for the financial year 2012-13, was trying hard to sound good — by resorting to statistical jugglery.

The bottom-line, however, is:

---

[102]The Charter of Farmers' Rights was drawn up by the leaders of different farmers' organisations in India together with representatives of social groups that participated in the National Consultation on Biodiversity, Farmers' Rights and IPRs. The Research Foundation organized it for Science, Technology and Natural Resources Policy and the Indian Trust for Art and Cultural Heritage in Delhi on 6 March 1993. For further information, contact: Third World Network-India, A- 60, Hauz Khas (2nd Floor), New Delhi - 110016, India. November 1993

This Budget not only comes as a huge disappointment for the entire peasantry, struggling against the markets, nature and policy vagaries for decades now, it actually comes as a cruel joke.

Like the previous budgets, this Budget too pays lip-service to the peasantry but in reality does exactly the opposite. Mr. Finance minister — despite his promises — continues to rob Peter to pay Paul.

The oft-repeated tools of intervention that he praises are food security and the Mahatma Gandhi National Rural Employment Guarantee Scheme (MNREGS). They, however, won't do any justice to farmers.

On the one hand the government gives higher wages to its own employees and widens the economic rift between the organized and un-organized classes, and on the other, it boasts of giving `2 per kg wheat to the poor. The Finance Minister can't deny that the poor would spend more money on crushing that wheat into flour.

The Finance Minister praises the MNREGS saying it has helped bring down poverty, but he shies away from telling us exactly how much he has allocated to the unorganized labour. We don't know how many more man days are being generated through the MNREGS and at what wage per day. If we knew that, we'd know how much a poor finally is earning. For, against the backdrop of rising salaries of employees under the wage commissions, the `125 per-day wage of a labourer under the MNREGS is too puny and unfair.

The Finance Minister emphatically boasts that the provision of 3 billion INR for the second green revolution for the eastern parts of India in the last Budget yielded good results. Paddy production, he says, went up enormously.

I want to humbly submit that increased production does not necessarily mean higher income for farmers, something that Commission for Agricultural Costs and Prices chairman Ashok Gulati, too, has recently admitted. Paddy farmers all over the country are selling their produce at distress prices far below the already dismal support prices. This Budget — like all his previous ones — doesn't even address the crisis of farm incomes.

On the contrary, he has very tacitly pushed the agenda of FDI in several sectors, while calling this a Budget of farmers. For instance, he says FDI in retail will ease the burden on farmers. Reality is exactly the opposite. Take but one example of his state of West Bengal. In a fertile district like Birbhum, where cold storage facilities are available, paddy and potato growers are killing themselves at a sickening pace. They are not even able to pay for the rent of the storage, forget recovering their investments.

This Budget speaks about the farmers getting a negotiable instrument for six months against their produce kept in storages. The moot question is when a farmer brings his produce to the local market; will he have the guarantee of higher prices? For, it has to account for his storage losses, transportation charges and additional interest on his crop loan for the time the produce is in storage etc.

Mr. Finance Minister says the fertilizer subsidy will continue, and be transferred through the Aadhar cards directly to the farmers. But so far the peasants don't have Aadhar cards.

He says the government has not reduced the fertilizer subsidy, but it has capped the potash and phosphate subsidies, and higher prices are to be borne by the farmers. The price of DAP was 485 INR in June 2011 and today it is 1,050 INR, despite subsidy. Barring urea prices, prices of all the other fertilizers are spiraling. It's not clear if urea prices will remain stagnant.

The Budget allocates 3 billion INR (Indian rupees) for irrigation in the Vidarbha region. In 2006, Prime Minister Manmohan Singh gave a special package for the beleaguered farmers of Vidarbha. It included 21.5 billion INR for irrigation. That money could bring no succor to the region's cotton farmers. How will this puny amount bring relief when 85 per cent of the land there doesn't have protective irrigation?

The Finance Minister speaks about the need to increase the production of pulses and oilseeds, but has not revealed how much money he has earmarked to motivate farmers to grow pulses and oilseeds. His bias against Vidarbha is obvious as he gave Echalkaranji, a textile and power loom hub in western Maharashtra, 700 million INR but gave short shrift to the handloom weavers in cotton growing area like Vidarbha.

The Budget gives more riches to the rich. Those who earn one million Indian rupees annual income will save more than 22,000 under direct tax sops, more than the annual income of one hundred thousands of monsoon-dependent farmers.

It is, therefore, clear that this Budget has disappointed farmers — more particularly a majority of the monsoon-dependent farmers who grow only one crop. It's in line with the policy framework that India adopted in 1991: imaginary carrots to the peasantry, cake to the service classes.[103]

---

[103]Vijay Jawandhia (2012), "A cruel joke on farmers", The Asian Age, March17, 2012

Conclusion

There are variations in economic, social, cultural and climatic conditions among countries. The developed countries desire to control the world and influence their supremacy in dictating the policies of the low-income countries. The developing countries fight against malnutrition, hunger, poverty, and diseases. These countries need development through industrialization; they borrow from the World Bank and other funding institutions; but they land in debt trap, high corruption and bad governance at home countries. The number of poor people grows at alarming speed and people die of hunger and diseases. In these developing countries war continues; rich cheats the poor; more budget outlays in defense; child sale continues, farmers commit suicides; yet there is possibility of achieving WORLD PEACE.

The farmers, small farmers, sharecroppers, agricultural labourers, artisans, agricultural traders and poor constitute three-fifths of total population in rural areas. So if farmers were utilized in productive processes, the world would definitely achieve peace everywhere. Hunger must be solved; humanity must be inculcated in everybody's mind; and we must adjust to live together in this world.

War does not result in peace; war creates enemies, war is not productive, and war comes from animal instinct. So let us live with humane characters and depend upon God's blessings. We can never say that there is no Super Power. What is harm if we help the needy people, which are starving? Let us make farming as an honored profession and allow the farmers to realize their dues from the society. We also feel that farming community could strengthen WORLD PEACE, as they constitute the largest section of people. They could be brought to 'peace forums' by economic and political means, which is also possible.

The farmers' organizations could change the disturbed earth into a peaceful world of tomorrow. They could make a heaven on the earth.

The poor farmer simply wants to live freely in peace. Most of the peasants are sharecroppers. They want a piece of land, where they could make huts for their living. They need engagement for a living. Cannot we provide the bare necessities of life to these uncared for people?

These people should be awarded their rights such as right to property, and right to food. But they are neglected as all lands belong to the state or to the landlords. They are neglected because they are poor and the leaders have 'no time' to hear their grievances. They are hungry because the bureaucrats and politicians are corrupt. They do not get justice because the legal system is more complicated and time consuming. A peasant, who grows food for others, forces him and his family members to go bed hungry. He is uncared for in hospitals, as he cannot purchase medicines.

A peasant adds his age quickly.

In this manuscript, we have searched for the possibility of FARMERS' involvement in strengthening WORLD PEACE. We have proposed few policy options for alleviating their sufferings for the purpose of achieving world peace.

We are confident that food security of the peasants and agricultural labourers would be the first step to achieve WORLD PEACE a reality.

Policy Options:

1. Food and Agriculture Organization (UNO)

FAO should prepare separate global reports on production, productivity, time of market arrivals of crops, fruits, flowers, other edible fruits, fibers, and market prices of all crops for the last 10 years for information of country governments, researchers and general public.

FAO should publish a Directory with the addresses of all Specialists who have received their Doctoral degrees in Agricultural Marketing, Agricultural Policy, Land Economics, and Agricultural Economics and may appoint them as FAO representatives for the district, state or country.

FAO should not employ NGOs, CSOs for researches in agriculture. A local researcher preferably an Agricultural Economist should be authorized to collect data, write report and send the report to the FAO, Rome office as and when necessary.

FAO's local representative should collect facts on the government policies in Agricultural Marketing, State Laws on procurement, subsidy in agriculture, distribution policy, storage, VAT, Insurances, traders license, cold-storages, warehouses, food processing industries, land policies, market policies and rice mills or wheat mills etcetera. The FAO should identity the surplus and deficit states in agriculture. The world is so great that none can draw a conclusion at the FAO HQ.

FAO should publish impact of globalization, working of the WTO, Import and Export Laws of all countries for the use of Governments, Universities and all Researchers. It should study the causes of farmers' suicides.

FAO works for the governments. FAO organizes conferences and produces reports. Who would be blamed for farmers' suicides? Who would explain why farm youths join the Terrorists, Maoists or Naxalites camps? It is because

farmers are neglected, tortured and are made beggars by government policies and programs.

Agricultural Services and Marketing (AGSM) of FAO has brought out several manuals to guide member countries in making better decisions in the area of marketing system improvement. All the publications should be free of cost and made available to all Agricultural Marketing Specialists.

FAO should directly monitor issues relating to WTO, the Commodity and Trade Division, the Agro-industries and Post-harvest Management Service and the Nutrition Division with specialists.

FAO should have a vast network of Agricultural Marketing Specialists or Agricultural Economists in each country and state for consultation purposes.

The issue of buffer stocking is very important, but while looking at the possibilities of regional cooperation, there is a need to distinguish between price-stabilization stocks and emergency food security reserves.

FAO should act as the policy advisory organization for all countries. It should aim at the welfare of all farmers, peasants, small farmers, sharecroppers, agricultural labourers and hungry people of the world. If the FAO were successful in planning and advising the farmers and governments, food security would be achieved.

2. Land Courts

Judicial delay is the greatest impediment to legal profession, justice to the people and the country. The poor suffers, as legal procedure is lengthy, expensive and could be manipulated in favour of rich people.

All land cases must be finalized within a year. It should not continue for generations. It can be finalized even in camp courts or can be decided with a note that it cannot be cited as a reference. The court should not permit the government or government agencies to apply to higher court as the government officials generally torture the sufferers. For each wrong decisions of the government, the services of concerned official might be terminated to restrict corruption and inefficiency in administration. This procedure would minimize vindictive cases in the court.

Corrupt judiciary induces poverty, illiteracy and lawlessness in Asia and Africa. Corruption free judiciary ensures peace, democracy, human rights, and economic development.

As justice is costly, a farmer fears to seek for justice; if he files a case, he has to sell his landed property and accept further misfortune. The peasants and rural people need immediate justice, **right or wrong,** because they are so poor that they cannot attend the courts on all dates the case is enlisted. The court must decide all land cases within a year. If it is not decided or delayed by the government, the judgment should be in favour of the farmer, the petitioner. A wrong judgment of the court also could save the farmer from torture and agony. The farmer accepts any judgment; hates his bad luck and remains silent. He accepts the path of sufferings. The learned judges could also finalize cases on the first date of listing of court cases too.

If hundreds of farmers commit suicide in a year, the court should start *suo motu* cases and call the government to explain the situation. The court, if convinced, that the implementation of government laws is defective or the officer has neglected in his duties, the court could award punishment directly to the government and/or the officers responsible for negligence in duty.

3. The Government

The government must award land rights to the tiller of the land at the earliest. A complicated land policy creates mass unemployment, increases the number of hungry people and encourages corruption. It derails democracy, humanity and rule of law.

The governments should not invite industrialists, multinational corporations, like Cargill, Tyson, and Smithfield and foreign nationals to enter into farm sector in both developed and developing countries. Farming through public-private-partnership or farmers' cooperatives or farmers' joint ownership or contract farming should not be encouraged by the government because it gives rise to corruption, power play and harassment to the peasants.

All advices by world organizations must be locally tested because of difference in climate, culture, people and local farm practices. Entry of billionaires into farm sector would increase farm yield, but it would encourage small farmers' suicides, international conflicts and growth of Maoists and Terrorists all over the world. Let all governments take steps to be self-sufficient in food grains. If they fail in agricultural production, they would ultimately loss their independence through uprisings and war between the government and people.

Industrialists need more agricultural and forest land to maximize profit through government patronage. A peasant needs land for peace, prestige, food and self-employment. He produces food grains for his family and the world. But the government is worried for the industrialists. Why?

Food Laws promulgated by the government necessarily control agricultural prices of wheat and rice, movement barrier, licensing of trade, Fair Price Shops, procurement policy, rescue plan, and subsidy in food grains. These Laws cause high storage loss, recycling in food grains and black marketing and corruption. The government can be more popular when price of food grains is cheaper as compared to industrial products. The government collects money from industrialists to fight elections and therefore industrial products are priced high after election in all countries. This results in farmers' suicides and poverty of farmers. The final result is that the farm-boys leave agriculture and rural areas for engagement in non-agricultural profession and opt for urban life. Hence, agriculture should be a free business and free trade to reverse the present trend. Let the farmers realize their dues from sale of rice and wheat. The farmers would achieve justice when the government declares and offers procurement prices of food grains as compared to rise of index numbers of all commodities with a base year or offering parity prices.

The prices of rice and wheat (essential commodities) should be at par with increase of pay and perks received by government employees or gold prices over a period of time for awarding justice to the vast majority of population.

If price of gold or pay of government employees increase by 10 percent per year, procurement prices of rice and wheat should be increased by 10 percent per year.

The government should award benefits to farmers directly to enrich them. Government would procure the minimum quantities of food to stabilize market or be ready to import cereals as per need for a couple of months in a year only. But government should declare higher prices for rice and wheat. The expenditure on farmers' insurance, health insurance, farmers' pension, declaration of higher prices would be much less than the subsidy to agricultural inputs (seeds, fertilizers, pesticides, tractor or pump sets, wastage at warehouses, F. C. I. storage loss etcetera). The government should not use force to collect rice and wheat from the farmers.

Existing course curricula in agricultural universities need to be strengthened to produce trained human resources in agricultural marketing and agro-processing. Each agricultural university must open a Post–Graduate department in Agricultural Marketing. Each government should start short course training centers in agricultural marketing in each district. This institute would impart training on grading, processing, packaging, quality control and storage.

There should be special markets for fruits and vegetables. The government should provide refrigerated transport facility to transport fruits to the consuming markets located in cities.

The Directorate of Agricultural Marketing must be headed by a Doctorate in Agricultural Marketing. The research cell under the directorate should undertake studies on marketing costs and margins on different agricultural commodities continuously. It should also forecast future prices and future markets to the producers, traders and consumers.

Market information systems need to be strengthened and geared to meet the requirements of farmers, business houses and market functionaries. In case of shortages, it should advise how to procure, store and maintain uniform supply to the consumers. Similarly in case of over-production, it should contact other governments or countries for exporting the surplus commodities to break glut in the local markets.

The government must advise all farmers to grow at least two crops; one crop, which is best, suited to the area and another crop, which could be sold exclusively for earning an income. The farmer would be in an advantage side if grows cash crops, vegetables, fruit trees for earning higher income. He could buy cereals from other farmers.

The government should popularize horticultural plantations or forest plantations in drought prone areas. The plants like mango, guava, kagzi lime, teak tree, sandal wood tree, Sal tree, and bamboo tree etcetera. The government should supply seeds, seedlings, saplings and plants to all farmers free of cost. These people would be richer than the farmers with irrigated land holdings. It would save the climate too. Horticultural plantations would be more profitable in un-irrigated areas. The corrupt governments borrow more funds for flow irrigation, where irrigation is not required or the land is not suitable for irrigation.

All mini banks for weaker sections should be closed. It gives loan to farmers without studying 'Return from the investment, Repaying capacity and Risk bearing ability' of the farmer. As a result, the farmer commits suicides if crop fails. All private loans must be declared as illegal.

The government should act as a guarantor of the loan amount borrowed from a nationalized bank within a limit, say 1000 INR (Indian rupees) for each cardholder. Each bank should have facility of zero-balance cash account for all adults in the country to facilitate bank transaction. But till date, neither the government nor the Banks have extended any help or assistance in bank loan to these poor people residing in rural areas.

The government may make a law that each individual can have only one bank account in one bank only.

Multiple of bank accounts are the sources of black money, corruption, and malpractice. If a family has 3 adult members, the family can have 3 accounts in total. Each industry or firm can have only one Bank account. Double accounts for a firm should be treated as illegal.

The government must accept that retailing creates employment.[104]

Even a peasant or an unemployed youth goes to the market with home-grown commodities such as pumpkin or arum or green leaves worth of 5 or 10 INR (Indian rupees) to the weekly market to sell. He/ she gossips with other retailers and return to his/her home with salt and kerosene with satisfaction. The poorest retailer too possesses self prestige and he gets satisfaction in local market (Haats) as he is free for talks with opposite sex.

Market is not only a place of economic activity but is also a social place where marriage proposals of youths (both sexes) are finalized. It is a recreation place for all people in the tribal areas.

The Directorate of Agricultural Marketing should try to convince the farmers to start local daily markets in morning hours for two hours only to sell their grains or fruits to local traders or consumers. The price chart prevailed yesterday for different commodities may be displayed in the Notice Boards for information. Market Extension service is also necessary to save the peasants. If all the villagers desire to start a daily market in their village, it would be a welcome venture. If village–A chooses Sun day, time 6 AM to 8 AM, the village-B could have Monday; village-C could

---

[104] Mallick, Suresh Chandra (1975), "Marketing of Rice in Orissa", Research Orissa Publications, CL – 21, VSS Nagar, Bhubaneswar-751004

have on Tues day and so on. So, all 7 villages in a cluster could have one market day in the village in a week. The result would be as follows:

(a) This would help the farmers to sell their surplus commodities in his village without any wastage of time.
(b) The consumers would also avail their necessities without wastage of time.
(c) It would create a market demand for other consumers and of other villagers.
(d) These village markets would create employment opportunity even in villages. The unemployed youths would become traders or itinerant traders and earn an income without government patronage.
(e) Retailing of agricultural commodities creates the maximum employment opportunity without any assistance of the government.
(f) Further, these peasants or youths might be interested to undertake processing, transportation, and may act as market informer of prices.
(g) The village market committee should create Market Pindies (an elevated rectangular trading place of 8′x4′) in rows in a centrally located place in the village. The village market committee should not charge any rent from the villagers or traders. It should be free. But it should ensure cordial market environment, prestige to both buyers and sellers and maintain peace at all cost.
(h) In village market, women participation would strengthen women empowerment and they would earn an income. This would assist in food security too.

If a peasant could sell his marketable surplus at a favourable price in his village market, he could plan to produce market-oriented vegetables, poultry birds or milk to earn an additional income. Single crop cultivation such as rice or wheat can award more pain than gain to the farmer. If crop fails, a farmer could commit any mischief including suicide. If we can create a market in each village, a poor man/woman can earn an income. If a person creates an employment for him and earns an amount and is free from loan, he would not commit suicide.

The planner must find ways for boosting the income of the vulnerable farmers to maintain the family.

False advertisement, wrong policy and corrupt government officials make the farmers' poor. So the government must take adequate steps to help the farmers.

In order to create more employment opportunities for farm women, the government should distribute 5 or 10 saplings of one horticultural plant to each farmer in the district. Suppose, the specialists identify a district is suitable for Kagzi Lime cultivation by studying its soil type, rainfall and marketing facility; it would be better to distribute the samplings directly to all rural women for creating employment opportunity and income. An example of plantation of one million Kagzi Lime in a district would add to the income of the farmers. Moreover, it helps in market development and usher an era of peace in the locality. All the districts could be allotted with different horticultural plants to safeguard the life and economy of the rural households. (Appendix1)

The government should not allow Foreign Direct Investment in retail sector. A big fish in a pond could eat all fingerlings. India is a country with 400 million hungry people. So SEZ in agriculture and FDI in retail sector must be withdrawn immediately.

A major share of subsidies allotted by the government, all donations by developed countries and all programs for awarding justice to the poor is simply eaten away by the politicians, bureaucrats, contractors and elected representatives of people in developing countries.

Farmers, peasants, and share-croppers would not be benefitted by Agricultural Produce Market Acts, Control Orders and Food Laws such as Rice Milling Industry Act, Rice Milling Industry (Regulation and Licensing) Rules, Rice Movement Control Orders, Food Grains Dealers' Licensing Orders, Rice and Paddy Control Order, Guest Control Order, Food grains Movement Restrictions Orders, Rice Milling Industry (Regulation) Act, Rice (Movement Control) Order and many other food grains orders as these laws simply empowers the corrupt government officials of the Consumer welfare department. These Acts and Control Orders control the peasants, traders and consumers in a country. It is a sign of a food deficit country.

Hoarding, profiteering and black marketing are illegal activities; hence government intervention is a must.

Each Government must ensure agriculture as a profitable enterprise; this would make the country surplus in food grains and award food security to all.

Each government must ensure that the farmers, peasants and agricultural labourers are food secured and they live in peace.

Wheat, Rice or Paddy (rice with husk) must be without government taxes for the entire country. There should not be any restriction on movement of these commodities in the country. This will create employment to 4 million youths as traders to support their families in India.

So the price of wheat and rice (with husk) must be fixed at 3000 INR per quintal as farm harvest price. The farmers must be assured parity prices as compared to gold prices, government employee's salary over a period of time (with Base year 1951, or 1961, or 1971). The farm labourer's wage should be at par with or nearer to industrial workers or city labourers.

Each senior citizen of the country must be assured of Pensioner's benefit. It should include farmers, peasants, agricultural labourers, artisans, small traders of both sexes; it should be uniform for all non-government employees. The farmers' pension amount would be $1/10^{th}$ of the retired highest government servant. Why only 3 percent people would get pensioners' benefits? What about others?

Let all senior citizens of the country be awarded pensioners' benefits. Let dearness allowance, medical allowance, house rent allowance and special allowance to only 3 percent of beneficiaries be scrapped or cut by the government to do justice to all people in the country. Reappointment of government employees after 60 years of age must be stopped by law. If not, their pension - benefits must be denied straightway.

The government should purchase these cereals at parity prices and store the commodities only for four months. Moreover, money spent on charity to farmers should be stopped, Fair Prices Shops be closed, free donations and free midday meals should be abolished. The money saved by the government through subsidy could be utilized in direct assistance to people through A/C payee deposits.

Dual price system for the same commodity is a political decision.

Free gifts of bicycles to girl students, Fair Price Shops, low cost wheat or rice to the poor must be stopped.

Award of thousands of acres of land to industrialists, higher salary and pensioners' benefits to government employees have widened the disparity between rich and poor.

Allow the farmers to sell their commodities with prices best suited to them. The government should declare parity prices for agricultural commodities for a year before the marketing season and in no case, a government should force the farmers for LEVY procurement.

Most part of the subsidies earmarked for agriculture is misappropriated by government employees, corporations, industrial houses and politicians or enter to the black market. Therefore all subsidies must be withdrawn at once.

The Supply Corporation, Cotton Corporation, Jute Corporation, the Food and Civil Supplies Department and the Cooperation Department of the government should be dismantled as these institutions have failed in their duties to protect the interests of farmers.

But Food Corporation of India should be squeezed to $1/10^{th}$ of its present capacity to serve to the people during war, famine, flood or cyclone.

Each country must encourage import and export of agricultural and horticultural commodities at the shortest possible time. So each country should have foreign tie-ups.

The governments must purchase and store minimum quantities of food grains to meet natural calamities like flood, cyclone, drought and war etc. It must dispose of all the stocks before the next procurement season. Wastage of food grains must be avoided. If the government feels that free flow of goods would not meet the market demand, it could import the required quantities from foreign markets.

Import of food grains would discourage farmers and farming. Each country must take adequate steps to meet its own requirement of rice and wheat. A chronic deficit country in food grains would lose its sovereignty to a rich country in future.

Budgetary support on charity for the farmers, peasants, and BPL families should be stopped. Fair Prices Shops and midday meals in schools should be abolished.

Subsidy in agriculture should be stopped as most of the amount is misappropriated by bureaucrats, politicians, government employees, corporations, contractors and business houses.

The money saved by the government by abolishing subsidy in all sectors could be better utilized in Pensioners' benefits to all senior citizens of the country including farmers. Moreover healthcare facility, drinking water facility to all could be reached. The government should fill up all vacant posts in the government. The pensioners' benefits should be channelized through A/C payee deposits only.

Food processing units could be started in rural areas by farm youths for income, employment and for checking wastage in horticultural produce such as prickle making, squash making, potato chips etc.

Government must encourage all the rural households to grow fruit trees and firewood trees for women empowerment, employment and income. Horticultural nurseries should meet the demand of the farmers.

Food security is possible through farmers in all the LDCs and developing countries provided agriculture is a profitable enterprise. But the government must invest in market infrastructure, strengthen market intelligence services, arrange foreign–tie up for export and import, and declare parity prices for agricultural commodities much before sowing season.

Public expenditure in agriculture and charity for the poor is mostly mis-utilized. The end result is that farmers become beggars; commit suicides and are hungry throughout their life. Yet the farming community provides food to all, a commitment for world peace.

4. Farmers' Organizations

There could be annual fares of farmers at block level, district level, state level, country level and international level. They could discuss about their problems and try to make solutions for establishing economic, social and cultural ties. Farmers are the fountains of world peace. They can create new horizon of peace and strengthen peace environment, as they believe in peace. The whole world is a family and all people are brothers and sisters.

Farmers supply food to the whole world for better health and peace. If their income is increased, they can fulfill their ambitions of sending their children to schools and colleges. The governments must allot a piece of land to all landless families free of cost with occupancy rights.

Although people differ in faith, religion, culture, custom and character, farmers of the world do not consider such dividing factors for a greater cause of World Peace. They consider that all human beings have aspirations for their children. They believe in the Almighty God.

They say 'All roads lead to Heaven for right deeds only'.

They express their thoughts among them, but they want to meet the government officials to explain their sufferings. But an individual farmer fears to meet rich or powerful people or the government machinery, as he does not possess the strength to absorb the shocks. He is pessimistic in character as he is uncared for, unprivileged and a sufferer from his childhood to the funeral. He produces food but he is unfed.

So both the government and farmers' organizations must try to see that farmers laugh, enjoy and live as human beings.

The farmers' organizations should not be at charity from political leaders; should not be controlled by few individuals for all time to come, but they should have only one aim of doing justice to the farmers' community.

The farmers should have a separate Political Party in each country. It is necessary and urgent. Justice should be achieved through ballot and not by bullet. The elected members of farmers' party should explain their grievances in the Parliament and be a part of Law making process for benefits of farmers.

The party should contest in General Elections as per election rules. It should be an ideal political party, which should not be indulged in black money, corruption, and should be free from caste or class or religion. It should have only one aim to make and implement laws for the benefits of largest section of society, the poor and venerable peasants. The country can stop beggary too.

5. Farmers

The farmers must remember that they work silently to provide food to the whole world. They are simple and obedient but they are sufferers. So their sincerity must be rewarded by the society, state, country and governments. They should take up farming operations with interest and zeal.

He should not borrow personal loan with higher rate of interest for daughter's marriage or construction of a residential building. A family function gives satisfaction but it is not an investment; it is simply wastage of money. A farmer losses peace when pays the interest of the principal. He suffers mental agony when his crop fails by heavy downpour or flood or drought or cyclone. It causes loss of his family peace.

A farmer knows what to do in agriculture. He should grow crops to sell in market. He should treat farming as a business for profit and survival. A farmer should be engaged to achieve prosperity. He should carefully decide the crops, bank loans and family expenses. A farmer needs justice to live happily. A farmer needs the following entitlements. These are:

(a) Right to land
(b) Parity prices for wheat and rice with gold, government service, land value or cement
(c) Pensioner's benefit as reward for his/her lifetime services to the nation
(d) Family insurance
(e) Single Bank Account for each voter in the country.
(f) The state laws should prohibit more than one bank account and one passport for an individual.
(g) A Voter identity card
(h) Disposal of land cases within a year
(i) Procurement prices of wheat, Rice, Paddy as per their legitimate dues.

(j) The Essential Commodities Act for Rice, Wheat and Paddy should be withdrawn to assist the farmers of the country. It can award profit and peace to the farmers as producers, traders and millers.

A farmer should not adopt a coercive step of committing suicide. He must know that suicide is the worst sacrilege in all religions.

A farmer should not borrow more funds to become rich overnight.

A peasant believes in the Almighty God throughout his/her life because he is poor.

All peasants need justice. They may be permitted to sell their produce at the price dictated by them. The governments and the officials torture the peasants even today. Peasants should not be evicted from their land for industrialists by the governments. One-third of geographical area in the country must be used for agriculture.

Each farmer must remember that he grows crops, vegetables, and fruits, condiments for the people of the world, which are enjoying life in towns or cities with higher income. But they look down upon the farmers as they are poor and hungry.

He has to live till he gets justice.

The peace-loving farmers of the world can strengthen WORLD PEACE. And it is possible.

THE END

Annexure 1

A Proposal of One Million Kagzi Lime Trees

To Support One Hundred Thousand Farmers in Jagatsinghpur District (Orissa State) INDIA

The Orissa State faces emerging problems of hunger, malnutrition, farmers' suicides, climate change, air pollution, water pollution and rise of Naxalites over a period of years. The high growth of industrialization and free flow of funds have changed the aspiration of people and youths. The state is proud of having hundreds of Engineering colleges, Management colleges, and more than 15 Universities. The spread of concretization of roads to remote villages, and construction of palatial buildings everywhere in the state have changed the status and scenario of the state.

But the state has not ensured food security to all the inhabitants. It has not provided employment opportunities to all youths. The easy availability of bank loans has created a chance to invest more in agriculture. But climate change, untimely rainfall has caused farmers' suicides. Lack of regular income of most of the farmers, peasants, artisans and agricultural labourers is the root cause of their mental agony; and they are dragged to revengeful activities in public life. But more than three-fourth of families in the state are not food secured.

Hence, it is necessary that all the rural people must be the partners of progress in the state.

A proposal for additional income is necessary to save the poor farmers from suicides, hunger and terrorism. This project would help the farmers, farmwomen and youths in the villages, who could earn an additional income daily or weekly and achieve satisfaction for at least 15- 20 years. This would induce the beneficiaries to praise the government and support the government because they would achieve peace, happiness and regular income. The state can boast that it exports agricultural commodities to Japan, Middle East and other countries.

The Project is to make Jagatsinghpur District a pioneer district in planting ONE million Kagzi lime saplings in the district that would award peace, happiness and would add to the income of one hundred thousand families.

Saplings of papaya and drumsticks could also be added for supplementing income of each family for local markets.

Saplings of Kagzi Lime (Nimboo or Citrusaurantifolia) would be purchased from Horticultural Farms of the State and Ministry of Agriculture, Government of India. These seedlings would be supplied to all the farmers, peasants, artisans and agricultural labourers free of cost. But these beneficiaries would make pits, apply compost, plant the saplings, and make adequate steps to water the plants. The beneficiaries would be owners of the fruiting plants and pick up the matured lime for sale. If every family were given 10 plants each, the following benefits would be achieved.

The benefits are:

(a) It would create an atmosphere of equality, a possession, a chance to gossip with others that his plants are growing better
(b) The womenfolk would take more care for irrigating and watching the fruit plants
(c) Others never steal Kagzi lime, so cent percent harvest without even watching.
(d) The monkeys never destroy the plants and never climb the Kagzi lime tree because of its pines.
(e) There would be easy marketability with profit
(f) The fruits can be dispatched to Rourkela, Bhubaneswar, Calcutta, New Delhi, Bangalore or Mumbai. The market could be a wider market as there would be daily transaction between the production center and distribution center.
(g) The fruit is less perishable and can be kept or dispatched without deterioration.
(h) Normally pickle industries and packaging industries would be started by farmers themselves or by private companies without any investment of the government.
(i) Transportation of commodities would be possible by traders, truck owners or railways as South Eastern Railways pass through the district.
(j) The income from 10 Kagzi lime plants could manage a family's immediate needs. Once, a farmer is induced to cultivate the plant; the family would try to increase the number of plants because he would a specialist of the plant by course of time.
(k) This project would utilize the services of all family members and would make the family – a heaven.

(l) One Million Plants would be helpful to reduce air pollution, soil pollution and water pollution of the district. It would reduce air pollution caused by moving vehicles and show some impact on climate change.

(m) The project would be a part of WORLD CANOPY program.

The trade name of Kagzi Lime produced in Orissa may be decided by the government as 'Orissa Kagzi Lime' to popularize the state among all consumers inside and outside the country.

The project would generate income each week, so the peasants would be food secured and at least shift their misfortunes for some days. It would also create employment opportunities in marketing of the produce such as village trader, itinerant trader or commission agent of exporters. It would be possible because the entire district would produce Kagzi Lime.

Nowhere in India Kagzi Lime has been undertaken in large scale and that too in a compact area. Once, this horticultural plant is popularized it could be adopted in other districts. If the farmers agree, we could advise them not to apply pesticides, insecticides, fertilizers or other herbicides to make the product free of toxins. The toxin free fruits could be sold at three time's higher prices in foreign markets. The fertilizer component could be available through home produced Farm Yard Manure or compost. Similarly, all diseases could be restricted or subsidized through application of Neem oil to the plant or simply through bio-treatment.

This project would convince the farmers, traders and exporters of Kagzi Lime to avoid toxin – free Kagzi Lime for foreign market. Colorization of vegetables has made consumption of vegetables as poisonous foodstuffs. This results in many complications to unknown people who utilize this as food. Even banana used for worshipping God in Bhubaneswar is poisonous.

Jagatsinghpur District:

The district is centrally located in the state. It includes the Paradip port and Jagatsinghpur town. It is well communicated to other parts of the country. It covers 8 Community Blocks and 194 Gram Panchayats and 4 Assembly Constituencies. The CD Blocks are Balikuda, Jagatsinghpur, Naugaon, Tirtol, Kujanga, Erasama, Biridi, and Raghunath Pur.

The project would be taken up in all the villages of the district and assist all rural people in achieving food security through additional income. If all the villages do not count one hundred thousand families, we would include Niali C D Block of adjoining Cuttack district and Kendrapara districtfor this plantation scheme. People are highly literate and they can adopt modern technology quickly. The district could be an export zone for Kagzi lime.

The project area is well connected with Bhubaneswar, Cuttack, Kendrapara, Puri and Calcutta by road. The Paradeep Port is an all-weather port, which is situated in this district. This plantation would render justice to all rich and poor people in the district. Research studies indicate that Kagzi lime could be better grown in Jagatsinghpur district. So this proposal would be a pioneering step to assist the rural people to have an additional and constant return with or without investment by the beneficiaries.

How to Proceed

We would try to convince the local leaders, youths and the ultimate beneficiaries that this project would award not only monetary benefits but also satisfaction without any cost. Their products would be exported to other states, countries and create a regular supply to the markets. The farmwomen would take better care because these plants would be preferred in the backside of their houses. There is no chance of theft or monkey – menace for Kagzi Lime. The specialists would convince all aspects of growing the fruit trees for profitability and pleasure. However, if toxin-free Lime is produced, we can enter to international market.

If farmers appreciate this program in Jagatsinghpur district, steps could be taken by the government to prepare schemes for all the THIRTY districts of the state to make National Horticulture Mission a success. The farmers, peasants, agricultural labourers and artisans would appreciate this project and a market for Kagzi Lime could be created in the state. And it is possible.

Funding of the Project - Necessary funds for the project could be available from the government budget or National Horticulture Mission project being operated in the State.

Kagzi lime for all rural families

The Kagzi lime (Nimboo or Citrusaurantifolia) is an important fruit of citrus group. It is very popular all through the tropics and is used as a necessary adjunct in everyday meal. It is regarded as a health-building food of great value. Limes are generally mistaken for lemons, but they represent two varieties of the same genus. The lime is smaller in size than the lemon, with a thin smooth skin. It has sweet smell and contains less juice than the lemon. The lime grows on a small, multi-branched tree up to 5 meter in height, with spiny branches, small green leaves and white and strongly scented flowers.

There are many varieties of limes, differing in size, color and shape. They are, however, classified into two main groups, namely, the sweet and the acid limes. The sweet limes contain a. higher proportion of sugar but they have an insipid taste and are not considered to be of high nutritive value. They are, therefore, not grown on any great scale. Acid or sour limes, on the other hand, are extensively cultivated, as their importance as food and medicine has been recognized for centuries. The two most popularly known varieties are *Pari* and *Kagzi niboo*. The lime is believed to have originated in India, where it has been grown since remote times. Arab traders are believed to have taken it to Eastern Mediterranean and Western countries in about l000 AD. The Spaniards took it to the New, World early in their colonization. It has since spread throughout the tropics, where it is the most commonly cultivated species of the acid citrus.

Food Value

Acid limes are excellent source of free citric acid, natural sugar, vitamin C, calcium and phosphorus. It contains by far more vitamin C than the lemon. It is generally used for its juice, which is taken in various ways. The best way to use it is to take with water. The lime juice forms an indispensable ingredient of salads. In fruit salads, it helps to retain the normal color of fruits and imparts tart flavour. It is often mixed with cooked pulses, soups, sauces and gravies to make them more tasty and palatable.

Food Value of Lime
Moisture: 84. 6%
Protein: 1.5%
Fat: 1.0%
Minerals: 0.7%
Carbohydrates: 10.9%
Fiber: 1.3%

Minerals and Vitamins
Calcium; 90 mg
Phosphorus: 20 mg
Vitamin C: 63 mg

Iron: 0.3 mg

Small amount of Vitamin B Complex

(Value per 100 mg's edible portion = Calorific Value – 57)

Natural Benefits and Curative Properties

The juice of fresh limes is being used in medicine from ancient times in India. In *Vedas,* lime has been mentioned as a sacred fruit. Cutting limes after reciting certain *Mantras* is considered an effective method for driving away the evil spirits. Charaka and Sharangdhara, the two famous physicians of ancient India, have mentioned about the therapeutic value of lime in various diseases of bones and joints. The vitamin C content in lime increases the body's resistance to disease, aids the healing of wounds and prevents damage to the eyes. Vitamin C is also helpful in maintaining the health of the teeth and other bones of the body. It prevents decay and loosening of the teeth, dental caries, toothache, bleeding of the gums and fragility of bones. The rind of the fruit also has medicinal properties. It contains a volatile oil, which is used in medicine for improving digestion and removing wind

Scurvy: As a rich source of vitamin C, the lime has been regarded as a food of exceptional therapeutic value. It has saved the lives of innumerable crews of ocean-going vessels from scurvy. The Boards of Trade regulations have made it compulsory for the crew to have a supply of lime juice when vegetables are not available.

Digestive disorders: Lime is considered highly beneficial in the treatment of digestive disorders. A teaspoonful of fresh lime juice should be mixed with equal quantity of bony. It should be licked to stop bilious vomiting, indigestion, burning in the chest due to high acidity in the stomach and excessive accumulation of saliva in the mouth. A teaspoonful of lime juice mixed with water and a pinch of soda bicarb makes an excellent remedy for reducing the acidity in the stomach. It also acts as a powerful carminative in case of indigestion. It produces a marked sedative effect in the stomach due to release of carbonic acid gas.

Constipation: The lime juice is of great value in constipation, when it is taken as the first thing in the morning in a glass of warm water. In chronic cases, it helps remove tire disorder by promoting biliary secretion from liver.

Peptic Ulcers: The citric acid in limes has an alkaline reaction in the system. This acid together with the mineral salts present in the juice helps the digestion by assisting in the absorption of fats and alcohol and by neutralizing excessive bile produced by the liver. The juice counteracts the effects of greasy food and reduces gastric acidity. It is, therefore, especially valuable in the treatment of peptic ulcers.

Common Cold: Lime is ideal in all types of fevers and cold if taken welt diluted. Vitamin C rich lime juice increases resistance, reduces toxicity and cuts down the course of the illness. Unless one is especially allergic to citrus fruits, onc should not avoid lime in cold. A glass of diluted lime juice prepared in warm water, to which a teaspoonful of honey is added, is an ideal remedy for cold and dry cough.

Tonsillitis: Lime has proved effective in the treatment o(acute tonsillitis. A fresh lime squeezed in a glass of warm water, with four teaspoonful of honey and a quarter teaspoonful of common salt, should be sipped slowly in such cases.

Gums: Lime is valuable in swollen gums. A glass of diluted fresh lime juice mixed with a pinch of rock salt should be taken in this condition. The squeezed lime rind should also be rubbed over the gums, before throwing it away.

Eye Disorders: Lime juice is valuable in eye disorders. Few drops of warm lime juice diluted with water should be instilled in the eyes in case of conjunctivitis. Its regular use with pure rose water in the ratio of 1:4 is helpful in preventing old-age cataract.

Cystitis: Lime has proved valuable in cystitis (Inflammation of urinary bladder). A teaspoonful of lime juice should be put in 180 gm. of boiling water. It should then be allowed to cool and 60 gm. of this water should be given every two hours in this condition. It gives relief to burning sensation and also stops bleeding in cystitis.

Scorpion Sting: When externally applied, fresh lime is highly beneficial in the treatment of scorpion sting. A crystal of potassium permanganate should be put over it. It will have effect in ten minutes.

Obesity: The lime juice is also excellent for weight reduction. It has a sedative effect on the nerves. Fresh juice' of a lime mixed in a glassful of water and sweetened with honey should be taken every morning on empty stomach in case of obesity. It will reduce the weight in two to three months' time. One should however, take low calorie diet to get the desired result.

Precaution: Limes should not be used in excess. The alkaline salts of the lime juice neutralize the free uric acid and precipitate it. It has; therefore, been found that its excessive use may cause the formation of renal calculi. Excessive sucking of fresh lime is also bad for teeth as the acid damages the delicate enamel of the teeth and makes them sensitive. Its excessive use weakens digestion and impoverishes the blood. **+++++**

AUTHOR INDEX

+++++

SUBJECT INDEX

+++++

AUTHORS

Professor Suresh Chandra Mallick (b 1944) was a faculty member of the OUAT, Bhubaneswar (India) during 1968 - 2004. He is a researcher, writer, thinker and social worker. He is an Agricultural Economist with specialization in Agriculture, Poverty, Marketing, Policy and World Peace to motivate people's involvement in peace process. He held the post of Vice President, Indian Society of Agricultural Marketing during 2003 - 05. At present, he is the Chairperson of the Institute of Development Studies & Policy Research, Bhubaneswar.

Pritam Mallick (1975–2006) was extremely noble, friendly and knowledgeable and possessed extraordinary memory. He received B.A. (Honors) from Utkal University, M.A. from Central University, Hyderabad and M. Phil. Degree from JNU and completed Ph. D. courses in JNU. He was a specialist in Monetary Economics and Econometrics. He remembered the Oxford Dictionary and Roget's Thesaurus to master English literature. He acquired deep knowledge in Astrology, Palmistry, Mathematics and Statistics. He contributed enormously for WORLD PEACE manuscripts as co-author. But his heavenly demise occurred on August 4, 2006.

Published – Published - Published

WORLD PEACE

BY

PROFESSOR SURESH C. MALLICK

AND

PRITAM MALLICK

Volume: 1	**:**	**Poverty and Peace**
Volume: 2	**:**	**Corruption and Peace**
Volume: 3	**:**	**War and peace**
Volume: 4	**:**	**Debt and Peace**
Volume: 5	**:**	**Farmer and Peace**
Volume: 6	**:**	**Food Security and Peace**
Volume: 7	**:**	**Humanity- A Religion**
Volume: 8	**:**	**Environment and Peace**
Volume: 9	**:**	**Politics and Peace**
Volume: 10	**:**	**Woman and Peace**
Volume: 11	**:**	**Governance and Peace**
Volume: 12	**:**	**Mind and Peace**
Volume: 13	**:**	**Terrorism and Peace**
Volume: 14	**:**	**Democracy and Peace**
Volume: 15	**:**	**Country and Peace**
Volume: 16	**:**	**Water and Peace**
Volume: 17	**:**	**Economics and Peace**
Volume: 18	**:**	**People and Peace**
Volume: 19	**:**	**Media and Peace**
Volume: 20	**:**	**Land and Peace**
Volume: 21	**:**	**Justice and Peace**
Volume: 22	**:**	**Health and Peace**
Volume: 23	**:**	**Culture and Peace**
Volume: 24	**:**	**Faith and Peace**
Volume: 25	**:**	**Life and Peace**

+++++

A MOVEMENT FOR A PEACEFUL WORLD